Orthodox Religion and Politics in Contemporary Eastern Europe

This book explores the relationship between Orthodox religion and politics in Eastern Europe, Russia and Georgia. It demonstrates how as these societies undergo substantial transformation Orthodox religion can be both a limiting and an enabling factor, how the relationship between religion and politics is complex, and how the spheres of religion and politics complement, reinforce, influence and sometimes contradict each other. Considering a range of thematic issues, with examples from a wide range of countries with significant Orthodox religious groups, and setting the present situation in its full historical context, the book provides a rich picture of a subject which has been too often oversimplified.

Tobias Köllner is assistant professor at the Witten/Herdecke University and board member in the Centre for Research on Transformation at Otto von Guericke University, Magdeburg, Germany.

Routledge Religion, Society and Government in Eastern Europe and the Former Soviet States

Series Editor
Lucian Leustean is Reader in Politics and International Relations at Aston University, Birmingham, United Kingdom.

This Series seeks to publish high quality monographs and edited volumes on religion, society and government in Eastern Europe and the former Soviet States by focusing primarily on three main themes: the history of churches and religions (including, but not exclusively, Christianity, Islam, Judaism and Buddhism) in relation to governing structures, social groupings and political power; the impact of intellectual ideas on religious structures and values; and the role of religions and faith-based communities in fostering national identities from the nineteenth century until today.

The Series aims to advance the latest research on these themes by exploring the multi-facets of religious mobilisation at local, national and supranational levels. It particularly welcomes studies which offer an interdisciplinary approach by drawing on the fields of history, politics, international relations, religious studies, theology, law, sociology and anthropology.

Monasticism in Eastern Europe and the Former Soviet Republics
Edited by Ines A. Murzaku

The Catholic Church and Soviet Russia, 1917–39
Dennis J. Dunn

The Making of the New Martyrs of Russia
Soviet Repression in Orthodox Memory
Karin Hyldal Christensen

Religion and Politics in the Orthodox World
The Ecumenical Patriarchate in the Modern Age
Paschalis M. Kitromilides

Orthodox Religion and Politics in Contemporary Eastern Europe
On Multiple Secularisms and Entanglements
Edited by Tobias Köllner

Orthodox Religion and Politics in Contemporary Eastern Europe

On Multiple Secularisms and Entanglements

**Edited by
Tobias Köllner**

Routledge
Taylor & Francis Group

LONDON AND NEW YORK

First published 2019
by Routledge
2 Park Square, Milton Park, Abingdon, Oxon OX14 4RN

and by Routledge
711 Third Avenue, New York, NY 10017

Routledge is an imprint of the Taylor & Francis Group, an informa business

© 2019 selection and editorial matter, Tobias Köllner; individual chapters, the contributors

British Library Cataloguing-in-Publication Data
A catalogue record for this book is available from the British Library

Library of Congress Cataloging-in-Publication Data
A catalog record has been requested for this book

ISBN: 978-1-138-49735-1 (hbk)
ISBN: 978-1-351-01894-4 (ebk)

Typeset in Times New Roman
by Taylor & Francis Books

To my parents Martina and Hartwig

Contents

Figures

Preface

This book is based on a conference held in October 2015 at the Otto von Guericke University Magdeburg with financial support by the German Research Foundation DFG (KO 4652/1–1). First draft papers were presented and discussed at this conference. Later on, we engaged in committed discussions amongst each other and tried to elaborate a more unified and coherent conceptual framework. Again and again we have circulated our ideas and drafts, and tried to improve them accordingly. Therefore my warmest gratitude goes to the participants of this workshop, and most of them have contributed material for this book and revised it several times before publication. In addition, I would like to thank all other participants during the workshop and in later discussions. To name just a few, I would like to thank Chris Hann, Bernhard Streck, Alexander Agadjanian, Julia Gerlach, Nikolai Mitrokhin and Jochen Töpfer. Thank you again for your insightful comments and helpful criticism during the workshop and later on!

Second, I would like to thank my former colleagues in Magdeburg where I have been hosted for more than three years. With their inspiring discussions and helpful criticism on provisional ideas, results and first theories they have been very helpful in so many ways. In particular, I would like to thank Heiko Schrader, Tatiana Golova, Frederik Schöne, Jacob Fruchtmann and Tatiana Samostian.

In addition, I am deeply indebted to my assistant Andreas Emcev at the Otto von Guericke University Magdeburg. He accompanied the book project for several years and was very helpful in organising the conference and caring for all the people attending it. Moreover, I would like to thank him for the fruitful discussions that were very important for the development of the book project. He very professionally organised the communication and helped a lot to keep all the contributors to the volume aboard. Thank you again very much, Andreas!

Since 2017, I have been based at the Witten/Herdecke University. Here I was made very welcome at the Witten Institute for Family Business where I discussed these topics again with my new colleagues, and received yet further stimulating insights. I am very grateful for this and thank Tom Arne Rüsen, Marcel Hülsbeck, Heiko Kleve, Arist von Schlippe and all my colleagues there.

I am also indebted to Peter Sowden, Rebecca McPhee and Lucian Leustean from Routledge publishers for their confidence in the book to become a success. From an early stage they were very helpful with their comments and later in the smooth and professional production of the book.

Last but definitely not least, I want to thank my family for their help and understanding during the writing-up. Especially I am grateful to my wife Sabine for her incredible patience, empathetic tolerance and support. Again and again I have told her that this project, as so many others before, is very, very important and has to be finished as soon as possible. But afterwards it certainly would become better ... Well, the bright future still has to come but at least this book is published and will not trouble us anymore. Thank you so much for your love and understanding, Sabine!

Witten and Magdeburg,
January 2018

Contributors

Nutsa Batiashvili is Associate Professor of Anthropology at Free University Tbilisi. She obtained her PhD from Washington University in St Louis. She is the author of the book *The Bivocal Nation: Memory and Identity on the Edge of Empire* (Palgrave Macmillan, 2018).

Ana Raluca Bîgu is an independent researcher specialising in educational studies, most notably in the fields of religious education and educational policies in Central and Eastern European post-communist countries. Awarded with a PhD in Philosophy from the University of Bucharest, she has published on various topics concerning education and religion, both from a Romanian and an East European perspective. Her most important works can be found in *Balancing Freedom, Autonomy, and Accountability in Education* (Netherlands: Wolf Legal Publishers, 2012) and *Faith and Secularization: A Romanian Narrative* (Washington DC: The Council for Research in Values and Philosophy, 2014).

Lucian Cîrlan is a PhD candidate in sociology of religion at Ecole Pratique des Hautes Etudes (Paris-Sorbonne) and member of the Research Center Groupe Sociétés, Religons, Laïcités (GSRL-CNRS) in Paris.

Alicja Curanović is Assistant Professor at the Institute of International Relations at the University of Warsaw. Her articles have appeared in renowned academic journals, such as *Politics and Religion* and *Religion, State and Society.* Among her most important publications is the monograph *The Religious Factor in Russia's Foreign Policy* (Routledge, 2012).

Romanița Iordache is currently the Romanian Independent Expert in the European Equality Law Network of the European Commission and the Senior Expert coordinating the Romanian team of the Fundamental Rights Agency FRANET while finishing her doctoral studies at Karl Franzens University, Austria and Università di Bologna, Italy on Diversity Management and EU Governance.

Daniel Jianu is a PhD candidate at Erfurt University with academic research and analysis experience on secularism, international relations theory and religion, the relationship between Eastern Orthodox Christianity and the foreign policy of countries such as Greece and Romania

Tobias Köllner is an assistant professor at the Witten Institute for Family Business at the Witten/Herdecke University, Germany. He has studied Russian Orthodoxy extensively in relation to economy, morality and politics. He is the author of *Practising Without Belonging? Entrepreneurship, Morality and Religion in Contemporary Russia* (LIT, 2012) and *Orthodox Religion and Politics: An Anthropological Perspective on Post-Soviet Russian Secularity* (Routledge, forthcoming).

Agata Ładykowska is a social anthropologist affiliated with the Institute of Archaeology and Ethnology at the Polish Academy of Sciences. She is interested in anthropology of religion (notably of Christianity, and especially of Eastern Christianity), historical anthropology, anthropological theory, political anthropology and anthropology of post-socialism/social change. She has obtained both an MA (Warsaw University) and a PhD (Martin-Luther University of Halle Wittenberg, Germany and Max-Planck Institute for Social Anthropology, Halle, Germany) in anthropology. In her research, she aims to bridge the disciplinary traditions of socio-cultural anthropology and history.

Vasilios N. Makrides is Professor of Religious Studies (specialising in Orthodox Christianity) at the Faculty of Philosophy of the University of Erfurt, Germany. Among his recent books are the following: *Christentum und Menschenrechte in Europa. Perspektiven und Debatten in Ost und West* (Frankfurt am Main: Peter Lang, 2016; co-edited with Jennifer Wasmuth and Stefan Kube).

Anna Ozhiganova (PhD) is an anthropologist, a researcher at the Institute of Ethnology and Anthropology Russian Academy of Sciences and a member of the Association of Medical Anthropologists (AMA). Her research interests concerns the intersections of religion, health and alternative social movements, as well as the teaching of religion in the post-secular societies.

Marten Stahlberg is a theologian and PhD student at the Humboldt University Berlin. He has been involved in the project of creating a Russian-German theological dictionary.

Detelina Tocheva is Research Fellow at the Centre National de la Recherche Scientifique and a faculty member of Groupe Sociétés, Religions, Laïcités, Paris (CNRS/ EPHE/ PSL Research University Paris). She is the author of *Intimate Divisions: Street-Level Orthodoxy in Post-Soviet Russia* (Berlin: LIT, 2017).

Dmitry Uzlaner holds a PhD in philosophy and religious studies (M.V. Lomonosov Moscow State University). He is a Research Fellow at Moscow School of Social and Economic Sciences (MSSES) and at Russian

Presidential Academy of National Economy and Public Administration (RANEPA). He is editor-in-chief of *Gosudarstvo, religiia, tserkov v Rossii i za rubezhom* journal and part of a five-year international research project 'Postsecular conflicts' (2016–2021) at the University of Innsbruck (Austria).

Nenad Živković is a theologian and a PhD candidate at the Chair of Orthodox Christianity at the University of Erfurt (Germany). He is currently finishing his PhD thesis on the link between nation-building strategies and the struggle for ecclesiastical autocephaly in the Republics of Macedonia and Montenegro in comparative perspective.

Part I

Introduction and historic overview

Introduction

Tobias Köllner

Orthodox religion today

This volume tries to fill an important gap in the social-scientific study of Orthodox Christianity as a majority religion in its relation to politics. A comprehensive study of Eastern Orthodox Christians has been demanded for some time (see Hann 2007: 403; Ghodsee 2009: 231f.), but Orthodoxy remains a largely neglected subject that has only recently received more attention from a comparative perspective and in its global relevance (Hann 2014; Hann and Goltz 2010; Leustean 2014; Roudometof et al. 2005; Roudometof 2014). This is somehow striking because Orthodox Christianity claims to have about 300 million believers (Adams 2015; Pew Research Center 2017). For this reason we are convinced that the subject deserves much more attention from the social sciences and in broader comparative perspective.

Not only is Orthodoxy poorly known, but it attracts strong essentialisations and generalisations about its impact on political life. Many authors and the media both inside and outside the region have contributed to a picture of Orthodox countries as stagnant states. The so-perceived evidence of a particularly close relationship between politics and religion is used to render countries with a dominant Orthodox religion as politically 'backwards' in contrast to Western Europe and the Anglo-Saxon world (cf. Huntington 1998: 70f. as the most prominent example). The crucial difference, according to these readings, is that Orthodoxy's mystical and magical traits form a main obstacle to modernisation. Such views, however, fail to recognise the great diversity of political and social associations that have been made with Orthodox religiosity by Orthodox communities (see also Makrides in this volume). To name just a few, Orthodox religion has sometimes served as the locus for identification (Karpov et al. 2012; Berglund and Porter-Szűcs 2013: 8; Filatov and Lunkin 2006); sometimes as a moral grounding for society (Benovska-Sabkova et al. 2010; Köllner 2012; Rogers 2009; Steinberg and Wanner 2008; Zigon 2011); and sometimes in its relation to culture (Ładykowska 2016: 230ff.; Rogers 2015: 211ff.; Scherrer 2003). In addition, it has to be kept in mind that there is no single Orthodox Church. Orthodox Churches are organised according to local and national traditions (see also Makrides in this volume). These local traditions have some common traits but could not be described as having one single coherent form of secularism or relationship between politics and Orthodox religion. For this reason there still is a lack of analytic concepts that describe these issues more precisely.

Moreover, most of the Orthodox Churches are located on the territory of the former Soviet Union and Europe's formerly socialist states. This means that Church, belief and believers are in the midst of substantial change and transformation. From the perspective of the host states alone, most are aiming to come to terms with the socialist past (post-socialism) and, at the same time, to enhance their future opportunities with and within the European Union. As a result, the relationship of religion and politics is in constant flux and evolution. Accordingly, the novelty and fluidity of both politics and religion makes apparent and observable how both processes influence each other, and how an action taken on one side reshapes the conditions for the other. Analysing this rapidly changing situation is very challenging but allows for new theoretical insights which are very relevant for the study of religion and politics in a broader perspective.

Orthodox religion and politics: contemporary theories and discussions

During the writing-up process we engaged critically with the scientific literature. In so doing, we have identified three theoretical issues where we think that our empirical material could provide an impetus for developing new analytic concepts and new inroads. First, due to the fact that recent interpretations of the interrelation between politics and religion still seem to be unable to overcome essentialisations and generalisations, fresh analytic concepts are highly desirable. Second, we have noticed a strong emphasis on the macro and meso level of analysis that neglects important developments on the micro level. Here we would like to provide new empirical material that is focusing on the micro level. The third and last point is that too little attention has been paid to the actual relationship between the local, the regional and the national level. There an analysis is needed that combines all three levels of analysis and provides a fuller picture.

Coming back to the first issue, the essentialisations and generalisations mentioned above, it becomes obvious that the interrelation between Orthodox religion and politics is guided by two dominant discourses. On the one hand, Eastern Orthodoxy is perceived to be submissive to the State authorities and largely driven by attempts to support them or to provide legitimacy to them (see for example Mitrofanova 2005 for the Russian Federation). Although the names for this are different, the guiding idea behind is the concept of caesaropapism coined by Justus Hennig Böhmer and used in the literature (Weber 1990: 200) that describes a dominant political authority that makes use of the religious realm for its own sake which is contrasted to Western Europe and the Anglo-Saxon world (see Makrides in this volume for more details). These descriptions of a very dominant state in its relation to religion, however, focus on the macro level and neglect that this is not equally true on the micro level. This pertains to the second theoretical contribution mentioned above. For this reason we demand a stronger emphasis on the micro level because here the relationship between Orthodox religion and politics is much more diverse and allows for different interpretations. On the micro level, for example, conflicts occur far more often and can have very diverse results. Here the dominance of the State authorities is not as clear-cut as it seems at first glance. The occurrence of conflicts and the different results of these conflicts might suffice as examples here. These are important limitations that have been largely ignored in recent analysis.

On the other hand, a number of authors propose a particularly collaborative relation between Orthodox religion and politics. Focussing on the collaboration of State and Church in post-socialist Russia, Furman and Kääriäinen (2007: 94) noticed a 'sort of "interchange" of popularity and authority [that] is taking place between the Church and the President of Russia, which enhances the further strengthening of the "pro-Orthodox consensus" and the role of religion as a symbol of national unity'. As a result, some of these disparaging notions of cooperation, then, are inverted and given a positive reading as the underpinning of a distinct civilisation. This is the so-called harmony (*symphonia*) of Church and State that proposes an idealised consensus between religious and political elites. As such, it is symphony that has attracted a lot of attention from those who were attempting to understand the relation between religion and politics in countries with significant Orthodox communities. Some authors continue to emphasise the importance of the concept of symphony because of its alleged inheritance from Byzantine symphony although they contend that it is more a societal ideal than a lived reality (Ghodsee 2009; Knox 2003; Meyendorff 1982). As a result, different additions have been made to the idea of symphony in contemporary Orthodoxy: James Warhola (2004: 97) talks about 'an imbalanced symphonia', John Anderson (2007) mentions 'assymetric symphonia' and Kristen Ghodsee (2009) puts forward the idea of 'symphonic secularism'. But these additional qualifications show quite clearly that the symphonic ideal is becoming more and more difficult to apply to research and analysis.

Therefore we found it difficult to apply any of the interpretations that describe the interrelation between Orthodox religion and politics as symphony. Here we have noted three main problems. First it has to be admitted that although the concept claims the importance of historic legacies it actually provides little historical evidence which can be applied easily to current relations. Here it is important to acknowledge that the concept underwent profound changes already in Byzantine time and even more so during the Ottoman rule (see Jianu in this volume). In addition, and secondly, 'a partnership between the church and state as two separate entities [did] not exist in Byzantium' (Hovorun 2016: 14). Moreover, thirdly, the idea seems to have little practical application for today because 'no single model of symphony from premodern times would satisfy the churches [today]' (Hovorun 2016: 17). On the contrary it could be noticed that, despite close cooperation, the outcomes are not determined and quite often lead to unexpected or even unintended consequences. In addition, the close cooperation, at least at times, seems to foster conflicts in these societies that are related to this close cooperation and the involvement of religious institutions in many issues (see Uzlaner in this volume). For this reason we suggest not to use the concept further in scientific discourse and to find new approaches, which describe the interplay between Orthodox religion and politics more correctly.

Moreover our research on the interplay between politics and Orthodox religion has identified a strong bias that focuses on the higher echelons of power (here the idea by Dobbelaere 2002 on the differentiation between three levels of secularisation was important for us). Most of the scientific and popular literature on the Russian Federation, for example, focuses on the impact of Vladimir Putin. Although he certainly is a highly influential person, the actual workings in everyday politics and the results might be quite different from his initial intentions. This is even more relevant for weak leaders in other states such as Moldova or Georgia. For the analysis Sonja Luehrmann's findings (2011: 10) about socialist times are important which could have parallels in recent developments. Luehrmann noted that the picture of an all-encompassing socialist state is wrong. To a large extent these socialist states were not able to provide the resources and means for country-wide indoctrination. Instead the central authorities were more occupied with formulating initiatives and with establishing incentives for implementation. As a result, most of the ideas and practices changed considerably and underwent profound transformation. Accordingly, they were adapted to the local situation and to the needs of local actors involved. This finding still seems to be relevant today. For this reason it is of crucial importance for us to see how events on the national, regional and local level are related to one another and what they could tell us about the interrelation between Orthodox religion and politics.

The exclusive focus on the macro level is related to yet another limitation. According to our perception it is not enough to change the focus to the micro level. Instead, it is an analysis of the interrelation *between* the micro, the meso and the macro level which is needed. For this it is important to draw attention to how actions on one level can have intended and unintended results on another. In a recent publication, for example, Köllner (2013a) has shown how donations by Russian businessmen on the local level are related to actions on the regional and national level: lavish donations for the construction of churches or memorials, then, are used by these businessmen to get access to political and religious elites on the national level. Therefore it is proposed to differentiate between national, regional and local level and to analyse how they are relate to one another. Quite often the initiatives developed on the national level are not spelled out in detail or lack the funding necessary for their implementation. As a result, people on the regional and local level have a lot of freedom to include their ideas and to adjust them according to their own understandings, needs and networks for implementation.

But this analysis needs to look beyond the boundaries of the nation state, as Kristina Stoeckl (2014, 2016), Alexander Agadjanian (2008), Alicja Curanović (2012 and in this volume) and Victor Roudometof (2014) have rightly argued. Orthodox Human Rights or 'traditional moral values' are such notions that have been put forward by Russian Orthodox groups in cooperation with the Russian State administration. Although most of these attempts have had only limited success (Stoeckl 2017), this is something that needs to be taken into consideration. Here it is very interesting to show how ideas, concepts, interpretations, models and institutions disperse from one country to the next. This takes place between countries with a significant Orthodox religious community and beyond as the involvement of conservative organisations in Western Europe and US suggests. In this context, it is essential to acknowledge that these models 'do not diffuse by themselves and they cannot be transferred without being translated' (Behrends, Park and Rottenburg 2014: 2). The actual practice, however, of how this takes shape has to be provided. Here we need much more analysis before we are able to show how models, ideas and concepts 'travel' between different countries (see Behrends, Park and Rottenburg 2014; Czarniawska and Joerges 1996; Ong and Collier 2005 for theoretical suggestions on this issue).

Drawing on these conclusions, we see a need that recent perspectives have to be re-evaluated critically. Both the debates on caesaropapism and on symphony seem to have reached an impasse. For this reason we demand an assessment of Orthodox religion 'in its own right' (Stoeckl 2016: 132 in her analysis of the Russian Orthodox Church) that, first, pays attention to different factions inside Eastern Orthodox groups (see Papkova 2011; Richters 2013; Stoeckl 2014; Verkhovskii 2003 for the Russian case) and, second, addresses the agency of Eastern Orthodoxy in a more realistic perspective. In so doing, we hope to be able to provide a more accurate and detailed picture of Orthodox religion in contemporary Eastern Europe and beyond.

Orthodox religion and politics reconsidered: a new perspective

For these reasons we have tried to find new approaches for interpreting the interplay between religion, politics and secularisation in contemporary Orthodox countries. This needs more than just the analysis of the interrelation between the 'State' and the 'Church', as it is common in recent sociology and political science (Chaves & Cann 1992; Pollack 2002; Minkenberg 2003; Fox 2011).[1] We have therefore taken a wide view of what constitutes the political domain and have considered phenomena such as schooling and media discourse alongside the programs of political parties and the rhetoric of decision makers. We also approach Orthodox religiosity as multi-vocal, following the nuanced approaches provided by Makrides (2005), Papkova (2011), Richters (2013) Roudometof et al. (2005) and Stoeckl (2014). In so doing, we aim to steer the discourse on Orthodoxy and politics on to a track that enables accurate comparisons between Orthodox communities and between Orthodox, Protestant and Catholic communities (see also Makrides in this volume). The key theoretical suggestion of our joint volume, then, is a critical revision of our thinking about the relation between politics and religion in countries with a strong Orthodox religious community based on the recognition that the relationship between both realms is highly dynamic, mutually constitutive, and cooperative and conflictual at the same time. Herewith we critically engage with the widespread tendency to search for unidirectional causal relationships which, according to our joint perception, diverted attention away from empirical studies that explore how political reforms and the re-emergence of Orthodox religion evolved in relation to each other. In so doing, we try to develop new theoretical concepts that try to provide a full picture of the complex interplay between politics and religion in countries with strong Orthodox religious communities.

One of these ideas is the concept of 'entangled authorities' that has been developed by Tobias Köllner based on his ethnographic fieldwork in the Russian Federation (Köllner 2018a, 2018b, forthcoming). With the idea of 'entangled authorities', the complex interplay of Russian Orthodoxy and politics is described in more detail. In so doing, attention is drawn to the fact that too many different ideas have been put into one single concept. On the one hand, as has been mentioned above, there has been a tendency to focus on cooperation and entanglements, and to neglect unintended consequences and conflict. Recent research, however, has shown the limits of this cooperation that is far from harmonious (see for example Stoeckl 2017; Köllner 2018a). Therefore it is more useful to describe the interplay between politics and Orthodox religion as a rivalry for scarce resources and authority in society. This, at times, allows for close cooperation but does not prevent conflicts and competition. Based on our empirical material we hope we are able to provide evidence for this.

On the other hand, we have to scrutinise the entanglements between politics and Orthodox religion in more detail. We have to ask *how* Orthodox religion and politics are entangled and where we have evidence for cooperation or conflict. In drawing on these questions we have noticed that at least three different forms of entanglements have been intermingled which have to be delineated and analysed separately: personal, ideological and institutional entanglements. Only then, so it is suggested, will we be able to describe, analyse and grasp the interplay between Orthodox religion and politics more fully and more accurately.

The first aspect of entanglement refers to the personal entanglements. Herewith we refer to the personal acquaintance among people from Orthodox communities and political actors. Both Orthodox religion and politics are addressed with authority in these countries and have to be considered as part of the societal elite. Therefore their representatives know each other quite well and meet regularly. Sometimes this takes the form of spiritual guidance where priests or monks serve as spiritual fathers for politicians (see also Köllner 2013b on this topic). These direct contacts are very important and helpful because they allow for mutual beneficial exchanges and initiatives.

The second form of entanglement pertains to the ideological sphere. On many issues people from both elites hold similar worldviews when it comes, for example, to the rejection of the official recognition of homosexual partnerships or the reaffirmation of the great historic tradition of the respective country. But this ideological convergence (see also Curanović 2012: 133, 146) often relates to vague notions such as tradition, heritage or national culture. Therefore it has to be handled with care because we agree with Herzfeld who emphasises that 'Even people who talk as though they fully endorsed and agreed upon the ideals of national unity do not necessarily mean the same things by it' (1987: 152). Nevertheless, these ideological entanglements are important for the understanding of the relation between Orthodox religion and politics, especially if they are combined with other forms of entanglement.

The last form of entanglement is the institutional. Herewith formal agreements between Orthodox religion and politics in different spheres are meant. One important issue in this respect is religious education in public schools (see Ładykowska, Ozhiganova and Bîgu in this volume). This issue has been and sometimes still is a source of heated discussion in these societies: how should religious issues be addressed in public schools, how should religious organisations be allowed to participate and, if so, which ones? But institutional entanglements are not confined to religious education. They are equally relevant in processes of law making, in international relations (see Curanović 2012) and for property restitution (Köllner 2018a) or for the organisation of new festive days with both religious and political notions (Köllner under review). Moreover, it is important to note that in practice all three forms of entanglement appear separately and in various combinations.

In a broader perspective the idea of entangled authorities relates to the topic of secularism. Secularism, however, as Talal Asad (1997, 2003) has aptly shown, is nothing that stands on its own but is a political doctrine which underlies historic changes and adaptations. Following this interpretation we suggest to define secularism as 'an enactment by which a *political medium* (representation of citizenship) redefines and transcends particular and differentiating practices of the self that are articulated through class, gender, and religion' (Asad 2003: 5, emphasis in original). Keeping this in mind it is obvious that secularism is nothing fixed and stable. Instead, we suggest that there are multiple secularisms or secularities with 'variations across time and space in how the religious-secular divide is understood and justified' (Wohlrab-Sahr & Burchardt 2012: 880). Accordingly, we suggest that there can be no single form of 'Orthodox secularism' or genuine relationship between Orthodox religion and politics. Strictly speaking there is even no single Russian, Georgian, Moldovan or Serbian secularism. In particular, the notion of personal entanglements introduced above allows us to show how distance or closeness, separation or entanglement between politics and Orthodox religion are actively produced and enacted, justified and structured. Of course this is not happening in a vacuum and so certainly 'not everything goes'. Cultural patterns, certain commonalities and historic legacies are important and have to be taken seriously. Nevertheless, we noticed significant differences within countries when we tried to describe the relationship between Orthodox religion and politics (see also Ładykowska in this volume where she shows that the situation in the Smolensk region is not the same as in the Rostov region of the Russian Federation).

When suggesting this we have to acknowledge that our ideas are by no means monolithic and ready yet. Our individual ideas and common grounds are still developing and deserve more efforts to become coherent and to be applicable in research and for further analysis. There is still a long way to go but we are convinced that our objections to previous interpretations and our initial analysis are worth considering. This edited volume, then, is a starting point that provides a comprehensive and new perspective on the entanglements between the spheres of religion and politics in several countries with a predominantly Orthodox Christian population.

Structure of the book

This edited volume is an empirical study of political and religious authorities that are described as deeply entangled phenomena. In this way we have attempted to address different questions and to document ongoing changes. Drawing on these findings, we suggest that beneath the flux there are continuities which are rooted in a longer history and shared across a wider region. In so doing, the authors of this volume, all researchers from the social and adjacent sciences, have attempted to provide fresh empirical material from countries with a strong Orthodox religious community. For this, the authors used different methods such as ethnographic fieldwork, media and textual analysis, and surveys to elaborate in more detail on the characteristics of this relationship. Thus, we have investigated the multiple ways in which the spheres of religion and politics complement, reinforce, influence and sometimes contradict each other.

After the introduction a chapter follows by Daniel Jianu who engages with the historical relationship between State and Church in the Byzantine and the Ottoman Empires. He describes the concept of *symphonia* (harmony) in great detail because it is discussed in scientific discourse and addressed in public debates in countries with a strong Orthodox religious community until today. In his analysis, however, Jianu strongly emphasises the changes symphonia underwent over the centuries. In so doing, he shows where legacies for today could be found that result in particular notions of secularism. At the moment this is challenged by different actors because these states with a strong Orthodox religious tradition actively engage with the European Union or other international agencies which adhere to different understandings of secularism and Church–State interrelation.

Part II includes three chapters by Lucian Cîrlan, Marten Stahlberg and Detelina Tocheva that engage with the relationship between Orthodox religion and politics in discourse and practice in contemporary states with a strong Orthodox religious community. Cîrlan is a sociologist and analyses the presidential elections in Romania in 2014. During these elections, he shows, Orthodox religion became important as an issue in order to prevent the candidate Klaus Iohannis, originating from the German ethnic minority in Transylvania and a Protestant Lutheran, from becoming president. His opponents gained some support from Romanian Orthodox clergymen and tried to initiate a discourse that described them as 'proud to be orthodox' during visits to monasteries and in the church. At the end, however, these attempts were unsuccessful and Iohannis won the election which, according to Cîrlan, shows that different notions of Orthodox religion have to be differentiated: identity issues (what he calls declarative) versus Orthodoxy as a lived and practised religion. In the next chapter Stahlberg, a theologian, analyses the discourses surrounding the Russian annexation of the Crimean Peninsula. These discourses, as Stahlberg is able to show, are highly charged with religious rhetoric and refer to religious symbols. One important point of reference is the comparison of the Crimea to the Temple Mount because of Prince Vladimir's alleged conversion to Orthodoxy in the city of Korsun. This is a serious challenge for the Russian Orthodox Church because it touches on sensitive issues such as the relation between State and Church in providing legitimacy for political decisions. In the last chapter of this part Detelina Tocheva, an anthropologist, analyses the relation between politics and Orthodox religion by referring to what she calls a 'resilient harmony'. According to her understanding, the social differentiation and gendered practices that govern Russian society are also valid inside religious communities. This is an interesting difference to, for example, some Protestant religious communities, where this differentiation is inverted. In her material, based on ethnographic fieldwork in religious communities of the St Petersburg region, this is not the case. Women, although very important in parish communities, have inferior positions and their efforts are often unrewarded.

Part III, with chapters by Ana Raluca Bîgu, Agata Ładykowska and Anna Ozhiganova, deals with Orthodox religion and politics by looking at religious education in public schools. Looking at textbooks used in religious education in public schools in Romania, Bîgu notices a strong religious bias in them. Romanian national identity is conflated with Romanian Orthodoxy and other religious denominations are described as potentially harmful and not suitable to the Romanian tradition. Throughout these textbooks, as Bîgu shows, an essentialist notion of Romanianness is fostered that has strong nationalist overtones. Quite often these books are written by believers or clergymen with the blessing of the Church and barely criticised by the State administration. In this way, the authors of these textbooks have an important role and mediate between Orthodox religion and politics with their works. The next chapter by Ładykowska, an anthropologist, deals with religious education in the Russian Federation. She uses her material for an analysis on issues of secularism and modernity. In so doing, she opposes to dichotomies based on a four-square model where education is associated exclusively with the public and religion with the private. Rather, it is that these secularist notions are not given but actively produced, as she shows in her material on religious education in the Russian Federation. The last chapter by Ozhiganova also deals with religious education in the Russian Federation. From yet another perspective it is shown that religious education in the Russian Federation is used more like in Romania, the case presented by Bîgu: it is a strong notion of identity. In this way notions of Russian Orthodoxy are used for nation building and adapted accordingly. But this faces strong disagreement in growing portions of the population and so these attempts have to be considered as unsuccessful, according to Ozhiganova's interpretation.

In Part IV on conflicts between Orthodox religion and politics, Romanița Iordache, Nutsa Batiashvili and Dmitry Uzlaner provide examples from Moldova, Georgia and the Russian Federation respectively that reveal strong disagreement between the Church hierarchy and the State or growing differences between the Church and society. As Iordache and Batiashvili have shown for Moldova and Georgia, political actors have attempted to come closer to Western states and the European Union and to fulfil their preconditions for closer cooperation. The introduction of new laws banning discrimination for reasons related to religion, gender and sexual orientation, however, has provoked harsh reactions and strong resistance from Orthodox religious communities. The repeal of laws prohibiting homosexuality (and the guaranteeing of human rights for sexual minorities) has been interpreted as a sign of moral decay, the dilution of local values and a promotion of homosexual propaganda. In some cases, local Orthodox Churches even have excommunicated politicians who support such new 'European' legislation. In his chapter Uzlaner focuses on growing tensions between Orthodox religion and Russian society. He notices that the 'pro-Orthodox consensus', so characteristic for the early post-socialist years, today seems to have vanished. Looking at broader trends, Uzlaner describes significant changes such as a growing number of ex-believers and open conflicts between the cultural sphere and Russian Orthodoxy that seem to contradict the high respect for Orthodox religion in opinion polls.

Part V, 'Orthodoxy in the International Arena', deals with attempts by Orthodox religion to gain more international recognition and with the relations between different Orthodox national Churches. Focusing on the interplay between the Russian Orthodox Church and the State administration, Alicja Curanović shows how *Russkii Mir*, a foundation supported by the State and the Russian Orthodox Church, or the growing interest in the Middle East and the Arctic aim at reversing the international hierarchy and at legitimating Russia's status as a superpower. In so doing, Curanović emphasises ideological entanglements which she describes as a symphony of views. In the next chapter Nenad Živković shows conflicts between several Orthodox Churches on the issue of official recognition. Based on his material from Macedonia, he analyses the political transformations and the emergence of new independent nation-states. Newly founded nations such as Macedonia have brought forward claims to religious autonomy or autocephaly, challenging the authority of the Patriarch in Belgrade who perceives these demands to be illegitimate and non-canonical. As a result, the issue of recognition became highly problematic for both religious and political representatives because they were accused of treason when they tried to find a compromise.

In the afterword, Vasilios Makrides elaborates on broader topics in Orthodox religion that have been addressed here only partially. Thus he gives a fuller historic picture of the complex relation between Orthodox religion and politics that provides a basis for future analysis. In his chapter he emphasises six key dimensions of Orthodox religion in history and today that might serve as a basis for future research: 1) the concept of symphonia; 2) the tension between imperial and national traditions; 3) the historic experience of Orthodoxy as a marginalised religion under Islam; 4) the relation between autocracy, totalitarianism and Orthodoxy; 5) Orthodox majority vs. minority status and 6) the East-West dimension.

Note

1 Nevertheless, these theoretical approaches have been important for us because they provide a continuum between different forms of relationship between politics and religion. But we still contend that our approach is more fine-grained because it includes macro, meso and micro level and the everyday practice which tends to be different from written constitutions or formal agreements.

References

Adams, Ch. J. 2015. 'Classification of Religion'. *Britannica*. Available at: https://www.britannica.com/topic/classification-of-religions/Conclusion#toc314840. Last accessed: 18 November 2016.

Agadjanian, A. 2008. 'Russian Orthodox Vision of Human Rights: Recent Documents and Their Significance', *Erfurter Vorträge zur Kulturgeschichte des Orthodoxen Christentums* 7/2008.

Anderson, J. 2007. 'Putin and the Russian Orthodox Church: Asymmetric Symphonia?', *Journal of International Affairs* 61(1): 185–201.

Asad, T. 1997. *Genealogies of Religion*. Baltimore, MD: John Hopkins University Press.

Asad, T. 2003. *Formations of the Secular: Christianity, Islam, Modernity*. Stanford, CA: Stanford University Press.

Behrends, A., S.-J. Park and R. Rottenburg (eds.). 2014. *Travelling Models in African Conflict Management: Translating Technologies of Social Ordering*. Leiden, Boston: Brill.

Benovska-Sabkova, M., T. Köllner, T. Komáromi, A. Ładykowska, D. Tocheva and J. Zigon. 2010. '"Spreading Grace" in Post-Soviet Russia', *Anthropology Today* 26(1): 16–21.

Berglund, B. R. and B. Porter-Szűcs, (eds.). 2013. *Christianity and Modernity in Eastern Europe*. Budapest, New York: Central European University Press.

Chaves, M. and D. Cann. 1992. 'Regulation, Pluralism, and Religious Market Structure', *Rationality and Society* 4(3): 272–290.

Curanović, A. 2012. *The Religious Factor in Russia's Foreign Policy*. London, New York: Routledge.

Czarniawska, B., and B. Joerges. 1996. 'Travels of Ideas'. In *Translating Organizational Change*. Edited by B. Czarniawska, B. Joerges and G. Sévon, pp. 13–48. Berlin: De Gruyter.

Dobbelaere, K. 2002. *Secularization: An Analysis at Three Levels*. Bern: Peter Lang.

Filatov, S. and R. Lunkin. 2006. 'Statistics on Religion in Russia: The Reality behind the Figures', *Religion, State and Society* 34(1): 33–49.

Fox, J. 2011. 'Separation of Religion and State and Seculariam in Theory and in Practice', *Religion, State and Society* 39(4): 384–401.

Furman, D. and K. Kääriäinen. 2007. 'Religioznost' v Rossii na rubezhe XX–XXI stoletii' [Religiosity in Russia at the turn of the twenty-first century], *Obshchestvennye nauki i sovremennost'* 2: 78–95.

Ghodsee, K. 2009. 'Symphonic Secularism: Eastern Orthodoxy, Ethnic Identity and Religious Freedoms in Contemporary Bulgaria', *Anthropology of East Europe Review* 27(2): 227–252.

Hann, Ch. M. 2007. 'The Anthropology of Christianity per se', *Archives Européennes de Sociologie* 47(3): 383–410.

Hann, Ch. M. 2014. 'The Heart of the Matter: Christianity, Materiality, and Modernity', *Current Anthropology* 55: 182–192.

Hann, Ch. M. and H. Goltz (eds.). 2010. *Orthodoxy, Orthopraxy, Parádosis: Eastern Christians in Anthropological Perspective*. Berkeley: University of California Press.

Herzfeld, M. 1987. *Anthropology through the Looking-Glass: Critical Ethnography in the Margins of Europe*. Cambridge, New York: Cambridge University Press.

Hovorun, C. 2016 'Is the Byzantine "Symphony" Possible in Our Days?', *Journal of Church and State* 59(2): 1–17.

Huntington, S. P. 1998. *The Clash of Civilizations and the Remaking of World Order*. New York: Simon & Schuster.

Karpov, V., E. Lisovskaia and D. Barry. 2012. 'Ethnodoxy: How Popular Ideologies Fuse Religious and Ethnic Identities', *Journal for the Scientific Study of Religion* 51 (4): 638–655.

Knox, Z. 2003. 'The Symphonic Ideal: The Moscow Patriarchate's Post-Soviet Leadership', *Europe-Asia Studies* 55(4): 575–596.

Köllner, T. 2012. *Practising without Belonging? Entrepreneurship, Religion and Morality in Contemporary Russia*. Berlin: LIT Verlag.

Köllner, T. 2013a. 'Ritual and Commemoration: State-Church Relationship and the Vernacularisation of the Politics of Memory', *Focaal: Journal of Global and Historical Anthropology* 67: 61–73.

Köllner, T. 2013b. 'Aspects of Religious Individualization and Privatization in Contemporary Russia: Religiosity among Orthodox Businessmen and their Relation to Priests and Parishes', *Archives de sciences sociales des religions* 162 (2): 37–53.

Köllner, T. 2016. 'Patriotism, Orthodox Religion, and Education: Empirical Findings from contemporary Russia', *Journal of Religion, State and Society* 44(4): 366–386.

Köllner, T. 2018a. 'On the Restitution of Property and the Making of 'Authentic' Landscapes in Contemporary Russia', *Europe-Asia Studies* 70(7): 1083–1102. doi:10.1080/09668136.2018.1484077.

Köllner, T. 2018b. 'Religious Conservatism in Post-Socialist Russia and its Relation to Politics: Empirical Findings from Ethnographic Fieldwork'. In *Eastern Europe's New Conservatives: Varieties and Explanations from Poland to Russia*. Edited by K. Bluhm and M. Varga. London, New York: Routledge.

Köllner, T. Forthcoming. *Orthodox Religion and Politics: An Anthropological Perspective on Post-Soviet Russian Secularity.* London, New York: Routledge.

Köllner, T. Under review. 'The Day of Family, Love, and Faithfulness: Orthodox Religion and Politics in Contemporary Russia', *American Ethnologist.*

Ładykowska, A. 2016. *Orthodox Atheists: Religion, Morality, and Education in Post-socialist Russia.* PhD thesis, Martin Luther University Halle-Wittenberg.

Leustean, L. N. 2014. *Eastern Christianity and Politics in the Twenty-First Century.* London, New York: Routledge.

Luehrmann, S. 2011. *Secularism Soviet Style: Teaching Atheism and Religion in a Volga Republic.* Bloomington and Indianapolis: Indiana University Press.

Makrides, V. (ed.). 2005. *Religion, Staat und Konfliktkonstellationen im orthodoxen Ost- und Südosteuropa: Vergleichende Perspektiven.* Frankfurt a. M.: Peter Lang.

Meyendorff, J. 1982. *The Byzantine Legacy in the Orthodox Church.* Crestwood, New York: St. Vladimir's Seminary Press.

Minkenberg, M. 2003. 'Staat und Kirche in westlichen Demokratien'. In *Politik und Religion.* Edited by M. Minkenberg and U. Willems, pp. 115–138. Wiesbaden: VS Verlag.

Mitrofanova, A. 2005. *The Politicization of Russian Orthodoxy: Actors and Ideas.* Stuttgart: Ibidem.

Ong, A. and St. J. Collier. 2005. *Global Assemblages: Technology, Politics, and Ethics as Anthropological Problems.* Malden, MA: Blackwell Publishing.

Papkova, I. 2011. *The Orthodox Church and Russian Politics.* New York, Oxford: Oxford University Press.

Pew Research Center. 2017. *Orthodox Christianity in the 21st Century.* Available online: http://www.pewforum.org/2017/11/08/orthodox-christianity-in-the-21st-centu ry/?utm_source=adaptivemailer&utm_medium=email&utm_campaign=17-11-08%2 0orthodox%20christianity&org=982&lvl=100&ite=1906&lea=413737&ctr=0&par= 1&trk=. Last accessed: 30 November 2017.

Pollack, D. 2002. 'Religion und Politik in Mittel- und Osteuropa', *Aus Politik und Zeitgeschichte* 42: 15–22.

Richters, K. 2013. *The Post-Soviet Russian Orthodox Church: Politics, Culture and Greater Russia.* London, New York: Routledge.

Rogers, D. 2009. *The Old Faith and the Russian Land: A Historical Ethnography of Ethics in the Urals.* Ithaca, London: Cornell University Press.

Rogers, D. 2015. *The Depths of Russia: Oil, Power, and Culture after Socialism.* Ithaca, London: Cornell University Press.

Roudometof, V. 2014. *Globalization and Orthodox Christianity: The Transformations of a Religious Tradition.* New York/London: Routledge.

Roudometof, V., A. Agadjanian and J. Pankhurst (eds.). 2005. *Eastern Orthodoxy in a Global Age: Tradition Faces the Twenty-first Century.* Lanham, MD: AltaMira Press.

Scherrer, J. 2003. *Kulturologie: Rußland auf der Suche nach einer zivilisatorischen Identität* [Culturology: Russia in Search for a Civilizational Identity]. Göttingen: Wallstein.

Steinberg, M. D. and C. Wanner (eds.). 2008. *Religion, Morality, and Community in Post-Soviet Societies.* Washington, D.C. & Bloomington: Woodrow Wilson Center Press & Indiana University Press.

Stoeckl, K. 2014. *The Russian Orthodox Church and Human Rights.* London, New York: Routledge.

Stoeckl, K. 2016. 'The Russian Orthodox Church as Moral Norm Entrepreneur', *Religion, State and Society* 44(2): 132–151.

Stoeckl, K. 2017. 'Russland als Verteidiger traditioneller Werte? Eine Idee und ihre Grenzen', *Russland Analysen* 335: 5–8.

Verkhovskii, A. 2003. *Politicheskoe pravoslavie: Russkie pravoslavnye natsionalisty i fundamentalisty, 1995–2001 gg.* [Political Orthodoxy: Russian Orthodox Nationalists and Fundamentalists, 1995–2001]. Moscow: Tsentr 'Sova'.

Warhola, J. 2004. 'Religiosity, Politics, and the Formation of Civil Society in Multi-national Russia'. In *Burden or Blessing? Russian Orthodoxy and the Construction of Civil Society and Democracy.* Edited by Ch. Marsh and N. Gvosdev, pp. 91–98. Boston, MA: Boston University Press.

Weber, M. 1990 [1922]. *Wirtschaft und Gesellschaft: Grundriss der verstehenden Soziologie.* Tübingen: J.C.B. Mohr.

Wohlrab-Sahr, M. and M. Burchardt. 2012. 'Multiple Secularities: Toward a Cultural Sociology of Secular Modernities', *Comparative Sociology* 11: 875–909.

Zigon, J. (ed.). 2011. *Multiple Moralities and Religions in Post-Soviet Russia.* New York: Berghahn Books.

1 Symphonia and the historical relationship between State and Church

Legacies from Byzantine times until today

Daniel Jianu

The legacy of the relationship between the State and Church in the Eastern Orthodox religion is reflected in its focus on the importance of identity as a guide to interest and action. The constitutive rules of Orthodox religion and the relationship between State and Church make up its norms; norms that define expectations for behaviour of actors or states within a given identity. That means that having an Orthodox Christian identity implies that particular forms of behaviour according to the norms that pertain to Eastern Orthodox religion is more likely. In this way, the norms both relate to Eastern Orthodox identity and regulate the behaviour of the actor or state that possesses this religious identity. Religion in general and the Eastern Orthodox one in particular is well positioned in giving a complete narrative of why things are the way they are. Acting in accordance with this religious narrative of their identity, actors' decisions are determined to a certain extent by the norms and constitutive rules of Eastern Orthodox religion.

It is, however, important to understand that religious identities are not unchangeable, and are not only constructed within the boundaries of clearly identified religious institutions or organisations. While religious identities are both constructed and constrained, new narratives are constantly emerging. Ongoing stories are disrupted by unexpected events and deliberate innovation, that is, religious identities are continuously constructed at the crossroads of religious tradition and new interactions. In the case of Eastern Orthodoxy, this aspect takes a dominant resonance. At the risk of generalising, Orthodox people on the European continent, right before modern times, lived 'outside of history', as they always lived under continuous threat of outside invasions, not only physically or territorially but spiritually as well; during times of conquest and uncertainties, all state and social institutions were either foreign or non-existent, *except* the Orthodox Church (Makrides and Roudometof 2010). The national history thus is connected fully and integrally with the history of the Church, a history that deepened the Eastern Church's predilections and tendencies for contemplative existence and actions; it also deepened its eschatological inclination and lack of trust in history and in contrast to the Western Church has not moved/graduated from the symbolic to dialectic reasoning, from a synthetic and organic perspective to an analytical and systemic reasoning.

Thus, in Eastern Orthodox Christian nations, this relationship between Church and State is guided by the notion of harmonic symphony, a doctrine stemming from the Byzantine times. The idea behind this concept is that the temporal (profane) and divine (sacred) powers should and need to work together in harmony with the end result that the contemporary ties between religion and nation are much more pronounced and organic in the Orthodox tradition than in the West (Byrnes 2006: 293). As Lucian Leustean (2009: 89) argues, 'While there is a separation between the completely lay character of the state and the religious status of the Church, symphonia promotes equality and an intimate relationship between these institutions, however, with different priorities and methods of operating'.

The proposed research method of this chapter is to look at the historical trajectory of the concept of symphonia at both the common traditional aspects of the relationships between Church and State and at the different dogmatic offshoots of the symphonia in relation to politics, culture and society. This chapter will also review the ways and means that symphonia or harmony has evolved over times and expressed itself in different incarnations starting from the Byzantine times all the way to the millet system of the Ottoman Empire and to the contemporary State-Church relations in countries and societies with a strong Orthodox religious affiliation. The legacy of the symphonia survives in the countries despite the fact that they have also undergone a process of secularisation to a large extent. The symphonic harmony between the religious and the secular in Orthodox countries is reflected in many privileged and hegemonic partnerships between the Church and State, and in the ways public administration had developed and established itself.

During the early Byzantine times, the concept of symphonia had never been a fully developed political or legal institution, but more of an ontological model to which the Church and State should both adhere to and pay respect. Gregory Nyssa (335–395), one of the Cappadocian Fathers and Bishop of Nyssa, is representative of the traditional meaning of symphonia where the understanding is that if the emperor and his subjects believe in God, then God would bless them and keep them safe and well. A 'symphonia of earth and heaven would result', reflected as well in the safety of the entire Christian empire from its enemies. This reflects the belief based on the biblical idea of God's protection of his covenant people (McGuckin 2003: 279).

John Chrysostom (349–407), Archbishop of Constantinople and early Church Father, argued that symphonia implies a differentiation between the functions of Church and State in the Christian empire. He looks at King Osias who had leprosy and argues that his disease was God's punishment for offering priestly incense to God and describes the two limits in his Oration to the Antiochenes:

> Therefore, stay within your proper domain. The government and the priesthood each have their own boundaries, even though the priesthood is the greater of the two. A king should not be judged merely on the

appearance, or valued merely from the gold and jewels in his costume. His domain is the administration of earthly affairs, whereas the jurisdiction of the priesthood is a power derived from above … Bodies are under the care of the King, souls under the care of the priest. The king remits earthly debts, the priest remits the debts of guilt. One uses earthly weapons, the other uses spiritual weapons, and it is the latter which bears greater power. This is why the King bends his head to the hand of the priest, and why, in the Old Testament, kings were always anointed by priests.

(McGuckin 2003: 279)

Hence, both the king and the priest had to support each other, to mutually reinforce one another and collaborate in harmony to please God. This concept had been expressed by the Sixth Novella of Emperor Justinian I (527–565). In the legal preface to his Sixth Novella issued in March 535, he promulgated his definition of the respective spheres of imperium and sacerdotium:

The greatest gifts that God's heavenly philanthropy gave to men are the *sacerdotium* and the *basileia,* of which the former serves divine affairs, and the latter presides and watches over human affairs, and both proceed from one and the same principle and regulate human life. So, nothing should be so much the care of the emperor as the saintliness of the priests since these constantly pray to God on his behalf. If the *sacerdotium* is in all ways blameless and acceptable to God, and the *basileia* rules justly and properly over the state entrusted to it, good harmony will result, which will bestow all that is beneficial on the human race.

(McGuckin 2003: 283)

We can see again the classical Byzantine sense of symphonia, the biblical doctrine of the conditional blessing from God based upon covenant fidelity. In Justinian's decree of May 535 he goes even further in the theory of the symphonia of the powers: 'The priesthood and the Imperium do not differ very greatly. Nor are sacred things so very different from those of public and common interest' (McGuckin 2003: 33).

According to John McGuckin, Justinian used this argument of harmony to justify his imperial role in the oversight of the Church's doctrine and dogmas and it is a learned biblical allusion to Psalm 131 (verses 8–12), which defines the Christian understanding of political symphonia: 'The king is blessed by God, he ensures the holiness of the priests who in turn pray for the welfare of the kingdom so that his throne shall endure' (McGuckin 2003: 283). Symphonia during Justinian's time returns to the meaning of the biblical doctrine of the conditional blessing from God based upon covenant fidelity as expressed by Gregory Nyssa (McGuckin 2003). This Justinian interpretation of the symphonia needs to be seen in the large scheme of things. It behoves to see that Justinian's arguments regarding symphonia were only a part of his fulsome effort to make the entire Byzantine society sacred not only through religious or legal efforts but also through his major building project of the capital which resulted in the restoration of Hagia Sophia and his codification of hundreds of years of imperial laws.

In the early Byzantine times, the Church consisted of the clerical hierarchy, the dogma and the traditions, and the physical buildings: the soul and the body of the empire. Soon though, the idea of the Church as a body or community had lost its meaning and slowly ceded this ground to the secular state. The Church accepted the premise of the Empire as a legitimate institution, but it denied the any moral authority over Christians. At the same time though, the Empire had not accepted either the legal existence or the moral authority of the Church. The dynamic between the Church and State becomes the problem of the relationship between two authorities, the secular and the spiritual within the state framework itself. These were exactly the issues that Justinian tried to manage with his legal and religious policies mentioned above.

Justinian was the first Roman and Christian emperor, bringing together all the previous attempts to unite empire and Church. At the beginning, the Christians represented a new and distinct community of believers, a sacred one distinct from the secular world. But starting with Constantine this community began to take over the whole Byzantine society and more or less became one with the larger secular world. As Alexander Schmemann argued, the doctrine and dogma of the Church had remained the same though and required a distinction between the realm of the secular world and the sacred one:

> The two communities have started to clash into different directions; the demarcating line or the border that before the Christianization of the society delineated two external spheres of the empire now has shifted this outwardly border between Christian and non-Christian into an inner one, between the two minds of the same Christian.
>
> (Schmemann 1963: 36)

Now the Christian belongs both to the secular world and the Church. The Church has merged with the world, but because this was a Christian world it has two claims to authority: the emperor and the patriarch.

The emperor and the patriarch held different offices but physically lived and worked in the same place and hence were forced to work together in a symphonic relationship between the two institutions, between the two spheres of power and legitimacy. There were certainly many cases where their political 'co-habitation' led to conflict between the emperor and patriarch and made it difficult to assess where the balance of power resided and to what extent the emperor had managed to exercise control over the Church. Early Byzantine conflicts between the emperor and patriarch were mostly about dogmatic issues such as Arianism, Monophisitism, Monothelitism, Iconoclasm and where the power and will of the emperor seemed to be ascending and winning over the Church and patriarch (Morrison 1964).

From all these conflicts and clashes between the two spheres, Deno Gea-nakoplos has identified a threefold division of areas of contention: first, the secular falling entirely under the control of the emperor; second, issues per-taining to the organisation and administration of the Church; and third, the esoteric, the dogma of the Church where the most interference from the empire took place but where it belonged in the end completely to the clergy alone (Geanakoplos 1965). These three spheres of conflict between emperor and patriarch are derived from the textual attempts of Justinian's Sixth Novella's preamble to regulate the relationship between Church and State. According to John Meyendorff (1979), we cannot understand the full sig-nificance of this text if we don't take into account that this text is only a preamble to a longer constitution on Church discipline where Justinian defines what he means by the 'dignity of the priesthood'.

The real object of the Sixth Novella is to legislate on the marital status of the clergy, on Church property, on episcopal residence, on clergy selection and education, on obstacles to ordination, and on the legal status of the clergy. 'Human affairs,' which the Emperor considered as being within his imperial competence, included all the legal aspects of the Church's structure, while the 'divine things' which were, according to the preamble, in the jurisdiction of the priesthood, consisted exclusively in 'serving God' (Meyendorff 1979: 48).

Meyendorff argues that the 'harmony' itself mentioned in the text is not a harmony between two powers, or between two distinct societies, the Church and the State, but rather it is meant to represent the internal cohesion of one single human society for whose orderly welfare on earth the emperor alone is responsible (Meyendorff 1979: 48). He interprets Justinian's legal arguments in such a way that does not allow any place for the Church as a society sui generis. He sees the Empire and the Church as one single body of the faithful administered by a twofold and God-given hierarchy, meaning the imperium and the sacerdotium are to be found in a balanced duality.

The physical, legal and religious Christian remaking of the Empire during Justinian's time harks back to Gregory Nyssa's arguments and represents one of the first efforts of legitimising through Christianity and through the con-vent with God, the 'state' or in our case, the empire's monopoly on legally accepted violence. If God conditionally blesses and protects the emperor and its subjects who have faith, then the corollary is that God punishes those who do not. Thus, symphonia, in a perverse reverted order, gives equal importance to both blessing and punishment from God to the Emperor and from the Emperor to its subjects. As we can see later, this arrangement is the opposite of Justinian's attempt to equalise the legitimacy of civil laws and religious canons by accepting the religious laws into the imperial legislation. The Emperor was attempting through the ideal of symphonia to legitimise his monopoly on punishment and on legal violence by using the Church's moral authority for his own purposes.

Within this context we need to place and understand the meaning of the Sixth Novella and the concept of symphonia. Justinian's efforts had exerted a tremendous influence over the future societies of both the West and the East and formed the incipient basis of the contemporary legal and public administrative systems.

Arian controversy (325–381)

The Arian debates represent more or less a vortex or a fulcrum of theological events that increasingly developed into a political conundrum. What started as a purely theological controversy regarding the true nature of Jesus had meta-morphosed into a State-Church intermingling of overlapping spheres of legit-imising power claims. The vision of the Christian world and implicitly the relation between empire and Church, between emperor and patriarch, was born and became the foundation of the Church's theological principles and teachings.

The dispute between the Early Church Fathers and the Arians was over the nature of the Incarnation. The central word in the controversy between the Fathers and the Arians was 'homoousios', 'equal in essence', or, as the Nicene Creed stated, homoousios tö patri, 'equal to the Father'. The Son of God, the Logos of the Father, is true God from true God. The Arians wanted to designate Him homoiousios tö patri, 'like the Father in essence'. The Bishop of Caesarea understood the Son to be infinite and procreated by God, but not equal to Him. The Incarnation, therefore, was not the historical revelation of God in the flesh, but the apocalypse of a lesser deity according to him. The Early Church Fathers believed Christ to be true man and true God at the same time. These beliefs were translated into political terms as the Arians' beliefs about the consubstantiality of Jesus and the independence of the Church from the Empire were complementary. Arians advocated for Christological subordination and the subordination of the Church to the State. Thus the Arians were more disposed to accept the will of an Emperor, because the canons, tradition and scriptural law reflected in the historical Christ could not take precedence over the living law of the Emperor ordained by the eternal God (Williams 1951).

The Arians looked at the Emperor as equal with the Father and at the Priest equivalent with the Son. The Emperor was the head of the imperium, sacerdotium and Church. On the other hand, the Fathers declared the Logos equal with the Father, hence undermining the imperium to the detriment of the sacerdotium. Together they governed the Christian commonwealth. The Arians saw the theology of the orthodox Fathers as a threat to their political theology, a 'rebellion' on the ontological level (Williams 1951).

According to Kartasheff (1946), incarnation is the key to understanding the Byzantine Christocracy meaning the formulation of the doctrine per Chalce-don (451) where 'one and the same Christ, Son, Lord, Only-Begotten, recog-nised in two natures, without confusion, without change, without division, without separation, the distinction of natures in no way annulled by their union' finds its political embodiment in Justinian's symphonia that we saw earlier on (Azkoul 1971: 432).

Leaving aside for the moment the legal and religious ramifications of our concept, David James Dunn argues that symphonia is not only a political doctrine, but a 'broader religious ethos deriving from the eschatological hope of the church as both early resistances to the empire and the church's later baptism of it were informed and motivated by eschatology' (Dunn 2010: 211). Before Constantine, the secular and the sacred had a more flexible and nimble relationship with both sides looking into and waiting for the 'future kingdom to come' without any specific claims of authority or primacy. After Constantine, the Church became the State or the State became Church and consequently the 'future' had been claimed by Christianity.

> *Symphonia* was the name given to this eschatological mission. The harmony sought between the affairs of the church and the state was proof that both were properly working together to make contemporary social and political life a more perfect icon of the kingdom of God to come.
>
> (Dunn 2010: 212)

In the West, almost parallel with these efforts in Constantinople, during the time of Emperor Anastasius (494), Pope Gelasius I forcefully argued for clear delineation between the two spheres and in a sense he had legitimised the autonomy and independence of the Church from the political body:

> There are two things, August emperor, by which this world is ruled: the sacred authority of the pontiffs and the royal power. Of these two the priests carry the heavier weight, as they must render an account to the Lord's judgment seat even for kings. Most merciful son, you know well enough that you surpass all mankind in your dignity, yet even so you must bend your head in submission to the ministers of divine things, and from them receive the pledge of your salvation. In receiving the heavenly sacraments, which it is their office to dispense, you must depend on their judgment and not desire to submit them to your will. In matters concerning public life, the ministers of religions understand that the imperial power has been given to you from above and they themselves will obey your laws.
>
> (McGuckin 2010: 285)

Although we need again to see these efforts within the historical and political context of the Acacian schisms, Gelasius's distinction between the imperial potestas, and the auctoritas of the Church had a huge influence in the subsequent development of the relationship between Church and State in the West.

These clashes over the imperial potestas and the auctoritas of the Church were also reflected in the many attempts of the Justinian imperial legislation of framing the relations between State and Church in proper and ordered arrangements. His Codex (529) contains the most provisions dealing with the Church, but he also issued many Novellae, laws of general interest and content through which he tried nonetheless to regulate many Church activities as almost all parts of the ecclesiastical organisation and administration were regulated by his laws. He and other emperors were careful though to allow for a functional difference between the civil laws from the Church laws such as Holy Scriptures, the canons of the synods and religious customs. That somehow changed with Novella 131 (545) which promulgated that the canons of the four ecumenical councils (Nicaea, Constantinople, Ephesus and Chalcedon) should have the status of law, meaning that by incorporating the religious canons into the legal order of the secular state, it decreed and legitimised the importance of both laws and canons to the same degree of political and secular authority. Suddenly both laws and canons had to be interpreted and implemented in the same manner and by using similar principles by both the State and Church. This conflict between canons and laws were never formalised in an institutional arrangement but most of the contradictions were tended to be resolved on an ad-hoc basis depending on the situation and historical circumstances of the issue at play (Macrides 1990).

As Ruth Macrides (1990) argues, although initially it appeared that this change was beneficial to the development and implementation of the canon law, subsequent interpretations showed how in reality the Emperor had given himself the power and role of the supreme legislator and how the equivalence of the nomos/laws and canons meant that any differences between them that were resolved using the reverse precedent principle results in the ability of the civil law to annul the older synodical canons. Hence, Justinian, instead of enforcing the canon laws, tried instead to assure a legal and institutional way for the empire to intervene and adjudicate the affairs of the Church. All these issues were left in a legal and conceptual limbo as there were no clarifications over how to proceed in cases where nomos and canon contradict each other which perfectly reflects the lack of formal Byzantine institutional arrangements for delineating clearly the two spheres of political and social legitimacy, the Emperor and Patriarch, the Church and State (Macrides 1990: 65).

The tug of war between Emperor and Patriarch, between Church and State, hence can be traced through the relationship between the civil and ecclesiastical laws. As laws and canons were fused and gave birth to nomokanons, the relationship between State and Church became more complicated and complex. The canons of the Church and the laws of the empire were bound at some point during this legal cohabitation to be included in the same collections.

The unresolved tension between the laws and canons when dealing with the same issue or political situation determined the inclusion of both in a different type of legal collection, the abovementioned nomokanons. The most important of these Byzantine collections are the Nomokanon of 50 (L) Titles and the Nomokanon of 14 (XIV) Titles. The second one is the collection of more legal importance and is the result of incorporating into the Syntagma of Canons of 14 (XIV) Titles of the provisions from the legislative effort of Justinian in regards to the Church affairs; it was most likely composed at the beginning of the seventh century and it quickly became one of the most important sources of law of the Eastern Church (Ohme 2012). Both the form and content of the Nomokanon reflect a vision of the Church whose structure and discipline are based primarily on conciliar canons and traditions handed down by the great fathers of the Eastern Churches, but they are also increasingly governed by direct imperial ecclesiastical legislation resulting in the Church authorities and the civil authorities in Constantinople becoming closely linked together to form one harmonious whole (Gallagher 2002).

Epanagoge (884–886)

The next affirmation of the relationship between State and Church is to be found during the debates over the meaning of the text of the Epanagoge. The Epanagoge or Eisagoge was published somewhere between 884 and 886 at the end of Basil I's reign and it represented the first official attempt in regulating the relations between the Church and State (Azkoul 1971). Before this text, the relationship between the two reflected the dynamic of two not separate spheres but rather two forms of the one Christian essence. The Eisagoge, on the other hand, introduced the theory of the 'two authorities', the idea that each one, emperor and patriarch, had specific rights and powers that were to be seen as equal forms of authority within the State (Azkoul 1971: 461). The Christian unity of the empire was to be replaced with the unity and pre-eminence of the State as unit of reference and conceptual gravity centre. This directive about different rights and obligations of the emperor and the patriarch was codified in Titles II and III. According to the text, the State is made up of members and parts like the human body and the biggest and most important ones are the emperor and the patriarch. The emperor was charged to the well-being of the people while the patriarch to their spiritual care, a formula much based on the Sixth Novella of Justinian with the only significant difference being that there was no functional separation between the two while now the two sides are starting to differentiate and assume different contours (Azkoul 1971: 462).

Thus, Title II declares:

> (1) The emperor (basileus) is a legal authority, a blessing common to all people, who neither punishes with antipathy nor rewards with partiality, but acts without prejudice in all matters which come before him. (2) The aim of the emperor is to guard and secure by his power that which belongs to his office; to recover by sleepless care those that are lost; and to draw by wisdom and justice those that yet remain outside his dominion. (3) The purpose set before the emperor is to confer benefits; hence, he is called benefactor. Yet, should he fail to be beneficent, he becomes, to use the words of the ancients, a forgery (para-charaxis) of the royal stamp. The emperor is expected to enforce and maintain not only what is declared in the holy Scriptures, but the dogmas established by the Seven Ecumenical Councils; and, to be sure, the Roman laws of his predecessors.
>
> (Azkoul 1971: 461)

As we can see, the emperor had to respect many legal precedents before issuing new laws, legal precedents such as the Holy Scriptures, the canons of seven ecumenical synods, and the previously approved Roman laws. At the same time, chapters 5 and 6 of Title III gave only the patriarch the right to interpret both the decisions of the synods and the common practice followed by the Church. The Emperor is defined as a 'legitimate authority,' subject not only to the directives from the Holy Scriptures and from the canons of the ecumenical councils but also to the civilian/secular laws which were in the process of codification at that time. In Title III, the Patriarch is defined as an 'incarnate and living image of Christ, who, by his words and his deeds, expresses the truth'. This seemingly allows the Patriarch to increase its attributes at the expense of the Emperor, though all these changes are still within the framework of harmonious collaboration of the symphonic ideal between the two spheres (Dagron 2003).

These two titles, II and III, set forth the spheres of influence and legitimacy of the Emperor and Patriarch and institutionalise for the first time the concept of the two equal powers with separate spheres of influence. As has been mentioned earlier, in addition to this clear demarcation of their responsibilities, there is a distinction made in their legal activities and capacities. The Emperor hence must respect the Holy Scripture, the canons of the seven ecumenical councils and also the Roman law. He is not to issue any new law which transgresses these precedents while it is the reasonability alone of the Patriarch to interpret the canons of the holy fathers and synods (Macrides 1990: 62).

Epanogoge was considered at the beginning only a law project, never officially published and enforced (Knox 2003). The Russian scholar Sokolsky argued that the Epanogoge was actually officially promulgated as law and had been used extensively in the Byzantine Empire and in Russia (even became part of the canon law) as well as in other regions. 'It was the first code to present detailed definitions of the relations between Church and State especially regarding the specific duties and obligations of the emperor and the patriarch' (Spinka 1941: 351). It is the first known and official attempt during the Byzantine Empire at regulating in some form the relationship between our two spheres of legitimacy, between our two variables, between State and Church, between sacred and profane.

It is argued, especially by Ostrogorsky (1969), that the Epanagoge, which was later incorporated in the Syntagma of Matthew Blastaris, represents the fullest expression of the incipient formation of the Church–State structure. Accordingly, Titles II and III of Epanagoge enforce a clear dual authority and legitimacy that influenced later historical events (Spinka 1941). This argument is based on the idea that many subsequent legal collections were based on it, especially Blastaris' Syntagma which had widely travelled throughout the Eastern Church during the Byzantine times all the way to the Ottoman Empire times (Hussey 2010: 310).

The Epanagoge's interpretation of the relationship between emperor and patriarch can be found expressed in today's Orthodoxy in the legacy relationship between State and Church. As Tobias Köllner argues, in today's society, 'emphasis is put on the entanglement between religious and political elites which will be described as entangled authorities' (Köllner 2018a). This entanglement between secular and religion reflects a strong interrelation between both spheres of legitimacy. This political and social alliance does not preclude the existence of separate and independent institutions belonging to Church and State respectively. Distinct functions are performed by each institution representing different forms of authority. Yet there is an important connection between the two in that they share a common end, the 'kingdom to come' largely defined by the Christian unity (Bhargava 2011). Despite this harmonious cooperation, however, the outcomes are not determined and quite often lead to unexpected or even unintended consequences (Köllner 2018a, 2018b).

Millet of the Ottoman times

The concept of symphonia has also found expression in the millet system of the Ottoman times as it has preserved the harmonic Byzantine arrangement for Orthodoxy. It strengthened the ontological aspects of the symphonic relationship between Church and State. There were three non-Muslim *millets* (religious communities) recognised by the Ottoman authority: the 'Rum' (Greek-Orthodox), the Armenian (Gregorian) and the Jewish millet. The first included all the Balkan or Asia Minor populations, subject to the authority of the Orthodox Patriarchate of Constantinople. The second included the Armenians primarily and all Christian religious groups that were not subject to the Orthodox Patriarchate. The third included all Jewish populations in the empire (Romaniotes, Ashkenazi and Sephardic Jews).

Under the millet system operated by the sultan, the patriarch of Constantinople was seen as the legitimate spiritual, and in some ways political, leader of all Orthodox believers living in the Ottoman Empire (Azkoul 1971: 431–464). This system recognised only one type of community, namely religious community, and consequently reinforced the Church's roles as guardian of national identity and a form of *de facto* statehood (Perica 2006: 176). More importantly, the millet has allowed the Eastern Orthodox Church at times to step in and become politically active, especially in circumstances in which the secular authority did not exist or could not function properly. The Church then becomes a provisional government of sorts until restoration of secular authority (Perica 2006: 176). This historical experience turned the Orthodox Churches into peculiar 'reserve governments' standing by ready to assume functions of political leaderships in times of crisis (Kalkandjieva 2010). These 'reserve governments' had departments for foreign affairs and conducted active policies regarding relations with other states and churches. Specifically, both before, during and after the Ottoman times, there are many examples of Church filling the political void left open by the secular authorities in the history of the Church:

Patriarch Nicholas Mystikos (852–925) was regent of the young Byzantine emperor Constantine VII Porphyrogenitus, while the Metropolitan Alexii of Moscow (1353–1389) ruled the Principality of Muscovy during the childhood of the Grand Prince Dmitry II Donskoy. The most extreme example or case is the Principality of Zeta in 1516 when the heir to the throne, Prince Georgi Chernoevich transferred the government of the state to the metropolitan of the local Orthodox Church. Until 1851, Montenegro was ruled by its metropolitans. In 1866, the Metropolitan Kliment of Tarnovo became PM of Bulgaria, while Archibishop Makarios III combined his duties as church head with those of the President of Cyprus between 1960 and 1977.

(Kalkandjieva 2010: 8)

Nicolae Iorga in his essay Byzantium after Byzantium (2000 [1848]) argues that Byzantium has survived as a political and cultural substance throughout many of the Ottoman Empire territories. The political, social and economic traditions of the Byzantium have continued and flourished during the Ottoman times and informed many of its legal and administrative practices. The millet system embraced these Byzantium cultural and political paradigms and parameters and built around them the necessary framework within which the Ottoman State ruled its non-Muslim subjects and specifically the Orthodox Christian minority. The Ottoman governmental bureaucracy dealt with the religious minorities not as individuals with specific religious beliefs but as members of a larger community legitimised by one person or office as the head of this community. This made the efforts of the Ottoman State to manage these religious communities much easier than having to implement and coordinate integration and assimilation strategies for the religious minorities of the Empire.

Incidentally, the Ottoman administrators found preciously invaluable intellectual and political support in the concept and tradition of the Byzantine symphonia; this allowed the State to mobilise its resources in defining each religious minority community on the basis of their individual essential characteristic, the religious identity. A complete merge between the community and their religious belonging ushered a long-term transformation and political legitimisation of the symphonic experience.

This relationship between the Byzantine traditions of symphonia, we have argued, stayed alive and meaningful even after the collapse of the Byzantine Empire, and the foundational framework of the millet system has been neglected and minimised. We cannot fully comprehend the millet without its deep connections to the State-Church arrangements that evolved before the Ottoman Empire. Benjamin Braude and Bernard Lewis (1985) have written eloquently about the foundational myths of the millet system and argued that this system has been more of a vague general approach than a fully developed Ottoman institution. Because of this flexibility the millet avoided the pitfalls of forced and direct rule of the Christian minority by adopting the traditions and political arrangements of symphonia, and consequently institutionalising the historical close relationship between State and Church.

Conclusion

As shown before, symphonia refers to an ideal and a theoretical framework of the relationship between Church and State in the Eastern Orthodox world. It represents the ideal of a harmonious partnership between Church and State that goes all the way back to the Byzantine times. This concept reflects the imperative of the sacred and profane domains to work together in harmony with the end result that the contemporary ties between religion and nation are much more prominent and natural in the Orthodox tradition than in the West.

The analysis of the contemporary relationship between the Orthodox Church and State has to take into account its social and political role in previous periods, dating back to the establishment of the autonomous nation states after the fall of the empire. The relationship between faith and state during the Ottoman times' millet system of administration granted the Patriarch both ecclesiastical and temporal authority over the Christian subjects of the empire. This peculiarity of the millet system also allowed the Orthodox Church to help instil and preserve a sense of belonging and common identity among Orthodox populations that even after the collapse of the empire continues to entangle the spiritual and temporal authorities between the State and Church (see also Köllner 2018a and 2018b on the concept of 'entangled authorities').

These 'entangled authorities' between State and Church are also reflected in the development and evolution of the public administration and management systems in Orthodoxy. The aim of the public administration reflects the needs common to the entire community, and whose decisions are binding as the public administration can use state coercion when necessary. The public administration belongs to the realm of the public sphere. The public administration can be understood as a system of institutions, including administrative structures which organise and effect the execution of the laws of the state. This is in tune with the way religion in pre-modern times had the same public authority in not only generating but also enforcing the laws of the land.

The public administration, in the rule of the law, is the main lever by which the values established at the level of the political realm are carried out and implemented. It has to be continuous, omnipresent, prompt and energetic, since it represents the state the whole time just as religion used to be. Religion makes itself present in the normative frameworks of public administration. Public bureaucracies developed out of the proto-bureaucracies dominated by clerics in the middle ages: the very word 'clerk' is a sign of this. Notions of hierarchy, regularity, due process, adjudication, checks and balances, record-keeping etc., are derived from ecclesiastical institutions.

This emphasis in the state public management structure on local autonomy and self-government reflects the attempts of the Church to be an autonomous legal institution on the same level field as the state. Both the symphonic partnerships between State and Church and the system of the public administration are based on the foundational values of Orthodox religious identity and formational characteristics. In Orthodoxy there is an argument to be made that the elements of this symphonic partnerships have an outsize influence in contemporary society. Many of its economic, political and cultural institutions are influenced by its history, which is to say that the institutional formation of governmental agencies, if not in their constitutional foundation, at least in the procedural and functional capacities, are much indebted to the historical close relationship between Church and State. Many of the public choices made in Eastern Orthodox societies, the way institutional and cultural reforms are accepted or rejected, seem to be fundamentally driven by an ideological *substance* created over their long history (Barbu 2001).

The Eastern Orthodox Church is profoundly public and emphasises tradition, group identity and group boundaries. The Church without doubt is resurgent and has re-emerged as a resource for the engagement of citizens in democratic politics. If we transcend the secular and modern tendency to minimise and wish-think away religion from political arenas, we can imagine a place and a time where faith and its social trappings do play a progressive role and where religion and modernity can happily co-exist. On the other hand, we also have to be careful and not ignore the possibilities of reactionary behaviour from the newly empowered Church. As a potential development to be further considered and properly analysed, we would like to mention the possibility of metamorphosis of Church actions into a political ideology squarely aimed at the secular political authority.

Political Orthodoxism, as a theory of state and politics to paraphrase Ayubi (1991), is a conceptual and symphonic construct. As distinctions between religious and political authority are historically absent in the Orthodox world, political Orthodoxism refuses to acknowledge the privileged status of the private sphere or the distinctions between private and public. Political Orthodoxism, as a sentient commingling of religion and politics, could develop into a 'modern' language of politics that could challenge Western secularist assumptions about religion and politics (Hurd Shakman 2008). It could raise important critical questions about the foundational principles of collective/communitarian life (Hurd Shakman 2008). Political Orthodoxism can be considered a continuous and historical presence as a resource for collective legitimisation. It contests the terms through which secularist epistemology organises religion and politics.

As Orthodoxy has never experienced Reformation or Enlightenment, its relationship to the state and the secular is less sceptical or adverse, and much more in 'harmony'. One of the challenges of globalisation that the Orthodox Church is facing lately in countries such as Greece, Cyprus, Romania and Bulgaria is the European Union and its associated demands for liberal and cosmopolitan principles including individual human rights, tolerance and equality for minorities and women, and the secularisation of the state. These issues are quite grating to the Orthodox Church as they challenge the unity and tradition of their immutable dogma. One such topic that lately permeates deeply the debate in these countries and touches on many fragile and historically sensitive nerves is homosexuality, gender identity and the civil partnership between same sex couples. The legalisation of homosexuality that happened in these countries as a precondition for joining the EU is still viewed in the eyes of the Church as a grave sin and an area of society where the Church intends to impose its authority and legitimacy over that of the civil secular government (see also Iordache and Batiashvili in this volume). At the same time, the Europeanisation of the Orthodox societies challenges their tradition of devotion to the form of national sovereignty and exerts pressure not only on the religious doctrine or dogma but also on their institutional and administrative structures.

Bibliography

Ayubi, N. 1991. *Political Islam: Religion and Politics in the Arab World*. London: Routledge.

Azkoul, M. 1971. 'Sacerdotium et Imperium: the Constantinian Renovatio according to the Greek Fathers', *Theological Studies* 32: 431–464.

Barbu, D. 2001. *Bizanț contra Bizanț: Explorări în cultura politică românească*. Bucharest: Nemira.

Bhargava, R. 2011. 'Rehabilitating Secularism'. In *Rethinking Secularism*. Edited by C. Calhoun, M. Juergensmeyer and J. Van Antwerpen, pp. 92–113. Oxford: Oxford University Press.

Braude, B. and B. Lewis (eds.). 1985. *Christians and Jews in the Ottoman Empire: the function of a plural society*. Teaneck: Holmes & Meier Publishers.

Byrnes, T. A. 2006. 'Transnational Religion and Europeanization'. In *Religion in an Expanding Europe*. Edited by T. A. Byrnes and P. J. Katzenstein, pp. 283–305. Cambridge: Cambridge University Press.

Conovici, Iu. 2015. 'Concepts of Church-State Relations in Romania: Beyond Symphonia and the Privileged Orthodox Church'. Available online: https://www.yumpu.com/en/document/view/15872830/concepts-of-church-state-relations-in-romania-units muohioedu.

Dagron, G. 2003. *Emperor and Priest: The Imperial Office in Byzantium*. Cambridge, UK: New York: Cambridge University Press.

Dunn, D. J. 2010. 'Symphonia in the Secular or How to Be Orthodox When You Lose Your Empire'. In *Power and Authority in the Eastern Christian Experience: Papers of the Sophia Institute Academic Conference*. Edited by F. K. Soumakis, pp. 209–218. New York: Theotokos Press.

Gallagher, C. 2002. *Church Law and Church Order in Rome and Byzantium*. London: Routledge.

Geanakoplos, D. J. 1965. 'Church and State in the Byzantine Empire: A Reconsideration of the Problem of Caesaropapism', *Church History* 34(4): 381–403.

Hurd Shakman, E. 2008. *The Politics of Secularism in International Relations*. Princeton, NJ: Princeton University Press.

Hussey, J. M. 2010. *The Orthodox Church in Byzantium*. Oxford: Oxford University Press.

Iorga, N. 2000. *Byzantium after Byzantium*, transl. L. Treptow. Oxford: Center for Romanian Studies.

Kartasheff, A. V. 1946. *The Restoration of Holy Russia*. Cited in Azkoul, M. 1971. 'Sacerdotium et Imperium: the Constantinian Renovatio according to the Greek Fathers', *Theological Studies* 32: 432.

Kalkandjieva, D. 2010. 'Eastern Orthodox Christianity and Democracy: Foes or Allies in a Globalizing World' (paper presented at the Italian Political Science Association (SISP) Annual Conference Venezia, Venice, 16–18 September 2010).

Knox, Z. 2003. 'The Symphonic Ideal: The Moscow Patriarchate's Post-Soviet Leadership', *Europe-Asia Studies* 55(4): 575–596.

Köllner, T. 2016. 'Patriotism, Orthodox Religion, and Education: Empirical Findings from Contemporary Russia', *Journal of Religion, State and Society* 44(4): 366–386.

Köllner, T. 2018a. 'On the Restitution of Property and the Making of 'Authentic' Landscapes in Contemporary Russia', *Europe-Asia Studies*. 70(7): 1083–1102. doi:10.1080/09668136.2018.1484077

Köllner, T. 2018b. 'Religious Conservatism in Post-Socialist Russia and its Relation to Politics: Empirical Findings from Ethnographic Fieldwork'. In *Eastern Europe's New Conservatives: Varieties and Explanations from Poland to Russia*. Edited by K. Bluhm and M. Varga. London: Routledge.

Leustean, L. 2009. *Orthodoxy and the Cold War*. London: Palgrave Macmillan UK.

Leustean, L. N. 2011. 'The Concept of Symphonia in Contemporary European Orthodoxy', *International Journal for the Study of the Christian Church* 11: 188–202.

Leustean, L. (ed.). 2014. *Eastern Christianity and Politics in the Twenty-First Century*. London and New York: Routledge.

Macrides, R. 1990. 'Nomos and Kanon on Paper and in Court'. In *Church and People in Byzantium*. Edited by Rosemary Morris, pp. 61–85. Birmingham: Centre for Byzantine, Ottoman and Modern Greek Studies.

Makrides, V. 2015. 'Eastern Orthodox and Western Latin Churches under Communism: Differences and Parallels'. In *Romanica et Balcanica. Wolfgang Dahmen zum 65. Geburtstag*. Edited by Th. Kahl, J. Kramer and E. Prifti, pp. 703–724. München: AVM.

Makrides, V. and Roudometof, V. 2010. *Orthodox Christianity in 21st Century Greece The Role of Religion in Culture, Ethnicity and Politics*. London: Routledge.

McGuckin, J. 2003. 'The Legacy of the 13th Apostle: Origins of the East Christian Conceptions of Church and State Relation', *St Vladimir's Theological Quarterly* 47 (3–4): 251–288.

McGuckin, J. 2010. *The Orthodox Church: An Introduction to its History, Doctrine, and Spiritual Culture*. New York: John Wiley & Sons.

Meyendorff, J. 1968. 'Justinian, the Empire and the Church', *Dumbarton Oaks Papers* 22: 43–60.

Meyendorff, J. 1979. *Byzantine Theology: Historical Trends and Doctrinal Themes*. New York: Fordham University Press.

Meyendorff, J. 1982. *The Byzantine Legacy in the Orthodox Church*. Crestwood and New York: St. Vladimir's Seminary Press.

Morrison, K. F. 1964. 'Rome and the City of God: An Essay on the Constitutional Relationships of Empire and Church in the Fourth Century', *Transactions of the American Philosophical Society*, New Series, 54(1): 3–55.

Ohme, H. 2012. 'Sources of the Greek Canon Law to the Quinisext Council (691/2): Councils and Church Fathers'. In *The History of Byzantine and Eastern Canon Law to 1500*. Edited by W. Hartmann and K. Pennington, pp. 24–114. Washington, DC: CUA Press.

Ostrogorsky, G. 1969. *History of the Byzantine State*. New Brunswick: Rutgers University Press.

Perica, V. 2006. 'The Politics of Ambivalence: Europeanization and the Serbian Orthodox Church'. In *Religion in an Expanding Europe*. Edited by T. A. Byrnes and P. J. Katzenstein, pp. 176–203. Cambridge: Cambridge University Press.

Schmemann, A. 1963. *The Historical Road of Eastern Orthodoxy*. Trans. L. W. Kesich. US: St Vladimir's Seminary Press.

Spinka, M. 1941. 'Patriarch Nikon and the Subjection of the Russian Church to the State', *Church History* 10(4): 347–366.

Williams, G. H. 1951. 'Christology and Church-State Relations in the Fourth Century', *Church History* 20(3): 3–33.

Part II
Current discourses and practices

2   'Proud to be Orthodox'

Religion and politics during the 2014 presidential elections in Romania

Lucian Cîrlan

Introduction

The collapse of the communist regime allowed Romania not only to launch a double political and economic transformation, but also to redefine the relationship between religion and politics (see Stan & Turcescu 2007; Conovici 2010; Carp 2013). The redefinition was called for by political leaders, Church representatives and the civil society, each feeling that new Church–State relations were needed after the authoritarian communist state gave way to a democratic state, and new, mostly Western-based, religious denominations entered the country to compete with old, more established religious groups. The advent of democracy and religious freedom forced the Romanian Orthodox Church (ROC) to confront the new political and religious reality. Under the centuries-long Ottoman occupation the Orthodox Church was not challenged by disruptive social, political, cultural and religious phenomena like the Reformation and the Enlightenment. After 1989, confrontation with the Western-style liberal democracy was inevitable. The Church was called to rethink its understanding of Church–State relations by abandoning the cherished Byzantine concept of symphonia in favour of a pluralist perspective denying any one faith the power to organise the whole of social life.

As part of the post-communist transformation effort, the other religious and non-religious groups were also called to embrace democracy. Thus, the interplay between religion and politics had to evolve because both terms of the religion and politics equation had transmogrified substantially, and old management mechanisms, communication channels, State commitments and Church objectives could no longer adequately reflect post-communist realities. The presence of new religious movements and of the humanist organisations is challenging the traditional religious Romanian society, in particular the religion and politics relation. In order to study the interaction between religion and politics in post-communist Romania, the general and presidential elections are suggestive case studies. With a large majority of Orthodox Christians (86 per cent),[1] a development of religious diversity and the EU integration process achieved in 2007, Romania represents a particular case in the post-socialist countries of Central and Eastern Europe.

In this chapter I will draw the overall picture of religion in the political discourse of the 2014 presidential elections in Romania, analysing the implications of instrumentalising the Orthodox confession in electoral scopes. The research question is: why has the strategy of involving religion as a main campaign theme failed? By using different sources, such as press articles, religious documents, electoral materials and political statements, I will argue that, despite the post-communist religious revival, the previous elections and the overwhelming majority and social influence of the Orthodox Church, the individual level of secularisation, especially of the young generation born around 1990, is the main cause for the unsuccessful mobilisation of religion in the electoral process. The moral behaviour of the 'orthodox' candidate, together with the secular character of the European Union and the Romanian diaspora situation, will complete the argument. After a short overview of religion and politics interaction in modern Romania, highlighting the transfer from symphonia to the post-communist Church–State cooperation, the 2014 presidential elections will be presented as a case study. The chapter ends with the analysis of the post-2014 elections developments on religious and political landscape and the Orthodox Church's position within contemporary society.

From symphonia to cooperation: religion and politics in modern Romania

One of Romania's most important redefinitions of Church–State relations was launched by Prince Alexandru Ioan Cuza (1859–1866), as a comprehensive reform programme inspired by the 1848 revolutions and touching on all aspects of life. In 1859, Cuza became the ruler of the united principalities of Wallachia and Moldova, the new state known as Romania when recognised by the European powers three years later. At the time the dominant religious denomination was the Orthodox Church, while smaller Roman Catholic, Jewish and Muslim groups were present in central Moldova, the large towns and Dobrogea. Cuza's choice of a religion and politics pattern that allowed the State to strictly control religious affairs was determined by his desire to champion the local Orthodox Church's independence from the Patriarchate of Constantinople to subordinate it to his own ambitious projects. Through his religious policy, Cuza established a pattern of control over the religious activities that would be followed in various forms during the entire modern history of the Romanian state (Enache 2016).

Invited to assume the leadership of Romania by the anti-Cuza faction of Liberal and Conservative politicians, Carol I converted to Orthodoxy, thus validating the ROC as a legitimising factor for political leaders. Subsequently, all Romanian kings who ruled in pre-communist times were baptised in the Orthodox faith, considered protectors of that religious group, and given most of the privileges accorded to Byzantine emperors. Like other Eastern European Orthodox kingdoms liberated from Ottoman rule in the nineteenth century, the young country assumed a form of nation-state infused with the concept of symphonia, whereby the head of the State was expected to be an Orthodox Christian, the Church and the State were to coexist harmoniously for the good of the 'Orthodox Christian' society, and the State was expected to support the preservation of an 'Orthodox Christian' culture (see also Jianu in this volume).

After the creation of the modern Romanian state following the incorporation of the multi-religious and multi-ethnic region of Transylvania into the Romanian Kingdom in 1918, Church–State relations were redefined, but the 1923 constitution did not provide for a democratic system permitting all religious groups to worship freely and the State to treat them equally. Article 22 read that 'the Orthodox and the Greek Catholic Churches are Romanian Churches. The ROC, being the religion of a majority of Romanians, is the dominant Church in the Romanian state; the Greek Catholic Church has priority over other denominations.'[2] While this privileged position fell short of full autonomy from the secular power, it granted the dominant national church important privileges, including government subsidies for clergy salaries and pensions. After 1989 the ROC called for a return to inter-war arrangements that awarded it so many privileges.

After World War II Romania became part of the communist block. Like its East European counterparts, the Romanian Communist Party initially saw religion as a capitalist remnant expected to wither away as its social basis disappeared, but the party's religious policy was ultimately determined by practical more than ideological considerations. The Law on Religious Denominations of 4 August 1948 gave the Ministry of Religious Affairs full control over religious life. In 1957, the ministry was downgraded to the level of a department, to signal the communist state's belief that the 'problem of religious denominations' was solved. Communist authorities persecuted but did not dismantle the ROC, recognising that a Church respected by the population could be used to further the party's economic and political goals (see Roberson 1996: 331–337; Leuştean 2005: 440). Until 1965 the State made considerable efforts to weaken the Church's role in society and bring its hierarchy under control by legally depriving the Church of its national church status and the right to pursue educational and charitable activities. Once the last remnants of resistance were crushed, the State forged a special partnership with the ROC that enlisted that religious group as an unconditional supporter of communist policies in return for the government tolerating a certain level of ecclesiastical activity (see Gillet 1997; Enache 2005; Leuştean 2009).

In sum, in mid-19th century Romania recognised the ROC as the main denomination, a position which de facto meant that the Church acted, and was treated, as a state church. That privileged status was ratified by the 1866 constitution, and upheld by the 1923 and 1938 basic laws, even after the Old Romanian Kingdom incorporated the multicultural province of Transylvania. While the ROC towered over other religious groups, it progressively lost ground to the modern Romanian state, which emancipated from Church dominance to become an independent governmental machinery able to use the Church in its nation-building and modernisation projects. Communist authorities favoured secularism and atheistic Marxism-Leninism, but in time realised the advantages of tolerating rather than completely eradicating religious denominations. During its consolidation phase, the communist state persecuted all religions, but by mid-1960s the ROC re-established a new foundation for collaboration with the authorities based on a distorted symphonia in which the 'emperor' was no longer a Christian Orthodox, or even religious, but a State seeking to subjugate the Church.

When it comes to religion and politics in post-communist Romania, the political class has tried to find the middle ground between winning and maintaining the electoral support of its mostly Orthodox constituencies, enjoying autonomy from all religious groups in the policy making process, and complying with the requirements of religious toleration and even-handedness imposed by European Union accession. The process of negotiating between such competing goals has turned proposals coming from political quarters into variants of the managed quasi-pluralist model by which the centralised state retained control over religious affairs through registration and fund allocation, while relaxing communist-era restrictions on religious activity and endorsing a privileged partnership with the ROC. Individual parties and politicians have forged close ties to different religious groups, but the State has refused to formally elevate any denomination above all others. From the viewpoint of the authorities, religious groups formally belong to the State-free areas of family, education and the arts.

While all sides realised the need to place Church–State relations on new foundations, agreement had not been reached (by 2006) as to what kind of model the country must embrace. As various actors pursued various goals, the shape and content of the proposed Church–State models differed substantially depending on the initiators, all of whom sought to gain the maximum scope for unfettered activity. Romanian actors have made constant references to the experience of Western Europe, but were reluctant to prefer one single model over all others. For example, rather than adopting the German model in its entirety, the ROC has selectively endorsed some of its elements, while silently discarding others. Its vision has blended German and British elements, although Greece is a more appropriate model for Romania, having also an overwhelming majority of Orthodox believers.

Therefore, the *Law on Religious Freedom and Religions*,[3] adopted prior to the EU integration in December 2006, has established two steps of State recognition of the religious organisations: as religious Cults (*Culte religioase*) and as religious associations. Currently, 18 churches and religious organisations have officially received from public authorities the status of '*Cult*', which provides financial support for priests' salaries, religious buildings and religious education in public schools. Despite the ROC position favouring the reestablishment of '*dominant religion*' status from the inter-war period, the new adopted legislation of Church–State relation is based on three principles: autonomy, neutrality and cooperation. Thus, the democratisation and Europeanisation process has forged the political class to move beyond the national Church and Byzantine symphonia concept, towards a more inclusive model of religious pluralism, implying the public institutions neutrality in terms of religious affairs. In sum, *de jure* the transition from symphonia to *cooperation*, between State and religions in educational, cultural and social sphere, is one of the most important achievements of the 2006 Law.[4]

However, *de facto* the ROC has sought to maintain a strong formal presence in politics. Informally, the Church has been a powerful political actor, so much so that the State often had to react to developments initiated by the Church without consultation with, and often in contradiction to, the political class (see Stan & Turcescu 2000, Stan 2005a, 2005b). For example, the Church offered religious instruction in public schools before parliament legislated the issue (see also Bîgu in this volume), and hampered attempts to decriminalise homosexual behaviour at the risk of endangering Romania's European Union integration (see also Iordache in this volume). Church direct and indirect political involvement at all levels has been endorsed by powerful Synod members, both conservative and reformist. In 1998, Archbishop Anania proposed that the Church select candidates for parliamentary mandates and priests urge believers during sermons to vote for people whom the Church trusted. Even respected Metropolitan Nicolae Corneanu of Banat further explained that the Church 'can neither be apolitical, as some fear, nor involved in political partisanship, as some wish,' since it 'must have a word to say in what goes on in the world, society and daily life.'[5]

The prominent social theologian and orthodox intellectual Radu Preda (2011: 344) investigated the Holy Synod of the ROC official decisions concerning every four years elections after 1989. In 1990, the ROC main body recommended the abstention from political engagement or active party members. Two years later, the decision was remembered to the orthodox priests, however no sanctions were defined for those who run independently or visibly supported one party. Before the 1996 elections the Orthodox bishops were forbidden to be politically involved or to run at the local level. Yet, it has still been possible for priests to run as local councillors, according to the Holy Synod. Only the 2000 elections introduced the sanction of being suspended from religious service for those religious leaders that will run as political candidates, during their mandate. But the radical change, according to Preda, came only in the 2004 elections, when the 'political' priests were to choose for life between a political or an ecclesiastic career. Despite this secular achievement, in the 2008 elections the Church leaders would return to the 2000 elections recommendations, allowing the possibility for clergy members to run as local councillors in their communities. As Radu Preda noted, this ambiguous, ambivalent and constantly changing position towards clergy involvement in elections shows the difficult task for ROC leaders to clearly separate religion from political affairs.

After the fall of communism, the theme of religion as an electoral campaigns topic was mainly present in local and general elections, but less in presidential elections. Using the public capital of the ROC, as one of the most trusted institutions in the country, different political parties have instrumentalised religion in their electoral strategies (see Stan & Turcescu 2007). The presence of politicians during religious holy days, pilgrimages or other religious activities prior to local and general elections, but also public statements of support for different candidates by religious leaders, are constantly part of the post-communist Romanian democracy each four years in the electoral process. On the other hand, in the 1996 presidential elections, during the last public debate between Ion Iliescu and Emil Constantinescu, the question of religion was relevant to the final outcome of the election. To this regard, Constantinescu's last question addressed to Iliescu was: '*Do you believe in God?*' underlying his opponent's identity as free-thinker in a major religious country. According to different studies, this 'religious' question made a significant difference between the two candidates in the final round. Since 1996, no other presidential electoral campaign has referred to the topic of religion as distinctive identity between candidates.

The Romanian democratisation process has developed tolerant and inclusive policies towards ethnic and religious minorities, spread across the country, in the last quarter of a century. Thus, apart from minor and regional disputes between ROC and new religious movements in the 1990s or the status of the Hungarian minority in Transylvania, no major ethnic or religious conflict has erupted after 1989. However, the 2014 presidential campaign placed the question of ethnic and religious identity in the core of political competition. Being twice in a minority position, as ethnic German and Lutheran, the right-wing politician Klaus Iohannis was the first presidential candidate who reached the final round as 'non-orthodox'. In the following section, I investigate, through a case study, how the 'orthodox' socialist candidate Victor Ponta politicised religion in political discourse, but also the ROC position during the electoral process.

2014 presidential elections and religion

After the collapse of Ceausescu's regime in 1989, socialists and liberal-democrats shared the Romanian presidency. Thus, from the left-wing political family and former communist party, Ion Iliescu was president between 1990–1992, 1992–1996 and the last mandate 2000–2004. On the other side of the political spectrum, Emil Constantinescu was elected president between 1996–2000 from the centre-right political alliance, followed by two mandates of Traian Basescu, 2004–2009 and 2009–2014. Since Iliescu's last mandate, the Socialist Democrat Party (PSD) has been struggling in vain to win the presidential seat. The 2014 presidential elections were considered the perfect timing for the socialist party to reach again the Controceni Palace and the most important position in the public administration of Romanian democracy. In addition, the young president of PSD and his position as Prime Minister of the Romanian Government since 2012, Victor Ponta, was increasing the hopes of left-wing supporters for a successful presidential campaign. It is worth noting that Victor Ponta had hesitations about his candidacy in 2014 elections, stating that his age and his function as head of the government in the middle of political mandate will make him a more suitable candidate for 2019. However, the PSD elected Ponta as presidential candidate with deep confidence in his chances to win the 2014 elections.

Mayor of Sibiu city in Transylvania, former European capital of culture in 2007, Klaus Iohannis was an enigmatic figure in the political arena. Representing the German community at regional level, with an historical presence since the 14th century, his public administration performances as leader of Sibiu were soon discovered and promoted at the national level. The German ethnic identity of Iohannis was a significant advantage for his public perception among Romanians, linking his political career to the royal family of Hohenzollern, who led the country to the modernisation era, from the mid of 19th century to the communist regime. In this regard, Iohannis was already on the list of the socialist party as Prime Minister during the 2009 presidential campaign. Five years later, he would join the National Liberal Party (PNL) and be nominated to run as candidate of the right-wing alliance for the presidential seat. By the mid of 2014, the two major forces of the political landscape had elected Victor Ponta and Klaus Iohannis as candidates for the November elections. Nevertheless, Iohannis's religious identity, affiliated to the Protestant Lutheran religious minority, was never raised until the 2014 presidential campaign started.

On 29 July, Victor Ponta launched his candidacy in Craiova, Oltenia region, introducing religion to the campaign political agenda. Despite no accusations regarding religion and ethnicity, Ponta started to defend his ethno-religious identity defining himself as 'proud to be born Romanian and Orthodox' in a major Orthodox country. Several days before this speech, 'Romanian', 'patriot' and 'Orthodox Christian' were the most important and desirable characteristic of the next president, according to the qualitative survey realised by Focus Avangarde.[6] Based on this study, the PSD leader strategy was to consider Iohannis as 'non-Romanian' and 'non-Orthodox'. In the following days, different leaders of PNL described the instrumentalisation of religion in electoral scopes as being 'ugly, immoral and unacceptable' (Petre Roman)[7] or 'damaging the peaceful religious and ethnic coexistence' (Catalin Predoiu)[8] in Romanian society. Former Minister of Education Daniel Funeriu moved further, criticising the ROC for being involved in the campaign and describing the use of religion as 'division strategy of those without God'.[9] Moreover, the Romania TV station, with close ties to the PSD party, announced Victor Ponta as the 'only Orthodox candidate'. To sum up, ethnic and religious identity was transformed into a political weapon against the 'foreigner' and 'non-Orthodox' Iohannis.

In response to the criticism against the ROC involvement, the Romanian Patriarchate press office qualified these accusations as 'unjust' and rejected the political competition that instrumentalised religion. By reaffirming the neutral position of the Church in political affairs, but also the interdiction for

Orthodox clergy to join political organisations, the ROC communicate was appealing to the political leaders to avoid using religion on the electoral battleground. The message ends with a list of Church priorities in society, such as pastoral mission, helping those in need or developing educational and cultural programmes for communities in Romania or abroad. It was the first press communicate that the ROC made publicly during the 2014 elections. On the same day, former Prime Minister Mihai Razvan Ungureanu, who preceded Victor Ponta, published an article titled 'The good Orthodox and the bad Orthodox',[10] deploring the ROC intrusion in the elections. According to his view, the Church hierarchy should counter religion's politicisation, highlighting the possible conflict with Victor Ponta's strategy and the indirect support for Klaus Iohannis as a misunderstood outcome. At the end of the article, Ungureanu challenged Ponta's religiosity and morality with several questions regarding abortion, homosexuality and new religious movements.

Following this first round of exchanges between political and religious entities, the PSD candidate started his 'religious campaign' tour. Religious feasts and pilgrimages were added on the map of Victor Ponta's road to the presidential seat. One of the most important pilgrimages in Romania takes place every year on 15 August at the Nicula monastery in Transylvania. Present at this large religious event,[11] Ponta expressed his administrative support for the local infrastructure in order to provide basic conditions for pilgrims. The day after, on the feast day of St Brancoveanu, according to the Orthodox calendar, the social-democrat leader and other ministers attended the religious service at St George Church in Bucharest. The Patriarch Daniel celebrated the liturgy, commemorating 300 years of Constantin Brancoveanu and his four sons' martyrdom in Istanbul. On his Facebook page, Ponta wrote 'I prayed yesterday at Nicula and today here for my family and Romanians, so we may live together in Romania as in our country and being proud of that'.[12] He also shared his religious experiences as child, attending very often the Orthodox services with his grandfather, an Orthodox priest. Ponta concluded with Brancoveanu's role model of preserving Romanian identity and values, underlying its relevance for contemporary society. The ethnic and religious identities were again present in his communication strategy. By the end of August, Ponta fulfilled his promises and allocated, from government reserve funds, 6 millions lei (1.5 million euros) for three religious locations: Nicula and Tismana monasteries and the Metropolitanate centre of Iasi, Moldova region.

October has gained the status of 'pilgrimage month' in the post-communist Romanian society. Each year on 14 October, believers from all around the country and abroad take part in the Sainte Parascheva feast in Iasi. One month before the November elections, political leaders from all parties do not miss the opportunity to be seen next to important religious representatives of the ROC. It has also become a place for 'political' pilgrimage towards winning elections (see Banică 2014). Victor Ponta did not neglect this 'tradition'. The day after, the government approved another 6 millions lei (1.5 million euros) for religious constructions: two cathedrals for the Romanian diaspora (Madrid and Barcelona) and two churches (Gorj and Cluj).[13] It's worth adding that other religious denominations were targeted to support Ponta's candidacy, like the Greek Catholic Church who received the visit of Vice-Prime Minister Liviu Dragnea, a short time after the governmental decision to fund the cathedral.[14] Attending the most important religious feast and pilgrimages prior to the elections, together with State support from public budget for religious buildings of different churches,[15] were on the top list of Ponta's electoral strategy to win votes from traditional and religious peoples.

Another dynamic of politics and religion interaction during the presidential elections was taking place at the local level. Posters, flyers and 'political-religious' icons showing Ponta as the only 'Orthodox' candidate were distributed to individuals. Some of them were posted online, stating that Orthodox Christians voters should not betray their faith and nation (*neam*)[16] by choosing Iohannis. The main argument was that 'Romania needs an Orthodox president'. On the other hand, the use of religion in campaign reached deep theological justifications. For example, one flyer urged 'Vote for the Left', arguing that the Orthodox believers were worshiping with the sign of the cross starting from the left side. Similar to this, an icon having on the front side the figure of Arsenie Boca[17] had the logo of the PSD party and 'Victor Ponta president' on the back.[18] The local Church representatives had always countered these electoral materials, affirming that it is impossible to control their distribution. In addition, there was no proof of religious leaders or local priests involved in these electoral affairs. From this perspective, replying to accusations of supporting Victor Ponta, from President Traian Basescu, the second ROC press release[19] during the campaign was based on the absence of evidence, denying Church political involvement.

The same didn't happen after the first presidential elections tour. With more than 40 per cent of votes, Victor Ponta was heading confidently to the Cotroceni Palace. His opponent, Klaus Iohannis, had only 30.37 per cent of votes. Thus, previsions had been fulfilled and the second tour of the pre-sidential elections had for the first time a non-Orthodox candidate. For the final confrontation, the PSD political mobilisation included the Church infrastructure at the local level. The participation of political leaders to the Sunday service before the 16 November final election and statements of high-level Orthodox priests during worships were clearly indicating Victor Ponta as the 'suitable' candidate. As a case in point I will give some examples, recorded and transmitted by media agencies. Bishop Iustin Sigheteanu of Mar-amures stated that: 'The President needs to be Romanian and Orthodox, who makes the sign of the cross'. Moreover, he urged the diocese priests to parti-cipate at the second presidential tour 'immediately after the Liturgy, together with all the community'.[20] The bishop of Oltenia, Irineu Popa, declared during the Sunday sermon: 'Let us pray that God will give us leaders who are orthodox, honest and correct'. In the Cluj diocese, a pastoral letter for the election of an 'Orthodox President' was sent to the local Church leaders.[21] As the second presidential tour was approaching, the ROC support for Victor Ponta became visible and was strongly publicised and criticised by civil society and orthodox intellectuals.

Before the second tour of the presidential campaign, most of the political analyst and sociological estimations were favouring Victor Ponta as winner of the elections. Yet, the final outcome was different and surprised everyone. Several political and sociological reasons made this possible. First of all, many problems were registered in diaspora during the first presidential tour, as Victor Ponta's government reduced the number of polling stations abroad. Therefore, Romanians living outside the country were protesting against the government and Victor Ponta's candidacy for not allowing them to vote. Pictures and videos with endless lines in front of polling stations were posted online, causing a massive reaction from the population. As a result, Romanians abroad were calling those inside the country to participate in the electoral process, motivating them to be present on the 16 November presidential elections. Secondly, the young generation's enormous mobilisation via social media produced a high rate of voter participation, countering Ponta's advantage from the first elections round. It was well known that Romanian diaspora and young generation were voting in majority for the right wing political option. In this unforeseen political and social context, Klaus Iohannis won the presidential campaign with 54.43 per cent of the vote, defeating Victor Ponta (45.56 per cent) and his supporters. The post-election analysis will be developed in the last section of this paper.

Although not publicly stating their support for the socialist candidate at the national level, by highlighting the political neutrality, the PSD-ROC alliance was functional at the local level. After the 2 November presidential tour, Victor Ponta's supporters were very optimistic and the political-religious alliance seemed to be the perfect strategy. As the second tour was approaching, the ROC support for the 'Orthodox' candidate was visible and highly contested by civil society and the young generation. On the afternoon of election day, realising the possible defeat of Victor Ponta, the Romanian Patriarchate press office released a communicate called the 'orthodox exit-pool'. By referring to the modern history of the Romanian nation, the Patriarchate was stating that, as an answer to people's prayers for freedom and national unity, 'God has also worked through foreigners, such as king Ferdinand and his queen Maria'. Being accused of political opportunism, as Iohannis was increasing his chances to reach the Cotroceni Palace, the ROC denied the electoral purpose of the press release. In fact, according to the press office, the message was an older sermon of the Patriarch from 2010, reposted online on the merciful Samaritan Sunday.[22] Despite the origin of the sermon, the 'orthodox exit-poll' was qualified by public opinion as ROC shifting support towards Iohannis. Let us now turn on the research question and analyse why the political strategy of involving religion has failed.

Religious revolution and secularisation

'God exists' and 'God is with us' shouted thousands of Romanians in December 1989. After almost 50 years of atheist propaganda in public schools, religious persecutions and religious freedom restrictions, the post-communist Romanian society was putting religion at its foundation. Religion has regained the public sphere and Romania has experienced one of the most important religious revivals in Central and Eastern Europe (Tomka 2010). Thus, in the new political and social environment, the ROC preserved its status of the largest religious confession and was highly credited by society. Nevertheless, the Byzantine symphonia, rebranded under the forced communist collaboration between Church and State, was kept alive after the fall of the totalitarian regime. Heir of the communist party, the socialist-democrat PSD had in the ROC a strong ally every four years during the elections. In fact, compared to other governments, the PSD has supported and financed most of the Church restoration programmes within society. In short, the post-communist religious revival was institutionally re-established by the ROC, with significant help from the political class in search for social legitimacy, headed by the PSD party.

In the light of previous elections, the 2014 presidential race brought religion to the centre stage. Drawing a comparative analysis between the 1996, 2004 and 2014 presidential elections, Andrei Alexandrescu (2015) argues that when some candidates assumed a certain political identity, which included the Orthodox religious dimension and support for certain issues on the agenda of the official church, the balance of popular vote didn't change decisively. In his view, ethnic identity and political ideology seem to be more important than religious identity and ROC support, when it comes to presidential elections. In other terms, affiliation with ROC image does not guarantee political success. On the other side, Iohannis's ethnic identity surpassed Ponta's religious self-identification as 'proud to be Orthodox'. Between Iohannis's double minority identities, as religious and ethnical, the German origins were positively perceived by the society. Thus, constructed as a disadvantage by the socialists' group strategy, Iohannis' ethnicity and 'foreigner' image were transformed into a successful outcome by the PNL party. His German ethnicity balanced his 'non-orthodox' religious affiliation.

But Iohannis had an advantage also on the religious ground. Among the five most important candidates on the 2 November presidential tour, the German candidate was in fact practising his religion without instrumentalising it. Furthermore, on several occasions the right-wing candidate refused to comment on his confessional belonging and criticised Ponta's strategy of using religion in political combat. Being religiously discrete and maintaining strict separation between religion and politics, Iohannis was leading in the morality field. Far from being the 'good Orthodox', Ponta's corruption scandals, plagiarism, his position as leader of the Government and the PSD party were not morally a virtue for him to be considered the suitable 'Orthodox' candidate. In this context, putting religious belonging at the first glance of the elections, but without proving his spiritual authenticity and moral vocation, Ponta's strategy turned against himself. Even if Romanians were to choose an 'Orthodox' as president, Victor Ponta was not a suitable person. The moral argument had a significant impact on the final result.[23]

In order to pursue the argument, next to ethnical and religious implications, it is important to add the political and social context. As mentioned in the previous section, following the deplorable election organisation in diaspora, demonstrations all over Europe were taking place. From abroad to inside the country, thousands of Romanians started to criticise the socialist government and Victor Ponta's candidacy. Underlying the intentional limitation of voting rights by the PSD government, millions of Romanians working and living in Western countries started a mobilisation campaign for the second tour of the elections. By using technological communications tools, such as emails, social networks, calls, videos and pictures posted online, Romanian diaspora have had an enormous impact on the massive voting participation for the final election. Therefore, the diaspora doubled its participation in comparison with the 2009 presidential elections.[24] In response, the 16 November final presidential tour registered an increase of 10 per cent, reaching 64.10 per cent of the voting population in the country and abroad. Despite Ponta's first tour result and its politicised religious affiliation, the diaspora conflict was crucial for the historical turn between the two presidential tours and his political defeat.

Focusing their political strategy on the conservative and traditional PSD electorate, the socialists neglected the young generation. It is widely known that young people do not have a high rate of participation in votes. The first presidential tour confirmed this social reality. However, as a consequence of the diaspora voting procedures, the young generation was mobilised via the social networks. The Facebook 'party' was smartly affiliated to the PNL strategy and Klaus Iohannis' official page became an important campaign tool. One step further, the political combat was uploaded on social media and the virtual world competed with real society. Ethnic identity and religious belonging was less important in social media political confrontation. In response, similar to the diaspora case, the young generation voted in a majority for Klaus Iohannis, or to put it in other terms, they voted against Victor Ponta. The anti-communist attitude of the young people against PSD party was predominantly put on the front page of the right-wing political propaganda. In the end, young people made the difference in the final election tour.[25]

The young generation's 'successful' participation in the 2014 presidential elections is also relevant for the Church–State relation and secularisation process of the Romanian society. Born around 1990, the young post-communist generation is becoming more secular, although it is still difficult to include them into Grace Davie's (1994) concept of 'believing without belonging'. Yet, in their view religion should stick out from political affairs. Favouring a clear separation between politics and religion and, sometimes, even between Church and State, the young people were against Victor Ponta's nationalistic exclusivism and confessional apartheid. Claiming the Church and State separation, it is important to note the advancement of the young generation's individual level of secularisation.[26] Moreover, there is an anticlerical spirit that was born during the 2014 election, hardly contesting the ROC mixture in the presidential campaign. Ignoring the voting population between 18 and 30 years, the PSD made another decisive step toward the unsuccessful result of the election.

Nearly one decade after European Union integration, Romanian society has developed a secular perspective on the relationship between religion and politics, challenging the Byzantine traditional symphonia. As Lucian Leuştean (2014) argues, the 'Romanian elections are a veritable religious revolution won by the secular nature of the European Union, with its emphasis on multi-religious and multi-ethnic dialogue'. According to the same scholar, the diaspora has become a key factor in winning elections. For them, Iohannis was the providential man, whose religion and ethnicity did not matter, who could embody Europe. The 2007 enlargement of the European Union led to a significant section of the population living abroad, many of whom have fully integrated into Western European countries. Whereas the religious card ensured the winning vote in previous post-communist elections, the employment of the Church no longer has the same effect. The 2014 'religious revolution', followed by the ROC involvement in presidential elections, is challenging the Orthodoxy role in a pluralistic, secular and European society. The election of a German and Protestant candidate is a maturity sign of the democratic and transitional process that Romania has undertaken in the last quarter of century.

Religious pluralism is an undisputed condition for liberal, democratic society. The ROC involvement in supporting the 'Orthodox' candidate was causing conflict between religious institutions, endangering the multi-religious coexistence. One example is the Seven Day Adventist Church's president, pastor Marius Munteanu, who published an open letter addressed to 'all citizens from Romania, the homeland of all Romanians'.[27] In his text, Munteanu condemns the use of religion as presidential criteria and asks for clear separation between ROC and political parties. Furthermore, he underlines that 'the 2014 elections are for President, not for the Patriarch of the Romanian Orthodox Church'. According to the Adventist leader, 'Romanian does not mean Orthodox, as Orthodox does not mean Romanian. The Orthodox faith belongs to the Orthodox believers, not to the Romanian nation'. The open letter ends with an appeal to all presidential candidates and religious confessions to stop polarising the society and spreading religious intolerance, because the 'president of Romanian is president of all Romanians', no matter his ethnicity, colour or religion. Thus, after a long process of social and confessional coexistence in post-communist Romania, not without conflicts, the 2014 election reignited the flames of older religious disputes.

Many Romanian intellectuals criticised the use of religion for political goals and suggested that the ROC should stick to religious affairs (see

Baconschi 2016; Papahagi 2017). According to Dragoş Paul Aligică (2014), a political scientist scholar, by involving in the presidential campaign, the ROC made a huge mistake, 'as big as its modern history'. In his article, Aligică underlined the deplorable organisations of elections and Church compromise rewarded with public funds for religious buildings. Visibly disappointed, he reminds that when the Church is choosing to engage politically, it is being subordinate to the State. Instead of being a moral force for its believers, the Church becomes a powerful tool in the political competition and undermines its social, cultural and religious role in the society, concluded Aligică. The famous social theologian Radu Preda stated that the Church has not learned an important lesson after the fall of communism. 'It is not the clergy who should be involved in politics, it is lay members of the Church role', concluded Preda.[28] Last but not least, a former right-wing politician, with close ties to Orthodox intelligentsia, Server Voinescu (2014) highlighted the Church's public image damage after the 2014 presidential elections. The major social mutations that followed confirmed Voinescu's previsions. The ROC was weakened after the presidential elections and has to counter anticlerical reactions, in particular from the young generation.

The 2014 presidential elections brought for the first time a 'non-Orthodox' candidate to the final stage. Thus, very confident in their strategy of using ethnicity and religious affiliation as political tools, Victor Ponta's electoral campaign team didn't give a chance to Klaus Iohannis, the right-wing candidate. The final outcome was a different one. In the last section of this chapter we analysed the main causes of using religion as campaign topic failing strategy. Despite the successful political alliance between PSD and ROC at local and general elections, the previous presidential elections were already unsuccessfully instrumentalising religion for political capital. Furthermore, Victor Ponta's moral standards were not suitable for the 'Orthodox candidate' to be elected. By refusing to address the issue of religious belonging, but also being discretely a Church attender, Klaus Iohannis was morally countering Ponta's strategy. Finally, the unforeseen social and political impact of diaspora community and the Facebook 'party', which mobilised young voters for the second presidential tour, was the decisive step towards Klaus Iohannis' victory. Last but not least, by supporting Victor Ponta's candidacy, the ROC was negatively impacted the most after the 2014 elections.

Conclusions

The post-communist religious revival has slowed the secularisation process within society (see Tănase 2008). Despite the public space recapture by the ROC, the 2014 presidential elections erupted into a religious revolution with secularising consequences on the religious landscape. In other terms, the institutional de-secularisation (see Karpov 2010) led by the ROC after 1989 has reached its limits, after a quarter of century of transition towards democracy and European integration. The end of the post-communist religious revival is fostered by an increase of individual secularisation, mostly among the young generation. Although Romania is still a highly religious country, when it comes to the declarative religion and religious belonging,[29] the secular views on moral issues or Church and State separation are gaining space in public discourse. Declarative religion is contradicted by lived religion. Ignoring the contradiction between the external religious affiliation and the internal spiritual and political beliefs, Victor Ponta's strategy team made a crucial mistake. In addition, the moral evaluation of the 'Orthodox' candidate, together with his undemocratic elections organisation in diaspora, are completing the failing political strategy of turning religion into a political weapon. However, if the PSD party lost an election, the ROC seriously damaged its public trust and image, turning the post-communist de-secularisation golden page towards the increase of secularisation and anticlericalism.

Following the religion involvement in political affairs criticism, the religious revolution started with the 2014 presidential campaign war pursued by several unhappy events for the Orthodox Church. In this line, the religious education in public schools was subject to legal changes, changing its status of compulsory class in the education system (see Bîgu in this volume). Moreover, the corruption scandal of the 'Colectiv' affair unbound anticlerical demonstrations against the Patriarch Daniel and the Church's privileged position within the society. Currently, the debates and religious mobilisation around the constitutional amendment for preserving the traditional version of marriage, supported by ROC, are politically exposing the main religious institution. Shifting from the traditional alliance with political parties, after the unsuccessful result of the 2014 elections, the ROC is currently focusing on its religious network in order to advance a conservative political agenda.

As Romanian society is entering into a new religious environment after the 2014 presidential elections, reassessing religion as private matter through an anticlerical spirit, the ROC's political actions will be carefully followed by civil society. In the same time, the ROC's involvement in political affairs will increase the rise of secularisation and secularism supporters. According to their position, strict separation of religion and politics is commendable because it allows both the state and the churches to be independent and autonomous from each other, and therefore permits for a radical break with the recent past. This radical break supposes also moving beyond symphonia when analysing post-communist religion and politics.

Notes

1 See National Institute of Statistics (INS) 2011 Census: www.insse.ro/cms/files/p ublicatii/pliante%20statistice/08-Recensamintele%20despre%20religie_n.pdf.
2 See The Romanian Constitution of 1923: http://www.constitutia.ro/const1923.htm
3 See http://www.culte.gov.ro/
4 Regarding the cooperation model in orthodox countries, see the concept of 'entangled authorities' where both religion and politics cooperate but compete for scarce resources as well. So the outcomes of this 'cooperation' very much depend

on personal networks of power, the situational setting and the topics at hand (see Köllner, 2018, forthcoming).

5　See 'Biserica Ortodoxă vrea reprezentare', *Evenimentul Zilei* (17 April 1998).

6　See http://evz.ro/sondaj-avangarde-profilul-de-prezidentiabil-al-lui-klaus-iohannis-nu-este-conform-cu-preferintelor-romanilor.html (28 July 2014).

7　Former Prime Minister (1990–1991) and significant leader of PNL party.

8　Vice-President of PNL party.

9　See http://www.hotnews.ro/print?articleId=17817194 (4 August 2014).

10　See http://adevarul.ro/news/politica/ortodoxul-bun-ortodoxul-rau-1_53df81dd0d13 3766a8001131/index.html (4 August 2014).

11　See http://gov.ro/ro/print?modul=stiri&link=primul-ministru-victor-ponta-a-participa t-la-slujba-de-sfanta-maria-la-manastirea-nicula (15 August 2014).

12　See 'Victor Ponta a asistat, alaturi de mai multi ministri, la slujba de la Biserica Sf Gheorghe cel Nou din Bucuresti' *HotNews.ro* (16 August 2014).

13　For the Madrid Romanian community Cathedral Madrid (Spain) 2.000.000 lei; Barcelona Cathedral (Spain) 1.000.000 lei; Lainici Monastery (Gorj) 2.000.000 lei and Greek-Catholic Cathedral (Cluj- Napoca) 1.000.000 lei.

14　See 'Armonia politico-religioasă de la Cluj. Guvernul dă bani, biserica face slujbe', *Actualul de Cluj* (22 October 2014).

15　See　http://www.hotnews.ro/stiri-esential-18901107-anul-electoral-umplut-vistieria -bisericii-cultele-primit-suplimentari-record-22-milioane-euro-guvern-2014.htm (22 December 2014).

16　See Bîgu in this volume for more details on this concept.

17　Arsenie Boca, a former Orthodox priest, imprisoned and forcedly defrocked by the communist regime, is considered to be a saint by many Orthodox believers, but the ROC has not officially canonised him yet.

18　See http://www.hotnews.ro/print?articleId=18402639 (29 October 2014).

19　See http://basilica.ro/implicarea-politica-partizana-a-bisericii-in-campania-electora la-trebuie-dovedita/ (3 November 2014).

20　See http://adevarul.ro/locale/satu-mare/video-iustin-sigheteanul-vicarul-episcopiei-maramuresului-satmarului-instructiuni-preotilor-va-puneti-fruntea-credinciosilor-bi serica-direct-vot-oamenii-voteze-crestin-ortodox-1_5461d7620d133766a8bfd7bc/in dex.html (11 November 2014).

21　See http://www.hotnews.ro/stiri-esential-18489810-video-mai-multi-preoti-ortodocsi-din-judetul-cluj-primit-circulara-mitropolia-clujului-prin-care-cere-spuna-credinciosil or-voteze-presedinte-care-fie-crestin-ortodox-roman.htm (7 November 2014).

22　See http://evz.ro/bor-explica-mesajul-misteros-rostit-de-patriarhul-daniel-in-ziua-votu lui.html (19 November 2017).

23　See Zigon (2011) and the concept of 'multiple moralities' in post-socialist societies, where the Church is one player among many others, but not the dominant one in all cases.

24　See Covaci (2015). In 2014, the percentage of Romanians abroad voters increased 70 per cent, in comparison with 2009 elections, and other thousands were not able to vote. On the first presidential tour, there were only 161,054 votes. Klaus Iohannis was the new Romanian president thanks to diaspora votes, where 378,811 Romanians voted. Therefore, Klaus Iohannis had 89.73 per cent and Victor Ponta 10.26 per cent diaspora votes.

25　See the post-election IRES survey on voting profiles for both candidates http://www.ires.com.ro/articol/278/cine-sunt-cei-care-au-votat-in-turul-2–la-alegerile-prezidentiale and http://adevarul.ro/news/politica/alegeri-prezidentiale-2014-analiza-ires-tinerii-fa cut-diferenta-iohannis-ponta-1_546a1b4a0d133766a8f86176/index.html (17 November 2014).

26　I am referring to Karel Dobbelaere's (2002) theoretic framework of three secularisation levels.

27 See http://mobile.hotnews.ro/stire/18527309 (11 November 2014).
28 See 'Religia, teren de luptă în campania electorală. Ce rămâne după?', *Decât o revistă* (15 November 2014), http://alegeri.decatorevista.ro/ultimele-articole/religia -element-de-manipulare-in-campania-electorala-ce-ramane-dupa/.
29 See the latest Pew Research Centre survey *Religious Belief and National belonging in Central and Eastern Europe*, (10 May 2017), http://www.pewforum.org/2017/05/ 10/religious-belief-and-national-belonging-in-central-and-eastern-europe/.

References

Alexandrescu, A. 2015. 'Identitatea religioasa si alegerile repzidentiale din 1996, 2004 si 2014 din Romania', *Polis* 3(9): 61–79.
Aligică, P. D. 2014. 'Lecția întâmplărilor recente: Biserica', *Revista* 22 (9 December), available online: http://revista22online.ro/51255/leciile-ntmplrilor-recente-biserica.html.
Baconschi, T. 2016. *Cetatea sub asediu. Însemnări despre credință, rațiune și terrorism.* Iasi: Doxologia.
Banică, M. 2014. *Nevoie de miracol. Fenomenul pelerinajelor în România contemporană.* Iasi: Polirom.
Carp, R. 2013. *Religie, politica si statul de drept. Secventele unei acomodari.* Bucharest: Humanitas.
Conovici, I. 2010. *Ortodoxia in Romania post-comunista. Reconstructia unei identitati publice.* Cluj-Napoca: Eikon.
Covaci, M. 2015. 'Factorul Facebook în alegerile prezidențiale' *Sfera Politicii* 1(183): 85–91.
Davie, G. 1994. *Religion in Britain since 1945: Belonging without Believing.* Oxford: Blackwell.
Dobbelaere, K. 2002. *Secularization: An Analysis at Three Levels.* Bern: Peter Lang.
Enache, G. 2005. *Ortodoxie și putere politică în România contemporană.* Bucharest: Nemira.
Enache, G. 2016. *Orthodoxy, Liberalism and Totalitarianism in Modern and Contemporary Romania.* Targoviste: Cetatea de Scaun.
Gillet, O. 1997. *Religion et Nationalisme: L'idéologie de l'Eglise orthodoxe roumaine sous le régime communiste.* Brussels: Editions de l'Université de Bruxelles.
Karpov, V. 2010. 'Desecularization: A Conceptual Framework', *Journal of Church and State* 52(2): 232–270.
Köllner, T. 2018. 'On the Restitution of Property and the Making of 'Authentic' Landscapes in Contemporary Russia', *Europe-Asia Studies* 70(7): 1083–1102. doi:10.1080/09668136.2018.1484077.
Köllner, T. Forthcoming. *Orthodox Religion and Politics: An Anthropological Perspective on Post-Soviet Russian Secularity.* London, New York: Routledge.
Leuștean, L. N. 2005. 'Ethno-Symbolic Nationalism, Orthodoxy and the Installation of Communism in Romania: 23 August 1944 to 30 December 1947', *Nationalities Papers* 33(4): 439–458.
Leuștean, L. 2009. *Orthodoxy and the Cold War: Religion and Political Power in Romania (1947–1965).* Basingstoke: Palgrave Macmillan.
Leuștean, L. 2014. *A Religious Romanian Revolution: The Orthodox Church and the 2014 Presidential Elections.* London: Translating Academy.
Papahagi, A. 2017. *Creștinul în cetate. Manual de supraviețuire.* Iasi: Doxologia.

Preda, R. 2011. 'Dileme ale relaţiei dintre ortodoxie şi democraţie'. In *Religie şi democraţie*. Edited by Camil Ungureanu. Iaşi: Polirom.

Roberson, R. G. 1996. 'The Church in Romania'. In *New Catholic Encyclopedia 19*. Washington, DC: McGraw-Hill.

Stan, L. 2005a. 'Religious Education in Romania', *Communist and Post-Communist Studies* 38(3): 381–401.

Stan, L. 2005b. 'Religion, Politics and Sexuality in Romania', *Europe-Asia Studies* 57(2): 291–310.

Stan, L. 2007. *Religion and Politics in Post-Communist Romania*. Oxford: Oxford University Press.

Stan, L. and L. Turcescu. 2000. 'The Romanian Orthodox Church and Post-Communist Democratization', *Europe-Asia Studies* 52(8): 1467–1488.

Stan, L. and L. Turcescu. 2007. *Religion and Politics in Post-Communist Romania*. New York, Oxford: Oxford University Press.

Tănase, L. D. 2008. *Pluralisation religieuse et société en Roumanie*. Bern: Peter Lang.

Tomka, M. 2010. *Expanding Religion. Religious Revival Post-communist in Central and Eastern Europe*. Berlin: De Gruyter.

Voinescu, S. 2014. 'Provocări la care Biserica nu răspunde bine', *Revista* 22 (8 December).

Zigon, J. (ed.). 2011. *Multiple Moralities and Religions in Post-Soviet Russia*. New York: Berghahn Books.

3 The Temple Mount comparison

A new paradigm of the relationship between State and Church?

Marten Stahlberg

As often in history, a crisis situation unleashes underestimated powers and brings to light intentions and motives that were more or less hidden before. The conflict concerning Crimea seems to be one of that order. President Vladimir Putin mainly in two addresses defends the 'reunification' of the peninsular to Russia which was in the international context mostly perceived as the annexation of a territory belonging to another sovereign country and, as a matter of fact, as violation of international law. Beside several other arguments Putin deals with the religious motive of the Temple Mount in order to highlight the immense importance of Crimea. How can this be understood: do we witness desecularising tendencies in Russian society and a growing importance of religious topics? Or is it rather to be seen as a strategic manoeuvre that uses or even misuses religious symbols and motives for political interests? And, what does it tells us about the relationship between politics and religion according to the principle of 'symphonia' (harmony) describing the traditional orthodox way of close cooperation between the political power and the Church?

Putin characterises the events on Crimea as a historic turning point (*perelomnyi istoricheskii moment*; Putin 2014a), what could be translated also as point of change or even point of fracture. Does the 'Crimean question' indicate a political turn-around not only in Russian spatial policy but also in the way of interacting with Orthodoxy?

In our examination which is based on a contextualising interpretation of statements and documents both from political and from Church officials we will focus on two crucial elements of the Russian mindmap – the territorial and the religious question which happen to occur in Putin's Temple Mount comparison. The analysis and comparison of the religious, in particular Christian, subtext in official narratives used both by political and Church elites does require our particular attention. These religious implications are an important indicator of how the role of religion is apprehended by these elites who, evidently, aim to model societal life according to their perceptions (see Gadinger, Jarzebski and Yildiz 2014). The focus on these narrative constructions seems to be crucial in order to come to a critical revision of how the relation between politics and religion is received. This might provide also the frame to re-evaluate the role that the concept of symphonia plays in the contemporary situation.

Therefore, after some general remarks, we will analyse certain particularly revealing paragraphs of the Presidential addresses concerning Crimea. To conclude, we will confront the religious implications of these texts to corresponding ideas promoted by the Russian Orthodox Church.

General remarks

The multiple challenges which set in with the collapse of the Soviet Union have been sufficiently analysed (Hann 2002). The Marxist-Leninist ideology which had served as a kind of glue of the multi-ethnic USSR became obsolete and, in fact, the central political power lost its adhesive function. The centrifugal tendencies of the federal republics of the Soviet Union finally caused the dissolution of the state which covered the largest territory in the world. Subsequently, the Russian Federation that succeeded the Soviet Union lost its place as an important player in global politics. So there was a need to reinvent 'the foundation upon which Russian national community is based' (Wozniuk 1997: 195). A new national idea was to be reformulated taking into consideration the new geopolitical situation: the multi-ethnic and multi-religious structure of the Russian Federation and the existence of a large group of Russians outside the boundaries of the new Russian state, as well as the existence of mainly two independent states (Ukraine and Belarus) which are populated with Eastern Slavic peoples stemming from the same cultural and historical source as Russia, the so called Rus.

In order to shape the national identity different narratives were developed. Several movements or ideologies, often based on revived pre-Soviet ideas, did occur for example the Eurasianism (see Riazanovsky 1967; Laruelle 2008; Bassin 2011) or a range of ultra-national movements (see Clowes 2011: 43–68). The intense search for a national identity entails the danger, as Hunter asserts, of moving to a kind of mono-cultural Russo-centrism (see Warhola and Lehning 2007: 934). The government is confronted with the problem of 'how to ensure that the reassertion of Russianness and the affirmation of the Russian culture and identity will not be at the expense of other major ethnic and cultural groups' (Hunter et al. 2004: 204). This explains why the official understanding of 'nation' is oscillating between two poles – a group of people linked by the same religion, culture and history, on the one hand, and a community sharing the same citizenship, on the other hand. These two aspects mark a certain dichotomy which is difficult to resolve. In any case, the last aspect underlines the actual challenge to create a strong civil society in Russia which is characterised by a broad sense of civic solidarity.

The role of Orthodoxy

Orthodox traditions are considered to be an eminent part of the Russian national culture and, subsequently, as an important factor for the development of the national idea (Ryžova 2005: 66–91). 'Most of the ethnic Russians

tend to identify themselves as "Orthodox" in terms of religion, but this identification does not necessarily possess a theological character, and even less an
overtly, religious practicing character' (Warhola and Lehning 2007: 934).
That might be one of the reasons for 'politicization of this cultural identity'
which causes serious complications as shown by the fact that 'xenophobia
and anti-Semitic attitudes have grown along with increasing Russian self-
awareness and religiosity' (Ryžova 2005:68). Following historical patterns, the
relation between Church and political power is conceived according to the
principle of symphonia which Rousselet characterises as a kind of bargaining
or haggling: facing the pluralisation of religious offers the Church obtains
several prerogatives and privileges. In return, the Church accepts the role of a
legitimating instance for the Russian state (Rousselet 2007: 63–85).

In this context, the question arises whether the 'hegemonic ecumenism'
(Warhola and Lehning 2007: 947) of the Orthodox Church can work in the long
run in such a deeply divided country. In other words, can Orthodoxy serve as an
unifying force in a multi-ethnic and poly-cultural society of today's Russia?

Russian space

Another way to fill the ideological vacancy is a growing interest in geopolitical ideas. On the one hand, this corresponds to a general trend that can be
observed in different scientific fields, the so-called spatial turn (Schlögel 2003:
19–77; Schroer 2006; Döring and Thielmann 2008). On the other hand, geopolitical assertions provide patterns to manage one of Russia's principal tasks
which is to master Russian space (Schlögel 2011: 1–25; Smith 1999: 40–70;
also Curanovic's chapter). This is far more than only a historical challenge.
The post-Soviet discourse about space deals mostly, as Schlögel observed,
with the question of identity: it is an attempt of self-understanding daring to
figure out what Russia represents after the dissolution of the USSR (Schlögel
2011: 11; see also Köllner 2018).

Fostered by a common feeling of uncertainty and danger created by the
very difficult economic and social situation in the Yeltsin era, the attention
was drawn to the old ideal of 'statehood' (*derzhavnost'*) with its important
elements: consolidation of the borders, isolationist foreign policy and a new
state-ideology composed of communism, imperial awareness and Orthodoxy
(see Ignatow 1998). Mastering Russian space is conceived as one of the pre-
eminent tasks of a strong and centralised state. In this context the principle of
territorial 'self-assertion' or even expansion as a fundamental axiom in Russian history gained new importance. In this regard the dislocation of the
Soviet Union is understood as a geopolitical tragedy or even catastrophe.
Thus, the restoration of the imperial or Soviet space seems to be a guiding
line in the territorial policy of today's Russia. This aspiration Ignatow characterises as a 'spatial obsession' and describes it very eloquently by stating:
'The initial task to collect the Russian lands skipped easily to the collection of
any land' (Ignatow 1998: 23).[1]

Summarising, for the quest of national identity Orthodoxy and the Russian spatial 'frame' are considered to be important issues. It is often claimed that the enormous size of the Russian territory moulds a particular Russian way, the Russian *Sonderweg* (special path), to organise state, culture and society (Ingold 2007). It is noteworthy, as Ignatow puts it, that in the Russian case we face a conception of prestige, which is founded on the territorial aspect of the state, on the number of physical square kilometres, and not on the dimension of merits of individuals (Ignatow 1998: 23).

The Crimean question

Putin's statements about Crimea illustrate the outlined general tendencies in a very concrete way. Leaving aside, among others, the important question concerning the concepts of nation and people, we will focus, as already mentioned, on spatial and religious aspects evoked by Putin. We will turn our attention especially to the meaning of Crimea as a part of the Russian state territory and the arguments put forward in order to underline this claim. In doing so, our analysis will face a range of patterns of argument dealing, at least at first glance, with Christian rationales.

Geopolitical assertions

In his address to the State Duma deputies Putin evokes as a basic frame the dramatic disintegration of the USSR which caused the break apart of the Soviet state territory. According to Putin Crimea was shifted, in breaking even the constitutional norms of that time, to the former Ukrainian Federal Republic. After the collapse of the Soviet Union the peninsular continued to be 'forgotten' there. This oblivion Putin conceives as a 'plundering' that Russia only accepted because of its weak condition in the 1990s. In that time the Russian Federation was in fact 'incapable of protecting its interests' (Putin 2014a). Since Ukraine was expected to be a reliable partner in assuring the Russian security issues, the status of Crimea was accepted by Russia in the early 2000s.

Because of the increasing influence of Western countries, especially the USA, and the loss, at least in Putin's mind, of its inner stability, Ukraine ceased to be a trustworthy partner for the Russian security policy. Pretending a danger for the stability of the region and a possible loss of the peninsular both for Russia and for Ukraine, Putin requires it to be under a 'strong and stable sovereignty, which today can only be Russian' (Putin 2014a). The respect for the territorial integrity of the Ukrainian state is clearly limited by Russian security issues. Here is the core of Putin's argumentation: Crimea is a strategic territory and it has to be under Russian control.

As to be expected in a political speech, Putin holds a discourse of power (security and sovereignty) to express the Russian claim for the peninsula. To demonstrate the 'Russianness' of the Crimean territory and to qualify it as an integral part of 'state forming territory' different arguments are used by him:

a   Crimea is tied to Russia by history, culture, language and values of civilisation. Very striking are the historical key parameters referred to by Putin: the baptism of Prince Vladimir and the adding of Crimea to Russian Empire in 1783. Furthermore, Putin points out that no influence of foreign powers is accepted on the 'historical territories' of Russia. How are these territories to be defined? Does this expression relate to the Grand Duchy of Moscow, the imperial Russia or the Soviet Union? Noteworthy is also the argument that the Bolsheviks shifted not only the peninsula but also an important part of the historical South of Russia to the Ukrainian Federal Republic. So, following the argumentation that Crimea is a historical Russian region, what is the case with the 'historical South of Russia'? Did it ought to be under 'strong and stable sovereignty' as well?

b   A second argument is related to the Russian people living on the Peninsula. Because of the fact that the majority of today's inhabitants are Russian and their pretended oppression, in Putin's words 'forced assimilation', Crimea has to be a part of Russia. The Russian nation (*narod*) which Putin describes as 'one of the biggest, if not the biggest ethnic group in the world to be divided by borders' (Putin 2014a), should be reunited in one Russian territory.[2] The 'old' motivation in Russian politics reappears: gathering the Russian lands. As the historical argument, this 'ethnic' pattern could be applied not only to Crimea but also to other regions of the former Soviet space where Russians represent the majority or a strong minority!

Religious assertions

Given the relevance of Orthodoxy for the ideological foundation of the Russian state, it is not surprising to find a religious subtext in political statements. So we do, when Putin refers in his 'Crimean Speech' to the holy Prince Vladimir who by being baptised had chosen Orthodoxy and thus 'predetermined the overall basis of the culture, civilisation and human values that unite the peoples of Russia, Ukraine and Belarus' (Putin 2014a). A number of interesting aspects are embedded in this narrative.

a   Putin's argumentation is based on the historical veracity of the baptisms of Vladimir on the Crimean peninsula. That Vladimir was baptised and chose orthodox Christianity as the official religion is doubtless, but that his baptism took place in Korsun is considered at least uncertain. We cannot discuss this question here in detail, but it might be enough to point out that a range of historians date the baptism of Vladimir at 987 and his campaign to Korsun at 989.[3] Putin's picture of Crimea as the cradle of Russian civilisation and its sacral source is collapsing like a house of cards. By the way, until Putin's intervention there was never a doubt that *Kiev* is the spiritual centre and the cradle of civilisation and culture of the Eastern Slavic statehood.

In using the legend of Vladimir's baptism in Korsun Putin consciously takes a kind of meta-historical position, hardly to be contested. He makes use of a finally a-historical origin myth to justify the claim of a concrete circumscribed territory. Referring to the performative effects of such 'basic'-narratives Putin shows his utilitarian approach of political language. How else could a single place, presupposed that Vladimir was baptised here, legitimate a contemporary political postulate? An event like the baptism of a prince could be considered as an initial spark to launch the process of formation of a spiritual, cultural and even political identity, but not as reason to claim a land.

b   There is no doubt that Vladimir is important for the Christianisation of the principality of Kiev. In choosing Orthodoxy the Byzantine way to conceive the interaction of the political and the spiritual power was adapted as well. Putin goes far in juxtaposing the baptism of Vladimir which entailed the somewhat offhand baptism of several citizens of Kiev (surely not all Kiev!) and the Christianisation of the whole Rus leading to the development of a 'centralised Russian state' (Putin 2014b). Different movements in the history of the Russian Church suggest that the Church–State relationship could be conceived in various ways (Döpmann 1967; Goehrke 2010: 240–246; Sazonov 2015).

Putin highlights the integrative and unifying force of the Christian faith for the formation of a Russian nation. Accordingly, the territory of Crimea can be considered to have 'strategic importance for Russia' because, as a result of the adoption of Christianity, 'the spiritual source of the development of a multifaceted but solid Russian nation and a centralised Russian state' (Putin 2014b) emanates from there. Noticeable is the use of the word 'strategic' in this context. At first glance, Putin seems to describe the spiritual 'benefits' of Christianity, but on a deeper scale, the Christian 'input' consists of providing a spiritual setting for the strategy of consolidation of the national coherence and the installation of a vertical political power.

Paying attention to the Russian text the basic message is far clearer: the unifying force is the 'spiritual ground/soil (*pochva*)' which enabled different people to realise/to become aware (*osoznavat'*) that they are one people (*narod*). In other words, Christianity procures the mould for the process of national awakening. But is it considered as the shaping force in this process?

Following Putin's reasoning, a nation[4] is formed by several elements such as ethnic similarity, common language, common elements of material culture, common territory, a common economy and government, and a kind of unifying spiritual force. In the more elaborated December address, Putin uses three times the word spiritual to explicate the relevance of Orthodoxy in the national search of identity. Is Putin illustrating, thereby, his vision to organise and govern the Russian Federation according to Christian principles?

Following the well-known governmental religious policy (see Sazonov 2015) Putin seems to conceive Christianity in a primarily functional way. It is a good soil in which to flourish patriotism and allegiance towards the political power. It is understood on the level of a 'spiritual force' (Agadjanian 2014: 56) and, thus, could be replaced by any other religion or even by an ideology like socialism. Against this background, the fact that Vladimir had chosen Christianity can be ranged in a row of historical accidents. In other words, importance is ascribed to Vladimir as a holy founding figure but not to him as a historical person or, in Christian terms, as a saint. This might explain why Putin's construction hardly bothers about the doubts of historians concerning Crimea as the place where Vladimir received baptism. The choice of Christianity is a historical fact and has to be taken in consideration as part of the national culture and mindscape. But as a kind of 'nationalised' religion it has to serve pre-eminently the raison d'état. As already stated, the today's political challenge is to manage the multi-ethnic and multi-religious reality of Russia. Therefore a 'managed pluralism' (Warhola and Lehning 2007: 936) or a 'diversity management' (Agadjanian 2014: 56) is needed which require narratives with integrative power. Can a mainly ethnic-centred Orthodoxy contribute to this political project?

Political sacrality

> All of this allows us to say that Crimea, the ancient Korsun or Chersonesus, and Sevastopol have invaluable civilisational and even sacral importance for Russia, like the Temple Mount in Jerusalem for the followers of Islam and Judaism.
>
> (Putin 2014b)

We observed already that Putin attributes to Christianity an unifying force, conceived as a kind of catalyst which permitted the 'forefathers for the first time and forevermore' to see 'themselves as a united nation' (Putin 2014b). It is evident that Orthodoxy bears an invaluable importance to the Eastern Slavic and later Russian project of civilisation. But how is the epithet *sacral* to be interpreted in this context?

In introducing the Temple Mount as an element of comparison, Putin refers to the widespread idea of sacral territory. As the Temple Mount in Jerusalem possesses an immense sacral value for Jews and Muslims, the territory of Crimea has a high sacral meaning to Russia. Since Putin strives to justify the claim for Crimea as a part of the Russian state territory, the sacral dimension refers clearly to the Russian state as the source of that sacrality.

Following the intern logic of the comparison, we would expect that, on the one hand, those who confess Islam and Judaism keep the Temple Mount in Jerusalem holy; on the other hand, those who confess Christianity accept the sacral importance of Crimea. In accordance with this premise the sacral meaning of the peninsular would occur as an object of faith, more precisely of Christian faith.[5] Does Putin designate Crimea as a sacral place in this sense?

If we fill into the 'blank space' of the comparison not Christianity but 'Russianity', Putin's words become more lucid. Like those who confess Islam and Judaism hold the Temple Mount in Jerusalem holy, those who confess 'Russianity' accept the sacral importance of Crimea. Christianity is only the setting which has to promote the real 'worship': to serve the interest of the Russian state. Russia is the object of veneration; all that and all those who serve Russia confess this 'civil religion'. In other words, the political sphere is gaining a kind of pseudo-religious character in Putin's assertions. Is it a sheer coincidence that the final expression of this paragraph '*otnyne i navsegda*' (from now and forever) reminds one of the last words of many orthodox prayers: '*i nyne, i prison, i vo veki vekov*' (now and ever and unto ages of ages)?

Based on this premise, the territory of Crimea has indeed a sacred importance for Russia. The Temple Mount comparison makes evident a tendency which more or less has tacitly determined the attitude of the political power towards Orthodoxy for a long time: Orthodoxy provides the historical and cultural 'equipment' for the cult offered to the Russian Imperia and its power. In order to fulfil this function even on the legal level a special place was assigned to the Russian Orthodox Church. Against the background of the post-Soviet loss of state legitimation and the need to manage the country's ostensible pluralism this has apparently been a reasonable option since the Church was 'reemerging as a dominant agent, claiming normative authority in the nation and largely retaining an image of a unifying pan-national institution' (Agadjanian and Rousselet 2005: 30).

The hegemonism of the Orthodox Church on the one hand, and the growth and radicalisation of other religious groups, especially in the Muslim community, on the other hand raise the question whether this option is the only one and, given the religious and ethnic divides in Russia, the most appropriate one. In other words, under a historical viewpoint, the choice of Orthodoxy might have been the best, but is this option still a good one under today's circumstances? Putin's statement concerning Crimea could be interpreted as a turning point which marks an 'official' orientation towards a national civil religion. This 'religion' holds as its creed the values of Russian civilisation (Gvosdev 2002: 75–88) and promotes the commitment to develop a 'multifaceted but solid Russian nation and a centralised Russian state'.

When Putin speaks of the two new subjects entering the Russian Federation, the republic of Crimea and the city of Sevastopol, he attributes to the first a value for culture and civilisation and to the second a military importance as the main port of the Russian Black Sea fleet. Sevastopol as well as other places connected with military deeds is designated as 'holy' (the official English version translates by 'dear to our hearts'). The epithet holy refers to their function as symbols of 'Russian military glory and outstanding valour' (Putin 2014a). This could be understood as an allusion to a new type of 'religion', based on Russian victory and (military) glory (Briskina-Müller 2015; Desnitsky 2015).

Given the imperial and Soviet heritage and the geopolitical situation of the Russian Federation, a serious question has to be faced if a sacralised cult of power and victory (Prochanov 2015) does not possess a significant higher potential for national integration as an often non-religious and non-practised Orthodoxy. If a Church hierarch states: 'The most important question for the Church is how to safeguard an absolute patriotism in the hearts and souls of our citizen, i.e. a perfect commitment to the homeland' (Metropolitan Pante-leimon 2015) it has to be asked: does Russia shift to an official patriotic reli-gion? Indeed, it is the notion of fatherland (*otechestvo*) that covers the public discourse with a kind of mysterious veil. In celebrating the central categories of power and victory, especially in memorising the Great Patriotic War, a pseudo-religious veneration is offered to the fatherland. Is thus a new 'religious' paradigm emerging in Russia?

What does this mean to the question of symphonia? Is the high performa-tive effect of Christian, in particular Orthodox, coloured language just a useful support in today's political discourse or could it be interpreted as a modern expression of symphony? If symphony could be paraphrased as 'har-mony of interests' or 'mutual cooperation', we have to consider now whether this 'regulative idea' is still working or not.

Orthodox symphony

After some observations concerning the use of key concepts such as space and Orthodoxy in official political narratives dealing with identity and state-hood, these aspects are now to be compared to the conceptual framework provided by the Orthodox Church. Though it reflects only a part of the orthodox mind map, here again we will focus mainly on the official Church discourse. In so doing, we strive to determine some elements that elucidate the question if a harmonic cooperation of the political and the religious sphere is still a reasonable option.

Symphony in Orthodox teaching

The Russian Orthodox Church (ROC) traditionally describes the relationship between political power and Church by referring to the Byzantine principle of 'symphony'. In the 'Bases of the Social Concept of the Russian Orthodox Church' (BSC) adopted in 2000 by the Bishop's Council of the ROC this basic pattern was reconsidered, taking into account the actual political situation and the Church's historic experience (see Chaplin 2000; Arola and Saarinen 2000; Wasmuth 2004, 2014; Uertz 2014). This 'reformulation' was also called a 'new symphony' (Arola and Saarinen 2000), recognising that 'a state is normally secular and not bound by any religious commitments' (BSC III, 2). In addition, the characterisation of the Church–State relationship as a harmonious coop-eration marked by mutual acceptance of the distinct sphere of action of each one and the principle of non-interference is considered to be an innovation. Though its elaboration and main impetus can be attributed to a more liberal wing in ROC, at that time, represented by Metropolit Kirill (Gundiaev), the document reflects different positions in the ROC.[6] With regard to political power, the Church recognises a duty of allegiance which is not to be confused with subservience. Noteworthy is the affirmation of a right of resistance, certainly mirroring the Church's experience in communist times, when the political power turned to be openly anti-religious (BSC III, 5).

In the document the interaction of Church and State – at least from the ROC's point of view – is clearly outlined. But the way in which the 'nation' is referred to remains somewhat ambiguous. The Social Concept of the ROC highlights the idea of the 'Orthodox nation' as a 'mono-confessional Orthodox community' which 'can in certain sense be regarded as the community of faith' (BSC II, 3). This concept excludes 'various minorities who do not confess Orthodoxy [...] from the spiritual mission of this nation' (Chaplin 2000: 116). In so doing, the ROC articulates its mono-ethnic or ethno-centred self-understanding in retaining the excluding categories of 'nation' and 'brothers by blood' (BSC II, 3; see also Wasmuth 2014: 23–25). Thus, the Church, on the one hand, restricts her universal mission (Rousselet 2007: 65; Payne 2007) and, on the other hand, instead of exploring a unifying force in society, supports the emergence of xenophobia and aggressive nationalism and national exclusiveness – phenomena that the Church herself characterises as 'sinful' and 'against Orthodox ethics' (see BSC II, 4).

To resume, the principle of symphony remains a core element in the Church's self-conception as an important player in the societal and political life of Russia. It is considered, with regard to the political power, as a kind of frame that regulates the interaction of State and Church. But symphony or 'new symphony' is, moreover, a dynamic and flexible concept that enables the Church to connect its own heritage and experience with today's circumstances (see Introduction to this volume and Jianu's chapter). Only timidly does the ROC refer to its experience as an institution that is habituated to deal with multi-nationality and national pluralism. So, it is noteworthy that the ROC recognises also the nation as community of citizens (BSC II, 3). If the Church continues to explore the dynamism of the symphonic idea in this domain the 'new symphony' could serve as a conceptual frame in order to strengthen civil society. If Christian patriotism as an important element of the Church's 'political' attitude is also due to the civic nation, the Church could thus enable herself to cooperate, in order to 'build' a strong civil society including values as social engagement, personal freedom and plurality of opinion. If so, the ROC might have to sacrifice her interpretational sovereignty concerning all aspects of society's life, granting to the society the same autonomy as to the state in the frame of the 'new Symphony' (Wasmuth 2004).

National religion

It is a commonplace today that the ROC is an integral part of the Russian political system. Constant allusions to religious, in particular Christian, figures in political discourses seem to prove a, we would call, 'pretended symphony'.[7] Against the background of an emerging Russian 'civil religion' (Hovorun 2014) the Church has to defend her prerogative to interpret religious patterns of meaning. Relating to the notion of fatherland the ROC states that an 'Orthodox Christian is called to love his fatherland [...] and his brothers by blood who live everywhere in the world' (BSC II, 3). This love for the native country is framed by the conviction that the 'spiritual homeland [...] is not earthly Jerusalem but the Jerusalem "which is above" (Gal 4: 26)' (BSC I, 3). The Church underlines that 'contrary to Orthodoxy are the teachings that put the nation in the place of God or reduce faith to one of the aspects of national self-awareness' (BSC II, 4).[8] Here the political narrative which promotes a Russian civil religion clashes with the Church's claim to denounce the false aspirations of that pseudo-religion (Prochanov 2015) which is characterised, inter alia, by nostalgia for the imperial and Soviet past (Hovorun 2014). In order to withstand all temptations to be part of this religion in sacralising the categories of victory and power the ROC could refer to her own spiritual treasure: the narration about the first 'Russian' saints, the princes Boris and Gleb, who paid with their lives the renouncement to earthly power and success (Poppe 2007), could be conceived as a kind of antithesis to secular heroism.[9] Succumbing to the risk of turning the people not to God but to the earthly fatherland (Rousselet 2007: 68), the Church would contradict her own credo, that is to make possible the transformation and purification of world, socium and state on the principles of God-commanded love (BSC I, 3) by perceiving 'world and society in the light of his ultimate destiny, in the eschatological light of the kingdom of God' (BSC I, 3).

Holy land

As discussed above on behalf of Crimea, the territorial aspect – the question of land and space – is another key element in the conception of Russian identity and statehood. The 'territorial discourse' of the Church oscillates between two poles: on the one hand, there is a kind of political conception concerning the land, based on 'physical square kilometres'. It allows the Church to circumscribe and, subsequently, to dominate the land. On the other hand, the land is conceived as a spatial entity (Schlögel 2003: 393) characterised by culture, history and the personal merits of its inhabitants.

Tempted by a discourse of power in order to defend her integrity and predominance the ROC refers to a political acceptation of the land in using the concept of canonical territory. The canonical territory outlines the sphere of exclusive jurisdiction or, in political terms, domination that covers most of the former Soviet territory (except Georgia and Armenia). Though it is based on

Old-Church traditions (Wasmuth 2014: 21; Payne 2007: 834–835), in today's geopolitical situation it seems to be foremost an instrument of the Church's policy to 'monopolize the goods of salvation' (Rousselet 2007: 69) even causing a couple of conflicts (Estonia, Moldavia). The Church is still struggling to define the canonical territory clearly, so, its application in the contemporary circumstances is not evident. For this reason it can be interpreted in different ways; even as a useful political instrument which helps to control the actual 'étranger proche' (narrow abroad), the former Soviet space (Rousselet 2007: 69).

At the same time the ROC fosters a territorial concept that emphasises the category of space. In this light it is noteworthy, that the initial spatial concept of the Rus was the 'Russian land' which was considered to become a holy land because of the saints living in it.[10] According to this idea, it is God who makes the land holy in granting through the saints, as the Tale of the Passion of the holy martyrs Boris and Gleb notes, the grace to forgive, to heal all sufferings and to calm the passions (see Müller 1967: 59f.). This concept of Holy Russian Land (*sviataia russkaia zemlia*), illuminated by the saints,[11] which later on became the Holy Rus includes neither a concise territory nor a compulsion to territorial expansion (Vodoff 2003: 23)[12]; it can be described as an open space for all people to convert to Christ. The Holy Rus, as Patriarch Kirill highlights, points to the ideal of holiness incarnated in a genuine Russian way (Patriarch Kirill 2015); it is neither an ethnic, political nor linguistic notion but a spiritual notion, transcending all political frontiers (Patriarch Kirill 2010).

In focusing on the narrative of the Holy Rus as first and foremost spiritual entity, the ROC could be an important counterbalance to all political acceptations of the land as a space of domination. Thus, the baptism of Vladimir would not appear as a catalyst for the development of a 'multifaceted but solid Russian nation and a centralised Russian state' but as the initial impulse for the emerging of a new spiritual space – the space or the land where Christian sanctity can flourish.[13]

To conclude, if we are not wrong in observing the emergence of a new paradigm in the relation between political power and the Church, the obvious secularisation of Christian ideas and the participation of the Church in matters of the raison d'état represent a serious challenge to the Church. Either the ROC will yield to the temptation of power and, subsequently, adapt its official discourse in the way that it becomes a mere duplicate of the political one, or the Church will make every effort to develop alternative narratives drawing inspiration from her proper traditions. Thus, the core elements of Russian identity could be conceived and developed according to a Christian prism. In doing so the Church could play, to put it in churchly terms, a prophetic role in Russian societal and political life. Maybe this will be a way to rethink the principle of symphony?

Notes

1 The religious 'coloured' motive of the collection of the lands of the Rus was already abandoned when in 1552 the Khanate of Kazan (in 1556 the Khanate of Astrachan) were conquered. Here is the watershed in the Russian territorial policy: the target of reunification of all the Orthodox East Slavs under the rule of the grand Duke was changed. The extension of both the sphere of power and the territory was in the beginning not an imperial ideology but a consequent use of the given opportunities. It was thus a search of power for the sake of power. The legitimation was provided later on und could change according to time and need (Goehrke 2010: 85).

2 Putin affirms later that Russians and Ukrainians are 'not simply close neighbours but [...] one people' (Putin 2014a). It would be of special interest to figure out the relation between this all-embracing, trans-national people and the notion 'people' used in regard to the Russian, Ukrainian and Belarus nations. It is not easy to situate the right of national self-determination which Putin affirms, on the one hand, and the notion of that kind of 'super-ethnos' having its cultural and historical roots in the Ancient Rus, on the other hand.

3 The Primary Chronicle or Tales of Times gone by (*Povest' vremennykh let*) is the main source according to which the baptism of Vladimir took place in Korsun in 988. Shachmatov recognises in the Primary Chronicle a compilation of different sources and doubts the chronology proposed in the document; following his analyse, based primarily on the '*Pamiat' I pokhvala kniaziu russkomy Vladimiru*'. Vladimir was baptised in 987 and afterwards, in 989 undertook the campaign to Korsun (see Shachmatov 1906 and 1908). Kartashev thinks that Vladimir was baptised in Vasiliev, near Kiev in 987 (see Kartashev 1959: 105–121). See also A. Poppe (1976: 197–244); Vodoff (2003: 259–264).

4 Putin's approach in the address pronounced in December is much more precise than in the statement delivered in March. In the paragraphs we are paying attention to, he uses the term people (*narod*) only once differentiating it clearly from nation (*natsiia*). While nation seems to be linked to the process of formation (*formirovanie/obrazovanie*) of national and political structures and occurs always in connection with Russian state (*Rossiiskoi gosudarstvo*) or statehood (*gosudarstvennost'*), the term people connotes a kind of spiritual or mystical dimension. It seems to be something organic which grows on a spiritual soil (*pochva*). One has to become aware of it.

5 According to biblical narratives the Temple Mount receives its religious meaning from the Temple as a place where God dwells. It is seen as a place of worship and sacrifice to God and thus, exempt from human appropriation (2 Chron 34, 14; Lam 1, 10).

6 This document expresses a kind of 'official' position; a broad reception of this position in all 'wings' of the ROC has not taken place yet (Novikov 2014).

7 It is often forgotten that the idea of symphony is promoted by the Church. Putin hardly uses this term to conceptualise the relation of politics and Church; compare also to the concept of 'advanced secularity' in Wood (2015).

8 Compare to the already cited phrase of Putin: 'It was thanks to this spiritual unity [Christianity as a unifying force] that our forefathers for the first time and forevermore saw [*osoznavat'* – realise, become aware] themselves as a united nation' (Putin 2014b).

9 See the interesting answer of Metropolitan Hilarion of Volokolamsk, head of the Department for External Church Relations, to A. Prochanov who proposes to canonise all victims and heroes of the Second World War. The bishop clearly points out that the criteria to become a churchly recognised saint are different from those historians or the society refers to in order to consider somebody as a hero.

Hilarion highlights the importance of personal holiness and piety (Metropolitan Hilarion 2015).

10 V. Vodoff notes that the geographic, politic and ethnic notion 'Russian land' is probably pre-Christian but only testified in Christian sources. By means of this notion the processes of identification of 'Russian land' and Russian Christendom can be made evident (Vodoff 2003: 19–29).

11 The Russian 'sanctity' is celebrated in the Church with a feast dedicated to all the saints who lighted up the Russian land.

12 It is noteworthy that some historians think that the policy of territorial expansion was a heritage of the Mongols, and thus, can hardly be considered as Christian.

13 A 'sacral space', according to Christian tradition, could be approached as a gift of land that 'becomes a true good, a real gift, a promise fulfilled when it is a place where God reigns. Then it will not just be some independent state or other, but the realm of obedience, where God's will is done and the right kind of human existents developed' (Ratzinger 2000: 17).

References

Agadjanian, A. 2014. *Turns of Faith, Search for Meaning: Orthodox Christianity and Post-Soviet Experience*. Frankfurt/Main: Peter Lang.

Agadjanian, A. and Rousselet, K. 2005. 'Globalization and Identity Discourse in Russian Orthodoxy'. In *Eastern Orthodoxy in a Global Age. Tradition Faces the Twenty-first Century*. Edited by V. Roudometof et al., pp. 30–57. Lanham, MD: AltaMira Press.

Arola, P. and Saarinen, R. 2000. 'In Search of Sobornost and "New Symphony": The Social Doctrine of the Russian Orthodox Church', *The Ecumenical Review* 54(1/2000): 130–141.

Bassin, M. 2011. 'Eurasian visions of Russian nationhood in space'. In *Mastering Russian Spaces: Raum und Raumbewältigung als Problem der russischen Geschichte*. Edited by K. Schlögel, pp. 47–64. München: De Gruyter Oldenbourg.

Briskina-Müller, A. 2015. *Power and Victory as Central Categories of the Russian Orthodox Public Discourse Today: An Observation*, lecture on the conference 'Political Orthodoxy and Totalitarianism', May, Helsinki (as paper received from the author).

Chaplin, V. 2000. 'Remaining Oneself in a Changing World: The Bases of the Social Concept of the Russian Orthodox Church', *The Ecumenical Review* 54(1/2000): 112–129.

Clowes, E. 2011. *Russia on the Edge: Imagined Geographies and Post-Soviet Identity*. Ithaca, NY and London: Cornell University Press.

Desnitsky, A. 2015. 'Die Orthodoxie und die "Religion des Sieges" in Russland', *Religion und Gesellschaft in Ost und West* 43(8/2015): 14–16.

Döpmann, H.-P. 1967. *Der Einfluss der Kirche auf die moskowitische Staatsidee: Staats- und Gesellschaftsdenken bei Josif Volockij, Nil Sorskij und Vassian Patrikeev*. Berlin: Evangelische Verlagsanstalt.

Döring, J. and Thielmann, T. (eds.) 2008. *Spatial Turn: Das Raumparadigma in den Kultur-und Sozialwissenschaften*. Bielefeld: Transcript.

Gadinger, F., Jarzebski, S. and Yildiz, T. 2014. 'Politische Narrative: Konturen einer politikwissenschaftlichen Erzähltheorie'. In *Politische Narrative: Konzepte – Analysen – Forschungspraxis*, pp. 363–386. Edited by F. Gadinger et al. Wiesbaden: Springer.

Goehrke, C. 2010. *Russland: Eine Strukturgeschichte*. Paderborn: Ferdinand Schöningh.

Gvosdev, N. 2002. '"Managed Pluralism" and Civil Religion in Post-Soviet Russia'. In *Civil Society and the Search of Justice in Russia*. Edited by C. Marsh and N. Gvosdev. Lanham, MD: Lexington Books.

Hann, Ch. (ed.) 2002. *Postsocialism: Ideal, Ideologies and Practices in Eurasia*. London: Routledge.

Hovorun, C. 2014. *Orthodox Civil Religion*, lecture at the conference 'Political Modernity and the Responses by Contemporary Orthodox Theology', January, Vienna. Available online: http://www.russ.ru/Mirovaya-povestka/Pravoslavnaya-grazhdanskaya-religiya (accessed 15 September 2015).

Hunter, S., J. L. Thomas and A. Melikishvili. 2004. *Islam in Russia: The Politics of Identity and Security*. New York: Routledge.

Ignatow, A. 1998. *Geopolitische Theorien in Russland heute*. Bonn: Bundesinstitut für ostwissenschaftliche und internationale Studien.

Ingold, F. Ph. 2007. *Russische Wege: Geschichte, Kultur, Weltbild*. München: Wilhelm Fink.

Kartashev, A. N. 1959. *Ocherki po istorii russkoi tserkvi* [Outline of the history of the Russian Church]. Paris: YMCA.

Köllner, T. 2018. 'On the Restitution of Property and the Making of 'Authentic' Landscapes in Contemporary Russia', *Europe-Asia Studies* 70(7): 1083–1102. doi:10.1080/09668136.2018.1484077.

Laruelle, M. 2008. *Russian Eurasianism: An Ideology of Empire*. Baltimore, MD: John Hopkins University Press.

Metropolitan Hilarion. 2015. *My deti Sviatoi Rusi* [We are the Children of Holy Russia]. Available online: https://mospat.ru/ru/2015/06/10/news119918/ (accessed 12 December 2015).

Metropolitan Panteleimon of Krasnojarsk. 2015. *Moshchi Sv. Valentina my privozim ne radi 'shou', a dlia istselniia dush i tel* [The relics of St Valentine are brought here not for show but for the healing of the soul and the body]. Available online: http://www.pravmir.ru/mitropolit-krasnoyarskij-panteleimon-moshhi-sv-valentina-my-privozim-ne-radi-shou-a-dlya-isceleniya-dush-i-tel/ (accessed 10 August 2015).

Müller, L. (ed.), 1967. *Die altrussischen hagiographischen Erzählungen und liturgischen Dichtungen über die Heiligen Boris und Gleb*. München: Wilhelm Fink.

Novikov, A. 2014. *Russkaia Tserkov' i russkii mir pered litsom ispytanii*. Available online: http://www.fondsk.ru/news/2014/02/09/russkaja-cerkov-i-russkij-mir-pered-licom-ispy ta nij-25646.html (accessed 10 September 2015).

Patriarch Kirill (Gundiaev). 2010. *Address in Chişinău (September 08, 2010)*. Available online: http://www.patriar-chia.ru/db/text/1254808 (accessed 15 September 2015).

Patriarch Kirill (Gundiaev). 2015. *Sermon Delivered on the Ceremony of the 1000th Anniversary of Saint Vladimir Death, July 28, 2015, Moscow*. Available online: http://www.patriarchia.ru/db/text/4180727.html (accessed 20 September 2015).

Payne, D. P. 2007. 'Nationalism and the Local Church: The Source of Ecclesiastical Conflict in the Orthodox Common-wealth', *Nationalities Papers* 35(5): 831–852.

Poppe, A. 1976. *The Political Background to the Baptism of Rus': Byzantine-Russian Relations between 986–989*. Washington, DC: Dumberton Oak.

Poppe, A. 2007. 'Losers on Earth, Winners from Heaven: The Assassinations of Boris and Gleb in the Making of Eleventh-Century Rus''. In *Christian Russia in the Making*. Edited by A. Poppe. Aldershot: Ashgate.

Prochanov, A. 2015. *Religiia pobedy*. Available online: http://zavtra.ru/content/view/prohanov/ (accessed 15 September 2015).

Putin, V. 2014a. *Address to State Duma Deputies, Federation Council Members, Heads of Russian Regions and Civil Society Representatives (Kremlin, March 18, 2014)*. Available online: http://en.kremlin.ru/events/president/ news/20603 (accessed 17 August 2015).

Putin, V. 2014b. *Presidential Address to the Federal Assembly (Kremlin, December 04, 2014)*. Available online: http://en.kremlin.ru/events/president/news/47173 (accessed 17 August 2015).

Ratzinger, J. 2000. *The Spirit of the Liturgy*. San Francisco, CA: Ignatius Press.

Riazanovsky, N. 1967. 'The Emergence of Eurasianism', *California Slavic Studies* 4: 39–72.

Rousselet, K. 2007. 'L'Eglise orthodoxe russe et le territoire', *Revue d'étude comparative Est-Ouest* 1 (La Russie: géographie des territoires): 63–85.

Ryžova, S. 2005. 'Tolerance and extremism: Russian Ethnicity in the Orthodox discourse of the 1990s'. In *Religion and Identity in modern Russia: The Revival of Orthodoxy and Islam*. Edited by J. Johnson *et al.* Aldershot: Ashgate.

Shachmatov, A. A. 1906 [2011]. *Korsunskaia legenda o kreshchenii Vladimira* [The Korsun Legend about the Baptism of Vladimir]. St Petersburg: Tip. Imperatorskoi akademii nauk.

Shachmatov, A. A. 1908. *Razyskaniia o drevneishikh letopisnykh svodakh*. St Petersburg: Tip. Imperatorskoi akademii nauk.

Sazonov, D. 2015. *Sud'by Rossii: Tretii Rim ili vtoroi Ierusalim?* [The Fate of Russia: Third Rome or Second Jerusalem?]. Available online: http://www.bogoslov.ru/text /4437 297.html (accessed 15 September 2015).

Schlögel, K. 2003. *Im Raume lesen wir die Zeit: Über Zivilisationsgeschichte und Geopolitik*, München: Fischer.

Schlögel, K. 2011. 'Raum und Raumbewältigung als Problem der russischen Geschichte'. In *Mastering Russian Spaces: Raum und Raumbewältigung als Problem der russischen Geschichte*. Edited by K. Schlögel, pp. 1–26. München: De Gruyter Oldenbourg.

Schroer, M. 2006. *Räume, Orte, Grenzen: Auf dem Weg zu einer Soziologie des Raumes*. Frankfurt/M.: Suhrkamp.

Smith, J. (ed.). 1999. *Beyond the Limits: The Concept of Space in Russian History and Culture*. Helsinki: Suomen Historiallinen Seura.

Uertz, R. 2014. 'Die Orthodoxe Kirche in Russland und ihr Verhältnis zum Westen', *Imprimatur* 8(47): 1–6.

Vodoff, V. 2003. *Autour du mythe de la Sainte Russie, Christianisme, pouvoir et société chez les Slaves orientaux (Xe–XVIIe siècles)*. Paris: Institut d'étude slaves.

Warhola, J. and A. Lehning. 2007. 'Political Order, Identity, and Security in Multinational, Multi-religious Russia', *Nationalities Papers* 35(5): 933–957.

Wasmuth, J. 2004. 'Sozialethik in der russisch-orthodoxen Kirche der Gegenwart. Die "Grundlagen der Sozialkonzeption" in kritischer Betrachtung', *Evangelische Theologie* 1/64: 37–51.

Wasmuth, J. 2014. 'Russian Orthodoxy between State and Nation'. In *Eastern Orthodoxy Encounters of Identity and Otherness: Values, Self-Reflection, Dialogue*. Edited by A. Krawchuk and Th. Bremer, pp. 17–27. Lanham, MD: Palgrave MacMillan.

Wood, M. 2015. 'Shadows in Caves? A Re-Assessment of Public Religion and Secularization in England Today', *European Journal of Sociology* 56: 241–270.

Wozniuk, V. 1997. 'In Search of Ideology: The Politics of Religion and Nationalism in the New Russia (1991–1996)', *Nationalities Papers* 25(2): 195–210.

4 A resilient harmony, or how the politics of social inequality in post-Soviet Russian society have informed Orthodox parish life

Detelina Tocheva

Orthodox symphony unbound: from the policies of the elite to politics on the ground

Recently, the idea of a symphonic relationship between State and Church in countries with a dominant Orthodox Church has most commonly been defined as the harmonious collaboration between these two centres where, respectively, political and religious power reside.[1] This commonsensical definition of symphony has come under scrutiny in different fields of the social-scientific study of the religious resurgence in post-socialist Eastern-European countries.[2] Most scholars note a specific entrenchment of the Orthodox Churches in the political sphere and, reciprocally, the states' interventionist approach to the Orthodox ecclesiastic organisations.[3] Consensus is sometimes the hallmark of this mutual influence.[4] But consensus is by no means the dominant model, as the chapters in this volume show, let alone a self-reproducing principle.[5] The existing relatedness does not rule out the pursuit of different agendas by Church and State officials. This relatedness often involves complex processes of negotiation that may result in compromise, as well as outright dissent (see Köllner in the introduction to this volume).

Yet, the commonsensical contemporary view of symphony as 'following of the same track' verifies in different areas and at different levels in the post-socialist setting. More precisely, a specific kind of a harmonious movement unfolds within the social fabric of Church life and society, far away from the highest political circles of the two organisations. In order to highlight this process, I move the focus from policies initiated by the headquarters of the Russian Orthodox Church[6] (hereafter 'ROC', Patriarchate of Moscow) and the top State officials to the social fabric of the Church and its distinctive embeddedness in society-wide politics.[7] How and why have some formal and informal complexes of relationships, that determine the life of the ecclesiastic organisation at its basic territorial level, directly replicated societal dynamics? My aim is to unpack the forms of and reasons for this coincident politics. Undoubtedly, power and authority play a role, but this politics stretches far beyond the milieus of the official power holders.

Social differentiation along the lines of wealth, status and gender, and their interlocking dimensions, as they unfold in parish life, are placed at the centre of my study. I have found that, since the fall of the Soviet regime in 1991, Church politics at the parish level has reproduced some of the dominant trends of disparity in Russian society. The study of other spheres can lead to very different findings and to the conclusion that the operation of specific rules and ideas singles out the Church from the rest of society. This is the case, for example, in the sphere of human rights. For example, Alexander Agadjanian has demonstrated that the Human Rights Doctrine of the ROC, an important document published in 2008, presents the Church to its members as 'an institutional, social and moral enclave, which uses the human rights rhetoric to create and protect its own niche, its own modest space within the global multicultural universe' (Agadjanian 2008: 18). In variance with the sphere of human rights, in the sphere of economic, social and gender inequality, the Church is precisely not an enclave. Throughout the post-Soviet period, within the structures of the parish and in inter-parish relationships, the Church has embodied some of the most widespread views about disparity and replicated society-wide dynamics of economic, social and gender differentiation. I call this coincident development in the politics of inequality *resilient harmony.*[8] It has resulted from a combination of choices made by the hierarchs of the ROC and grassroots engagement with growing Orthodoxy since the early 1990s in a context of overall policy-driven systemic transformation. In other words, the continuously interacting dynamics of Church, State and society directly inform the basic territorial level of the ROC, determining the structure and dynamics of the inequalities.

Below, I begin with an ethnographic note about two neighbouring parishes that shows how precisely in this case the most common dynamics and criteria of economic and social differentiation have permeated the functioning of the ROC's basic territorial level.[9] Then I proceed to a detailed examination of social stratification, Church decisions and the concrete dynamics whereby the gap between well-off and worse-off parishes, between influential and modest ones, has practically taken root. Furthermore, I demonstrate that differentiation along the lines of gender is enmeshed in the structure and operation of internal Church inequalities, with the low-paid and precarious work of women being instrumental to the everyday operation of the churches. My analysis draws mainly on ethnographic fieldwork that I conducted in Orthodox parishes in a small city in the region of St Petersburg, which began with a one-year fieldwork in 2006–2007 and shorter additional trips in the following years.[10] I also refer to official Church documents.

Unequal parishes

After 1991, deep inequalities took root in Russian society – along the lines of income, wealth, status, gender, ethnicity, housing, geographical region, all having interlocking dimensions.[11] The levels they have reached in Putin's era are particularly high: 'Currently, Russian society faces unprecedentedly high levels of income and wealth inequality, which is exacerbated by high levels of spatial and social inequality' (Oxfam 2014: 31). The NGO Oxfam made this assessment in a report drawing on extensive statistical data. Further, the report claims that the actually implemented state policies are unlikely to remedy the situation. The magnitude of inequality in contemporary rural Russia is also stunning (Wegner 2014). Notably, social and economic disparities have been one of the most sensitive issues for the population over the last 25 years.[12] Overall, the place that one occupies in relation to the market and to the political authority largely determines one's position in society. I claim that these two criteria directly influence the extant inter-parish disparities. In fact, processes that are usually approached as specific to the realm of the post-Soviet Orthodox religion, such as large-scale church (re)construction, the expansion of church commerce, the new canonisations and dynamics in the worshipping of saints, are deeply enmeshed in dynamics of inter-parish differentiation.

There is a large spectrum of degrees of material wellbeing on which the parishes of the ROC can be situated. Here I bring a short ethnographic account of two urban parishes which, in the local context, have cultivated opposed identities based on their different economic wellbeing. These two parishes could be placed in the well-off zone of the spectrum, even though certainly not on its extreme. Indeed, if there are no starving priests in these churches, and the buildings and beautification are of reasonable quality, they cannot compete with their homologues directly placed under the authority of the highest hierarchs of the ROC. Neither could they compete with churches strongly supported by top state officials and the wealthiest businessmen, or those that have become flourishing pilgrimage destinations. Yet, an analysis of the differences between these two local parishes sheds light upon the forms and dynamics of disparity, and their centrality in church life, as well as upon the ways in which they are inbuilt in the encompassing social fabric of Russia's unequal society.

In the city where I conducted most of my research, the central church is the centre of the largest parish and the centre of the deanery. I call it 'central' because it is centrally located on the main pedestrian street. This church remained open during Soviet times, has maintained strong relationship with the local authorities, and benefits from businessmen's large donations. Wealthier local families tend to choose this church to celebrate weddings and baptisms. The rector of this church, who is also the head of the deanery, has good connections to the hierarchs in St Petersburg. Members of the city government and important businessmen usually attend major celebrations in this church. The strong bonds between this church and local men in power are also expressed on a more private terrain. For instance, during a relatively modest, but open to the public, ceremony in the church for the fiftieth birthday of the rector, the most prominent businessmen and the head of the city's administration came to congratulate him and to offer him flowers.

A church that houses the relics of a saint is nowadays not only more prestigious on the scale of spirituality, but it tends also to be economically more prosperous, because it attracts pilgrims. None of the local churches could boast the relics of a saint before 2007. The rector of the central church initiated a process of canonisation of a new martyr saint, a local nun who passed away while she was imprisoned by the Soviet authorities during the bloody repressions against religion in the 1930s.[13] Thanks to his influential connections with the hierarchy in St Petersburg, the canonisation succeeded. The new female saint was recognised as an 'all-people revered martyr' (*vsenarodnaia prepodobnomuchenitsa*) in 2007. The church obtained the relics, brought there during an impressive ceremony co-organised by the city government. Soon after, groups of pilgrims started visiting this church.

The second largest church in the city was rebuilt by local enthusiasts over ten years, starting from the beginning of the 1990s when the building was given back to the ROC.[14] This church, first erected little before the 1917 revolution as the urban representation of a convent (*podvor'e*), was closed down during Stalin's repressions in the 1930s. Locally, this church has a very different image from the central one.[15] It is frequently mentioned in both churches that the salaries are lower in this reopened church. The central church is said by local people to offer expensive services and items, while the reopened one is said to be cheaper, less central, 'village parish' (*derevenskii prikhod*) and overall poor. In contrast, it is usual to hear comments pretending that the central church would find all possible ways to make money. Members of the core community of the rebuilt church felt like victims of the dominant position of the central church when the powerful deanery rector took over the process of canonisation of the new saint. Indeed, the saint, during her life, was a nun and belonged to their church, which was then an urban church part of a distant convent.

The difference that local people and committed churchgoers saw between these two churches belongs to a wider pattern. During the early period of post-socialist Orthodox revival, social-economic differentiation took a specific form. On the one hand, there were spontaneous initiatives of church (re-) building by local enthusiasts with scarce resources (Tocheva 2011; Kormina and Shtyrkov 2015: 37–41). On the other hand, churches were rapidly erected thanks to generous donations made by businessmen, often with a political intent (Köllner 2013). These two contrasting versions of church construction were given distinct moral assessments. Churches built with money donated by rich businessmen were said to be 'built with gold', while churches built with benevolent labour of worse-off enthusiasts were said to be 'built with tears' (Benovska-Sabkova et al. 2010: 19; Köllner 2011). In this locality, the popular perception of church construction as the embodiment of economic differentiation has been replaced by new controversies around the canonisation of new martyrs.

Such strong dichotomy between two churches is not necessarily found in every locality. Nonetheless, this example of differentiation of two neighbouring parishes illustrates a much wider situation. Within the large spectrum of degrees of wellbeing among individual churches, it is always possible to distinguish between, on one side, parishes that are well connected, generously supported by donors and successful in selling items and providing religious services and, on the other side, parishes that are less privileged in terms of income from trade, donations and in terms of influential connections.

The gap between well-off and worse-off parishes has become a durable characteristic of the post-Soviet ROC. The contemporary situation is reminiscent of the pre-revolutionary state of affairs where the material wellbeing of the parishes varied widely from one locality to another and from one church to another (Bernshtam 2005: 134–147; Freeze 1983: 51–101; Rozov 2003: 39–40 passim; Shevzov 2004: 54–94). There are several substantial differences, however.

An important specificity of the post-Soviet Orthodox resurgence resides in the unprecedented policy of church (re)construction, a process along which inter-parish differentiation emerged already from the early 1990s. The number of parishes belonging to the ROC grew dramatically in the post-Soviet period. There were less than 7,000 parishes on the territory of the Soviet Union in 1988, the year of the celebration of the Millennia of the baptism of Rus', which marked the beginning of the so-called Orthodox rebirth. According to a recent official Church report, there were 35,496 parishes in the beginning of 2015.[16] A new impulse was given to church construction directly from the top around 2015.[17] During a meeting of the hierarchs of the ROC, held in February 2015, Patriarch Kirill emphasised that one of the most central tasks of the Church must be to build new churches and to contribute to a more dynamic parish life, with the integration of new members as a key mission.[18] My ethnographic example above depicts a local configuration in which the established church is clearly more prosperous than the one rebuilt with enthusiasm and meagre resources. But there is material inequality among the new churches too, and at the same time, the status of an older church does not guarantee economic ease.

It is reasonable to ask how deep material inequality within the ROC is possible in the context of overall supportive state policies. I will first sketch the general terms of state policies regarding the ROC and will turn then to specific Church regulations and internal politics. On the one hand, the separation between the Church and the Russian state was adopted during the revolutionary period in 1918. This provision has remained unchanged in the post-Soviet period, being integrated in the constitution of 1993. This means that the state does not collect taxes for the Church. On the other hand, however, Presidents Putin (2000–2008, 2012–present) and Medvedev (2008–2012) did much to facilitate 'the rebirth of Orthodoxy', not least regarding the church economy. The state has started proving substantial support for church renovation in the case of buildings recognised as cultural heritage sites. Furthermore, the ROC has become the largest real estate owner in the Russian Federation since the Law on the Transfer to the Religious Organisations of

Property of Religious Significance under State or Municipal Ownership came into force on 3 December 2010.[19] Noteworthy is the fact that these policies are in favour of real estate acquisition, but do not support the material base that makes the life of the parishes effectively possible. In this latter respect, a key aspect of state policy is treating church money as a donation (*pozhertvo-vanie*) free from income tax, including all income from goods and rituals for religious use, which comprises virtually everything. But this disposition plays a role only once the church has earned income.

The most important source of inter-parish economic inequality derives from Church regulations whereby every parish is a self-provisioning unit. Moreover, there is no top-down allocation of resources, excepting in two marginal cases mentioned below foreseen in the official texts of the Church. The parish, through the deanery, hands over part of its income from commerce and donations to the diocesan bishop, who is directly accountable to the Patriarch and the Holy Synod, but receives no money from it.[20] Church regulations stipulate that it is the parish members who are obliged to provide for their clerics and for the upkeep of their church.[21] Still, there is no official parish affiliation; the status of a lay parish member is granted only on an informal basis. There are no registers of church members (see also Agadjanian 2011: 27–28).[22] Under the conditions of self-sustaining parishes, the salaries of the priests and other parish employees directly depend upon the income of the parish, which often boils down to income from sales and donations made to the church or to the priests in person. The diocesan bishop defines the tax that each parish pays. After important amendments of the Statute of the Russian Orthodox Church in 2008 and later in 2011 under Patriarch Kirill's ruling, the tax burden on the parishes has significantly increased. This new situation directly derives from the Patriarch's attempt to strengthen his own and the Holy Synod's power upon the two lower levels, the eparchies and the parishes, (and monasteries, educational institutions, etc.), as Kathy Rousselet has argued (2013).[23]

Consequently, the higher the turnover of a given church, the higher the income of the staff it employs, officially or not, and the larger the number of parish workers. In addition, good connections to political and economic leaders provide better access to economic resources and visibility in the public media.

Against the background of this instituted inequality, the hierarchs of the post-Soviet ROC have never supported any model of top-down redistribution of resources. Overall, their commitment in terms of material support is limited to providing the basic liturgical material to the parish churches.[24] It is only recently that the idea of controlling the material conditions of the parish clergy and church workers has received official support from the top hierarchs of the Church. In 2013, the Council of Archbishops adopted a statement about material and social support to be provided to 'servants of the sacred', church servants, workers in the religious organisations affiliated with the ROC, and members of their families. The statement recommends creating commissions at the level of the eparchy to identify problems and find solutions. For example, the commission should find ways of providing support to clergy and church workers living under the state-defined subsistence minimum, and guarantee income to the family members of clergymen and church workers who are deceased or temporarily unable to serve. The document also formulates an expectation that the parish rectors should prevent substantial differences from arising between the salaries of parish priests, and that the rectors should provide adequate official payment for other positions, such as parish bookkeepers and choir directors, taking levels of education into account. The priests heading a deanery should report to the eparchy about the payments provided to their clergy and workers.[25] These dispositions, however, do not imply that the Church hierarchy has taken any further control over the kinds and levels of various material resources available to a parish or over the overall parish incomes. More importantly, there are no guidelines, let alone formal rules, for preventing clerics and other church workers from entering poverty in the first place.

In these circumstances, unequal access to resources from trade, paid-for rituals and services, donations and relationships with influential persons, plays a fundamental role in the ongoing dynamics of inter-parish differentiation. Some priests have openly criticised these conditions that de facto oblige the parish priests to endorse the role of businessmen.[26] Institutionally enshrined unequal access to material resources means that deep economic disparities lurk behind much publicised policies of church construction and 'restitution' of real estate property to the ROC.

Trying to keep up with the 'law of the market', small churches in remote places strive to establish themselves as pilgrimage destinations. Usually, they advertise a 'holy spring', a local saint, a spiritual guide (known as *starets*) and the beauty of the surrounding landscape. Some are relatively successful in attracting visitors, others much less. Since the parishes directly depend on their turnover, the post-Soviet growth of the Church meant an unprecedented growth in trade. The churches offer a large range of cheap and expensive rituals[27] and items for religious use.[28] They have specialised in catering for a variety of faithful. For the committed and less committed Orthodox, participation in religious life involves, in one way or another, what is commonly, and imperfectly for the case in hand, termed 'consumption': buying religious items, paying for specific clerical services and rituals. Society-wide inequalities along the line of wealth and status translate into distinctive uses of Orthodoxy. Part of the top clergy caters for the economic and political elite. Wealthy businessmen have their 'private' confessors to whom they make donations; top political leaders have their own spiritual advisors. The companies organising pilgrimages offer another example. Cheap pilgrimages, massively advertised in the parishes and typically using for transport old buses, have little in common with expensive pilgrimages for pious and well-off people to prestigious destinations, including abroad.[29] Even some saints 'specialise'. Kormina and Shtyrkov (2011) show that among the faithful who worship Saint Xenia of Petersburg, women, especially the single, the elderly and the needy, are overrepresented. In all these respects, one's position in society determines one's access to specific Church services, activities and goods.

Women in parish life: visible, active, unrewarded

The second kind of embedded disparities addressed in this chapter are those running along the lines of gender. Women participate in mass in crucial areas of the post-Soviet ROC, ranging from head positions in the most popular Orthodox media to parish education and door-keeping. The female Orthodox elites have eagerly assumed important, new roles. Women are particularly active as leaders in Orthodox publishing and media (books, newspapers, Internet publications). As Nadieszda Kizenko emphasised, the significant participation of such women in the Orthodox revival has contributed to the expression of different opinions and more generally to the emergence of complex, multi-vocal post-Soviet Orthodoxy (Kizenko 2013). Feminisation has also taken place beyond the elite circles. Lay women play a key role as informal parish elite, in particular in parish education (Ładykowska and Tocheva 2013). But no matter what the specific job they occupy and no matter how high the esteem in which fellow parishioners and priests hold them, they are given modest material rewards and no recognition within the official hierarchy of the Church.[30] Below, I demonstrate how parish jobs reserved for women, far from being some sort of an isolated employment cluster governed by its own rules and logics, represent in a nutshell various combinations and levels of the discriminatory criteria of gender and age, characteristic of the Russian employment market. The female parish hierarchy is totally informal but quite consensual. Very low-paid jobs are reserved for elderly, retired women. Middle-level service, bureaucratic and commercial jobs are reserved for the middle-aged, preferably for those considered trustworthy by the parish rectors. The more prestigious positions of catechist, parish school leader, pilgrimage organiser, or head of the parish newspaper (these often overlap in practice), are occupied by women with a degree from the university. There is no statistical data about the level of women's salaries and their general employment conditions in the parishes. Nonetheless, direct observation and the interviews I have conducted show that they are given meagre economic reward.

On the most unprivileged side, women usually occupy door-keeping functions, essential to the practical life of every church. Such jobs link low-paid service work to old age. These women may also sell in the church shop (*svechnitsi*), but most often they work as cleaners (*uborchitsi*). Such women are sometimes empathically called 'little grannies' or 'little old ladies' (*babushki, starushki*). On the negative side, they are also perceived as grumpy, sanctimonious zealots who feel confident enough to use disparaging remarks in order to correct visitors' behaviour in the church. Under Soviet rule, the image of the old woman was associated with church life. Elderly women were indeed overrepresented among churchgoers. The combination of old age and female gender made them relatively immune to the official expectation addressed to every single member of the Soviet society to profess atheism. Immediately after the liberalisation of religious practice, these were precisely women occupying low-level service jobs in churches who assumed the informal office of teachers of correct behaviour in a church. Even today, an occasional visitor entering a church is more likely to see such women rather than the priests. Yet, their role as informal guides has been significantly eroded with the expansion of priestly guidance, Sunday schools and various Orthodox classes, and especially with the impressive proliferation of Orthodox publications. They mostly tend to withdraw to technical tasks.

Some of these women are employed occasionally, some on a permanent basis, some on an official contract, others outside of any such formal frame. In the latter case, the church declares officially that they work as volunteers. In fact, they do receive payments, and among priests these payments are considered as a normal reward for their work. Whether stable income or occasional payment from helping in the church and cleaning during important celebrations, this payment is always a welcome addition to their tiny pensions. This income is even more attractive in the context of growing insecurity regarding elder care. Indeed, in Russia, the search for welfare arrangements beyond the public services has been rapidly expanding as a result of the shrinking state support that goes together with the implementation of neoliberal schemes in the welfare sector (Caldwell 2007; Hemment 2012). This encompassing context has made the working elderly, especially women, an intrinsic feature of Russian society. The place such women occupy at the bottom of the informal church hierarchy directly replicates the one that Russian society has ascribed to them with an unvoiced agreement also outside of the walls of the church, that of low-paid, mostly undeclared jobs. Often, their work is absolutely crucial for the practical operation of the church.

On the more prestigious side, one finds the jobs of church shop seller, bookkeeper, secretary and other middle-level bureaucratic jobs. Jobs at the church stall are often held by the wives of the priests or by middle-aged women, considered pious and trustworthy by the priests. Bureaucratic tasks are also reserved for women who are closer to the priests. Some have work experience from the private sector as bookkeepers or secretaries.

The case of women catechists is particularly interesting. They are on the top of the informal female hierarchy in the parishes. Sunday schools and classes for adults have been now established in nearly every parish. Agata Ładykowska and I have shown that in post-Soviet Orthodoxy the clergy and the laity have endowed women teachers of Orthodoxy with unprecedented credit and didactic authority (Ładykowska and Tocheva 2013). This authority is founded in professionalism; priests and the laity recognise these women's educational and organisational expertise. Frequently, the same women act as the actual managing directors of the Sunday schools, although priests are the official heads. It is usual for a Sunday school teacher to take care of the parish newspaper and to organise public events in the parish. I came across several cases where a female teacher, or a woman acting as the managing head of the Sunday school, had graduated as an Orthodox choir director in St Petersburg and indeed directed a church choir. Some of these women, usually well educated and appreciated by the priests, also work as parish bookkeepers.

Women engaged in parish education often combine two or more jobs in order to make a living, one in the parish (which is often already a combination of several jobs) and one in a state school or university, often also as part-time medical staff, secretary or employee in a private company. These experiences largely resonate with those of women in post-socialist Central and Eastern Europe (e.g. Gal and Kligman 2000). Nevertheless, in my field site, they choose to work in this sector, because they see it as a morally higher, cultured enclave amidst Russia's rude, often brutal relationships. Their commitment to spreading the faith is for them a way to reach out to the youngest generations whom they aspire to teach amiable social relationships, and to thus improve society.

The parishes have reproduced the striking discrepancy characteristic of employment in Russia between high female participation and low payment. In the sphere of parish schooling, it has also reproduced the ambivalent legacies of female participation in Soviet education. On the one hand, this strongly feminised profession still holds the high symbolic status acquired in Soviet times. On the other hand, however, throughout the Soviet period women have always occupied lower professional positions and have received lower salaries. Despite the fact that official Soviet discourses emphasised women's emancipation, state policies were far from emancipatory, which was visible already from the post-war period (Lapidus 1978; Engel 2004; McMahon 1994). In practice not only did women grapple with the double burden of reproductive matters and of participating in salaried labour, but also occupied the most poorly paid jobs (Lapidus 1978: 143, passim, 172, 185–187). Salaries in Soviet education gradually decreased in comparison to the national average (Lapidus 1978: 190–191). Beyond the sphere of education, the Gorbachev period and the later economic changes brought the feminisation of poverty (Pilkington 1996). This trend has continued in the Putin-Medvedev era:

> Although there is no noticeable gender gap in employment rates in Russia, the gender pay gap remains very high; on average, women are paid 64 per cent of the pay of men for their work. This gap is related to relatively high levels of gender segregation in Russia's labour market, where women traditionally dominate in lower-paid public sectors; for example, the number of women working in the healthcare sector is almost four times higher than the number of men and in education there are more than five times more female than male employees. […] women and men are paid differently even when they do exactly the same work.
>
> (Oxfam 2014: 21)

Conclusion

I have argued that resilient harmony is the consequence of specific configurations of politics at different levels and of different kinds. Criteria of economic and social differentiation at work in Russian society have provided a blueprint for the social fabric of the ROC, and inter-parish disparities more specifically as the Orthodox Church expanded after 1991. The ambivalences of the structural and symbolic unequal position of women in Russian society have been replicated on church grounds. I have demonstrated two things. First, in these two areas, resilient harmony between church and societal developments appears as an unintended result, rather than as an outcome of the pursuit of a symphonic model of a sort. Here my ethnographic material provided evidence that the ROC is not a monolithic bloc. For this reason, various actors, intentions and aims have to be differentiated. Second, the study of this unwittingly achieved harmony can help renew the organisational analysis of the ROC. And perhaps it can be extended to the analysis of other dominant Orthodox churches in post-socialist Eastern Europe.

Notes

1 There are no similarities between this contemporary definition and the Byzantine archetype of symphony formulated by the Emperor Justinian I in the sixth century (Kalkandjieva 2011; Hovorun 2016).
2 For a broad picture of the relations between Orthodox churches and political transformations after 1989 within and beyond Europe, see Leustean (2014).
3 About the political influence of the Russian Orthodox Church (Patriarchate of Moscow) in post-Soviet Russia and the irrelevance of the model of Byzantine symphony in that context, see Knox (2003).
4 Kristen Ghodsee advanced the idea that a Byzantine symphonic model of consensus has been revived in post-socialist Bulgaria, a model that she called 'symphonic secularism'. She included in this model not only the Bulgarian Orthodox Church and the State, but also the religious minorities of the country and Bulgarian society altogether (Ghodsee 2009).
5 For the case of the Russian State and the Russian Orthodox Church, Papkova (2011) and Richters (2013) argued that the agendas of these two organisations diverge in many spheres and that the influence of the Church on society is rather weak.
6 As for example in *The Basis for the Social Concept* (ROC 2000).
7 I am indebted to Alex Agadjanian for having summarised my idea as 'politics instead of policies'.
8 I prefer 'harmony' to 'symphony' in order to avoid any possible association between the situation that I examine and the Byzantine ideal.
9 Monastic institutions need a separate analysis. I also leave out of the scope of this chapter Orthodox charitable organisations, rehabilitation centres and programmes. For more detail on the number and types of official sub-organisations and formally established centres affiliated with the ROC, see http://www.diaconia.ru/viceprem er-rossii-olga-golodec-vstretilas-s-uchastnikami-v-obshhecerkovnogo-sezda-po-so cialnomu-sluzheniyu.
10 I do not provide the name of the city and the names of my informants in order to protect their privacy.
11 In some respects, this was in continuity with Soviet trends (McAuley 1979).
12 Although inequalities along the lines of material wellbeing and status characterised the late Soviet period, Soviet Russia was far more homogenous than post-Soviet society. Sociological surveys conducted in the 1990s found that a large majority of

Russians expected 'equality of material life' (Shlapentokh 1999: 1172) and social justice, while polarisation was thriving, with the political elites holding popular ideas of equality in almost complete disdain (Shlapentokh 1999).

13 In the year 2000, the Council of Archbishops canonised 860 new martyrs and confessors. By 2015, the ROC had canonised 1,776 new saints. The new martyr saints are those who fell victim of violent death under the Soviet anti-religious repressions. The category of saints confessors encompasses persons who stood for their faith under the regime but their death was not caused by the authorities (Rousselet 2007, 2011; Kormina 2013; Christensen 2015).

14 For another case study of an enthusiastic church rebuilding, see Kormina and Shtyrkov (2015).

15 This case is discussed extensively in Tocheva (2011).

16 See Patriarch Kirill's report: http://www.patriarchia.ru/db/text/3979067.html.

17 Civil protests have arisen around the 'Programme 200', initiated in 2015, aiming to erect in Moscow 200 new churches 'within walking distance'. See http://www.portal-credo.ru/site/?act=news&id=112120. In other large cities too, local dwellers oppose church construction. About controversial church construction in St Petersburg, see http://www.portal-credo.ru/site/?act=news&id=112153. About the controversy around the 'transfer for use during 49 years' to the ROC of the St Isaak Cathedral in St Petersburg, a building belonging to the city of high cultural and artistic significance to its population, see, for example, http://www.portal-credo.ru/site/?act=news&id=126915.

18 Meeting of the Archbishops on 2 February 2015. Source: http://www.patriarchia.ru/db/text/3977933.html.

19 Source: http://www.rg.ru/2010/12/03/tserkovnoedobro-dok.html.

20 Sometimes money is given back by the central authorities for particular projects and participation in competitions.

21 This 'obligation' of the laity is specified in point 3.33 of the Statute of the Parish. http://www.patriarchia.ru/db/text/133141.html.

22 http://www.patriarchia.ru/db/text/133141.html.

23 Source: https://mospat.ru/en/ documents/ustav/xiv/, https://mospat.ru/en/documents/ustav/xiii/, and https://mospat.ru/en/documents/ustav/xviii/.

24 The clergy is entitled to a minimal old-age pension, provided by the State to everyone who has reached retirement age. During my fieldwork, I found that in the St Petersburg region, the parishes usually add an extra pension, the size of which varies from one parish to another.

25 Source: http://www.patriarchia.ru/db/text/2775729.html.

26 Source: http://www.portal-credo.ru/site/?act=news&id=116006.

27 The most frequently listed rituals are: baptism; marriage; funeral service at the cemetery or in the church; mentioning of the name of a person in prayers at the altar during 40 days, 6 or 12 months; single mentioning of the name of a living or deceased person in different kinds of prayers; individual prayer for a living or deceased person; the blessing with water of apartments, houses, offices, cars; photograph and video recording of a ceremony.

28 The main producer of religious paraphernalia is the factory Sofrino (*sofrino.ru*), belonging to the Patriarchate of Moscow.

29 Mount Atos in Greece and Bari in Italy, where the relics of Saint Nicolas of Myra are kept, are among the prestigious destinations.

30 These women find no recognition in the hierarchy of the organisation, however with the notable exception of the monastic sphere. Women have been active in the establishment of sisterhoods and the revival of monasticism after the fall of the USSR (Medvedeva 2015). In addition, the wives of the priests hold a semi-recognised position known as *matushka*. Western Orthodox theologians have argued in favour of the ordination of women in the Orthodox Church. Karras

(2008) offers a well-argued example, including an extensive overview of the theo-logical literature. In Russia, the issue hardly appears in public debates. Among the teachers, the parish clergy and parish activists, I have never heard anyone even vaguely approaching the topic of the ordination of women.

References

Agadjanian, A. 2008. 'Russian Orthodox Vision of Human Rights'. In *Erfurter Vort-räge zur Kulturgeschichte des Orthodoxen Christentums 26*. Erfurt: Universität Erfurt Religionswissenschaft Orthodoxes Christentum.

Agadjanian, A. 2011. 'Prikhod i Obshchina v Russkom Pravoslavii: Sovremennye Protsessy v Retrospektive Poslednogo Stoletia'. In *Prikhody i Obshchiny v Sovre-mennom Pravoslavii: Kornevaia Sistema Rossiiskoi Religioznosti.* Edited by A. Agadjanian and K. Rousselet, pp. 15–36. Moscow: Ves' Mir.

Benovska-Sabkova, M., T. Köllner, T. Komáromi, A. Ładykowska, D. Tocheva and J. Zigon. 2010. '"Spreading Grace" in Post-Soviet Russia', *Anthropology Today* 26(1): 16–21.

Bernshtam, T. A. 2005. *Prikhodskaia Zhizn' Russkoi Derevni: Ocherki po Tserkovnoi Etnografii.* Saint Petersburg: Ethnographica Petroplitana, Peterburgskoe Vostokovedenie.

Caldwell, M. 2007. 'Elder Care in the New Russia: The Changing Face of Compas-sionate Social Security', *Focaal: European Journal of Anthropology* 50: 66–80.

Christensen, K. H. 2015. *The Making of the New Martyrs of Russia: Soviet Repression in Orthodox Memory.* Ph.D. dissertation, University of Copenhagen.

Engel, B. A. 2004. *Women in Russia, 1700–2000.* Cambridge: Cambridge University Press.

Freeze, G. 1983. *The Parish Clergy in Nineteenth-Century Russia: Crisis, Reform, Counter-Reform.* Princeton, NJ: Princeton University Press.

Gal, S. and G. Kligman. 2000. *The Politics of Gender after Socialism: A Comparative-Historical Essay.* Princeton, NJ: Princeton University Press.

Ghodsee, K. 2009. 'Symphonic Secularism: Eastern Orthodoxy, Ethnic Identity and Religious Freedoms in Contemporary Bulgaria', *Anthropology of East Europe Review* 27(2): 227–252.

Hemment, J. 2012. 'Nashi, Youth Voluntarism, and Potemkin NGOs: Making Sense of Civil Society in Post-Soviet Russia', *Slavic Review* 71(2): 234–260.

Hovorun, C. 2016. 'Is the Byzantine "Symphony' Possible in Our Days?', *Journal of Church and State* 59(2): 280–296.

Kalkandjieva, D. 2011. 'A Comparative Analysis of Church-State Relations in Eastern Orthodoxy: Concepts, Models, and Principles', *Journal of Church and State* 53(4): 587–614.

Karras, V. A. 2008. 'Orthodox Theologies of Women and Ordained Ministry' In *Thinking Through Faith: New Perspectives from Orthodox Christian Scholars.* Edited by A. Papanikolaou and E. H. Prodromou, pp. 113–158 Crestwood, NY: St Vladimir's Seminary Press.

Kizenko, N. 2013. 'Feminized Patriarchy? Orthodoxy and Gender in Post-Soviet Russia', *Signs* 38(3): 595–621.

Knox, Z. 2003. 'The Symphonic Ideal: The Moscow Patriarchate's Post-Soviet Leadership', *Europe-Asia Studies* 55(4): 575–596.

Köllner, T. 2011. 'Built with Gold or Tears? Moral Discourses on Church Construc-tion and the Role of Entrepreneurial Donations'. In *Multiple Moralities and*

Religions in Post-Soviet Russia. Edited by J. Zigon, pp. 191–213. New York: Berghahn Books.

Köllner, T. 2013. 'Businessmen, Priests and Parishes: Religious Individualization and Privatization in Russia', *Archives de Sciences Sociales des Religions* 162: 37–53.

Kormina, J. 2013. 'Canonizing Soviet Pasts in Contemporary Russia: The Case of Saint Matrona of Moscow'. In *A Companion to the Anthropology of Religion.* Edited by J. Boddy and M. Lambek, pp. 409–424. Chichester: Wiley Blackwell.

Kormina, J., and S. Shtyrkov. 2011. 'St. Xenia as a Patron of Female Social Suffering: An Essay on Anthropological Hagiography'. In *Multiple Moralities and Religions in Post-Soviet Russia.* Edited by J. Zigon, pp. 168–190. New York: Berghahn Books.

Kormina, J. and S. Shtyrkov. 2015. 'Eto nashe iskonno russkoe, i nikuda nam ot etogo ne det'sia: predystoria postsovetskoi desekuliarizatsii'. In *Izobretenie religii: desekuliarizatsia v postsovetskom kontekste.* Edited by J. Kormina, A. Panchenko and S. Shtyrkov, pp. 7–45. Saint-Petersburg: European University at Saint-Petersburg.

Ładykowska, A. and D. Tocheva. 2013. 'Women Teachers of Religion in Russia. Gendered Authority in the Orthodox Church', *Archives de Sciences Sociales des Religions* 162: 55–74.

Lapidus, G. W. 1978. *Women in Soviet Society: Equality, Development, and Social Change.* Berkeley: University of California Press.

Leustean, L. N. (ed.). 2014. *Eastern Christianity and Politics in the Twenty-First Century.* London and New York: Routledge.

McAuley, A. 1979. *Economic Welfare in the Soviet Union: Poverty, Living Standards and Inequality.* Madison: University of Wisconsin Press.

McMahon, P. 1994. 'The Effect of Economic and Political Reforms on Soviet/Russian Women'. In *Women in the Age of Economic Transformation: Gender Impact of Reforms in Post-Socialist and Developing Countries.* Edited by A. Aslabeigui, S. Pressman, G. Summerfield, pp. 59–73. London: Routledge.

Medvedeva, K. 2015. 'The Landscape of a Religious Workspace: The Case of a Russian Christian Orthodox Sisterhood', *Russian Sociological Review* 14(2): 70–81.

Oxfam. 2014. *After Equality: Inequality Trends and Policy Responses in Contemporary Russia.* Discussion paper. Available online: https://www.oxfam.org/sites/www.oxfam.org/files/file_attachments/dp-after-equality-inequality-trends-policy-russia-100614-en.pdf.

Papkova, I. 2011. *The Orthodox Church and Russian Politics.* New York: Oxford University Press.

Pilkington, H. (ed.). 1996. *Gender, Generation and Identity in Contemporary Russia.* London: Routledge.

Richters, K. 2013. *The Post-Soviet Russian Orthodox Church: Politics, Culture and Greater Russia.* London: Routledge.

Rousselet, K. 2007. 'Butovo: La Création d'un Lieu de Pèlerinages sur une Terre de Massacres', *Politix* 77(1): 55–78.

Rousselet, K. 2011. 'Constructing Moralities around the Tsarist Family'. In *Multiple Moralities and Religions in Post-Soviet Russia.* Edited by J. Zigon, pp. 146–167. New York: Berghahn Books.

Rousselet, K. 2013. 'L'autorité Religieuse en Contexte Post-Soviétique: Regard sur le Fonctionnement des Paroisses Russes Orthodoxes', *Archives de Sciences Sociales des Religions* 162: 15–36.

Rozov, A. N. 2003. *Sviashchennik v Dukhovnoi Zhizni Russkoi Derevni.* St Petersburg: Aleteia.

Russian Orthodox Church. 2000. *The Basis of the Social Concept.* Available online: https://mospat.ru/en/documents/social-concepts/.

Shevzov, V. 2004. *Russian Orthodoxy on the Eve of Revolution.* Oxford: Oxford University Press.

Shlapentokh, V. 1999. 'Social Inequality in Post-Communist Russia: The Attitudes of the Political Elite and the Masses (1991–1998)', *Europe-Asia Studies* 51(7): 1167–1181.

Tocheva, D. 2011. 'Ot Vosstanovleniia khrama k Sozdaniiu Obshchiny: Samoo-granichenie i Material'nye Trudnosti kak Istochniki Prihodskoi Identichnosti [From the Rebuilding of the Church to the Creation of a Community: Self-Limitation and Material Hardship as Sources of Parish Identity]'. In *Prihody i Obshchiny v Sovre-mennom Pravoslavii: Kornevaia Sistema Rossiiskoi Religioznosti* [Parishes and Communities in Contemporary Orthodoxy the Basic System of Religiosity in Russia]. Edited by A. Agadjanian and K. Rousselet, pp. 277–297. Moscow: Ves' Mir.

Wegner, St. K. 2014. *Rural Inequality in Divided Russia.* London, New York: Routledge.

Part III
Religious education in public schools

5 National heroes, martyrs of the faith and martyrs of the people

Mixing political and religious discourse in the post-communist Romanian Orthodox religious education textbooks

Ana Raluca Bîgu

Introduction

Religious education (RE) returned to the Romanian school curricula after almost 50 years of socialist and communist leadership, but the discussions concerning whether religion should or should not be taught in Romania's public schools remained a hot topic throughout the last few years. With the overwhelming majority of Romanians declaring themselves 'Orthodox' (86.45 per cent according to the last census from 2011),[1] RE meant for the vast majority of pupils Orthodox teachings, throughout primary and secondary school, with no alternative subjects offered. The critics (mainly from civil society) addressed various concerns regarding teaching religion in public schools, from the fact that RE was an elective-compulsory subject taught in a confessional manner to the design and content of the RE textbooks, most notably the Orthodox ones.[2] The debate concerning the Orthodox RE textbooks touched mainly upon the moral dimension of the textbooks' teachings and the means chosen by the Romanian Orthodox Church to promote its understanding of a moral and civic education, with little attention paid to other questionable approaches, such as the treatment of other denominations – part of the post-communist Romanian religious landscape. The discussion also lacked almost any academic dimension and appeared constantly in the media, often in a sensationalist manner, focusing extensively on the simplistic way several Orthodox RE textbooks treat certain behaviour as sin.

While most of the critiques echoed the secular tendencies affecting Western Europe and a growing trend toward a non-confessional and intercultural approach to organising RE classes, teaching RE in Romanian public schools remained, as I will show in the following, confined to a nationalistic discourse, both at the level of the syllabuses and of the textbooks (even if to a lesser degree in the former), that sees religion as a key element of building national identity throughout the centuries.

The present research will thus shift the focus from the ongoing debate concerning RE in post-communist Romania, choosing to analyse both the way in which the Orthodox RE textbooks reflect the dynamic religious landscape after the fall of communism and how their presence in Romanian pretertiary public education became one of the key battlegrounds where politics and religion intermingled and reinforced each other in post-communist Romania. While the nature of such a mutually beneficial relation, I will argue, might be properly described as a post-communist 'symphonia' – at least in a modern interpretation of the term[3] – the relation is not symmetrical, as one entity (the denominations, especially the Orthodox one) is for its most part financially dependent on the other, in the form of State subsidies. Still, this relation can be seen as 'symphonical', with mutual benefits for the two actors implied. On the one hand, we have the expressions of support guaranteed to denominations by the Constitution[4] and Law no. 498/2006 on Freedom of Religion and the General Status of Religions. Moreover, political positions are offered to members of the Church hierarchy in parliament, 'while the state dominated the Church, transforming it into a state institution which served its political interests', as Lucian Leuştean (2008: 425) notes.[5] On the other hand, we have the Church acting as an electoral agent and promoting a political agenda at election times but also depicting its political donors in frescoes in its churches.

My research will deal primarily on how this concept of post-communist 'symphonia' is operationalised in the field of education, by arguing that this will take the form of an 'indirect' symphonia, operating through third parties (in our case the RE authors of textbooks), so as to maintain the official separation between State and Church, as highlighted in the Constitution. While not pretending to be an exhaustive analysis, due to limitations which appeared when trying to reach some of the textbooks, the research will simultaneously offer an account of how the Orthodox Church, through the voice of the textbook authors, is using education to promote a discourse aimed at consolidating its position in a post-communist nation where it was already perceived as a key actor in society. More specifically, the chapter will show how the Orthodox RE textbooks acknowledge and address the evolving diversity of the country's religious post-communist landscape by seeing this diversity as a threat. This led to several strategies of 'resistance'. These strategies, I will argue, will gradually give shape – throughout the textbooks – a complex concept of Romanian 'national identity' ('Romanianness'), comprising both elements of political and religious identity (see Stahlberg, Cîrlan and Ozhiganova in this volume), but also to a comprehensive framework for excluding other denominations and beliefs from the post-Communist Romanian religious landscape.

In shaping this concept, the Orthodox RE textbooks will make use of ethnicity, the Orthodox faith and a biased view of history to justify the perceived threat from other faiths, but also to re-affirm the pre-eminence of the Orthodox spirituality in the Romanian psyche.

When dealing with this concept, I argue, the textbooks often conflate being 'Romanian' with being 'Orthodox', while ascribing to the 'Romanianness' a moral dimension that comes almost automatically with being Orthodox. This conclusion is 'facilitated' by the way various other denominations are presented throughout the textbooks, and the limited space they receive within Orthodox RE textbooks. This interconnectedness between religion and ethnicity that I will analyse in the Orthodox RE textbooks can be best referred to, as I will argue in the following, as a typical example of 'ethnodoxy', as coined by (Karpov et al. 2012) to describe:

> a belief system that rigidly links a group's ethnic identity to its dominant religion and consequently tends to view other religions as potentially or actually harmful to the group's unity and well-being and, therefore, seek protective and privilege status for the group's dominant faith.
>
> (Karpov et al. 2012: 644)

The situation can be also be described as an instance of an 'ethno-religion', as used by Martin (2005: 32) when presenting religious post-communist developments in Eastern Europe in the context of evangelical expansion, but the insufficient characterisation of the concept will not allow me to use it further.

In the end, the chapter will offer a detailed exemplification of how this concept of 'Romanianness' is put to work in the RE Orthodox textbooks, by showing how the legends and historical data about some local personalities seen as 'martyrs' are interpreted and discussed by some authors to fit the nationalistic cliché which boasts that 'Romanians have been Christians almost from the beginning of their history'.

On a more general level, the chapter suggests the Romanian Orthodox RE textbooks are the perfect example to show how the constant interplay between past politics (history) and religion is used to make a political statement concerning Romanian identity now, but also how the textbooks deliberately make use of this statement to justify the importance of the Orthodox faith in the present, and thus to gain more influence, protection and subsidies from government. On the other hand, by approving these textbooks, the State gives, as I will show in the following sections, an official 'blessing' to the vision of the RE textbook authors (and thus indirectly to that of the Church), contributing to a de facto symphonical consensus between religious and political elites in today's Romania (see Curanović in this volume).

Methodological considerations

The research proposes a systematic discourse analysis[6] taking as sample a number of 13 Orthodox RE textbooks and auxiliary materials[7] used in Romanian public schools at the pre-tertiary level, but also a perspective on the syllabuses for Orthodox education. More specifically, the research can be described as an occurrence-based word analysis, looking into the presence and context in the orthodox RE textbooks of various words and expressions dealing with nationality, ethnicity and historical context, such as 'patriot/patriotism', 'nation', 'fatherland', 'Romanian people', 'kin' and 'country'.

The reason why the research draws on the RE Orthodox textbooks is two-fold: firstly, the Orthodox RE textbooks have recently been the main target of criticism from numerous actors and NGOs, and secondly, the role played by the Orthodox Church in Romania's history helps us hypothesise that there is a greater probability of finding nationalistic elements in the Orthodox textbooks than in any other Romanian RE textbooks.

In order to offer a broader perspective of RE textbook design in today's Romania, the research extends the methods employed when analysing the Orthodox RE textbooks and auxiliary materials to Greek Catholic RE textbooks used in pre-tertiary public schools in Romania. The Romanian Greek Catholic Church is an autonomous Eastern Catholic Church, created following the Habsburg conquest of Transylvania at the end of XVII century.

The decision to include Greek Catholic RE textbooks was justified by considerations of similarity: the Romanian Greek Catholic Church appeared in Transylvania after the conversion of numerous Orthodox believers and continues to maintain many Orthodox observances and traditions. Greek Catholicism thus seems to be the closest religious denomination to Orthodoxy. My analysis explores if there are significant differences between the RE textbooks despite many similarities in religious teachings. I keep in mind the huge difference in the number of believers (86.5 per cent Orthodox versus 0.8 per cent Greek Catholics, according to the last census).

Teaching RE in Romania's public schools: a post-communist perspective

The last few years have witnessed an unprecedented debate about the role of religious education in public schools in Romania, as various voices from civil society issued multiple concerns about the topic. The criticisms varied from the fact that RE is an elective-compulsory subject, taught in a confessional manner, without any alternative on offer, to the way the Church influences the content of the RE syllabuses and textbooks, in order to promote its own understanding of a moral and civic education.

The Orthodox Church was at the forefront of such debates, often portrayed as a powerful actor, which continued to impose its view on teaching RE in public schools. Thus, in 2010, the Orthodox Church succeeded in removing from the draft of the Education Law the proposal to have an alternative course to RE in the form of a 'history of religions' or 'history of culture and arts' course. More recently, the same church succeeded in convincing the authorities to have RE studied for one more year in public education (in preparatory class), bringing the total number of years of RE study in Romania to 13.[8]

One must also mention that Romania is an overwhelmingly Orthodox country, where 86.45 per cent from a population of approximately 20 million people are declaring themselves Orthodox and where the Constitution guarantees religious education in State schools (Article 32, Par.7). While 18 religious denominations are officially recognised by the Romanian State, the Orthodox faith is usually considered an essential part of the 'Romanian identity' throughout centuries, and thus often invoked in nationalistic rhetoric in politics and in art.[9]

Since the fall of the Communist regime over two decades ago, the Romanian educational system, along with other former Communist ones, undertook several reforms, most significantly by introducing private education alongside public schools. Still, after more than two decades since the fall of Communism, the overwhelming majority of Romanian pupils (96 per cent) are still enrolled in public educational structures, while the private ones are concentrated at the kindergarten and tertiary level. Furthermore, the Romanian education system is still heavily centralised, especially in what concerns the curriculum and the funds received, with little power left to the schools or to local authorities.[10]

The reinstatement of RE in public schools was the one of the first requests of the denominations in post-communist Romania and, in 1995, religious classes were introduced by the previous Education Law (Law no. 84/1995), later amended in 1997. The legal framework for teaching RE in public schools is still offered by Education Law no.1/2011, which states that RE is an elective subject (integrated in the field 'Man and Society' within the core curriculum) that schools have to offer compulsorily for one hour a week – but with one important amendment. Until November 2014, in Article 18 (par. 1), the law stated,

> The framework curricula for primary, lower secondary, high school and professional education include the subject Religion as a part of the core curriculum. Students who belong to state-recognised religious denominations are ensured, irrespective of their number, their constitutional right to attend Religion classes in accordance with their own religious faith.[11]

Still, while students could 'opt out' at the written request of parents or legal tutors, there was no alternative offered. Thus, according to the law,

> At the written request of students of adult age, of parents or of legal guardians in the case of minors, students are able not to attend religion classes. In such cases, the overall average mark is computed without that subject. A similar procedure is applied for students for whom, for objective reasons, the conditions necessary for the attendance of religion classes could not be ensured.
>
> (Art.18, par. 2)

But this 'opt out' clause proved to be one of the most problematic issues regarding teaching RE in schools, as the article assumed that students were enrolled *by default* in religion classes, instead of opting *before* enrolling.

In November 2014, a Romanian Constitutional Court (CCR) decision declared unconstitutional Article 9, par. 2 of the Education Law and installed an 'opt-in' system in which the parents should make a request if they want their children to be enrolled in religion classes, as it happens in many countries around Europe (Robbers 2011). For the next academic year, the Romanian Education Ministry set 6 March as the deadline for parents to decide and by that deadline, 89.5 per cent of parents opted for enrolling their children into religion classes – a result promoted as a big success by the Romanian Orthodox Church.

Over the last five years at least, the public debate concerning RE in State schools has focused on the way RE textbooks (in particular the Orthodox ones) draw a religious, moral and behavioural landscape (see also Köllner 2018 for Russia) that critics see as inadequate, intolerant and outdated for a modern and democratic society. Thus, the textbooks have sparked strong criticism from both mass media and NGOs, while the calls for dropping or redesigning certain textbooks has increased dramatically and continues to appear in the mainstream media from time to time. Critics accused the Orthodox RE textbooks of promoting an agenda of intolerance toward other confessions, of displaying an excessive ritualism, but also of using a discourse that embraces nationalist elements together with a distorted view of history.

More recently, the debate concerning RE in Romania took a new turn, as teaching RE in Romanian schools received fresh support from a newly created NGO called '*Asociația Părinți pentru ora de religie – APOR*' (Parents' Association for RE Classes), that hails itself as 'non-confessional' but is keen to display a strong connection with the Orthodox Church. This moment is particularly important given the fact that until then, teaching RE in public schools in Romania had been supported mainly by the clergy of different denominations, but not by a civic initiative with such visibility and presence in the public sphere.

The RE textbooks debate in Romania

The fall of Communism marked the official end of the era of the 'single textbook per subject' taught in the Romanian schools. Now each school is able to choose between alternative textbooks produced by private publishing houses, which first have to be approved by the Ministry of Education. Therefore, neither the government nor the denominations are directly involved in the preparation and production of textbooks, thus allowing private enterprises to control these processes.

In the case of Orthodox RE textbooks, the authors are mainly professors and academics specialised in the field of theology, while the advisors or coordinators are teachers at the Departments of Theology across the country and/or important members of the clergy. While the denomination had a crucial role in licensing the RE teachers,[12] the final approval in the case of the RE textbooks belongs to the Ministry of Education. But in most cases this is only a formal step, once the blessing from the Patriarchy is ensured.

The syllabuses for Orthodox religious education include teachings about the Old and New Testament, catechesis, elements of Christian ethics, aspects related to the mission of the Church, but also depictions of other denominations and beliefs. Gradually, students are familiarised with the history of the Romanian Orthodox Church, historical figures, local clergy and saints, and elements of the Orthodox art and architecture.

Beginning with high school, the syllabus includes a chapter dedicated to 'Orthodoxy and National Culture', featuring numerous historical events and figures that have a special relevance for the history of Romanian Orthodoxy, but also key Romanian thinkers and writers known for their religious faith. Still, the way the authors choose to cover the themes presented in the syllabus varies heavily, as it happens when describing other beliefs and religious denominations. In recent years, this variation prompted numerous accusations of biased treatment and lack of tolerance from the part of Orthodox textbooks, but all these accusations had little effect. The vast majority of the textbooks approved remained in place, while the Ministry of Education promised, but never actually started, a reform to redesign the RE textbooks (see Ozhiganova in this volume for the Russian case).

Nationalism and religiousness in Romania: a historically proven symphony?

Theoretical framework

The Romanian Orthodox Church has a long history of interweaving with politics, so relying on a heavily nationalistic discourse to achieve its goals would not come as a surprise. Still, for the purposes of the present analysis, when using terms such as 'nationalism' and 'nationalistic', I will not step into the broad discussion about nationalism and its various interpretations, but will stick to a working definition – favoured by a number of scholars in the field (see Verdery 1996; Hastings 1997) – that would work more conveniently when applied in a post-communist context about teaching RE in public schools in Romania. This interpretation will grant a special place to the idea of a 'nation', understood as an entity comprising all those of a cultural sameness – a decision justified by the way the national idea emerged and evolved in the specific cultural and political context of the Romanian and Central and Eastern European societies in the 18th, 19th and 20th centuries.

The proposed interpretational framework is justified in the case of Romania by the emergence of the Church as an important actor promoting 'Romanianness' and 'Romanianism', strongly related to the birth of Romanian national ethnic consciousness after Greater Romania incorporated Transylvania in 1918.[13] As highlighted in Stan and Turcescu (2007: 43), the Romanian Orthodox Church borrowed the Transylvanian Greek Catholics' nationalist discourse centred on the Latin character of the Romanian language in order to gain legitimacy, as well as more recognition from the State.

This discourse gradually adopted a more visible nationalist stance, especially when Orthodoxy was linked to fascist politics, as many Orthodox priests joined the pro-fascist Iron Guard movement. During the Communist times, as the initial internationalism was gradually replaced by a more national political approach, with the coming to power of Nicolae Ceaușescu, the Orthodox Church unearthed this discourse, as reflected in the Church history textbooks, thus bringing 'its own contribution to the thesis of the Romanian ethno-genesis and historical continuity', as described by Stan and Turcescu (2007: 48).

Later, in post-communism, confronted with a growing religious competition[14] and a perceived West-mirrored secularisation, the Orthodox Church felt threatened and started re-using the rhetoric of pre-communist times about its place in history, synthesised in the famous phrase 'Romanians have been Christians for 2.000 years'. Actually, the phrase became so embedded in national consciousness, than no later than several years ago, the Minister of Education at that time, Ecaterina Andronescu, used it when interviewed at a television channel to justify the presence of religion in public schools. The echoes of this rhetoric were also present in the way the Orthodox clergy got involved in the national elections (see Cîrlan in this volume), but also in the insistence of the Orthodox Church to construct a 'Romanian People's Salvation Cathedral' (*Catedrala Mântuirii Neamului Românesc*), relying heavily on State subsidies.

These historical considerations help justify why an ethnical understanding of the 'nation' best suits the Romanian context, from the pre-communist times to post-communist developments. Within this framework described above, I will use the term 'nationalism', following mainly Verdery and Hastings as meaning the practice/process of 'invocation of one's own cultural and linguistic sameness toward political ends' (Verdery 1996: 102), when this sameness, understood as the basis of a more complex concept of 'national identity', 'is considered especially valuable and need to be defended at almost any cost, through creation or extension of its nation-state' (Hastings 1997: 4f.). Understood in this way, nationalism can be tactically used to serve as a basis for a successful exclusion of those who do not share the same sameness, but also in order to gain support and to fuel demands from an already powerful actor, under the guise of a perceived threat. This, I will argue, will be the strategy employed by the Orthodox Church, using education (through RE Orthodox textbooks in this case), in order to build a powerful legitimising discourse that will reconfirm its place in Romanian society after 1989.

Romanian identity and Orthodoxy – a 'natural' bond?

The deep interweaving of the political and religious can be easily observed in almost all the RE textbooks analysed. This connection is nevertheless treated as a 'natural' bond, one that explains why the Romanian culture and people occupy such a unique place in the history of mankind. This Romanian 'exceptionalism' can be explained, as one Orthodox RE 9th grade textbook argues (Boldea et al. 2004: 53), by the misfortunes that the Romanian people have had to endure during the centuries, connected with a deep embracing of the Orthodox faith, with the result of creating an unique Latin Orthodox culture.

Throughout the textbooks, the authors construct a legitimising discourse for the Orthodox Church by constantly relating it to the history of the Romanian people from its early beginnings in order to prove that Orthodoxy is the sole genuine faith and that the Orthodox Church deserves the status of 'national church'. Thus, the Orthodox faith is usually referred to as the 'belief of our ancestors' or as the 'church of the people'. Combined with no other specifications regarding the existence of other confessions on the Romanian territory – in several passages in the textbooks – this may induce the idea that the Orthodox faith was the only faith, or at least the only genuine faith, of the Romanian people.

Beyond this direct characterisation of the Romanian Orthodoxy, the textbooks offer, on some occasions, derogatory portrayals of other faiths, by describing them as non-natural, 'aggressive strategies' of proselytism (Lemeni et al. 2006: 90), that plan to lure the believers and distract them from embracing the true faith. For example, the same textbook describes the 'Neoprotestant proselytism as a lack of respect for the freedom of the Christian to believe in God', while the Greek Catholic Church is portrayed as the result of an 'aggressive strategy' of the Catholic Church (Lemeni et al. 2006: 90).

The idea of 'linking a group's ethnic identity to its dominant religion, while treating other religions as harmful', in order to receive a privileged status for the group faith was described by (Karpov et al. 2012; 638) as the main components of a belief system called 'ethnodoxy'. The concept, coined to fill a gap when discussing instances of mingling ethnic identities with particular faiths, describes fully the preference of Orthodox RE textbooks for portraying the Orthodox faith as innate to Romanian people, while marginalising, ignoring or demonising other faiths (see also Ozhiganova in this volume).

Treatment of other denominations in the Orthodox RE textbooks: a case study

The post-Communist religious landscape in Romania is usually addressed by Orthodox RE textbooks at the level of high school, in chapters dealing with 'Christianity and the problems of the contemporary world', 'Christianity and the problems of the youngsters' or the 'The religions of mankind'. From the beginning, we are facing a dichotomy: on one side, we have 'Christianity', seen as a whole, and on the other, the 'problems' it is facing in the contemporary world. But this initial dichotomy is proved to be false: the chapters will subsequently oppose Orthodoxy, portrayed as the only authentic and true form of Christianity, to other faiths, including other Christian denominations. Moreover, by describing other religious options from the beginning as 'problems', we get a first glimpse into how other denominations will be treated throughout the textbooks, as it is highly improbable to use a derogatory term into the title of the chapters and maintain a neutral tone afterwards.

By contrast, the Greek Catholic textbooks will generally discuss other confessions and beliefs from the assumed standpoint of Christianity, sticking to a descriptive historical level, while avoiding documenting an open conflict between denominations. Still, as in the Orthodox RE textbooks, the religion can be 'true' or 'false', and may contain 'errors', as in the case of non-Christian faiths. In that context, Christianity is seen as 'the last and ultimate form of religiosity, wished by God, the fulfilment of all the non-Christian beliefs, and the specific path to redemption', as the Greek Catholic RE textbook for the 9th grade (Marțian et al. 2005: 65) states in a description of the Christian faith.

On the other hand, in the Orthodox RE textbooks, the authors seem to be particularly preoccupied with a specific religious context – one in which the new religious movements and Neoprotestant Churches that arrived in Romania after the fall of Communism are successful in recruiting new believers – but also with its relations with the Greek Catholic minority.

At another level, this preoccupation expressed in the textbooks reflects a more general concern of the Orthodox Church that witnessed, in the last years, a decline in the religiosity expressed by the Romanians, even not at the level of people declaring themselves Orthodox (see Uzlaner in this volume).[15] On the other hand, the Greek Catholic textbooks do not seem to share the same concerns: Even confronted with the same decline in religiosity, the Greek Catholics did not face the same exodus of believers to Neoprotestant movements, so these movements are not perceived as a threat or described in the textbooks in details. Moreover, as long as the discussion remains at the level of comparing Christianity with other religions, these movements will show no particular interest for the Greek Catholic authors of textbooks, since they are Christian.

For the Orthodox RE textbooks, the main argument for proving the Orthodox belief is the true one lies in the assumption that a true belief does not need proselytes, as its truth will reveal itself. Orthodoxy, argues (Lemeni et al. 2006: 91), 'never made proselytes', so Orthodoxy is the only true belief. By contrast, the argumentation goes, these new religious movements eager to attract new believers represent a 'real danger to society', one about which the Orthodox textbooks felt obliged to raise concerns in 'a realistic manner'. Their common feature is their 'aggressiveness' and their shared common goal is the 'spiritual corruption', for which they should face legal action, as suggested by Timiş et al. (2004: 111): 'It is thus mandatory to know the psychology of these groups, for their mission shall not deceive us, affecting the family and the community of the Church. Which are the specific forms of proselytism?' By acting 'as wishing the good', these faiths attract believers 'using means incompatible with the Christian mission, such as: indoctrination, bribe, blackmail, exploiting the poor or fanaticism', argue Lemeni et al. (2006: 91), citing one popular Romanian orthodox priest.

For the Orthodox textbooks, all other denominations 'sin' by making proselytes, so usually their condemnation is proclaimed for all, without feeling the need to specifically mention or go into details about certain cases. Still, some textbooks go a little further in their biased treatment of other faiths by further denouncing, in harsher and more derogatory terms, some denomination or religious movements. Interestingly enough, these harsher condemnations are not declared directly by the textbooks' authors, but cited from several popular theologians, and thus conferring more authority and justification to the 'truths' they express.

In some cases, the distorted view of other denominations is taken to a whole new level of derogatory treatment. In the same chapter devoted to 'Orthodoxy and contemporary world problems', a RE Orthodox textbook for 10th grade (Lemeni et al. 2008: 94), states that

> many forms of so-called spirituality proposed today, which promise miraculous powers, are often arising from the direct influence of the demons. Magic, spiritualism or certain yoga practitioners' powers, which confer supernatural powers, are closely related to the work of demons. (...) Unlike yoga, Christianity is a religion of life and resurrection (...) Yoga reincarnation theory predisposes to fatality (....) Christianity loves life, while yoga, in all its forms, despises life and sees it only as suffering.

In some cases, other religious faiths are mentioned (and highlighted using Aldines) only when a character in a story presented in a textbook committed a misdeed, as in the case of a Muslim Tatar leader who ordered the killing of a local Romanian saint. By doing this, the textbook manipulated the way in which information is provided to pupils in order to suggest that the Orthodox faith and its followers suffered from the actions of non-believers.

The victimisation process highlighted in the Orthodox RE textbooks is taken one step further by presenting patriotic religious figures who died for their faith at the hands of foreign invaders, notably of other faiths than the Orthodox one. The victimisation is also applied when describing how episodes of Romanian history affected by misfortunes were surpassed only with the help of the Orthodox Church, a central pillar of the Romanian spirituality. The Orthodox faith is thus portrayed as saviour of the national self, as well as bringing a special element to an already unique spirituality.

Nevertheless, this biased coverage of other denominations went unnoticed or was ignored by the authorities for a long time in Romania. In 2007, the National Council for Combating Discrimination (the government agency charged with fighting discrimination) finally acknowledged that the way one Orthodox RE textbook described the Bahá'í religion was discriminatory and intolerant and recommended that the textbook should gradually disappear from the Romanian schools. Despite the recommendation, in the absence of any effective monitoring, the textbook continued to be used and still could be found in Romanian bookshops.[16]

The Orthodox RE textbook concerned was published in 2006 by the Ministry of Education and Research under the direction of the Secretary of State for Religious Affairs (Lemeni et al. 2006) and describes the emergence of the Greek Catholic Church in the eighteenth century as a consequence of 'Catholic proselytising', while the Jehovah's Witnesses, the Bahá'í religion and the Mormons are sects that pose 'a real danger to society'. Moreover, the textbook insists that these sects proselytise through methods such as brainwashing, bribery and blackmail but also by exploiting the poor. As described by the US authorities in their assessment of Romania's respect for religious freedom in 2010, representatives of Jehovah's Witnesses and the Bahá'í religion confirmed that the textbook was neither reviewed nor withdrawn from the schools, although the Romanian government declared otherwise. Later, when the National Council for Combating Discrimination confirmed that the textbook had not been modified, the representatives of the Bahá'í religion decided to sue both the Ministry of Education and State Secretariat for Religious Affairs.

On a more general level, the de facto withdrawal of such textbooks remains a problem waiting to be solved in Romania, since the Ministry of Education passes the responsibility for withdrawal to the schools, arguing that these have the duty to respect its list of approved textbooks. If someone takes notice that a textbook has not been withdrawn and one school continues to use it, a parent can write a note to the county inspectorate and it will analyse the case (see Hotnews 2014).

The Orthodox textbooks display numerous cases of discriminatory and derogatory treatments of other faiths. However until now, few complaints have been filed. Instead, there were numerous calls asking for a complete overhaul of the Orthodox textbooks, but the critiques were issued mainly by voices from the civil society (Andreescu et al. 2007) or from the political spectrum (US Embassy 2010) and not by the religious leaders of the denominations attacked.

The attack on other faiths documented so far enables us to state that the Romanian Orthodoxy is feeling threatened by the evolution of the post-communist religious landscape and it is using the RE textbooks in order to prove that this threat is real and 'resistance' is needed.

Interweaving religion and history in building Romanian identity: a deconstruction

The resistance documented so far took the form of a generalised attack on other faiths over their perceived eagerness to proselytise. But the RE textbooks have another strategy for resisting the perceived threat: the constant linking between the Orthodox Church and the history of the Romanian people from its early beginnings, in order to justify the role that the Orthodox Church should have in a post-communist Romanian religious landscape, which the institution feels is controlling less and less (see also Stan and Turcescu 2007).

The idea behind this strategy is that people should adhere to teachings of a faith that is deeply intertwined with the history of their own nation. For that, the Orthodox textbooks will deploy a complex mixture of historical, religious and national elements in order to prove the essentialist principle according to which being 'Romanian' necessary presupposes being an 'Orthodox', and thus to gradually shape a complex concept of a 'Romanian national identity' as related to an Orthodox one.

My analysis so far has documented the deep interweaving of the political and religious elements in almost all the Orthodox RE textbooks analysed. But at this point, the research will take a step back, by deconstructing the argument used by the Orthodox RE textbooks in order to 'prove' that you cannot be a 'true' Romanian without being a true Orthodox.

For that, I argue, the textbooks make use of two major simplifying and somehow mystifying assumptions. One is that we can have a glimpse about Romanian identity throughout the centuries by presenting a numbers of representative figures – political, cultural and religious leaders who served as models throughout the history of the Romanian people. But this assumption can be seen as highly controversial, as one can question why some chosen rulers or members of the cultural or clerical elites should be considered representative for the Romanian people, given the fact that occasionally these elites had foreign origins.

The second assumption that the textbooks get wrong is that these elites presented as models can be satisfactorily described by highlighting only two dimensions – their highly praised political/social/cultural achievements, together with their strong religious (Orthodox) faith – while neglecting other biographical elements, and thus offering a simplified, if not distorted, perspective on historical reality.

These historical figures are usually described as exemplary Orthodox believers, whose deeds reflected their strong faith, no matter if that meant building churches as political rulers or dying for their faith, as artists and writers held in communist prisons. But the problem is that the Orthodox textbooks suggest that their Orthodox faith was in fact the guiding light behind several actions that kept or sustained a vulnerable national identity through the centuries. For the textbooks, these models acted as good Orthodox believers, but aware or with the clear intent of doing patriotic acts for their nation, as suggested by subtitles like 'The national unity in the works of Romanian high clerics' (Lemeni et al. 2008: 80f.). These exemplary Romanians acted in a praiseworthy fashion – the argument in the textbooks goes – not just because they were animated by patriotic feelings or just lived in a territory where the ethnic and cultural sameness indebted them to call themselves 'Romanians', but because they were necessarily, and in the same time, good Orthodox believers and good patriots.

As said, the bi-dimensional method of portrayal is not confined to describing political or cultural leaders, but used by the authors of the textbooks to describe some important religious figures as well (most commonly education reformers), who were also great 'patriots' and who died as martyrs after refusing to surrender to external pressures. It is the case of an important

Orthodox cleric such as Varlaam (1580/1585–1657), who is described by one RE Orthodox textbook for 11th grade (Timiş et al. 2004: 97) both as a martyr of the faith and as an 'enlightened patriot'. The description is also applied indiscriminately to all the important religious figures presented by the textbooks, without suggesting or explaining whether the term 'patriot' reflects the authors' opinion on the presented cases or it is an assumed conviction by the clerics themselves.

Summarising the discussion above, in most cases, the characterisation of the personalities intended to serve as models, both religious and political, follows the classical pair patriot-Christian, with political rulers as exemplary Christians, and the Orthodox clerics as exemplary patriots. In addition, the portrayals are deliberately described to fit the existence of a two-dimensional characterisation, while neglecting other biographical elements, and thus presenting a biased view of the historical reality. The most obvious cases presented in the textbooks are those of a political ruler: Stephen the Great (1433–1504), sanctified by the post-communist Orthodox Church, who is presented as a living saint who devoted his life to stop Turkish and Tatar invasions, while ignoring his tumultuous personal life – and of a writer, Nichifor Crainic, a theologian known for his association with the far-right Iron Guard,[17] but presented only as an Orthodox martyr by a 12th grade RE Orthodox textbook (Timiş et al. 2004: 80). Moreover, by portraying these personalities only in a bi-dimensional manner, the textbooks resort to the same process of 'mythification' one can observe in the Romanian history textbooks, where rulers like Mircea the Elder, Stephen the Great, Michael the Brave and Constantin Brâncoveanu are often described using highly selected events to create unambiguously heroic and pious characters.

Moving to the vocabulary level, when presenting the exceptional character of a person, RE textbooks usually describe his exceptionality using adverbs whose meanings are related to the main domain of activity of that character. To be more precise, an exceptional ruler (who is also a Christian) is described as sacrificing himself as 'hero', while in the case of a religious figure (who is also a patriot), his sacrifice makes him a 'martyr'. There is one notable exception to this general situation, and its presence shows that the nationalist stance adopted by RE textbooks can advance further.

The example comes from Timiş et al. (2004), in a chapter dedicated to Romanian writers and thinkers who are hailed as pious orthodox believers. In the end of the chapter (p. 82), after a brief portrayal of each of these personalities, they are collectively characterised by a new formula – 'martyrs of the people' (*martiri ai neamului*)[18] – that combines the vocabulary typically used when describing the model clerics who died for their faith (martyrs – *martiri*) with that employed when presenting the life of political rulers, as heroic fighters for their country (people – *neam*) – thus taking one step further in the direction of a nationalistic stance adopted by the Orthodox Church.

Thus, by 'borrowing' the term 'martyr' – used so far only in connection with someone's religious faith – to describe rulers or writers, who were also religious, the textbooks are bringing the sacrifice from the level of the individual to the level of the whole nation, and thereby suggesting that the Romanians have a moral duty to respect and honour these figures, as long as the level of *neam* is involved.[19]

The notion of *neam* requires a special treatment in the discourse analysis of the textbooks, since its understanding, close to that of 'kin' or 'nation', but preferred by the authors – and, at a more general level, by the patriotic literature – is that of an ethnic community with a clear historical and cultural lineage. This understanding of *neam* was enriched to include the Christian element by authors like Dumitru Stăniloae, an important theologian in the Romanian Orthodox literature, who saw it as 'the spiritual synthesis of [mainly] Dacian, Latin and Christian Orthodox elements', which 'has its own individuality and a unity that goes beyond its components'.[20] This idea of a special individuality of the *neam*, closer to a personified one, is also reflected by the Orthodox RE textbooks, when the authors speak of the protection of the '*neam*'s being' as of the protection offered to a person (Timiş et al. 2004: 60).

Even before engaging in quantitative analysis, in the textbooks the occurrences of *neam* clearly surpass those of the modern term 'nation', with the latter appearing mainly in two formulas: 'National Church', as shown in a 3rd grade Orthodox RE textbook (Timis et al. 2008) and 'national unity', as in Timiş et al. (2004).

This shows interestingly that even the Romanians are presented in a dual role, both as Orthodox believers and citizens, enforcing thus a strong connection between the two dimensions. But the idea that the Romanian Orthodox believer has a duty towards their country is present in the Orthodox RE textbooks beginning with 4th grade, when a 'pupil's prayer' at the end of the 4th grade Orthodox RE textbook (Teodorescu et al. 2006: 63) states clearly the duties the children have towards their people and country. Here we can see clearly how the political and the religious dimension mingle, blurring the lines that separate the duties that citizens have towards the State from the duties of the members of a religious community, thus suggesting that the nature of such duties is the same. Another interesting example comes from the new RE syllabuses for 5th–8th grade that recommends at the 5th grade level teaching the pupils to 'serve their own people', in a chapter dedicated to Christian life along the others. While the new syllabuses seem to address more openly the respect for religious diversity than the previous one, they also remained committed to a rigid view that fails to distinguish between religious and lay duties. On a more general level, the examples given above are just a few of the cases where the authors use rhetorical means and techniques.

It is important to note that the views described so far belong to the authors of the Orthodox RE textbooks and do not reflect any direct attempt by the State or by the Church to promote patriotism through religious education. Nevertheless, these views reflect opinions held by people with close connections with the Church, that gain approval from the Church hierarchy through the benedictions offered by important clerical figures to the RE textbooks.

Although textbooks require also a government approval (from the Ministry of Education), this approval is formal, once the textbooks got the denomination's acceptance. This situation – in which the two actors (the State and the Church) cooperate, with the State choosing not to interfere de facto[21] in designing the content of RE textbooks as long as they respect the guidelines offered by the syllabuses for RE – can be described as an 'indirect symphony' (or, at least, a 'symphony of views') between the Church and State – in which, officially, the main actors remain the textbooks' authors, acting as mediators between the religious and political elites.

Church and State in Romania – a symphony in a 'secular' age?

The analysis undertaken so far exposed – without pretending to be exhaustive – a clear intention by the textbooks (and thus by the Church) to appeal to nationalist feelings and discourse in order to gather mass support on a religious market in which the Orthodox faith is feeling threatened both by the competition of the newcomers' arrival in the aftermath of the fall of communism, but also by a growing public discontent to towards its projects (Romanian People's Salvation Cathedral) or clergy behaviour.

The nationalistic discourse used by the textbooks mainly includes the appeal to the essentialist principle according to which being Romanian presupposes being an Orthodox as a strategy to legitimise and consolidate the position of the Orthodox Church in a State where it already accounts for the vast majority of believers. For that, this chapter shows, the textbooks use factual inaccuracies and biased interpretations, victimisation and scapegoating, but also a stereotypical image of Orthodox Church and a distorted view of others faiths.

As documented so far, the Orthodox Church is indirectly presenting itself, with the help of the authors of textbooks, both as the guardian of a national self and as a constitutive element of a Romanian national identity; following the essentialist principle according to which being 'Romanian' necessary presupposes being an 'Orthodox'. One flaw is that the treatment completely and consciously ignores several important aspects concerning the Romanian history and culture that would convey a more realistic image of the past. Another flaw rests in the idea of resorting only to rulers or members of the elites from the Romanian history and culture to reconstruct a more complex and controversial concept of national identity, only to justify the special place of the Orthodox faith on a Romanian post-communist religious market in which it feels more and more threatened.

Here my discussion offers a detailed treatment of the Church discourse and fills – albeit only cursory – an important gap in the study of the consensus reached by the Romanian authorities and the Romanian Orthodox Church. By approving the RE textbooks designed by the persons related with Church, the State is thus legitimising the presentation offered by the Orthodox Church in the textbooks as a key actor of building Romanian national identity, and also the important role it should play today on a more competitive religious market. This particular situation – comprising in a de facto non-interference of the State in the designing and content of the RE Orthodox textbooks – was analysed throughout the chapter as documenting a mutually beneficial relationship that can be best described as an 'indirect symphonia', where the relation between Church and State was mediated by a third party: the textbooks' authors.

Notes

1 Pew Research Center (2017) places it at 86 per cent.
2 A detailed presentation of RE teaching in post-Communist Romania will be offered in a separate subchapter.
3 For the present purposes, I will follow Hovorun (2016: 288), where State and Church interact as different entities – different from the so-called 'Byzantinian symphonia', where State and religion formed 'a single theopolitical entity'.
4 According to the Constitution, Art. 29, 'All religions shall be free and organised in accordance with their own statutes, under the terms laid down by law' (paragraph 3), and 'Religious cults shall be autonomous from the State and shall enjoy support from it, including the facilitation of religious assistance in the army, in hospitals, prisons, homes and orphanages' (paragraph 5).
5 See also Hovorun (2016: 280).
6 For the methodological insights I am indebted to Fairclough (2003) and Salkie (1995).
7 The research also includes textbooks that are not currently on the list of approved textbooks issued by the Ministry of Education because they are still used in some Romanian schools.
8 For a further analysis of teaching RE in Romania see Bîgu (2014).
9 Law no. 498/2006 on Freedom of Religion and the General Status of Religions acknowledges the 'important role played by the Romanian Orthodox Church and the other Churches and denominations in the Romanian national history'. In neighbouring Bulgaria, however, the correspondent law, according to Ghodsee (2009: 239) seems to ignore the contribution of other denominations to the creation of Bulgarian statehood.
10 For more details concerning the post-socialist educational system in Romania, see Bîgu (2012).
11 The translation belongs to the author of this chapter.
12 In Romania, the RE teachers are paid by the State. According to the Education Law, 'the subject Religion may be taught exclusively by qualified teaching staff, as provided by this Law and under the protocols concluded between the Ministry of Education, Research, Youth and Sports and the officially recognised religious denominations' (Article 18, Par. 3). The Orthodox RE teachers are graduates from the Faculties of Theology around the country, professors in State theological high schools ('seminarii teologice') or priests – that take the approval from the local metropolitan (archbishop) in order to take part at the exams organised by the Ministry of Education. The approval takes the form of a benediction and is obtained following an interview, but only after the prospective teacher first obtains recommendations from a priest. The requirement that RE classes to be taught only by qualified staff prevent a situation described by Köllner (2016: 374f.) in Russia where RE teachers 'are not required to have any prior training or detailed knowledge of religion', so 'many of the teachers of religious education are former teachers of Marxism-Leninism'.

13 For the presentation of the historical elements highlighting the discourse of the Romanian Orthodox Church in the 18th, 19th and 20th centuries I am indebted to Stan and Turcescu (2007, chapter 3).
14 The Neoprotestant Churches are just one example: the number of Pentecostals grew from 220,824 (1992 census) to 363,314 (2011 census).
15 According to a survey conducted by the polling company Gallup, the number of Romanians declaring themselves 'religious' dropped from 85 per cent in 2005 to 77 per cent in 2014. Still, according to the National Institute of Statistics, the percentage of Orthodox in the Romanian population remained constant with 86.81 per cent (1992), 86.79 per cent (2002) and 86.45 per cent (2011).
16 As the author can certify by finding it in two central bookshops in the Romanian capital in 2014.
17 A far-right movement and a political party in Romania created in 1927 and dissolved in 1941.
18 The Romanian term translated here as 'people' (*neam* in Romanian) has two senses: i) extended family (a group of families related by blood or marriage), and ii) an ethnic group whose members share a common cultural tradition. As a result, belonging is seen as similar to belonging to a family, in an extended sense.
19 The same term (*neam*) appears in the Romanian name of 'Romanian People's Salvation Cathedral' (*Catedrala Mântuirii Neamului Românesc*), confirming once again the Orthodox Church's wish to conflate ethnical and religious dimensions when describing its contribution to Romanian history and identity.
20 See *Telegraful Român*, year 88, no. 4, 1949, p. 1–2, as mentioned by Stan and Turcescu (2007: 45).
21 The only case (to my knowledge) when the State reacted to the content of RE textbooks was when the National Council for Combating Discrimination acknowledged the discriminatory treatment of the Bahá'í religion by one Orthodox RE textbook and recommended that the textbook should be withdrawn.

References

Andreescu, L., L. Ardelean, C. Remus, S. Enache, J.-A. Kacsó, E. Moise and E. Szokoly. 2007. *Educaţia religioasă în şcolile publice* [Religious Education in Public Schools]. Tîrgu Mures: Pro Europa (http://www.proeuropa.ro/educatie.html).
Bîgu, A. R. 2012. 'Romanian Educational System'. In *Balancing Freedom, Autonomy, and Accountability in Education*, vol. 2, pp. 435–450. Nijmegen: Wolf Legal Publishers.
Bîgu, A. R. 2014. 'Becoming Secular? Dynamics of Teaching Religion and Ethics in Central and Eastern Europe: A Comparative Study Focusing on Romania'. In *Faith and Secularisation: A Romanian Narrative*. Edited by W. Dancă, pp. 67–76. Washington DC: The Council for Research in Values and Philosophy.
Fairclough, N. 2003. *Analysing Discourse: Textual Analysis for Social Research*. New York: Routledge.
Ghodsee, K. 2009. 'Symphonic Secularism: Eastern Orthodoxy, Ethnic Identity and Religious Freedoms in Contemporary Bulgaria', *Anthropology of East Europe Review* 27(2): 227–252.
Hastings, A. 1997. *The Construction of Nationhood: Ethnicity, Religion and Nationalism*. Cambridge: Cambridge University Press.
Hotnews. 2014. *Lecţie dintr-un manual controversat de religie: Dacă minţi, atunci vei fi călcat de maşină*. Available online: http://www.hotnews.ro/stiri-esential-16427224-lectie-dintr-manual-controversat-religie-daca-minti-atunci-vei-calcat-masina.htm.

Hovorun, C. 2016. 'Is the Byzantine 'Symphony' Possible in Our Days?', *Journal of Church and State* 59(2): 280–296.

Karpov, V., Lisovskaya, E. and D. Barry. 2012. 'Ethnodoxy: How Popular Ideologies Fuse Religious and Ethnic Identities', *Journal for the Scientific Study of Religion* 51 (4): 638–655.

Köllner, T. 2016. 'Patriotism, Orthodox Religion and Education: Empirical Findings from Contemporary Russia', *Religion, State and Society* 44(4): 366–386.

Köllner, T. 2018. 'On the Restitution of Property and the Making of "Authentic" Landscapes in Contemporary Russia', *Europe-Asia Studies* 70(7): 1083–1102. doi:10.1080/09668136.2018.1484077.

Leuştean, L. 2008. 'Orthodoxy and Political Myths in Balkan National Identities', *National Identities* 10(4): 421–432.

Martin, D. 2005. *On Secularization: Towards a Revised General Theory.* Burlington, VT: Ashgate.

Pew Research Center. 2017. *Religious Belief and National Belonging in Central and Eastern Europe.* Available online: http://www.pewforum.org/2017/05/10/religious-belief-and-national-belonging-in-central-and-eastern-europe/.

Robbers, G. (ed.). 2011. *Religion in Public Education.* Trier: European Consortium for Church and State Research.

Salkie, R. 1995. *Text and Discourse Analysis.* London and New York: Routledge.

Stan, L. and L. Turcescu. 2007. *Religion and Politics in Post-communist Romania.* Oxford: Oxford University Press.

US Embassy. 2010. *International Religious Freedom Report for Romania.* Available online: http://romania.usembassy.gov/2010-irf-ro.html.

Verdery, K. 1996. *What Was Socialism, and What Comes Next?* Princeton, NJ: Princeton University Press.

Orthodox and Greek Catholic RE textbooks (selection)

Boldea, F., V. Boldea, V. Pop and L. Lazăr. 2004. *Religion Orthodox Faith, 9th Grade.* Deva: Corvin Publishing House.

Marţian, N., O. David and S. Zetea. 2005. *Religion Greek-Catholic Faith, 9th Grade.* Cluj-Napoca: Dacia Publishing House.

Lemeni, A., G. Păunoiu, S. Tudose and D. Ştefănescu (eds.). 2008. *Religion Orthodox Faith, 10th grade.* Bucharest: Corint Publishing House.

Lemeni, A., J. Nedelea, G. Păunoiu and S. Tudose (eds.). 2006. *Religion Orthodox Faith, 11th Grade.* Bucharest: Corint Publishing House.

Teodorescu, L., Iu. Martin, and A. Chirilă. 2006. *Religion Orthodox Faith, 4th Grade.* Bucharest: Aramis Publishing House.

Timiş, V., G. Hagău, C. Orăştean, D. Ciacoi, M. Oros, I. Timiş-Râza, L. Dragoş and I. Râza. 2004. *Religion Orthodox Faith, 11th Grade.* Cluj-Napoca: Dacia Educational Publishing House.

Timiş, V., I. Corujan, D. Bumbu, I. Râza, A. Dâmbean and N. Vladu. 2008. *Religion Orthodox Faith, 3th Grade.* Bucharest: Corint Publishing House.

Websites

Coalition for Family (www.coalitiapentrufamilie.ro)
Ministry of Education, Research, Youth and Sport (www.edu.ro)
National Institute of Statistics (www.ins.ro)
Official site of the Romanian Patriarchate (www.patriarhia.ro)
State Secretariat for Religious Affairs (www.culte.gov.ro)

Legislation

Constitution of Romania (English) (http://www.cdep.ro/pls/dic/site.page?id=371)
Education Law No. 1/2011 (Romanian) (http://www.uaiasi.ro/ro/files/legislatie/LEGEA
    %20nr.1_05.01.2011_Legea%20educatiei.pdf)
Educational Law No. 84/1995 (Romanian) (http://legislatie.resurse-pentru-democratie.
    org/84_1995.php)
Law No. 489/2006 of Freedom of Religion and the General Status of Religions
    (Romanian) (http://www.arhiva.culte.gov.ro/detaliu-legislatie/vrs/IDleg/18)

6 The shifts between

Multiple secularisms, multiple modernities and the post-Soviet school

Agata Ładykowska

Multiple secularisms and multiple modernities

This contribution is based on a 12-month-long fieldwork conducted in Rostov-on-Don in 2006–7, during which I examined post-Soviet educational practices among middle-aged teachers of religion with long professional careers.[1] Having converted to Orthodoxy relatively late in their lives, these teachers display a propensity to employ Soviet imagery, discourses and techniques in their current work in religious education. At the same time, having been endorsed by the State and introduced to school curriculum, Orthodoxy has become a new source of self-assertion for these teachers, contributing to the renewal of their secular social status which had declined in the wake of changes to state educational policy after perestroika. By transferring certain values born of another historical experience and adding them to the cultural repertoire of both school and church, they modify both these institutions from the inside.

Teachers held a unique position in the USSR, since it was they who were directly responsible for raising the New Soviet Man. This process took shape through the activities of *vospitanie* – 'moral upbringing', an ideologically formulated understanding of education that was placed at the centre of the entire educational process. Atheism was one of the key principles of Soviet education and a characteristic of Soviet modernity. After its demise, religious sources of inspiration gained popularity within state education (Halstead 1994; Glanzer 2005) and, as a result, both secular and religiously inspired models of moral education pronounced the virtue of pluralism. However, despite official claims that moral education in state schools would draw on democratic values, questions of Russian national identity and Russian Orthodoxy have emerged as its major theoretical foundations. Eventually, the subject 'Foundations of Orthodox Culture' (hereafter: FOC) appeared in the curriculum as the primary resource for moral education.[2] It is a creative proposal that is nominally secular but suffused with Orthodoxy, and thus eligible for adoption in nominally secular schools. This was possible thanks to the adoption of the controversial Law on Freedom of Conscience and Religious Associations (1997). This law gives preferential status to Russian Orthodoxy for its 'special contribution' to the development of Russian history, culture and statehood, and adopts a distinction between traditional and non-traditional religious associations. International observers (US Department of State 2012) and political-social scientists (e.g. Richters 2013) consider that the law's enactment undermines the religious neutrality of the State and blurs the constitutional separation of Church and State.

As the notion of the secular is historically and socially contingent (Taylor 2007; Asad 2003; Cannell 2010), my aim is to explore its specifically Russian, post-Soviet expressions and the implications these may have in social life. As the dominant strains in social theory are premised on Western (culturalist) assumptions emphasising the link between modernity and secularity and making it normative, I ask what implications the growing salience of Ortho-dox ideals within Russian State education has for definitions of 'the secular' and 'modernity'. The majority of scholars addressing the topic of FOC (e.g. Glanzer 2005; Mulders 2008; Papkova 2009; Richters 2013; Mitrokhin 2004a, 2004b; Ozhiganovain this volume) tend to view it critically as a manifestation of the Russian Orthodox Church's (ROC) quest to increase its influence and the State's favouritism towards it. In these accounts, FOC is diagnosed as simultaneously violating the constitutional principles of: 1) the separation of Church and State, 2) the State's commitment to secular public education, and 3) religious pluralism guaranteed by religious freedoms. The claims both of these authors and of international observers are in line with contemporary Western secularist discourses that relegate religion to the private sphere, as evident in the desired construction of the relationship between Church and State, and between 'education' and 'religion'. Ideally, in modern democratic societies, these realms are configured as separate and distinct. Such a config-uration of Church–State relations was shaped by the Enlightenment approach to religion and thus by values deemed central to European identity: tolerance, hence plurality of beliefs, and secularism. The influence of these ideas has culminated in two central precepts: State neutrality towards religious bodies and the privatisation of religion, which have led to the separation of the two institutions of Church and State. In this sense, the critical scholarship on FOC I invoked above tends to support the classic 'four-square' model of 'public-education/private-religion' conventionally associated with the modern state. This 'four-square' model – conceived as a two-by-two grid in which 'public' is placed above 'education' and 'private' appears above 'religion' – gives the impression that religion and education are conceptually discrete (Stambach 2006: 2). In fact, such a configuration is fundamental for 'modernity'.

Secularism is a political doctrine (Asad 2003). Its conceptualisations are ingrained in a discursive field formed by the historical process whereby the epistemological legacies of the Enlightenment are either embraced or dis-carded. These discourses are often distorted by a Protestant bias: they ideo-logically privilege a notion of religion that prioritises personal private faith over collective public practice. This makes them inherently discriminatory toward religious traditions in which public manifestations of religion are privileged, such as Eastern Orthodox Christianity where religion is a constitutive element of ethnic and national identity (Agadjanian and Roudometof 2005). The adoption of such a version of secularism implies the acceptance of its ideology, which frames the ideal configuration of the Church–State relationship as separate. Importantly, critics of secularisation theory (e.g. Casanova 1994) have reified its core underlying premise, namely the separation of Church and State.

Genealogies of secularism often ignore any non-Western antecedents: they often begin with the Protestant Reformation which clearly bypassed many non-Western societies (Asad 1997; Taylor 2007; Cannell 2010). However, adopting Asad's critique of secularism as an Enlightenment-based political project, and considering 'the secular' a historically produced, politically institutionalised and programmatic category (not an inevitable process or fact) enables other conceptualisations of 'the secular' to emerge as equally relevant. This step allows for seeking alternate sources of 'the secular' and opens space for anthropological explorations of their ideological underpinnings. For instance, the Russian Orthodox perspective cannot be comprehended from the position founded in the context of the European Enlightenment (cf. Hovorun 2016). Symphonia, emerging at the time of the Great Schism that rendered Christendom into Eastern and Western halves (1054), is imagined to have had a continuous influence in shaping Church–State relations in Orthodox societies (Ghodsee 2009) and consequently to have furnished an alternative conceptualisation of secularism. Sociologically speaking, symphonia is today a rather mythical idea (see also Köllner 2018 and in the introduction to the volume). Although it is explicitly invoked by the ROC as the ultimate model of its relationship with the State, social scientific scholarship is rather suspicious of the harmony underlying this bond.[3] However, it is precisely in the area of education where one can see how religion and its 'proper' domains are being defined by the State, despite the constitutional separation of the two.

The secularisation thesis has been criticised more often in relation to religion than in relation to education. Although the secularisation thesis, with its idiomatic assumption that religion declines as modernity expands, has been subjected to many critical interventions, these critics retain a narrow vision of education as a field that promotes one kind of (secular) modernity (Stambach 2006: 4f.). This association carries a hidden historicist argument in which education is regarded as a catalyst for a particular kind of change. This association of education with modernity and of religion with challenges to secularisation perpetuates a religion-education, private-public divide (Stambach 2006: 4f.). However, precisely this argument, in which education is linked with attaining modernity, is well assimilated by middle-aged teachers of religion as a legacy of Soviet educational ideology.

Postsocialism was one among many analytical categories that has provided anthropologists with a variety of stances on modernity (e.g. Hann 2002; Buyandelgeriyn 2008; Brandtstädter 2007), but at the heart of the matter remains the attempt to get an analytical grip on continuity and change. In line with these attempts, this chapter too looks for analytical propositions on how to account for a shift in the social significance of concepts of religion or atheism in everyday realities and how people deal with this shift in political rhetoric. One way towards this goal is studying Orthodoxy's interplay with the 'modernities' intrinsic to socialist and Western (post-socialist) projects by looking at the dynamics of religious schooling in post-Soviet Russia.

In the view of many parents and teachers, education in post-Soviet era Russia has lost its previous modernising potential. A disintegration between the school curriculum and a moral curriculum, the collapse of ideological infrastructure, a pluralism of views, de-statisation and competing approaches to native and Western pedagogies and their philosophical infrastructures have all contributed to the overall feeling that the emancipatory potential of education, previously seen in the integrative character of the ideological and bureaucratic infrastructures, has been lost. This feeling of loss primarily concerns teachers: the agents of Soviet modernity. While the position of education has collapsed in post-Soviet Russia, religion has experienced a revival, offering new avenues for a renewal of teachers' status.

Post-Soviet reconfigurations

Since the demise of communism the social position of teachers has been gradually collapsing. Teachers' economic rewards had already been steadily declining since the 1960s and this process has simply accelerated during the 1990s (Eklof and Seregny 2005: 205). The profession's previously high level of social prestige had translated into a popularity of teacher training institutions among students. However, already by the late Soviet period these were underfunded, rigidly structured places that attracted less competitive students. Twelve per cent of all teachers are pensioners, and their training and experience place them among the most conservative parts of society (Eklof and Seregny: 204). Teachers are employees of local municipalities and are beneficiaries of the public funds. Their salaries are more than modest (in 2007 educators with a 20-year-long career reported ca 7,000 rubles, which equalled roughly 180 euro.)

This chapter is devoted to the peculiar effect which the combination of the religious and educational aspect is having on reconfigurations of social status within the post-socialist context. Related to this I find apposite the argument discussed by Chris Fuller (2003). Exploring the particularities of Indian secularism, Fuller noted that the status of priests in Tamil Nadu had risen, after an earlier sharp decline, due to a State-sponsored demand for more education in Agamic ritual texts. Fuller illustrates that in conforming to expectations that they should raise the level of education, the priests' commitment to authority and the legitimacy of tradition had been reinforced. Yet:

> [P]riestly traditionalism also goes hand-in-hand with the growing adoption of a range of modern attitudes and values about the importance of

education, training, and professionalism, as well as money-making and economic rationality ... The priests have become better informed about the wider world and less provincial in their outlook ... Priests with an Agamic education, especially if they are well educated in the secular system, too, also tend to display a positivist attitude towards book-based knowledge, and in their eyes both types of education are about acquiring rational knowledge that may be used reflexively to examine and reform religious and social practices.

(Fuller 2003: 5f.)

That these priests have become both more traditionalist and more modernist may look contradictory, but '[I]t does so only through the lens of a pre-dominantly Western misconception about modernity driving out tradition' (Fuller 2003: 5f). Education is usually interpreted as modernist and religion is not, so that one remains at odds with the other. Fuller uses the Indian model to account for an alternative configuration of this relationship. Bearing this in mind, I wish to illustrate a case that I think on the theoretical level is analo-gical to Fuller's. Provincial teachers from the vicinity of Rostov, whose status has weakened over the last two decades, were directly invited by State agen-cies to modernise it through the adoption of the FOC course in their schools. This step was considered by the local authorities as a moral response to what the State perceives as an inability to live up to the challenges of the modern world.

Welfare provision, religion and education: the State and the Church's parallel paths, and parallel rationales? New professional opportunities for teachers

In the morning of 6 March 2007, Svetlana Sergeevna and I were sitting in a chauffeur-driven car, taking us to Antratsit,[4] a small semi-urban settlement located in the Rostov *oblast'*. As the name suggests, the settlement belongs to a myriad of once prosperous sites of coal production in this mining region. At a distance of about 50 kilometres, we could already see the industrial land-scape: quarries, hills, and piles of stones and abandoned machines, now in need of a new purpose and otherwise left to decay. Antratsit, on the contrary, was a clean, green place, where one could see that the administration was careful to keep the streets tidy and lawns neat. My companion, Svetlana Ser-geevna, born in the mid-1950s, was a lay representative of the Rostov-on-Don Eparchy. She had invited me to accompany her to an event she knew would interest me: a meeting with the Eparchy representative, organised by the city's district administration for the district's pedagogical cadres. The aim was to encourage them to introduce the Foundations of Orthodox Culture course in their schools. The meeting was open only to the invited participants, and my inclusion on the guest list was possible only thanks to Svetlana, one of the VIPs of the event. Other VIPs were the mayor, the chief executive officer of the district's department of the Ministry of Education, priests representing different levels of the Church administrative hierarchy, and an ataman – a representative of the Don Cossacks who held the rank of colonel. Other invited guests included the headmasters of all State-funded public educational institutions of the district, including kindergartens. All of them had been invited to hear bureaucrats reporting on the steps already taken, and the administrative measures to be taken in the nearest future, leading unfailingly to the introduction of the Foundations of Orthodox Culture course in State schools. Svetlana Sergeevna was to report on the didactic aids at the Eparchy's disposal, and to encourage the introduction of the FOC course by assuring that pedagogical support would be offered to prospective teachers. Photographs I have taken to record this event show the mayor at the centre of the presidium table, with Fr Mikhail to his right and the local executive officer of the Ministry of Education to his left. To the left of the executive officers sits Svetlana Sergeevna. It is inconceivable that the seating and speaking order behind the presidium table was unintentional: it represented a particular conjuncture of ideas represented by leading local figures within the area of State administration, Orthodox hierarchy, educational administration and Orthodox education.

The audience was majority female: I was seated among about a hundred ladies in their fifties and older. I could not help but see them as casualties of post-socialist modernity, especially when confronted with the youthful vigour of the priests: these ladies' outlook, status and role in the school and society at large derived anachronistically from a previous era, in which an exclusive modern authority was vested in the builders of the Soviet project. This community's best prospect was, it seemed to me, to conform to the new project of national identity. We were listening to something that was very interesting for a researcher interested in the entanglements of religion and education, and which demonstrated the existence of multilevel connections between State administration and the Church. Most distinctly, it attested to a rhetorical forging of a very specific notion of modernity, where conceptual links between teaching religion and the welfare of citizens were made. The meeting was organised to explain to the headmasters that the FOC course would be introduced from the top down. As encouragement, additional payments for teaching the course were offered for disposal by school headmasters, who were now tasked with choosing the proper people for this activity. These people were now to be professionally trained to carry out the FOC course, a task ensured by cooperation between the Eparchy and the municipality, who would provide the educational aid and financial support, respectively.

To account for this, the executive officer from the educational department explained that the municipality had done extensive research in another region to learn from their experience. For this, he and a high-ranked priest had been sent together to Smolensk, a city considered as a successful example of introducing the FOC course in a variety of ways. The Smolensk administration had discovered the demand for the subject by conducting surveys. The officer described in detail how the system of cooperation between the Eparchy and the administration in Smolensk had been creatively developed in order to avoid transgressing the legal separation of Church and State, and how he wished to implement this model in Antratsit. The officer continued:

> In Smolensk, the task has been treated seriously by the oblast authorities, by the department of education and by the Eparchy. The best evidence of this is the fact that the issue is being administered by the educational department at the level of the oblast', and not at the city level. A number of additional officers specialising in moral upbringing have been appointed there, and an institute of advanced training for teachers has been affiliated. This year, together with the Eparchy, this institute released its first 200 graduates. With regard to the Eparchy: all of us understand that the issue in question generates costs, from the local budget, as well as from the oblast budget, because it involves the work of competent people who should be paid a decent salary. For the first year – the salary was calculated together by the administration and by the Eparchy. The system of teacher training was established on the basis of the institute of advanced training for teachers. The lecturers there were carefully selected: these were people with academic degrees, who can guarantee a 100 percent quality of education. The Eparchy made available its premises, reimbursed travel expenses, provided full board, accommodation, etc. This means that all those who went through an advanced training in teaching FOC did so for free. How did they come up with this? This is elementary. They explained to us that in principle we proceed along two parallel paths: the Eparchy is engaged in moral upbringing, especially of the Orthodox culture in Russia; we are engaged in the same. But these paths have not crossed so far. In Smolensk, these paths crossed exactly in 2003. Anyway, the normal working situation there is as follows: the Eparchy, in order to comply with the law that maintains that the church and the state be separated, did not insist that the clergy stays at the premises at the time of the course, nor that it teaches there. They have their own environment, they have their own Sunday schools – this system is well developed in Smolensk. 180 children voluntarily visit the Eparchy every Sunday. This means that 90 percent of children receive a parallel education in the 'History of Orthodoxy in Smolensk' in our, secular, schools.

The officer concluded that there had already been 'very positive' results. His speech was very convincing, as he was careful to illustrate his arguments with appropriate statistics on how critical factors for pupils' wellbeing and the standing of the school used as a 'model' by the Antratsit municipality have generally been improving since the school introduced the FOC course: 'In the period 2003–07, the level of juvenile crime has been dropping by about 6 to 7.5 percent per year'; the number of grants the school attracted had increased; the number of teachers with academic degrees had increased; the number of scientific and social programmes sponsored by municipalities in which the school actively participated had increased; and the overall professional profile of the school was outstanding and still improving.

During his short speech, the officer showed the headmasters a pile of documents containing the scales of additional salaries planned for prospective FOC teachers, which had already been accepted and signed by the appropriate authorities. His presentation was followed by a series of speeches: by Svetlana Sergeevna, who reviewed a range of available textbooks and other methodological resources for teachers, and by priests. All the speeches were in favour of this initiative and shared words of gratitude. Further, the audience was invited to ask questions. Three persons wished to make comments. None of them were critical. Instead, they underlined how they appreciate the project or stated that they have already taken steps in their schools to follow a similar path. The headmaster of a Cossack gymnasium made a speech about the low moral standing of pupils being a direct effect of the dissolution of Soviet forms of collective upbringing, and shared his observations that the FOC course run once by a priest had brought 'a very positive effect in pupils' behavior and in the way they interact with each other.' He concluded with a plea for more funds to continue the project. Clearly, everyone was in favour of the administrative proposal. The additional financial opportunities sketched by the officers were immediately recognised and highly appreciated.

But the most intriguing element was the concluding speech of the mayor. As the decision-maker, he felt the need to substantiate his decision with a series of arguments that developed conceptual links between economic development, religion, moral education, teachers' authority, priestly authority and the provision of welfare for the citizens of the region:

> Distinguished guests,
>   What we are doing today is an objective necessity – I am fully aware of this. Why? Well, one would think that with such an experience as we have [in matters of education], all that remains is to work, work, and work. But … Each year when I summarise the results of the year and define the tasks of my entire administration for the next year, I deliver the mayor's address in which I outline concrete directions [of action] and decisions. This year, I asked myself: what needs to be done, so that in 2007 the citizens of the district, my electorate … will have a better life. I set two tasks … 1) to develop a precise strategy of the development of our district; 2) to outline all the basic directions of economic activity in our district, so we could obtain an economically effective result, such that each citizen of our district would experience it in their home budget. In other words, that their wages rise or that basic urban facilities improve. This means a well thought out and precise strategy of development for our district. And this is what we actually do: we develop. We have constructed an industrial complex worth 39 million euro. One could say that a gigantic sum of money has been invested in the production sector. We

are currently in the process of constructing a complex of five production plants. This includes a brickyard, and several other sites, into which 60 million euro, that is 1.2 billion rubles has already been invested. Now, we have three other investments, big industrial plants in the district, into each of which huge resources have been invested. One could therefore conclude that we have everything [that is needed] to economically develop our district.

The second strategic direction I set for myself is the improvement of the quality of life of the population of our region. In my understanding this means concretely: a reduction of the mortality rate, an increase of the life span of our people and the improvement of the life conditions of our citizens. There are indexes, classic measures in twenty-one areas, indicating improvement of quality of life. Take the housing industry: it is considered normal if, per capita, there is one square meter of housing built per year [sic]. In the Rostov oblast, this rate amounts to 0.32. In our district: 0.12. So, from this it is clear what our goal is: it is clearly delineated. Let's work on this. But, thinking about the problem [of quality of life], I concluded that ... well why? Why, when we create new jobs, can we not find people to fill them? So they will work there? Can you see what I mean? So let's think about schools ... I consulted Fr. Mikhail, whom I respect deeply. And he said: go to the teachers. To our school headmasters, directors of kindergartens: it is to them, that all the parents go. For they can see clearly what kind of people arrive at school and who they are when the leave. And I can see that too.

For example, take Antratsit, the plant that we currently construct. The governor came, [because] they invited him, [but do you know] for what? No, not to boast about how excellently the construction work is progressing, no. He was invited for another purpose. To [show that there are difficulties with finding staff and] to ask him to establish [an additional sum of money] for attracting a quota of 800 people that could be hired for the purpose of constructing this plant. Can you see the problem?

And I understood that it is impossible to solve this problem without a spiritual-moral upbringing, without a spiritual message. Without a spiritual-moral basis how can we talk about a strategic development of our district of any kind? How can we talk about an improvement of the quality of life of our population? Yes, I admit, it is the authority, me personally, who is guilty of not having created the conditions for people to strive and to obtain, to make money and secure a more decent quality of life. And this is why this event [in which we all participate today] was conceived. This is not a spontaneously invented enterprise. I consulted in these matters with Fr. Mikhail and Fr. Andrei, whom I respect deeply, I commissioned a research into how this work is being conducted in more successful oblasts. And today, having heard all the speeches, I feel that this is the best direction. [You may] do whatever you want. But administrative pressures will be exerted. I am the authority here, and I will try to show you whatever support is needed in the realisation of these questions, namely teaching the FOC course. And in the case of resistance I will ask: why do you resist? Each of you [who is still not convinced], be so kind and think of the situation which we are in at the moment. Read the newspapers, watch television, see how our politicians and state activists speak about this problem. Just recently I read *Izvestiia*, where a journalist concludes [his article]: 'Russia can be saved either by God or by Stalin'. Well, consider whom to prefer. We chose the first way. And I believe this way consists in maintaining a spiritual-moral education. That is why in this matter I invited all the headmasters of all the educational institutions of our district, and I want to assure you that you can count on my support. Not only a moral support but also a material one. I direct this request to the clergy present here: you need to act, you have to act not only in this area, but in all other areas of our secular life on the territory of our district. Fr. Mikhail has already agreed to organise meetings in all settlements. And this does not mean we want to shake off our responsibility for the problems that citizens report to us and make the clergy responsible for fixing them, no. All I want is to make sure that the clergy is aware of and can see the ways in which the authorities in our district deal with this topic and solve the problems. That's why we speak openly: Fr. Mikhail, Fr. Pavel, Fr. Sergei, we are open for this kind of communication, in which you also [participate].

I find this official utterance important enough to present it at length, for the specific rhetoric and argument invoked here makes this case an example of a nexus of modernity and traditionalism for which conventional theories of secularism do not account. The pragmatics of everyday life, in what appears to be a social crisis, enable the cooperation of Church and (State) schools to be presented as an attractive option with the potential to remedy social problems. Also, the State views teachers and schools as nodes of contact with society, and recognises their potential for providing solutions in areas recognised as social problems, such as welfare provision and the quality of citizens' lives. As many anthropological studies suggest, religion in post-Soviet Russia is a meaningful field where one can seek satisfaction and it is in this sense that we can seek answers to the questions potentially raised by the case illustrated above: why is the social resonance to such incentives presented by the State positive? This is so not only due to the material rewards promised, but because religion can actually serve as a source of fulfilment. Teachers, once an important cog in the Soviet nation-building machine, are directly invited to see the new State-backed project as an opportunity to modernise their status. Thus, becoming 'more traditionalist' does not necessarily mean that teachers simply aim to achieve temporary political or material gains. Rather, as this case suggests to me, being 'more traditionalist' may just as well mean adherence to the Orthodox tradition as a preservation of the educational authority assured by the importance accorded to education by the Soviet State-building project.

This case provides me with arguments for engaging in another discussion concerning the actual significance of religion in the public sphere. Matthew Wood's (2015) reassessment of sociological literature on public religion and secularisation in England urges readers to pay attention to the nature of the evidence provided in favour of or against the secularisation thesis. He traces discussions of the role of religion in educational or welfare provision through a focus on the scope of religious authority as potentially played out in these spheres. Wood concludes, in opposition to some of the authors of studies he reviews, that the increased number of faith-based organisations involved in the provision of such services does not allow the conclusion that religion manifests itself strongly in public. The religious impact of these organisations is limited, if not entirely obstructed, since in order to be able to deliver public services they must compete for funding with other organisations and comply with the requirements of secular authorities. The latter are very often at odds with the missionising culture of these organisations and, as a result, a thoroughgoing reformulation of these organisations' public service provision along secular lines has occurred. Wood calls such 'institutional isomorphism' an 'advanced secularisation'. What is occurring in contemporary Britain is:

> [T]he thoroughgoing *co-optation* of religious authorities by secular ones and the embracing of this by religious actors. This marks a form of social differentiation in which the ventures of religious organizations become subsumed into other societal sub-systems but without having any discernible impact upon those spheres. These ventures are simply rendered subservient to the secular regulations and modes of operation in those sub-systems. Whilst this, to a certain extent, brings religious organizations back into the public sphere, it paradoxically does so only through a furthering of privatization since the religious rationales, actions and values that underpin the interests of religious organizations and personnel in these ventures are now either excluded or pushed into the private background.
>
> (Wood 2015: 264)

Such a realistic assessment is illuminating for understanding how an interlinked and mutually reinforced declining scope of religious authority at the macro-, meso- and micro-levels contributes to deepen secularisation despite an ostensible 're-emergence' of public religion. It highlights that what in de-secularisation theory has often been taken as a 'blurring' of the boundaries between 'the secular' and 'the religious', in reality translates into a heightening of the distinction between them. But evidence of the interactions of the mainstream Christian Church with the public secular authorities in Russia, on various, micro-, meso- and macro-levels, shows that these two actors' long-term goals may not be very different from each other. Their immediate rationales may be coloured by a short-term political aim, but what is at stake – a co-optation for the sake of the building of the larger national identity – does not require significant compromise and allows 'parallel action'.

The case presented here is difficult to account for through the available theories of secularism and modernity. Yet, it is revealing and instructive because it shows how an alternative project of social and cultural modernity enabled by a 'symphonic' coalition of Church and State, and the protracted effects of the socialist importance accorded to education has concretely worked itself out among a group of people who espouse both the values of tradition/religion and progress through schooling. This case illustrates how modernity can engender traditionalism, but also how traditionalism can constitute and promote modernity while simultaneously reinforcing the authority of the Church.

Notes

1 Rostov-on-Don, a city with a population of over 1,000,000, located in southern Russia, is predominantly Orthodox. My 12-month ethnographic research focused on Soviet-trained middle-aged teachers of Foundations of Orthodox Culture. It consisted of such activities as general participant observation in a number of state schools, Sunday schools and various institutions providing educational training for future teachers of religion. The focal point of the fieldwork was an intense participant observation in two local state schools and in the Sunday school of the parish where these particular state schools were located. Moreover, I conducted over 50 formal, semi-structured interviews with people relevant for the project due to their profession: school teachers, headmasters, deputies, professors of Rostov State University, Orthodox priests, Orthodox Sunday school teachers and officers of the administration of the local division of the Ministry of Education.
2 In 2009 the Ministry of Education replaced the FOC with a subject named 'Foundations of religious cultures and secular ethics', aiming at regulating the relations between Orthodoxy and other recognised traditional religions in a secular state. In the years to follow, further modifications were introduced (see chapter by Ozhiganova). Nevertheless, my aim in this chapter is to focus on bigger implications the entanglements of religion and education may have for our understanding of secularisms, thus I focus on the state endorsed Orthodox education.
3 The political and sociological scholarship critically discusses the role of the Church vis-à-vis the State by focusing on the ROC's leadership's political ambitions and its involvement in politics. The vast majority of political scientists assess the Church–State cooperation as a subjugation of the ROC resulting in unquestioned support for the government and the Kremlin, and see in this a continuation of the loyalty the ROC declared to the Soviet government. For instance, Anastasia Mitrofanova (2005) claims that the State is attempting to instrumentalise the ROC in order to provide moral legitimacy for itself. These researchers see the ROC as continuing its service to the State, without pursuing its own interests. In opposition to these voices, other scholars see the FOC issue as an attempt at a clericalisation of the State and an infiltration of its agencies with a catechetical agenda (Papkova 2009; Mitrokhin 2004a, 2004b), a view which is in line with a popular anticlerical trend in Russia. Katja Richters (2013: 7f.) emphasises the ROC's own political agenda, which it has formulated independently of the State and 'which it seeks to implement by all available means'. In her view, the ROC strives to revive the ancient competition with the Ecumenical Patriarchate for the position of the first among equals in worldwide Orthodoxy and, in order to achieve this goal, is turning to the Russian State for support. Access to secular education is presented in these works (Richters 2013: 36–56, Mitrokhin 2004a, 2004b) as a strategic opportunity to exploit state resources

and impose a new national identity centered on Orthodox values. The ROC is of value to the State as a source of symbolic capital and legitimacy. The work of Anastasia Mitrofanova (2005) suggests that the secular authorities reap even more benefits from this mutual cooperation than do the clergy. As early as 1991, the Russian clergy had been singled out as one of two (along with the army) 'eternal institutions of [Russian] statehood' (Dunlop 1995: 19). Prior to Vladimir Putin's emergence on the political scene, surveys showed that Russians trusted the ROC more than any other public institution, in a list including the law courts, trade unions, mass media, military, police and government (Kaariainen & Furman 2000: 14; Simons 2005: 14). Throughout the early 2000s, Patriarch Aleksii II was ranked in the top 15 of the country's most influential political figures (Knox 2005: 533). Under Putin, only the presidency has rated higher in such statistics (Papkova 2009: 292). The available research claims that the State seeks to exploit the ROC's symbolic resources through this created and continuously maintained ecclesiastical alliance.

4 A pseudonym.

References

Agadjanian, A. and V. Roudometof. 2005. 'Introduction: Eastern Orthodoxy in a Global Age – Preliminary Considerations'. In *Eastern Orthodoxy in a Global Age: Tradition Faces the Twenty-First Century.* Edited by V. Roudometof, A. Agadjanian and J. Pankhurst, pp. 1–26. Lanham. MD: Altamira Press.

Asad, T. 1997. *Genealogies of Religion.* Baltimore: John Hopkins University Press.

Asad, T. 2003. *Formations of the Secular: Christianity, Islam, Modernity.* Stanford, CA: Stanford University Press.

Brandtstädter, S. 2007. 'Transitional Spaces: Postsocialism as a Cultural Process', *Critique of Anthropology* 27(2): 131–145.

Buyandelgeriyn, M. 2008. 'Post-Post-Transition Theories: Walking on Multiple Paths', *Annual Review of Anthropology* 37: 235–250.

Cannell, F. 2010. 'The Anthropology of Secularism', *Annual Review of Anthropology* 39: 85–100.

Casanova, J. 1994. *Public Religions in the Modern World.* Chicago, IL and London: The University of Chicago Press.

Dunlop, J. 1995. 'The Russian Orthodox Church as an "Empire-Saving" Institution'. In *The Politics of Religion in Russia and the New States of Eurasia.* Edited by M. Bourdeaux, pp. 15–40. Armonk, New York and London: M.E. Sharpe.

Eklof, B. and S. Seregny. 2005. 'Teachers in Russia: State, Community and Profession'. In *Educational Reform in Post-Soviet Russia: Legacies and Prospects.* Edited by B. Eklof, L. E. Holmes and V. Kaplan, pp. 197–220. London and New York: Frank Cass.

Fuller, Ch. 2003. *The Renewal of the Priesthood: Modernity and Traditionalism in a South Indian Temple.* Princeton, NJ and Oxford: Princeton University Press.

Ghodsee, K. 2009. 'Symphonic Secularism: Eastern Orthodoxy, Ethnic Identity and Religious Freedoms in Contemporary Bulgaria', *Anthropology of East Europe Review* 27(2): 227–252.

Glanzer, P. L. 2005. 'Postsoviet Moral Education in Russia's State Schools: God, Country and Controversy', *Religion, State and Society* 33(3): 207–221.

Halstead, M. 1994. 'Moral and Spiritual Education in Russia', *Cambridge Journal of Education* 24(3): 423–438.

Hann, Ch. (ed.). 2002. *Postsocialism: Ideals, Ideologies, and Practices in Eurasia.* London, New York: Routledge.

122   *Agata Ładykowska*

Hovorun, C. 2016. 'Is the Byzantine "Symphony" Possible in Our Days?', *Journal of Church and State*, 1–17.

Kaariainen, K. and D. Furman. 2000. 'Religioznost' v Rossi v 90–93 gody' [Religiosity in Russia between 1990 and 1993]. In *Starye tserkvi, novye veruiushchie: Religiia v massovom soznanii postsovetskoi Rossii* [Old Churches, New Believers: Religion in Mass Consciousness of Postsocialist Russia]. Edited by K. Kaariainen and D. Furman, pp. 7–48. Moscow and St. Petersburg: Letnii Sad.

Knox, Z. 2005. 'Russian Orthodoxy, Russian Nationalism, and Patriarch Aleksii II', *Nationalities Papers* 33(4): 533–545.

Köllner, T. 2018.'On the Restitution of Property and the Making of 'Authentic' Landscapes in Contemporary Russia', *Europe-Asia Studies* 70(7): 1083–1102. doi:10.1080/09668136.2018.1484077.

Mitrofanova, A. 2005. *The Politicization of Russian Orthodoxy: Actors and Ideas.* Stuttgart: Ibidem.

Mitrokhin, N. 2004a. *Klerikalizatsiia obrazovaniia v Rosii: k obshchestvennoi diskusii o vvedenii predmeta 'Osnovy pravoslavnoi kul'tury' v programu srednikh szkol* [The Clericalization of Education in Russia: On the Societal Discussion about the Introduction of the Subject 'Foundations of Orthodox Culture' in the Program of Middle Schools]. Available at: http://religion.gif.ru/clerik/clerik.html.

Mitrokhin, N. 2004b. *Russkaia Pravoslavnaia Tserkov: Sovremennoe sostoianie i aktual'nye problemy* [The Russian Orthodox Church: Contemporary Condition and Current Problems]. Moskva: Novoe Literaturnoe Obozrenie.

Mulders, J. 2008. 'The Debate on Religion and Secularization in Russia Today: Comments on Kyrlezhev and Morozov, with Focus on Education', *Religion, State and Society* 36(1): 5–20.

Papkova, I. 2009. 'Contentious Conversation: Framing the "Fundamentals of Orthodox Culture" in Russia', *Religion, State and Society* 37(3): 291–309.

Richters, K. 2013. *The Post-Soviet Russian Orthodox Church: Politics, Culture and Greater Russia.* London and New York: Routledge.

Simons, G. 2005. *The Russian Orthodox Church and Its Role in Cultural Production.* Stockholm: Almquist & Wiksell International.

Stambach, A. 2006. 'Revising a Four-Square Model of a Complicated Whole: On the Cultural Politics of Religion and Education', *Social Analysis* 50(3): 1–18.

Taylor, Ch. 2007. *A Secular Age.* Cambridge, MA: Belknap Press of Harvard University Press.

US Department of State. 2012. *Russia 2012 International Religious Freedom Report.* Available online: http://www.state.gov/documents/organization/208572.pdf.

Wood, M. 2015. 'Shadows in Caves? A Re-Assessment of Public Religion and Secularization in England Today', *European Journal of Sociology* 56(2): 241–270.

7 Religious education in Russian schools

The false symphony[1]

Anna Ozhiganova

Introduction

The way of teaching religion in public schools is important for the analysis of the relations between the State and religious institutions. In Russia, the debate about religious education arose in the context of the growing influence of religious organisations, primarily, the Russian Orthodox Church (ROC), and has been associated with the search of a new national idea. Initially, in 1990s (in some regions in the late 1980s) the subject 'Basics of Orthodox Culture' became to appear in the schools as a regional educational component. Under different names it was taught in more than 11,000 public schools.

Then, in 2012, compulsory religion classes on the subject 'Basics of religious cultures and secular ethics' (BRCSE) were introduced into the school curricula throughout the country as a Federal educational component. This course includes six optional 'modules': Orthodox Culture, Islamic Culture, Buddhist Culture, Hebrew Culture, Secular Ethics and the World Religious Cultures. According to the 'Order of the module selection', worked out by the Ministry of Education, the parents need to choose one of the modules for their children and the school must provide teaching of all selected modules even if some of them are selected only by one pupil. Pupils study BRCSE only in the fourth grade of primary school (age 9 to 10 years), one hour in a week. The marks on this subject are not exposed.

A lot of publications devoted to the problems of religious education in Russia were released in the period of 2000–2012 (Mitrokhin 2000, 2004, 2005; Willems 2006; Lisovskaya and Karpov 2010; Shnirelman 2011, 2012). In part, this interest was inspired by a desire to deal with a phenomenon, which was completely new for Russia. At the same time, some of these publications caused violent public reactions to the introduction of religious lessons in schools and, in turn, became a part of the public debate. Tatiana Shaposhnikova (interview in 2016), my informant and the expert on religious education, talked about the situation of the 1990s: 'The regional prosecutor's offices were simply overwhelmed by the letters of indignant parents demanding the abolition of the lessons of the "God's Law"'. The significant episode of the protests against the 'clericalisation of education' was the Open Letter of Russian academicians to the president Vladimir Putin in 2007: 'We cannot remain indifferent when the attempts are made to call in question the scientific knowledge, to eradicate 'the materialistic vision of the world' from the educational programs, to substitute the knowledge accumulated by science for faith' (Open Letter 2007).

In recent years, the influence of the ROC on the public sphere in Russia increased greatly and was supported heavily by the State. The law protecting the religious feelings of Russian citizens of 2013, the programme of construction of new churches, the transfer of museums to the ownership of the Church are among topical issues on the agenda, which divide society and contributes to the formation of local civil protest (see also Köllner 2018). At the same time, after 2012 the protests against the introduction of religion lessons are almost inconspicuous, this topic only occasionally is covered in media. The heated debates erupted in 2006–2009 have subsided gradually. Many parents felt that one lesson a week would not cause great harm for the children and treated BRCSE as 'another delusion of the school life'. The most significant expression of the hidden protest became the Petition on the Change.org. platform, with the demand to abolish the teaching of religion in schools, which collected more than 100,000 votes in 2015.

In the period after 2012, noticeably fewer articles on the problem of religious education in Russian schools were published (Köllner 2016; Ozhiganova 2016). Undoubtedly, it was due to the achievement of a certain status quo between the ambitions of the ROC, the State educational politics and public attitudes. This chapter presents an overview of the current situation with the BRCSE lessons: their implementation and the ideological content. I will analyse how the relations between the Church and the State are reflected in the teaching religion in school. Where do the goals of the State and the Church coincide, where do they diverge? Can we expect the active protests against the actions of the ROC in this sphere? Do we witness a new symphonia between the State and the Church, as Patriarch Kirill proclaims? Are we dealing with an 'asymmetrical symphony', where the president being clearly the dominant partner 'allows Orthodoxy a position of primus inter pares, so long as its leaders continue to use that position to play a generally supportive role in society' (Anderson 2007: 198). We could suppose that we observe here a kind of false symphony, where each participant has its own interests, and their relationships concealing a potential or already existed, but hidden conflict.

The data

This chapter is based on the data of official surveys and monitoring of the BRCSE module conducted at request of the Ministry of Education and my own field data. I took a series of structured interviews with teachers attending special BRCSE training courses in February–April 2015 (50 respondents) and parents, whose children were beginning to study BRCSE in April 2015 (92 respondents). I also conducted semi-structured interviews with the parents (15) and teachers (total 12, in focus 5) in the period 2014–2016 and an expert interview with Tatiana Shaposhnikova, one of the authors of the BRCSE program and the editor of the BRCSE textbooks of the publishing house 'Drofa' (2016). I also used the records of the BRCSE teaching classes (9 hours, 2015) and the materials of the conference 'Introduction of the BRCSE course into educational institutions in 2014–2015: Problems, decisions and perspectives' which was held at the Academy of Advanced Training and Professional Retraining of Educators (Moscow, 2015). Since I conducted all interviews in Moscow, the materials of this conference and informal conversations with its participants provided the information according to the teaching around the country.

The introduction of BRCSE

In order to better understand the current situation around BRCSE, it is important to remember that there was no request for the introduction of the subject either by the Ministry of Education, or by religious organisations or the parent community. Behind the introduction of BRCSE there are only the ambitions of the Russian Orthodox Church to increase its influence in the public sphere. In 1999, Patriarch Alexy II called for organisation of the Orthodox culture learning in the State and municipal educational institutions. The Coordinating Council for Cooperation between the Ministry of Education and Science and the Russian Orthodox Church was established.

Tatiana Shaposhnikova, the expert on religious education and one of the authors of the BRCSE programme, said:

> The situation with the Orthodox culture classes was completely unsettled for almost 20 years. The teaching was conducted on the basis of incomprehensible and often odious textbooks. It was completely unknown who the teachers were or how these lessons were conducted. The state practically did not interfere in this process, did not examine the textbooks, no one controlled it. Everything was decided at the regional level. It was convenient for the ROC representatives, for they have done what they wanted. Therefore, in 2008, the Administration of the President has launched a new concept: Since Russia is a multinational and multi-confessional country, the situation that only Orthodox Christianity was taught in schools became unacceptable. In accordance with the Law on Religious Organisations, the modules of the main traditional religions of Russia (Islam, Buddhism and Judaism) were introduced into the program;[2] and also, as in the West, the modules for atheists were added: World religions and Secular Ethics. The program and the first textbooks on the new subject were created very fast: The working group was formed in September 2008 and in January 2009 the first pilot schools began to study on these textbooks.[3]

(Interview Shaposhnikova 2016)

The introduction of BRCSE is only a first step of the global program of the ROC in the sphere of education, announced by Metropolitan Mercury, the Head of the Department of Religious Education and Catechism of the Russian Orthodox Church, in 2010. The program proposes, first, the creation of a system of continuous Orthodox education from kindergarten to high school, and secondly, the integration of the educational component on the basis of religious traditions in the secular school (Metropolitan Mercury 2010).

It becomes increasingly obvious that the implementation of BRCSE does not suit the Russian Orthodox Church. At the XXIII Christmas Reading in January 2015, Patriarch Kirill declared the intention to extend the school course of religion to all grades and sent an official letter to the Minister of Education to consider the matter. However, in April the Ministry of Education made a statement that it did not recommend strongly the extension of the course. It becomes evident that so far there is no political decision to expand the teaching of BRCSE. Moreover, it is clear that the government has no definite opinion on the activities of the Church and even that there exists certain resistance to its growing influence.

At the IV Christmas Parliamentary Meetings in the Federation Council (29 January 2016) Patriarch Kirill (2016) once again stated the importance of studying BRCSE[4] and connected it to the threat of international terrorism:

> Ultimately, it is the question of the preservation of our multinational Russian civilisation, of the spiritual security of the state [...] We love our young people and trust them our common future. Therefore, they must be fully armed to reflect the dangerous ideas including religious extremism aimed at destroying our world.

Despite its relevance, the issue received little attention by the media. It was discussed between the representatives of the Church and the experts in education and culture on a popular TV program in December 2014. During this telecast, the influential Moscow priest and head of the Patriarchal Commission for Family, Maternity and Childhood Dmitry Smirnov stated that 'the study of religion should become the main subject, the core of the entire school curriculum'. One of his opponents, a well-known educational specialist, a corresponding member of the Russian Academy of Education, Alexander Abramov, said that he would do everything it would not happen: 'Today we have revealed a huge number of problems and risks. This means that the concept of the subject is absent. There are no obvious arguments in its favour, there is no consensus on the prospects for its development'. Another participant of the discussion, a historian, director of the museum-estate 'Ostankino', Gennady Vdovin, spoke even more categorically: 'This course is one more nail into the coffin of our Constitution' ('Basics of Orthodox Culture in secular school?' 2014).

This discussion revealed an existing conflict between supporters and opponents of BRCSE, a conflict which many experts have predicted. A well-known apologist of religious education, author of a number of monographs on this subject, Feodor Kozyrev, wrote that 'the increasing role of RE in schools can easily become either a contribution to dialogue or a factor of conflict'. He also pointed to the three main obstacles for the development of RE in Russian school: 'extreme politicalisation of religious issues, low standards of civil conduct and a lack of modern educational theory and methodology dealing with religion in secular environment' (Kozyrev and Fedorov 2006: 193). Karpov and Lisovskaya noted that the popular support for religious education in Russia was infused with religious intolerance, and predicted that 'further attempts to desecularize Russia's state schools "from above" may fuel ethnoreligious tensions' (Lisovskaya and Karpov 2010: 277).

So far, despite all the efforts of the ROC, the expansion of the course has not occurred, although every year the draft programs for all classes, from first to eleven, and new textbooks are proposed. In March 2017, the head of the information service of the Synodal Department of Religious Education and Catechism of the Russian Orthodox Church, Hieromonk Gennady (Voitishko), reported that the Church has not abandoned the efforts to introduce religious lessons to all classes and plans to implement this program within the next 5–10 years (Voitishko 2017).

The implementation of BRCSE lessons: public opinion, experts, teachers, parents

We know very little about the implementation of BRCSE teaching within the country. Only the selection of the modules is monitored regularly by the Ministry of Education. This monitoring shows that about a third of 4-graders study the module 'Basics of Orthodox Culture', whereas more than 60 per cent of all fourth graders votes for the study of the so-called 'secular' modules. In 2016–2017, for example, 35 per cent voted for the 'Basics of Orthodox Culture', 43 per cent for the 'Basics of Secular Ethics', 18 per cent for the 'Basics of the World Religious Cultures' ('The results of monitoring ...' 2016).

It is necessary to pay attention to a relatively small number of pupils who have chosen the modules of the *traditional* religions of Russia. Only 4 per cent of 4-graders study Islamic Culture (almost half of them are schoolchildren of the Chechen Republic), 0.4 per cent (5,458 people) study Buddhist Culture and 0.02 per cent (357 people) Hebrew Culture. These figures are incommensurable with the actual number of representatives of these denominations in the Russian Federation.[5]

It becomes obvious that the choice of the module depends not so much on the religious traditions of the region as on the decision of the regional administration. In Rostov, Kursk, Belgorod, Tambov regions the selection for the 'Basics of Orthodox Culture' is close to 100 per cent. At the same time, some regions declined teaching 'religious modules' in favour of 'secular' ones. For example, in Kabardino-Balkaria and Tatarstan, where significant parts of the population traditionally practise Islam, no one studies 'Basics of

Orthodox Culture' or 'Basics of Islamic Culture'. Despite the discontent of the Patriarch himself, the authorities of Tatarstan openly declares: 'We do not hide our position that the integrated course (*World Religious Cultures – A.O.*), that promotes tolerance, not separation of pupils on the basis of religion, would be the most rational decision'.

The dioceses exert significant pressure on the local departments of the Ministry of Education, on the process of teacher training, on the school administrations. An illustrative example is the incident with the dismissal of the school director in the Saratov region, which got quite a wide resonance in the media. The director got in conflict with the local diocese and was accused of hindering pupils from choosing the module 'Basics of Orthodox Culture' ('Khvalynsky patriotism' 2015).

In Karelia, representatives of the diocese participate in the parents' meetings on the choice of modules in accordance with the decree of the republican Ministry of Education. As a result, the number of those who selected the Orthodox Culture rose from 3 per cent to 11 per cent in the 2014/2015 academic year (Vasilieva 2015: 36).

Tobias Köllner in his article written on the basis of field research in the Vladimir region, which presented similar examples of violation of the principle of free choice of the module, noted:

> Quite often the choices for parents are rather limited from the start and dependent on the school's resources and goals. As a result, it is common practice for the opinions of minorities not to be taken seriously and they end up having to join the module chosen by the majority or selected by the school.
>
> (Köllner 2016: 372)

The lack of a real choice in many cases is just one of many problems of the BRCSE implementation. As follows from the results of a sociological survey (2015), experts from regional educational authorities have identified a number of negative consequences of the BRCSE teaching: privileging one of the modules, separation of pupils in terms of religion or ethnics, compulsion to religion and faith, a formal attitude towards religion and faith, intolerance of cultural and religious differences, conflicts among parents of pupils on national and confessional grounds. The overwhelming majority of respondents (80 per cent of specialists from the regional educational departments, 79 per cent of teachers and 89 per cent of parents) noted that the knowledge provided within the BRCSE course could be taught to children during the study such subjects as literature, history and art (analysis of survey data 2015).

The majority of primary school teachers who participated in my survey in February–April 2015 demonstrated their loyalty to the introduction of the BRCSE course. They answered that modern people need knowledge about religion. The overwhelming majority agreed that it is the best variant to start teaching religion in the primary school and that this course would be interesting for the 4th grade pupils. On the other hand, the larger part of teachers decided that a course on religion in the school should be optional not obligatory, as now. They agreed that the course should give objective information about the content, history and the social role of different religions. The overwhelming majority spoke strongly in favour of the modules 'Basics of Secular Ethics' and 'Basics of the World Religious Cultures'. In respect to the division of pupils into groups more than half of the respondents supported the idea of division. It turned out that the teachers did not accept the practice of separating students into groups of religious principle as a violation of human rights and contrary to the Constitution. They were convinced that the course refers to cultural studies (survey among BRCSE teachers 2015).

The results of a parents' survey are similar to the results obtained in the survey of teachers. They also demonstrated a high level of loyalty to the introduction of the BRCSE course. Parents think that modern people need knowledge about religion. More than half of the respondents agreed that the course should be extended to all classes in secondary school. At the same time, all of them agreed that the course on religion in the school should be optional (survey among parents of BRCSE students 2015).

In 2016, I conducted a series of interviews with teachers of Moscow schools, who already had experience of BRCSE teaching. The teachers take these lessons as an extra job, confess that they do not understand who needed this subject and ask when it will be cancelled. Very often lessons are held in the form of presentations from an electronic application to the course, reading aloud or rewriting paragraphs from the textbook. However, even when I talked with highly motivated teachers who had completed the special two-year training in BRCSE teaching, they did not hide their embarrassment: 'I understand that this subject has no future. Nobody needs it. I guess I wasted my time on these courses' (Interview 1, 2016).

Natalya Lvovna, a schoolteacher at Lublino district of Moscow, says that at their school, two-thirds of parents choose the 'Basics of Orthodox Culture' and one-third 'Basics of Islamic Culture'. However, the director conducts an explanatory conversation with the parents and after all everyone studies 'Secular Ethics'. It can't be done otherwise, explains Natalya Lvovna: it is difficult to divide the class into groups, it is unrealistic financially and it can lead to conflicts with parents. It should be noted that Lublino is one of the new regions in the southeast of Moscow, where newcomers from Central Asia and the Caucasus are living and the problem of nationalism is very acute: this is one of the places where Russian nationalists' actions are held. Natalya Lvovna admitted that it is completely impossible to learn with the textbook ('Basics of Secular Ethics' by the Publishing House 'Prosveshchenie'): 'Tell me, how can I explain 4-graders, for example, the topic *Reasonable Self-ishness*?' She complains that the children are bored on the lessons: 'Religion, ethics are not interesting for them at all'. The school is multi-ethnic, and the problem of tolerance education is very acute, but Natalya Lvovna is convinced that in the 4th grade it's too early to talk about it: 'Tolerance should be discussed with elder pupils, when the relationships become a problem'. She believes that the best solution would be the return to the subject 'World Art', which she previously taught in all classes, as well as the lessons of Moscow Studies (*Moskvovedenie*), which were abolished in schools a few years ago: 'Children are still waiting for these lessons' (Interview 2, 2016).

The State gymnasium located in the Moskvorechye-Saburovo district also does not implement the multi-module system: here all pupils study 'Basics of the World Religious Cultures'. The lessons are held by Tatyana Alekseyevna, who is a highly qualified teacher. She says that the lessons are interesting and pupils like them. The problem is that they cannot realise their interest and knowledge outside the school: 'At the competition of the BRCSE projects, for some reason, there is only the Orthodox Culture, the same is at the Olympiad for schoolchildren. How come?' She also regrets that the lessons of 'World Art' were cancelled: 'It was a wonderful subject! What textbooks! We understand everything, but it would have been better to save World Art lessons than to introduce BRCSE'. Throughout our conversation, Tatyana Alekseevna asked repeatedly with perplexity, why I am talking about religion: 'These lessons are not about religion, they are about culture' (Interview 3, 2016).

Since 2014, the Ministry of Education has tried to streamline BRCSE teaching and requires all teachers to take special training courses, which are conducted by the Academy of Advanced Training for Teachers and some other State institutes. However, in many schools there is a semi-legal practice of sending teachers to the courses on Orthodox culture opened at some monasteries. Five of the fifty teachers, who participated in the survey, have already finished these courses and six of them are planning to do it in the nearest future.

The Orthodox believers in general have no clear vision of advantages and disadvantages of the BRCSE lessons. Among Orthodox parents, with whom I spoke, there are those who are satisfied with these lessons: 'They are better than in our Sunday school' (Interview 4, 2016). At the same time, many of them are categorically opposed to the teaching of religion in schools, since they are sure that the teachers do not have sufficient knowledge and competence. One of my respondents had a sharply negative attitude towards these lessons: 'No, none from our parish will give up his child to study the "Basics of Orthodox Culture", because they are afraid that after these lessons they could not bring them to the church' (Interview 5, 2016). Many of the Orthodox believers are convinced that it is best for children to study the module of the World Religious Cultures. There is an opinion shared by many people, both experts and parents: 'This module is addressed to all: Believers, atheists, and those who did not define themselves in relation to religion. Its goal is to acquaint children with religion as important phenomenon of the human world' (Kulakov 2015: 100).

The situation with the teaching of religion in the regions remains understudied. There is evidence that in many schools, there are lessons of Orthodox culture in the schedule, which are officially selective but in practice are compulsory for all pupils. A teacher from Khakassia explained:

In the 4th grade we do not end up talking about the religious culture, we are just beginning. This conversation goes on during the literature lessons (5–6 grades) and the special course 'Christian plots and characters in Russian and world culture' (10–11 grades).

(Baranova 2015: 29)

In the Millerovo district of Rostov region pupils study 'Basics of Orthodox Culture' in primary and secondary school, and even in the kindergartens, and 'Basics of Orthodox Morality' in the higher secondary school (10–11 grades) (Zhiricova 2015: 71f.).

The problem of textbooks

The federal list of textbooks includes about 20 textbooks for the BRCSE course from seven publishing houses. Most of the schools (83.5 per cent) use the textbooks of the publishing house 'Prosveshchenie', 9 per cent textbooks of the publishing house 'Drofa' and about 6 per cent textbooks of other publishers, including the publishing house 'Russkoye slovo'.

The publishing house 'Exam' edits a new version of the textbook by Alla Borodina who had already fallen into disrepute in the early 2000s. The first textbook by Borodina was released in 2002 and earned a sharply negative assessment from the experts, who saw in this tutorial a threat to the principle of secularity of education. Willems (2006: 237) marked that this textbook presented the tradition-based approach, where 'the actual questions, or the examination of everyday life experiences, were not even included'. Nevertheless, it is not the biggest problem of this textbook as far as Borodina proclaimed the idea of the original dominance of the Russian Orthodox culture over the entire territory of Russia. The historical and ethnographic facts are rigged to justify the merging of Orthodoxy with the State, to confirm the idea of primordiality of Russian ethnicity, the continuity of statehood and culture over the centuries from the birth of ancient Russia to the present day. It was repeatedly noticed by different authors that the textbook contains confessional and nationalist ideas, as well as incorrect statements, incitement of religious and national hatred (Mitrokhin 2005; Willems 2006; Shnirelman 2012).

However, after a little processing the textbook was reprinted. Borodina has created not just a tutorial, but a full course of the Orthodox culture study for all 11 years of schooling. Many schools are going to use the program by Borodina, being offered a variety of bonuses, for example, raising the status of the school to gymnasium. Borodina's educational materials have been approved by the most influential priests who did not criticise her main arguments, including xenophobic ones (Shnirelman 2012: 267).

A series of textbooks on BRCSE released by the publishing house 'Prosveshcheniye' received in 2010 an unambiguously negative assessment from the experts of the Russian Academy of Sciences. However, they are republished virtually unchanged and used by the majority of schools. Tatiana Shaposhnikova explained:

> These textbooks could not be decent in principle. How could anyone prepare textbooks for such a period? We were assembled urgently at the request of the Ministry of Education in the publishing house 'Prosveshchenie' in September 2008. There were no specialists. There was nothing to rely on. The existing textbooks on the 'Basics of Orthodox Culture' by Borodina could not be used. Instead of three years, the textbooks were written in three months.
>
> (interview Shaposhnikova 2016)

The author of the most widely used textbook – 'Basics of Orthodox Culture' of the publishing house 'Prosveshcheniye' – is protodeacon Andrey Kuraev. In comparison with the textbook by Borodina it does not contain openly xenophobic and nationalistic statements. As a representative of the Church, Kuraev does not hide his missionary aims and is engaged, first of all, in explanation of the Orthodox faith and religious practice: in this textbook he tells children how to pray, how to venerate icons, etc. However, many parents and teachers, even not Orthodox, like it for 'alive language, understandable for children'. The other textbooks of the series written by secular authors are also not free from religious indoctrination. An appeal to the proclaimed cultural approach seems to be purely rhetorical; in all of them the concept of culture is superseded by the concept of religion.

The textbook 'Basics of Secular Ethics' begins with an unconvincing attempt to separate the concept of 'secular' and 'religious' ethics: 'Secular ethics presupposes that the person himself can determine what is good and what is evil; that depends on the person, whether he acts well or badly' (Daniluc 2013: 7). Still it does not explain what in that case should be understood by 'religious ethics'. Virtually all the tutorial is full of the definitions of culture, morality, ethics, duty, morality, shame, conscience. To illustrate the lesson 'Morality features' there are photographs of the conference room of the State Duma, the Russian coat of arms and the Constitution. Thus, the textbook is in effect propaganda of the statist ideology. According to the stories of the parents, the first lesson of the course is usually devoted to the story about President Vladimir Putin's merits, which indicates that the proper idea of the BRCSE teaching is not to acquaint pupils with religious traditions, but the patriotic education and the construction of some kind of a state political religion.

A series of textbooks on BRCSE released by publishing house 'Drofa' was written after negative peer reviews on the previous series and seems to be a big step forward. Its dialogic form of lessons is an apparently good invention. For example, a schoolboy Igor and his elder sister Julia, a student of philosophy, are discussing ethic themes. The 19th century characters, herd boy Vanya and monk Basil, are talking about the salvation of the soul and the importance of forgiveness in Orthodoxy. Grandfather explains to his grandson Itsak what it means to be a Jew. Grandmother Rabia acquaints her grandchildren Ilias and Camilla with Muslim customs. The so-called 'not ordinary lessons', for example, the trial of Socrates, a virtual tour to the Orthodox Church, a visit to Jerusalem, seem to be an interesting idea.

The desire of authors to emphasise the interrelation of the world religions is especially noticeable. The textbook 'Basics of Islam culture' explains that the names of some of the old streets of Moscow are connected with Muslims who have lived there before. The textbook 'Basics of Jewish culture' notes that there were the prophets who worshipped in Judaism as well as in Christianity and Islam, and quotes the founder of Islam, Muhammad, who called Jews the people of the book. The textbook 'Basics of Islamic culture' tends to avoid potentially harmful issues. According to one of the experts, the textbook 'is a forced tolerant' (Maltsev 2012: 7). Thus, the authors warn students of a simple understanding of the word 'jihad'. They explain that 'actually "jihad" is the desire to do something good, useful and necessary to others, for example, to help mother: Go to the store or look after the kids' (Shaposhnikova 2012: 132f.).

Tatiana Shaposhnikova, the editor of a series of textbooks from the publishing house 'Drofa', is convinced that she creates a 'real multicultural education' in Russia. In fact, these textbooks are also constructing the artificial Russian Orthodox and Russian imperial identity. It is not by chance that in the textbook on Orthodox culture the characters of archaic Russia are displayed as protagonists.

Chimera of BRCSE: 'God's law', patriotic education and culturology

No subject of the school curriculum has such a powerful ideological burden as BRCSE. The main objectives of this training course are: 'Spiritual and moral development; the formation of sociocultural identity and multicultural competence; awareness of the value of the family as the basis for the belonging to the multinational people of the Russian Federation; the development of patriotism and civil solidarity'; and even 'the strengthening of national security'. The exceptional importance of spiritual and moral development and upbringing is declared 'a key factor in the development of the country, strengthening the spiritual unity of the people, political and economic stability of the state' in the document entitled 'The Concept of spiritual and moral development and education of the personality of a citizen of Russia', which is the methodological basis of the State educational standard (Daniluc et al. 2009).

Now, after almost 10 years' experience and on the basis of the surveys and monitoring data we could argue that this training course does not fulfil any of the tasks assigned to it. It does not serve the formation of civic identity and cultural competences but, on the contrary, increases the risk of conflicts on ethnic and confessional grounds. The case of BRCSE is not, as it often happens, a good idea in a poor performance. There are two different approaches, two discourses in the BRCSE concept: *clerical* (participation of the Church in the educational process, religious indoctrination of schoolchildren) and *modernising* (strengthening the role of the school in socialisation and the formation of students' identity, patriotic education). These concepts merge into a single, though internally contradictory reality (see also Ładykowska in this volume). This contradiction was noted by Willems (2006: 236), who wrote that the Russian advocates of religion education try to accommodate varying educational aims:

> On the one hand there are aims such as those of traditional moral education (e.g. acceptance of traditional gender roles and sexual ethics in accordance with church teaching) and of the patriotic integration of state and society [...]. On the other hand, explicit religious aims are included, such as 'salvation of the soul' [...]. As a justification for this connection, representatives of the ROC claim that Orthodoxy should have a specifically moral potential and that it represents national values.

The Ministry of Education officials are trying to declare this project a part of modernisation process, aimed at the better implementation of freedom of conscience and freedom of religion (Daniluc et al. 2009). However, this so-called modernisation of education is closely related to religion: 'The government is trying to modernise the system of education and training, that's why it is natural to appeal for the help and support to similar systems, which in this case is a religious culture' (Kitinov 2015: 82).

The representatives of the Russian Orthodox Church have repeatedly proposed the revision of the principle of secularity of state, as laid down in the Constitution. It is not entirely clear whether it is a question of abolition of the relevant article of the Constitution, or a peculiar interpretation of the principle of secularism of the State. For example, Metropolitan Hilarion (Alfeyev) of Volokolamsk stated at a joint meeting of the Federation Council and the State Duma on November 20, 2015: 'It's time now to reject such an understanding of the separation of Church from the State and schools from the Church, which suggests that religion should not be present in the secular educational space' (Metropolitan Hilarion 2015). Igor Metlik, professor of St Tikhon's Orthodox University, the author of 'Religion and education in public school' (2004), said that the principle of secular education implies nothing more than a 'joint, distributed competence of the state and religious organisations'. According to Metlik, secular principles imply a division of labour between State and religion rather than 'anti-religiosity' or an 'equal distance' between State and various denominations and a separation of the Church from the State. In his view, a division of labour brings about a 'symphony of spiritual and secular power' (Metlik 2014).

The authors of the BRCSE conception emphasise that it is a secular subject, whose aim is cultural study. At the same time, this so-called *culturological* approach is opposed to religious studies as an *atheistic* discipline. Borodina tries to prove that 'culture' is 'religion', because Russian culture has been created by Orthodoxy. That's why Borodina expresses the conventional view among the ROC hierarchs that BRCSE should be considered as 'cultural studies', but in no case as 'religious studies'. She claims that 'atheistic religious studies' comes into contradiction with the Constitution of Russian Federation and the Law 'On Education' because this attitude:

> insults the feelings of believers, and does not provide the knowledge and skills that can be useful in life, does not improve the culture of dialogue, does not promote respect for people and for the successful education and socialisation of young people.
>
> (Borodina 2010: 5)

She is echoed by Metlik, who says that religious education must be distinguished from religious studies. He refers the BRCSE to the so-called *religious and cultural education*, which 'is realised for the purpose of studying a certain tradition, culture, as it is accepted and understood in the relevant religious organisation' (Metlik 2014).

Religious and cultural education should be considered in the context of the State's heightened interest in issues of culture, which was clearly demonstrated in the 'Fundamentals of State Cultural Policy' (2014). As Ilya Kalinin wrote, a specific understanding of the *culture* as a 'national tradition', 'heritage of the past', 'common memory', 'historical experience', 'cultural code' becomes the main strategic resource of the state, the basis of the national-patriotic idea (see also Stahlberg and Bigu in this volume). Under this approach, 'culture' is considered 'not as a set of mechanisms for the production of meanings, values and practices, but various ways of preserving and reproducing a single historical mental matrix' (Kalinin 2014: 88).

The Ministry of Education, referring to the international practice of school religious education, presents this project as evidence for the modernisation of the school, aimed at the realisation of freedom of conscience and freedom of religion. In fact, the study of religion in Russian schools radically differs from current projects in other countries. While religious education in Western Europe raises questions of the growing religious diversity, such phenomenon, as 'believing without belonging', changing of religious institutions in conditions of a secular state (Beaman and Van Arragon 2015), the objective of religious courses in Russia is to give children 'spiritual and moral education', the main feature of which is the promoting of patriotism and so-called traditional values (see Bigu in this volume). In fact, even such an important document as Toledo Guiding Principles on Teaching about Religions and Beliefs in Public Schools (Toledo Guiding Principles 2007) has not yet been translated into Russian and known only to a narrow circle of specialists in religious studies.

In Russia, the discussion on religious education actualised in a radically different context than in Western Europe: the growing influence of religion and religious institutions was associated with the search for a new national idea by the State. The result was the birth of a strange chimera, combining religious indoctrination, culturology and patriotic education (see Bîgu in this volume).

Feodor Kozyrev insists that the main difference between this approach and both confessional and atheistic approaches is its openness, invitation to dialogue, the opportunity for the student to ask questions and 'the development of the student's ability to be move free in the semantic field, not marked up in the zones of correct and incorrect answers' (Kozyrev 2010: 45). This is fine in theory, but we must keep in mind the hidden curriculum, which, in the conditions of total violation of freedom of conscience, negates all the best undertakings.

Conclusion

In sum, we must admit that there is no public consensus on the presence of religion in school education, just as there is no open discussion how to teach knowledge about religion. It is important to note the difference of languages in which people talk about this issue. Contradictions are rooted not in the fact that there are different points of view and different value systems but that these points of view, in most cases, are themselves self-contradictory, unreflected, as they are to a large degree created by propaganda.

Thus, in the implementation of the main objective of BRCSE, namely the patriotic education, the interests of officials and the Church merge (see the concept of ideological entanglements by Köllner 2018; 2016: 381f.). In this situation, the danger of the lessons of religion is not so much the *clericalisation* of education as the threat of conversion of the school into a mechanism for transmission of a new state ideology 'without an idea' that appeals to the mythologeme of *traditional spiritual values* (see Uzlaner in this volume). Since the key to the successful spread of this ideology is the absence of a critical, rationalising view, the goal of school education is upbringing of a 'new Orthodox': incapable of reflection, loyal to the authorities.

In accordance with the Constitution, Russia is a secular state, one of whose tasks is providing a secular character of education. In order to prevent possible accusations of violation of the law, the insertion of BRCSE into the school curriculum is justified by the necessity of multicultural education. However, textbooks on BRCSE give an example of the outright indoctrination of conservative and statist values: piety, patriotism, attachment to family life and traditionalism.

Thus, we can state that religious education has been introduced under the guise of an ideologically neutral ('cultural') discipline for a comprehensive school. The study of this discipline presupposes the separation of pupils on religious grounds. According to the words of A. Guseynov,

> a division of students into believers and non-believers is act of savagery, it amounts to dividing them on basis of their political sympathy or ethnicity.

It comes into flagrant contradiction with the canons of education and the laws of the state.

(Guseynov 2012)

The BRCSE conception advanced the idea that Orthodoxy is an essential component of Russian national identity. The data of official surveys announce that more than 80 per cent of the country's population are Orthodox and creates an illusion of Russia as an Orthodox country (Furman, Kaariainen and Karpov 2007: 55; Willems 2006). However, in reality the number of traditional Orthodox believers has remained virtually unchanged since the early 1990s and remains a minority of not more than 3 per cent (Mitrokhin and Sibirieva 2007; Levada Centre 2013, 2014). Belonging to the Orthodox Church for one-third of so-called 'Orthodox by culture' does not imply faith in God and almost for two-thirds belief does not play any significant role in their lives (Dubin 2014: 187f.). As Agadjanian noted, Orthodoxy in Russia transforms into cultural-religious identity: 'Modern 'Orthodox identity' is to a large extent, a mythologeme that arose as a response to the need for a new identity' (Agadjanian 2000: 10). Boris Dubin points to a correlation between the mass appeal to Orthodoxy and the respect for the State and the authorities: 'The authorities are using Orthodoxy as a national symbol, but the Church became the image of unity without real unity, "symphony" exists only in a symbolic pledge' (Dubin 2014: 188). The fact that the majority of Russians consider themselves 'Orthodox by culture' demonstrates not a religious revival but the addiction to the State and religious symbolism.

Indeed, the citizens are divided into two unequal camps: those who unconditionally support the actions of the ROC and those who in one or another way are opposed. However, this division is carried out not on the basis of believing or non-believing but on the principle of loyalty to the existing political regime. There are numerous examples when Orthodox believers oppose the construction of new temples in the park area of Moscow, the introduction of compulsory lessons of Orthodox culture and Orthodox morality, the enforcement of the law on insulting the feelings of believers and other activities of the Russian Orthodox Church. The BRCSE course on a whole does not cause a significant protest but the expansion of the teaching of religion is fraught with serious conflicts.

The public attitude to the ROC activity clearly shows that there is no broad support of the Church (see Uzlaner in this volume). The 'symphony' turns out to be merely a propaganda technique – a false symphony. There are all reasons to suppose that in a situation of growing economic stagnation mass social and political protests spread out in Russia and the tensions between State and Church will become more and more obvious.

Notes

1 The study was carried out with the financial support of the Russian Foundation for Basic Research, project No. 16–06–00282a.

2 The concept of four so-called 'traditional religions' was formulated in the Law 'On Freedom of Conscience and Religious Associations' (1997). Beside 'Russian Orthodox' identity Islam, Judaism and Buddhism enter as local identities. This framework draws on the Russian imperialist (Eurasian) concept, which has no room for any other religion (in particular, Catholicism, Protestantism, new religious movements). Also this law 'gave the Orthodox Church full legal privileges and awarded it certain financial and material benefits that are in many ways tantamount to establishment' (Marsh 2014: 27).

3 In 2009–2011, the BRCSE teaching was carried out in a number of regions as an experiment.

4 In August 2016, the former Minister of Education, Dmitry Livanov, was dismissed. The new minister was Olga Vasilieva, a head of the department of state-confessional relations of the Russian Presidential Academy of National Economy and Public Administration. Her appointment as minister is associated with an influential bishop, Tikhon (Shevkunov).

5 The confessional composition of the population of Russia is not exactly defined, since the confession is not taken into account in the All-Russian population census, and it is the subject of heated discussions. According to the latest census of 2010, the number of traditionally Muslim peoples in Russia (Tatars, Bashkirs, Chechens and other peoples of the North Caucasus) was about 15 million people (about 10 per cent of the country's population). The Muslim Spiritual Directorate of the European part of Russia claims that the number of Muslims is more than 13 per cent of the country's population. The number of representatives of the peoples traditionally professing Buddhism (national republics of Buryatia, Kalmykia, Tuva) is about 900,000 people (0.5 per cent of the country's population). At the same time, the Buddhist Association of Russia estimates the number of Buddhists to be between 1.5 and 2 million. According to the census, the number of Jews is 200,000. Jewish organisations report about 1.5 million members of the Jewish communities (see Rossiiskaia gazeta 22.12.2011 available online https://rg.ru/2011/12/16/stat.html).

References

Agadjanian, A. 2000. 'Religious Pluralism and National Identity in Russia: The Religious Diversity of the Russian Federation', *International Journal on Multicultural Societies* 2(2): 97–124.

Analysis of the survey data. 2015. BRCSE website: http://orkce.apkpro.ru/doc/%D0% 90%D0%BD%D0%B0%D0%BB%D0%B8%D0%B7%20%D0%B4%D0%B0%D0% BD%D0%BD%D1%8B%D1%85%20%D1%81%D0%BE%D1%86%D0%BE%D0% BF%D1%80%D0%BE%D1%81%D0%B0.pdf

Anderson, J. 2007. 'Putin and the Russian Orthodox Church: Asymmetric Symphonia?', *Journal of International Affairs* 61(1): 185–201.

Baranova, N. A. 2015. *Cultivating Spirituality – Thinking Out Loud: Introduction of the Course BRCSE into Educational Institutions in 2014–2015: Problems, Decisions and Perspectives.* Conference July 6–8, Moscow.

Basics of Orthodox Culture into the Secular School? 2014. Telecast 'Tem vremenem', TV company 'Cultura', 23 December. Available online: http://tvkultura.ru/video/ show/brand_id/20905/episode_id/1152662/video_id/1113162/viewtype/picture/.

Beaman, L. G. and L. Van Arragon (eds.). 2015. *Whose Religion? Issues in Religion and Education.* Leiden: Brill.

Borodina, A. 2010. *Basics of Orthodox Culture: The World Around and Inside Us.* Moscow: Exam.

Daniluc, A. J. 2013. *Basics of Religious Cultures and Secular Ethics.Basics of Secular Ethics.* Moscow: Prosveshcheniye.

Daniluc, A., A. Kondakov and V. Tishkov (eds.). 2009. *Concept of Spiritual and Moral Development and Education of the Personality of a Citizen of Russia.* Moscow: Prosveshcheniye.

Demidov, G. V. 2015. 'Patriotic Upbringing is the Main Vector of BRCSE Activity'. *Introduction of the Course BRCSE into Educational Institutions in 2014–2015: Problems, Decisions and Perspectives.* Conference 6–8 July, Moscow.

Dubin, B. 2014. 'The Faith of the Majority'. In *Mounting and Dismounting of the Secular World.* Edited by A. Malashenko and S. Filatov. Moscow: Carnegie Centre.

Furman, D., K. Kaariainen and V. Karpov. 2007. 'Religiosity in Russia from the 1990s through the early 21st century'. In *New Churches, Old Believers – Old Churches, New Believers: Religion in Post-Soviet Russia.* Edited by K. Kaariainen and D. Furman. Moscow: Letnii Sad.

Hilarion of Volokolamsk, Metropolitan. 2015. *Address by Metropolitan Hilarion of Volokolamsk at the joint meeting of the Federation Council and the State Duma on November 20.* Available online: http://www.patriarchia.ru/db/text/4276260.html.

Guseynov, A. 2012. 'Morals Is Not a Matter of Choice', *Nezavisimaya Gazeta – Religions*, 20 June.

Kalinin, I. 2014. 'Our Locomotive … Cultural Policy as an Instrument of Modernization', *Neprikosnovennyj zapas* 06(98): 85–94.

Kirill, Patriarch. 2016. *Speech in the Federation Council*, 29 January. Available online: http://www.patriarchia.ru/db/text/4362065.html.

Kitinov, B. U. 2015. 'Basics of Religious Cultures and Secular Ethics and Pedagogical Potential of History.' *Introduction of the Course BRCSE into Educational Institutions in 2014–2015: Problems, Decisions and Perspectives.* Conference 6–8 July, Moscow.

Khvalynsky Patriotism. 2015. 'Class Hour', broadcast 'Radio Svoboda', 21 April. Available online: http://www.svoboda.mobi/a/26970006.html.

Köllner, T. 2016. 'Patriotism, Orthodox Religion and Education: Empirical Findings from Contemporary Russia', *Religion, State and Society* 44(4): 366–386.

Köllner, T. 2018. 'On the Restitution of Property and the Making of 'Authentic' Landscapes in Contemporary Russia', *Europe-Asia Studies* 70(7): 1083–1102. doi:10.1080/09668136.2018.1484077.

Kozyrev, F. and Fedorov V. 2006. 'Religion and Education in Russia: Historical Roots, Cultural Context and Recent Developments Religion in Education'. In *A Contribution to Dialogue or a Factor of Conflict in Transforming Societies of European Countries.* Edited by R. Jackson, S. Miedema, W. Weisse and J.-P. Willaime. Hamburg: University of Hamburg.

Kozyrev, F. N. 2010. *Humanitarian Religious Education: A Book for Teachers and Methodists.* St Petersburg: RXGA.

Kulakov, A. E. 2015. 'Problems of Scientific and Methodological Support of the Module "Basics of Religious Cultures of the Peoples of Russia"'. In *Introduction of the BRCSE Course into Educational Institutions in 2014–2015: Problems, Decisions and Perspectives*, pp. 98–101. Conference 6–8 July, Moscow.

Levada Center. 2013. Available online: http://www.levada.ru/24-12-2013/rossiya ne-o-religii.

Levada Center 2014. Available online: http://www.levada.ru/30-04-2014/soblyudenie-velikogo-posta.

Lisovskaya, E. and V. Karpov. 2010. 'Orthodoxy, Islam, and Desecularization of Russia's State Schools', *Politics and Religion* 3(2): 276–302.

Maltsev, B. 2012. 'Islam. View from the Outside/Publishing Business', *Nezavisimaya-Gazeta – Religions.* 5 September.

Marsh, Ch. 2014. *From Atheism to Establishment? The Evolution of Church-State Relations in Russia.* Available online: http://www.academia.edu/2568553/From_Atheism_to_Establishment_The_Evolution_of_Church-State_Relations_in_Russia.

Mercury, Metropolitan. 2010. *Report of the Bishops' Conference on 16 July.* Available online: http://www.pravmir.ru/episkop-zarajskij-merkurij-rossijskomu-obrazovaniyu-nuzhno-vernut-vospitatelnuyu-funkciyu/.

Metlik, I. V. 2004. *Religion and Education in the Secular School.* Moscow: Planeta-2000.

Metlik, I. 2014. 'New about the Study of Religion and Education of Schoolchildren in the Law "On Education" in the Russian Federation', *Vospitanieshkol'nikov* 7: 24–35. Available online: http://www.verav.ru/common/mpublic.php?num=2876.

Mitrokhin, N. 2000. 'Religion and Education in Russia: The Religious Diversity of the Russian Federation', *International Journal on Multicultural Societies* 2(2): 44–71.

Mitrokhin, N. 2004. *Russian Orthodox Church: The Current State and Actual Problems.* Moscow: Novoe literaturnoe obozrenie.

Mitrokhin, N. 2005. *Clericalization of Education in Russia. To the Public Discussion on the Introduction of the Subject "Fundamentals of Orthodox Culture" in the Secondary School Curriculum.* Moscow: IIF.

Mitrokhin, N. and O. Sibireva. 2007. 'Do Not Be Afraid, Little Flock!': On the Assessment of the Number of Orthodox Believers on the Basis of Field Research in Ryazan Region', *Neprikosnovennyj zapas* 1(51): 243–258.

Ozhiganova, A. 2016. 'Battle for School: Modernisers and Clericalists', *Neprikosnovennyj zapas* 2(106): 92–105.

Open Letter. 2007. *The Open Letter of the Academicians to President V. Putin.* Available online: https://www.skeptik.net/religion/science/10academ.htm.

Results of monitoring the BRCSE integrated training course in 2015/2016 academic year 2016. BRCSE website http://orkce.apkpro.ru/doc/%D0%9E%D1%82%D1%87%D0%B5%D1%82%20%D0%BE%20%D0%BF%D1%80%D0%BE%D0%B2%D0%B5%D0%B4%D0%B5%D0%BD%D0%B8%D0%B8%20%D0%BC%D0%BE%D0%BD%D0%B8%D1%82%D0%BE%D1%80%D0%B8%D0%BD%D0%B3%D0%B0%20%D0%9E%D0%A0%D0%9A%D0%A1%D0%AD.pdf.

Shaposhnikova, T. D. (ed.) 2012. *Basics of Religious Cultures and Secular Ethics: Basics of Islamic Culture.* Moscow: Drofa.

Shnirelman, V. A. 2011. 'Russian Christ: The Struggle of the Russian Orthodox Church to Introduce Religion into the Curriculum in the First Decade of the Twenty-first Century', *Journal of Educational Media, Memory, and Society* 3(2): 1–22.

Shnirelman, V. A. 2012. 'Russian Orthodox Culture or Russian Orthodoxteaching? Reflections on the Textbooks in Religious Education in Contemporary Russia', *British Journal of Religious Education* 34(3): 263–279.

Toledo Guiding Principles on Teaching about Religions and Beliefs in Public Schools. 2007. ODIHR OSCE.

Vasilieva, N. V. 2015. 'Interaction with Religious Organisations in the Framework of the Introduction and Implementation of a Comprehensive Training Course BRCSE'. *Introduction of the Course BRCSE into Educational Institutions in 2014–2015: Problems, Decisions and Perspectives.* Conference 6–8 July, Moscow.

Vojtishko, G. 2017. 'In Russia, the Rudiment of Atheistic Thinking Still Educates the Mind', *Vesti.ru*, 13 March. Available online: http://www.vesti.ru/doc.html?id=2865177&cid=520.

Willems, J. 2006. 'The Religio-Political Strategies of the Russian Orthodox Church as a "Politics of Discourse"', *Religion, State and Society* 34(3): 287–298.

Zhiricova, N. N. 2015. 'The Experience of Teaching Orthodox Culture in Educational Institutions of Millirovo Region'. *Introduction of the Course BRCSE into Educational Institutions in 2014–2015: Problems, Decisions and Perspectives.* Conference 6–8 July, Moscow.

Surveys and interviews

Survey among BRCSE teachers; Moscow, February–April 2015 (50 respondents).

Survey among parents of BRCSE students; Moscow, February–April 2015 (92 respondents).

Interview with Tatiana Shaposhnikova (2016), Moscow.

Interview 1 (2016) Interview with BRCSE teacher Elena Petrovna, Moscow.

Interview 2 (2016) Interview with BRCSE teacher Natalya Lvovna, Moscow.

Interview 3 (2016) Interview with BRCSE teacher Tatyana Alekseevna, Moscow.

Interview 4 (2016) Interview with a parent of BRCSE student Elena, Moscow.

Interview 5 (2016) Interview with a parent of BRCSE student Ludmila, Moscow.

Part IV
Conflicts between Orthodox religion and politics

8 The dichotomy between Europeanisation and the revival of Moldovan Orthodoxy

The strategy of the Moldovan Orthodox Church in relation to equality legislation

Romaniţa Iordache

Introduction

Instead of highlighting close and cooperative relationships between politics and religion, this chapter emphasises the opposite: attempts of religious actors to undermine political agendas. The frame of reference for this is the adoption of the non-discrimination law in the Republic of Moldova during the process of coming closer to the European Union and in attempts to receive visa liberalisations for its citizens.

In the context of a wider research on how European integration and Europeanisation processes in the specific area of promoting equality and combating discrimination affect domestic norms, policies, politics and polities in the European neighbourhood, with a focus on the Republic of Moldova, a more specific question on the position of the Orthodox Church in the Europeanisation process emerged. Due to the focus on the dynamic between the EU, the international and the different domestic actors, and the competition between messages promoting European identity(ies) and counter-messages focused on the development of an ethnic and national identity, the Moldovan case study brought light on the interrelation of politics and religion in Republic of Moldova. Given the self-assumed role of the Moldovan Orthodox Church (MOC) (*Biserica Ortodoxă din Moldova*) in the coalescing of illiberal resistance against what was described as EU-imposed legislation, and its final role as self-described defender of the nation against European-ness, a new dynamic emerged as a departure from the traditional *symphonia* (see Jianu in this volume).

Media monitoring, monitoring of the legislative process, and media and textual analysis of news and public statements of religious leaders and decision makers had been used in order to map out the new dynamic of the relation between religion and politics affecting the human rights agenda and featuring the re-assertion of Orthodoxy in the public sphere as an outspoken anti-Europeanisation actor, with Orthodoxy being publicly constructed as a fundamental constitutive element of the nationhood, a distinct feature of civilisation and of 'Moldovanness', endangered by and actively opposing to 'the Europeanisation' package.

Background

The European Union as a transformative space strives to be defined by its support for the rule of law, fundamental rights and liberties, pluralism as well as respect for equality, recognition of otherness (*altérité*) and pro-active combating of discrimination. Accommodating diversities and promoting the equality and non-discrimination principle became a priority for the EU both internally as well as in its relation with third countries, including with the Republic of Moldova, a country which was often times described as the leader in the European Neighbourhood Partnership (Soloviev 2014) and navigated its way from the Partnership and Cooperation Agreement and the ENP Action Plan to EU-Moldova Association Agreement (AA), including a Deep and Comprehensive Free Trade Area (DCFTA) and an Association Agenda. However, visa liberalisation was probably the strongest incentive and probably the most tangible achievement eyed by Moldovan politicians and society alike given the particular situation of Moldova, taking into account that official statistics indicated that up to 20 per cent (informal studies indicate more than 30 per cent) (Moşneagă 2012) of the Moldovan population lives and works, either legally or illegally, in the EU and visa liberalisation would simplify visa requirements and, subsequently, their lives.

The Republic of Moldova, often times referred to as the poorest country in Europe[1] or the nearest frozen conflict in the neighbourhood of the European Union,[2] is a relatively new state, having no independent existence on its own prior to 1991.[3] The lack of an independent national past and of its own national myths due to Moldova's historical incorporation either in Romania or in Russia meant, after 1991, that the Orthodox Church had the role to fill the gap and oftentimes Orthodox Christianity was used as the binding element for the Moldovan social construct. It also implied that Orthodox traditional values were perceived as one of the legacies to be cherished in affirming the identity of the new state. While the reassertion of Orthodoxy in the public sphere did not come as a surprise, more surprising was the positioning of the Orthodox leadership in a wider geo-political context as leading strategic player on an anti-European platform, invoking religious freedom to seek limitation of other fundamental rights and warning against Europeanisation as a threat.

In order to assert an independent nation-state, the concept of symphonia came in handy as this mechanism of harmonious and mutually beneficial coexistence between State and Church was endorsed by the Russian Federation and used in Romania at the beginning of the 19th century.[4] The Russian influence can be explained as Moldova was dominated by Tsarist Russia for more than 100 years after 1812 and the link to the Russian Orthodox Church is essential to the Moldovan clergy given the canonical subordination of the

Moldovan Orthodox Church to the Russian Patriarchate. The Romanian influence can be explained as the neighbour/sister model often times perceived aspiration country. Notably, there are two main Orthodox Churches in Moldova: *Biserica Ortodoxă din Moldova* (Moldovan Orthodox Church) which is an autonomous church under the authority of the Russian Orthodox Church, and the Metropolitan of Bessarabia (*Mitropolia Basarabiei*) which is an autonomous Eastern Orthodox Metropolitan bishopric of the Romanian Orthodox Church.

The Republic of Moldova made its position towards Europeanisation felt since 2009 when the political changes in Chișinău brought into power a pro-European coalition of parties. The EU proposed an Action Plan on Visa Liberalisation in January 2011 with much more specific 'roadmaps', linking the extremely popular desideratum of visa free travelling to tough conditionalities regarding not only the reform of the institutions involved in border management or of the law enforcement bodies, but also with conditions addressing external relations issues (including human rights and fundamental freedoms) linked to the movement of persons such as the substantive and procedural aspects of the comprehensive anti-discrimination law or specific elements regarding the protection of minorities.[5]

From the equality and anti-discrimination bill to the law on ensuring equality: the plot and its outcome

The de facto reality of an un-assumed multi-ethnic society[6] with inter-ethnic relations being sharply divided due to old as well as ongoing historic constraints[7] meant that the Moldovan social construct was based on acceptance of the principle of equality as a legacy of the ubiquitous, though fake, equality rhetoric in the Communist era. The specific arrangements on minority rights were also determined by the experience of the USSR past and of the Transdnistrian conflict and Moldova's multi-ethnic constituency. In spite of the rhetoric, a sociological research conducted in 2009–2010 showed prevailing sexism and intolerance in the form of homophobia or pervasive discrimination against Roma, challenges which were long term present and evidenced.[8] Besides the naturalisation of difference using ethnicity as a marker as featured in other states in Eastern Europe, it was noted that Orthodoxy also became a relevant marker. Indeed, 'Orthodoxy has become the defining element of Moldovan identity, hence replacing the former atheism of the Soviet era' (Munteanu 2015, see also Stahlberg in this volume for the Russian case).

To the external observer, it did not come as a surprise that, among the milestones prioritised by the international actors, a conditionality in relation to visa liberalisation was a draft law on anti-discrimination with the objective of creating institutional safeguards meant to ease ethnic and religious tensions. The 2005, the First Joint Action Plan was the first document which mentioned anti-discrimination legislation as conditionality as the obligation to: 'Put in place and implement legislation on anti-discrimination and legislation guaranteeing the rights of minorities, in line with European standards.'[9] Addressing outstanding human rights commitments became a priority for the pro-European Alliance which came into power after 2009 and was eager to make some progress towards the desired Association Agreement or Visa Liberalisation Plan.

A first draft law on anti-discrimination dates from 2006 and it was pushed for by the Communist government but blocked in the Parliament.[10] Another bill was prepared by NGOs with support from international actors, and underwent a round of public consultations in June–July 2009, but was not submitted to Parliament. A second bill was initially submitted for public consultations in June–August 2010, finalised in January 2011 but subsequently withdrawn by the government from the Parliament in March 2011, following the pressure from religious groups. The same draft was still discussed in April 2011 during the EU–Republic of Moldova Human Rights Dialogue and its withdrawal generated the protest of many NGOs working with various vulnerable groups.[11]

As soon as the lack of progress in adopting an anti-discrimination law was registered by the EU as a delay affecting the closure of the first stage of the Visa Liberalisation Action Plan, the Moldovan Ministry of Justice rewrote the bill and the law was adopted in the second attempt in May 2012 amid wide protests organised by religious actors.[12]

Law 121 of 24 May 2012 on Ensuring Equality was adopted under a title indicating itself the need to mitigate its impact and trying somehow to disguise its scope. Even more important are the significant substantive and procedural limitations in the Law 121 which are a result of political trade-offs, as well as of lack of understanding of the legal standards or of equality and non-discrimination as value. The weak mechanism of enforcement and the lack of adequate remedies for victims of discrimination (see Grecu et al. 2015) suggest that the adoption of Law 121/2012 was merely a token gesture and were correctly identified as 'a version of compromise' (see Grâu 2013). Sexual orientation was deleted as ground protected against discrimination and it is mentioned as protected ground only in relation to discrimination in employment and occupation. A simple and effective institutional mechanism to secure revue was replaced by a limited mandate for the national equality body and a convoluted mechanism of referral to courts leading to de facto lack of remedies for cases of discrimination (see Grecu et al. 2015). Furthermore, different from all similar laws in the region or in Europe, Law 121 includes exceptions from the application of the equality and non-discrimination principle which are carved out to appease religious fears. Paradoxically, after listing the EU Directives establishing the standards in equality and anti-discrimination norms across Europe, Law 121 introduces additional exceptions for entities with a religious ethos in Art. 1(2) of the Law:

> The provisions of the law do not cover and cannot be interpreted as touching upon: a) the family which is based on the marriage freely entered into

by a man and a woman; b) adoption; c) religious denominations and their components in regards of their religious beliefs.[13]

These unusual exceptions which came as last minute amendments were meant to appease religious fears.

Though adopted in May 2012 with considerable limitations, legal European standards being significantly diluted in order to get it adopted, the Law on Ensuring Equality and its promoters came shortly under attack and close scrutiny and generated further wide societal debates. In March 2013, a draft law seeking to abrogate the Law on Ensuring Equality had been filed with the Permanent Bureau of the Parliament of the Republic of Moldova.[14] In the supporting note, the MP who authored it, later to become Moldovan President, wrote:

> Liberalisation of the homosexual practices in the Republic of Moldova through the adoption of the Law on Ensuring Equality is a direct defiance of the moral values accumulated by the nation throughout the centuries and cultivated by each citizen in the family, which these 'European values' have been imposed by the European Union and accepted by the previous leadership in return to the visa liberalisation regime.[15]

In June 2013, more than a year after the adoption of the Law on Ensuring Equality, the Orthodox clergy issued a statement threatening to excommunicate officials who support the law and mentioning that it will call for national protests if the protection for sexual minorities is not rescinded.[16] Reportedly, some of the Orthodox Church officials also warned that if Law 121 is not reversed they would bar public officials from participating in the rite of communion and might excommunicate them. The Orthodox Church basically 'warned of the necessity of protecting believers from the "spread of spiritual death in our society"'.[17] In 2014, Law 121 became the topic of a meeting of the Synod of the Moldovan Orthodox Church and the subject of one of its public documents of condemnation – a novelty in terms of the involvement of the Church in the public sphere.[18] The statement entitled 'Condemnation of gay marches and of the consequences of adopting the Law on Equality of Chances'[19] states the disappointment of the Church that its pleas had not been heard and that 'indecency and sexual amorality had been turned into law, as expressed by the Law on Equality of chances'. The Synod concludes:

> we hope that at least now, after strenuous attempts, the State will hear the people which entrusted him the power to rule and will show justice and determination, in order to repeal a law shameful as well as dangerous for us all, both on the short run but mostly on the long run.[20]

The attacks against Law 121, the national equality body and the promoters of the equality and non-discrimination principle are paradoxical given that a

2014 survey reveals that tolerance is an important social value for 53.8 per cent of the respondents.[21] However, the way in which toleration and equality are communicated by the Church frame the public attitudes and beliefs as the same sociological survey finds that 57.6 per cent of the respondents have the highest trust in the priest and 83 per cent of the interviewees would not accept in the society LGBT people.[22]

The role of the Moldovan Orthodox Churches and their affiliates: the framing

In Moldova there are two main Orthodox Churches: the Moldovan Orthodox Church affiliated to the Russian Orthodox Church and the Metropolitan of Bessarabia linked to the Romanian Orthodox Church.[23] Similar to the Russian Law on Freedom of Conscience granting a privileged status to the Orthodox Church, Orthodoxy is recognised as a primus inter pares by the Moldovan Law on Freedom of Conscience, Thought and Religion. Article 15 (5) of the Law on Freedom of Conscience, Thought and Religion states that 'the state recognises the special importance and the most important role Orthodox Christianity and respectively the Moldovan Orthodox Church has had in the life, history and the culture of Republic of Moldova's people'.[24]

Both main Orthodox churches present in Moldova left aside their internal conflicts and worked against the adoption of the anti-discrimination law. Given that more than 93.3 per cent of Moldovans declared themselves Orthodox believers in the 2004 census,[25] the constituency of the critics of the Law seemed impressive and many politicians reacted to the messages conveyed by the religious actors.

During the debates generated by the draft law and subsequently after Law 121 was adopted, the most vocal actor was the Moldovan Orthodox Church and its affiliates, including unexpected allies such as Scott Lively, an evangelical pastor, known and condemned in the United States for being outspoken against homosexuality and 'the LGBT lobby', as well as an occasional Holocaust revisionism.[26] Also very present were Pro Familia and Moldova Creştină, two Orthodox NGOs affiliated with the Metropolitan of Bessarabia who participated not only during the debates for the adoption of the Law but also during the hearings for the nomination procedures for the members of the Steering Board of the national equality body established in 2013 based on the requirements of Law 121/2012. This cooperation between the otherwise competing religious strongholds however managed to aggregate around the campaign against the law other religious communities such as Baptist, Neoprotestant or Jehovah Witnesses with whom the relations were usually conflictual, reconfirming Stoeckl's (2016) insight of 'norm protagonism' of the Russian Orthodox Church as proposer of 'traditional values' in an attempt providing alternative interpretations to human rights standards. The aggregation of diverse platforms under the same interests/representation proved to be effective. Following Lively's visit, as well as the calls of Moldova's

Orthodox Church, leading members of Parliament said they would not consider discussing the bill until the 'sexual orientation' reference were removed.[27]

The pressure of religious groups was much more visible outside Chișinău where local authorities were enlisted and declared 'homosexuals' free zones' or 'areas of true Moldovanness'. Thus, the cities of Bălți,[28] Soroca, Drochia, Cahul, Ceadîr Lunga and Hiliuți, as well as the Anenii Noi, Fălești and Basarabeasca districts, adopted norms to prohibit the 'aggressive propaganda of non-traditional sexual orientations' and, in one case, 'Muslim activity'.

The religious actors presented the proposed norms as going against religious tenets, infringing the religious freedom of the majority, putting in peril the health and morals of the Moldovan society. The critics of the anti-discrimination legislation adopted three types of often overlapping messages. Firstly, they promoted an anti-European discourse, of Russian influence, depicting the EU as the end of the national state and as being in a secular tradition. The same message permeates further communication of the Moldovan Orthodox Church as evidenced by a 2014 statement of the Synod of the Moldovan Orthodox Church regarding 'the secularising provocations of the European Union'.[29] The 2014 statement of the MOC Synod presents Europe as 'an example of existence without God. The West not taking into consideration His Commandments and Prohibitions'. The Synod warns against 'same-sex marriage, euthanasia, abortion and other social illnesses – great dangers which might destroy a whole Orthodox civilisation'.[30]

Embedded in the anti-European, anti-Western message the critics of Law 121 built an anti-human rights message, also influenced by the current Russian public discourse as observed by Stoeckl (2014: 32) who notes that human rights are 'depicted as a political instrument through which the West seeks to destabilize Russia, because human rights supposedly strengthen national, religious and ideological minorities at the expense of Russian collective identity'. Stoeckl (2014: 49) also highlighted the conceptual opposites spelled out by the Metropolitan Kiril in 2000 as:

> foundations of a clash of cultures between the East and the West. In this clash the West stands for liberalism, secularism and individual human rights, while the East, that is Orthodox Christianity, is the guardian of traditionalism, religion and the rights of the community, nation, family.

Even more specific, the third type of message is anti-homosexual, confirming Barry Fitzpatrick's (2007) warning regarding the incompatibility between some religious beliefs and acceptance of LGBT rights as 'one of the most acute dilemmas confronting European and national equality law and policy'. As the European Social Survey (ESS), published in August 2013 by City University London, has reported a notable decrease in tolerance of homosexuality in a number of Eastern European countries,[31] it is obvious that in the Moldovan case, similar to the Russian Federation or Ukraine, homophobia provided a convenient scapegoat. In an unprecedented statement entitled 'Condemnation of gay marches and of the consequences of adopting the Law on Equality of Chances'[32] the MOC Synod states in September 2014 the disappointment of the Church that its pleas had not been heard and that 'indecency and sexual amorality had been turned into law, as expressed by the Law on Equality of Chances'.

The anti-discrimination law was never presented by its promoters – domestic or international – as ensuring equal access and protection to persons with disabilities, religious or ethnic minorities, as creating a fair and equitable framework for women, younger or older citizens, for those socially disadvantaged. Instead, the religious groups successfully labelled the draft as 'the homosexual bill' from the very beginning and managed to present the content of the bill as promoting homosexuality. Thus they managed to claim that 'ending discrimination against gays would be the first step towards the "homosexualisation" of society and would be followed by granting gay people the right to marry and adopt children'.[33]

The misinformation and homophobia paid off – following the calls of Moldova's Orthodox Church, significant members of Parliament declared they would not consider discussing the anti-discrimination bill until the reference to 'sexual orientation' (meaning the protection clause covering sexual orientation as protected ground against discrimination) was removed.[34] The religious-nationalist calls came from across the entire political spectrum. Igor Dodon, at that time the reformist leader of the Communist party, since 2016 President of Republic of Moldova, joined the choir of criticisms:

> Even more worrying are all sorts of weird initiatives which aim to legalize and promote sexual relations that go beyond normality and the traditional Moldovan common sense, says. Moldova has always been shunned to accept such 'habits' and I hope God protects us from them and from now on.[35]

From the other side of the political spectrum, the Liberal Democrat Valeriu Ghiletchi joined:

> I became deeply sad when I heard about the Government's decision to pass the bill regarding prevention and combating of discrimination to the Parliament … Without any doubt, this draft law presents potential danger for integrity of the family and freedom of expression for the Church in terms of moral issues … if the 'sexual orientation' phrase is erased, then the law per se does not represent any danger for society … I think the best solution would be to reject the bill completely.[36]

Similarly, the leader of the Liberal Party was quoted stating:

> We are liberals, but we are healthy and we want a healthy family. Homosexuality is a deviation, nature is nature, but it doesn't mean that

we need to put them [homosexuals] in the forefront. We don't take patients from psychiatric institutions to bring them on our main square. With all the respect for them, I will not vote.[37]

The end of symphonia?

The history of the Moldovan anti-discrimination legislation evidences what happens when European norms, or their related collective understandings as defined by a particular group of interests in the Orthodox Church, are successfully communicated as not being compatible with values at the local level and instead they are actually depicted as threatening local identity. The case is also relevant in showing the power of the Orthodox Church in delegitimising the efforts of the Moldovan authorities towards Europeanisation. More than the mere attempt to ensure the revitalisation of the position of the Church in the society, the Moldovan case suggests how religious actors try to position themselves as regional deal-breakers or gate-keepers, sometimes promoting agendas at odds with the interests of their constituencies.

The success achieved by the religious groups in the reframing of the substantive provisions of the Law 121 and the dilution of the institutional mechanisms for equality and non-discrimination in Moldova were not perceived as satisfactory and Law 121 and the pro-European political elite came repeatedly under attack, with leaders of the Moldovan Orthodox Church being the organising vectors in the coalescing of otherwise diverging forces on an anti-European platform. The strategy used by the Moldovan Orthodox Church to block or prevent the adoption of equality legislation in 2011–2012, the public statements, protests and the threats with a prohibition to share Holy Communion for the politicians who supported the Law in 2012, and, eventually, the decisions of the Holy Synod of the Moldovan Orthodox Church from 2014 condemning 'the EU-driven way of life' and criticising the Law on Ensuring Equality suggest that Moldovan religious actors are claiming an added, ultimate power in an attempt to reframe the dynamic of the relation between State and Church. In this context, Europeanisation was depicted as a threat to the revival of the Orthodox Church and rejected as a new enemy. The geo-political interests of some members of the clergy or the drive of the Orthodox clergy to play a more significant role in framing domestic and regional politics disrupted the harmony of the prior arrangement between state and church which had predominant elements of symphonia, a balance in the relationship between state and church.

Notes

1 Human Development Report Moldova (2009). In 2005, 20.8 per cent of the population lived under the absolute poverty line and registered an income lower than US $ 2.15 per day and Moldova's Human Development Index is below the world average.

2 See http://www.stratfor.com/weekly/20101118_geopolitical_journey_part_4_moldova (20.11.2010).

3 After developing as one of the Romanian medieval states, the Eastern part of the Principality of Moldova known as 'Bessarabia' was ceded in 1812 by the Ottoman Empire to Tsarist Russia and turned into the 'Oblast of Moldavia and Bessarabia' while the Western part remained as an autonomous principality and joined the Romanian state in 1859. In spite of a policy of forced assimilation, Bessarabia declared its independence and conditional union with Romania in 1918; however, this was not for long: In 1939, when the Soviets signed a nonaggression pact with Nazi Germany, Bessarabia was also ceded to the Soviets which by 1940 rebranded Bessarabia as the 'Moldavian Soviet Socialist Republic'. One year later, the territory was seized by Hitler during the Axis invasion and, when Stalin got it back in 1944, the new power took measures of ethnic cleansing and population shifts for forced Russification as well as carried out a famine also geared to 'pacify and control the region', see King (2000).

4 See Stan and Turcescu (2007: 20) who describe the young Romanian national state as being defined in terms of symphonia – 'the head of the state was expected to be an Orthodox Christian, the church and the state were to coexist harmoniously for the good of the "Orthodox Christian" society, and the state was expected to support the preservation of and Orthodox Christian culture'.

5 See Action Plan on Visa Liberalisations: EU-Republic of Moldova Visa Dialogue, available online: http://www.gov.md/doc.php?l=en&id=3397&idc=447.

6 Republic of Moldova, National 2004 Census in Republic of Moldova: 75.8 per cent Moldovans, 8.4 per cent Ukrainians, 5.9 per cent Russians, 4.4 per cent Găgăuz, 2.2 per cent Romanians, 1.9 per cent Bulgarians and 1.0 per cent other nationalities, available online: http://www.statistica.md/newsview.php?l=ro&id=2358&idc=168. Accessed 20 August 2014.

7 Victor Munteanu (2015) briefly presents the challenge of the Moldovan identity in the following terms: 'In the case of the Moldovan people, a group's understanding of its identity can differ from the same group's spoken language. This sensitive issue leaves Moldova a society deeply and irreconcilably divided between those who identify and speak Romanian, considering the country and its people to be a part of the Romanian nation, versus those who uphold the idea of a sovereign Moldovan nation and language. In addition to the division between the two groups, another category of Moldovans affiliates themselves with the Romanian nation 'but with different markers of identity".

8 See http://soros.md/files/publications/documents/Studiu%20Sociologic.pdf.

9 See EU-Moldova Action Plan, available online: http://ec.europa.eu/world/enp/pdf/action_plans/moldova_enp_ap_final_en.pdf.

10 See Governmental Decision 1459 from 24 December 2007.

11 Briefing submitted on 24.03. 2011 as a part of the contributions within the Human Rights Dialogue, *MOLDOVA: Discriminatory attitudes, impact on society and negative consequences from the Human Rights Perspective,* by the Non-discrimination Coalition, the Human Rights Resource Group supported by Soros Foundation – Moldova and the Legal Resources Centre, Moldova. See also memo signed by 74 human rights and social services NGOs in support of the Anti-discrimination Law from March 2011.

12 See Moldovan Law 121/2012, Lege cu privire la asigurarea egalităţii din (Law on Ensuring Equality), 25.05.2012.

13 See Moldova, Lege Nr. 121 din 25.05.2012 cu privire la asigurarea egalităţii (Law on Ensuring Equality), Law 121/2012, 25 May 2012. Art. 1(2).

14 Information on the draft Law for abrogating Law on ensuring equality Nr. 121 of 25 May 2012 published on http://parlament.md/ProcesulLegislativ/Proiectedeacte legislative/tabid/61/LegislativId/1649/Default.aspx. Accessed 10 March 2013.

15 Explanatory memorandum for the draft Law for abrogating Law on Ensuring Equality nr. 121 of 25 May 2012 available at: http://parlament.md/ProcesulLegisla tiv/Proiectedeactelegislative/tabid/61/LegislativId/1649/Default.aspx. Accessed 15 May 2013.
16 Statement of the Orthodox Church of Moldova from 20 June 2013, available at: http://mitropolia.md/en/the-synod-of-the-orthodox-church-of-moldova-met-on-the-20th-of-june-2013-at-the-metropolitan-administration/.
17 Radio Free Europe/Radio Liberty, *Gloves Come Off In Moldova's Church-State Battle*, available online: http://www.rferl.org/content/moldova-orthodox-church-eu/25035131.html (3.07.2013).
18 Sinodul Bisericii Ortodoxe din Moldova, 3 September 2014, No. 1, Condamnarea paradelor gay și a consecințelor adoptării Legii cu privire la egalitatea de șanse.
19 Note by the author: By Law on Equality of Chances, the Synod wrongly referred to the Law on Ensuring Equality.
20 Sinodul Bisericii Ortodoxe din Moldova, 3 September 2014, No. 1, Condamnarea paradelor gay și a consecințelor adoptării Legii cu privire la egalitatea de șanse.
21 Consiliul pentru Prevenirea și Eliminarea Discriminării și Asigurarea Egalității, sociological survey carried out in 2014 available online: http://egalitate.md/media/files/files/sondaj_sociologic____fenomenul_discrimin__rii_ain_republica_moldova-_percep_aia_cet__aeanului____3832326.pdf, p. 11.
22 Consiliul pentru Prevenirea și Eliminarea Discriminării și Asigurarea Egalității, sociological survey carried out in 2014, available online: http://egalitate.md/media/files/files/sondaj_sociologic____fenomenul_discrimin__rii_ain_republica_moldova-_percep_aia_cet__aeanului____3832326.pdf.
23 The Mitropolia Basarabiei was established in 1923 but was inactive between 1941–1991. It was re-activated on September 14 1992. Its recognition was however granted by the Moldovan authorities only following the ECtHR judgment in *Metropolitan Church Of Bessarabia And Others v. Moldova*, from 13.12.2001, application number 45701/99.
24 Moldova, Lege Nr. 125-XVI din 11.05.2007 privind libertatea de conștiință, gândire și de religie available online: http://www.legislationline.org/topics/country/14/topic/78.
25 Census information available online: http://www.statistica.md/newsview.php?l=ro&idc=168&id=2358.
26 The visit was reported by US human rights groups: http://www.humanrightsfirst.org/2011/03/11/two-influential-americans-make-separate-visits-to-europe%E2%80%99s-poorest-nation/.
27 See http://www.rferl.org/content/moldova_us_antigay_activists_homosexual/2333089.html.
28 The Resolution adopted by the city of Balti on 23 February 2012 stated: 'Considering particular importance and historic role of the Moldovan Orthodox Church as a state-establishing institute of the Republic of Moldova; considering traditional values of Moldovan society; incompatibility with modern democratic standards of aggressive intrusion of sexual behaviour forms on the majority, which are characteristic for the most insignificant part of population; bearing responsibility for security (including ethical and moral one) of Bălți city residents'.
29 See Sinodul Bisericii Ortodoxe din Moldova, No. 4 from 3 September 2014, Declarația Sinodului Bisericii Ortodoxe din Moldova referitor la provocările secularizante ale Uniunii Europene.
30 See Sinodul Bisericii Ortodoxe din Moldova, No. 4 from 3 September 2014, Declarația Sinodului Bisericii Ortodoxe din Moldova referitor la provocările secularizante ale Uniunii Europene.

31 Warren, Adrienne, *State-Sponsored Intolerance: Homophobia in the Eastern Part-nership.* Available at: http://eastbook.eu/en/2013/08/country-en/moldova-en/lega l-intolerance-homophobia-in-the-eastern-partnership/.
32 See Sinodul Bisericii Ortodoxe din Moldova, 3 September 2014, No. 1, Condamnarea paradelor gay şi a consecinţelor adoptării Legii cu privire la egalitatea de şanse. (Synod of the Orthodox Church from Moldova. Condemnation of the gay pride parades and of the consequences of adopting the Law on Equality of Chances).
33 See http://www.humanrightsfirst.org/2011/03/11/two-influential-americans-make-sepa rate-visits-to-europe%E2%80%99s-poorest-nation/.
34 See http://www.rferl.org/content/moldova_us_antigay_activists_homosexual/2333089. html.
35 Igor Dodon, Communist MP on 17th of March 2011, statement available at: http://unimedia.md/?mod=news&id=31336.
36 Valeriu Ghiletchi, MP in the Liberal Democratic Party, 8th of March 2011, avail-able at: http://valeriughiletchi.org/2011/03/proiectul-de-lege-privind-combaterea-dis criminarii/.
37 Mihai Ghimpu, leader of the Liberal Party, MP during the protest against the anti-discrimination law on 17 March 2011 available at http://www.azi.md/ro/story/ 17174.

References

Fitzpatrick, B. 2007. 'The "Mainstreaming" of Sexual Orientation into European Equality Law'. In *Equality Law in an Enlarged European Union – Understanding the Article 13 Directives.* Edited by H. Meenan. Cambridge: Cambridge University Press.
Grâu, L. 2013. *Contribuţii la Parteneriatul pentru Dezvoltare dintre România şi Republica Moldova. Un parteneriat pentru nediscriminare.* Available online: http://www.ape.md/lib.php?l=ro&idc=156.
Grecu, P., N. Hriptievschi, R. Iordache, Iu. Ionescu and S. Macrinici. 2015. *Analysis of Compatibility of the Moldovan Legislation with the Equality and Non-discrimination Acquis Communautaire.*
King, Ch. 2000. *The Moldovans: Romania, Russia, and the Politics of Culture.* Stanford, CA: Hoover Institution Press.
Moşneagă, V. 2012. *Moldovan Labour Migrants in the European Union: Problems of Integration.* San Domenico di Fiesole: Robert Schuman Centre for Advanced Studies.
Munteanu, V. 2015. 'Behind the Curtain: The Relationship between the Moldovan State and Church.' In *Traditional Religion and Political Power: Examining the Role of the Church in Georgia, Armenia, Ukraine and Moldova.* Edited by A. Hug. London: The Foreign Policy Center.
Soloviev, V. 2014. 'Moldova: The Failing Champion of European Integration', *Global Transitions, Transitions Forum.*
Stan, L. and L. Turcescu. 2007. *Religion and Politics in Post-Communist Romania.* Oxford: Oxford University Press.
Stoeckl, K. 2014. *The Russian Orthodox Church and Human Rights.* London, New York: Routledge.
Stoeckl, K. 2016. 'The Russian Orthodox Church as Moral Norm Entrepreneur', *Religion, State and Society* 44(2): 132–151.

9 Between Europeanisation and the Russian-Georgian brotherhood

Nationalism, Orthodoxy and geopolitics of the Georgian Church

Nutsa Batiashvili

Introduction

The collapse of the communist regimes witnessed the rise of religious nationalism in many of the post-Soviet states. Georgia was no exception in this respect (Waal 2011). Especially the early 1990s was marked by the kind of ethnonationalism that some have referred to as 'ethnodoxy' (Karpov et al. 2012). Crisis of legitimacy that the state institutions experienced, as is always the case in most of the postcolonial societies, enabled the Orthodox Church and its Patriarch Ilia II to become the locus and the ultimate source of authoritative power (see Figure 9.1). But this was due, not solely to the inherent nature of religious institutions to emanate divine power and sustain the sense of certainty that comes with its hierarchical cosmology, but to the distinctly powerful bond that in the Georgian national imagination exists between the Christian faith and the Georgian nationhood. The vision of this indissoluble bond is embedded in historical representations and popular memory, going back to centuries-long history of Georgia's nation-making.

From the early medieval texts to the 19th century letters by 'founding fathers' the narrative of conversion is construed 'not only as a story of Georgia becoming Christian, but as a process of the formation of Georgia's body politic...' (Aleksidze 2016: 227). Particularly ethnocentric and nationalist discourses that have evolved during post-Soviet era, but have roots in earlier discursive traditions, have obviously placed extensive emphasis on the link between Christian faith and national identity. To be more precise, in such conceptions of nationhood, Georgianness is exclusively circumscribed to and equated with the Orthodox faith.

> Georgia is reckoned to consist of those spacious lands in which church services are celebrated and all prayers said in the Georgian tongue. Only the Kyrie eleison, which means 'Lord, have mercy', or 'Lord be merciful to us', is pronounced in Greek.[1]

This often quoted excerpt from the 10th century hagiographic account is dominantly used to inscribe Georgian nationhood into the domain of

Figure 9.1 The hegemony of the Church ideology and its authority among Georgian
public is revealed not only in the political domain but is manifested in the
peculiarity of everyday practices. This photograph of a makeshift shrine I
took in a store in the centre of Tbilisi depicts a somewhat typical scene that
one can encounter in stores, salons, taxi cabs, mini buses and most certainly private homes. For a wonderful account and the anthropological
analysis on the post-Soviet religious practices in Georgia see Keti Gurchiani's
work (2017).

Christianity as well as to define the boundaries of the 'body politic' (as
Aleksidze (2016) shows in his above quoted text) by marking the territory
where prayers are pronounced in Georgian.

Thus, the linkage that in Georgian experience exists between religious
institution and national politics goes beyond the idea of *symphonia*, and the
conventional understanding that such a relationship entails; particularly
because rather than there being a mutually complementary alliance, the relationship can more aptly be characterised as one in which the Church has been
substituting the State throughout the long periods of invasions and conquests.
Part of this chapter is dedicated to showing how this interchangeability
between Church and the State, nationhood and faith is represented and
articulated in dominant memory narratives and how such a conception of this
bond shapes modern political thought among Georgians.

Yet, most of the ethnographic episodes discussed in this chapter are used to
explicate the notion of 'Orthodoxy' as it evolved in Georgia's colonial
experience with Russia, most significantly its role in the public discourse for

contemplating, criticizing or justifying complexities of Russian-Georgian relations. It is here, in this discussion, that we can understand how Orthodox faith can become not only a matter of politics, but of geopolitics as well and how it can shape the ways in which individuals imagine the world order and the place of their nation in it.

The mosaic of the colonial 'friendship'

In the times of the Russian Tsarist Empire and long since then a route that lay through Dariali valley from Russia's Northern Caucasus to the capital of Georgia, known as the Georgian Military Road, was considered the only safe way of getting through the troublesome region of the Caucasus – Russia's own Orient – to the countries south of the mountainous range. On this mountain-mantled route, somewhere near the point where the highway begins to follow the river Aragvi, there is a sightseeing spot, popular among travellers visiting Georgia. It is a stop point on the edge of the summit with a 360-degree view, literally *framed* by a somewhat whimsical, belvedere style, construction: a semi-circular mosaic wall with twelve arches, each one crowning a balcony that overlooks the valley (see Figure 9.2). The wall is something like a curtaining partition that screens off the bare nature from a viewer until a certain point. As if one approaching the viewing point needs to be prepared for the sheer magnitude of the place, not only of its naturalistic beauty but of geo-historical significance that this site embodies.

The mosaic is what creates the narrative frame for experiencing the scene and its central element is a monumental figure of a woman with a pigeon in her right hand and a child leaning against her lap (see Figure 9.3). Right from her is an image of the Georgian Orthodox Church and left from her is an image of the Russian Orthodox one. The monument was erected in 1983 to commemorate 200 years of Russian-Georgian 'friendship'. What one can tell from this mosaic pane is that Orthodox Christianity is the single most important node for enshrouding Russian-Georgian relations into the narrative of peaceful relations. What one cannot tell from this is that nowhere else is the term 'friendship' so gravely charged and contested as it is in the context of this geo-political and historical tangle.

This chapter, then, is also about this contested notion of 'friendship' as a construct of imperial imposition and subjectification that is in its entirety built

Figure 9.2 The mosaic construction on the 'military road'. Photo taken by the author.

Figure 9.3 The centrepiece of the mosaic. Photo taken by author.

upon and amplified through the discourse on the 'common Orthodox faith' (Georgian: *ertmortsmuneoba*, Russian: *edinoverie*). I want to unravel this tension that exists between words 'friendship' and 'occupation,' to show how these competing narratives fall across the lines of division between notions of 'east' and 'west', 'Russophilia' and 'westernism' and how they become vocal in the struggle for the ultimate authority between Georgian Church and the State. Making my way through this discussion, what I want to show is how 'Orthodox faith' functions on three distinct levels of cultural imagination: a) as a mnemonic construct embedded in national myths and historical narratives, b) as an ideological currency that mobilises power by merging the religious with the nationalist, and c) as a geopolitical category that embodies the organic bond between the colony and the Empire and as such dictates distinct kind of postcolonial order. I begin my discussion with the history of the Russian-Georgian relations and the politically charged memory discourse that is inevitably tied to this triadic paradigm of Orthodoxy.[2]

The Orthodox bind and Georgian national memory

Russian annexation of Georgian territories began in 1801 but the story of Russian-Georgian relations goes back to the late 18th century and the national memory of these inceptive events are as challenged and challenging in the public discourse as the idea of 'Russian-Georgian friendship' itself. In 1783, under the pressure experienced in the context of the rivalling powers of

Russian and Persian Empires, the Kingdom of Kartl-Kakheti (Eastern Georgian Kingdom) signed a treaty (Traktat) with Russia at Georgievsk in the North Caucasus. The treaty constrained the power of Georgian monarchs in many ways and subordinated the Catholicos-Patriarch[3] to the Russian Synod (see Rayfield 2012). As popular memory discourse has it, allying with Russia would help Georgia 'get rid of' its non-Christian oppressors and finally find the escape route from the shackles of the Persian Empire.

For Georgians the '1783 Georgyevsk Traktat' represents what some refer to as the 'difficult past' (Vinitzky-Seroussi 2002) as a historical moment which set the stage for ensuing full annexation of Georgian kingdoms. Hence, it is here, with Erekle's decision to sign this treaty, that many of the disputes on Russian-Georgian relations unfold. In many conversations I have been part of, the disagreement on the 'Russian issue' somehow leads to mention of Erekle's decision as a fateful act of a man upon which the destiny of an entire nation has hinged. 'Erekle's decision' has been an issue of contention and contestation not only today but in the 19th and early 20th century intellectual terrain, and this is reflected in poetry and prose as well (e.g. N. Baratashvili's poem *Fate of Georgia* 1839).

One of the reasons we can talk about '1783' as a form of the 'difficult past' is because on the one hand, ramifications of this event continue to act on the present geopolitical context. On the other hand, it represents an unsettling memory narrative because of its incongruity with the dominant national myth which frames the nation's past in terms of the perennial struggle for freedom and independence. This idea of the perennial struggle against alien powers, unwillingness to subdue and subordinate to foreign cultures is one of the most powerful sentiments of the national self-awareness. Georgians are socialised into this cultural knowledge from early on in their childhood, not only through school education (history curriculum, Georgian language and literature classes) but through legends, media sources and everyday representations of the historical past. Thus, for many Georgians (if not all) these patterns, these reoccurring historical acts do not just set the ground for the national politics, but fundamentally reveal the essential character of an archetypical Georgian. It is from this perspective that, in memory discourse, one finds it hard to get over Erekle's decision. Yet, the framing of his decision in terms of the desperate attempt to free Georgia from Persia's cultural oppression and its religious animosity provides very strong justificatory grounds for King Erekle. In order to have a clearer perspective on where this kind of framing fits in the dominant myths of the nationhood, consider the following quote by one of the 'nationalist' historians as an ample illustration of the memory truths that shape normative understanding of the past:

> In its struggle against various invaders Georgian selfhood (identity) and its culture of statehood have been formed. Historically, some intruders were capable of tearing apart Georgia or partially incorporating it into another state. In such times, the Georgian church remained as the

guarantor of the Georgian state's indissolubility, while the Georgian people never complied with the occupant.

(Putkaradze, n.d.)

What such a view on the statehood and nationhood suggests is that preserving national spirituality is a mission of a much higher order than sustaining a political entity. Its ultimate 'moral impulse' (White 1981) is that Georgians preserved their nationhood under the rule of various invaders because of cultural and spiritual steadiness. While the passage above belongs to an extremely nationalist historian, especially well established in the religious circles, nevertheless, the narrative frame that he employs represents a somewhat general and generic mode of reasoning in this matter. For instance, Nino a 17-year-old Georgian student (one of the subjects of my ethnographic field research) has very similar understanding of the national historicity:

> The history of our nation is an endless struggle for preserving the integrity of the nation. For almost twenty centuries our ancestors have been defending Christian belief with the spear ... They fought with Iranians, Arabs, Turk-Seljuqs, Mongols, Kizilbashs, Russians ... None of the enemies have inflicted as much damage on our nation as this latter [i.e. Russia]. Russia began annexation of Georgian Kingdoms since 1801 and in a matter of few years it managed to 'enslave' the entire country. The enemy that came as a friend and the commonality of the faith seduced our kings, Erekle II among them and with signing of the Georgievks Treaty the situation worsened [for Georgia]. Integration with Russia resulted in forgetting traditional old culture that we had shed our blood to preserve.

And it is here, in these formulations, that we can see how Orthodoxy – *martlmadidebloba* in Georgian – becomes a dominant cultural force preserving the national 'body politic'. It has to do with Georgian nationalism just as much (if not more) as with faith and religiosity, because one's belonging to the Georgian Orthodox Church is intricately tied to one's vision of the Georgian nationhood and the ideas about statehood. This is so, as noted earlier, not solely due to the Church's ideological authority in the context of post-communist moral crisis, per se, but because of how Orthodox faith ties into the Georgian collective memory and the narrative of constant resistance to the advances of the various alien forces against Georgian culture, statehood and spirituality.

Thus, on the one hand while culturally normalised memory discourse posits Georgians' historical identity in terms of constant and persistent struggle against any form of foreign domination, instead 1783 represents an instance of voluntary submission of the national sovereignty to the outside power. Nino, as many other Georgians, sees this as a submission by seduction, seduction in which the idea of a 'common faith' played a crucial role in disguising 'the enemy' as a 'friend'. Yet, it is the same reasoning logic that when projected on the historical context enables Erekle's justification. Particularly the idea that the nation needs to be preserved spiritually exonerates Erekle II.

This is why Erekle represents a paradigmatic figure, but not only because of the historical momentum that he was an indissoluble part of, but because his own image incorporates the dual paradigm of Georgianness[4] and invokes the ambivalence of Georgians in judging the king whose heroic and benevolent character has been the subject of diverse folkloric encounters. As such, in popular imagination Erekle is both a venerated king, defender of Christianity, skilful and brave warrior as well as an uncertain, naive, misguided, failed politician who carries the burden of the nation's 'tragic' fate. This is how the authors of an unpublished history textbook on 200 years of Russian-Georgian relations frame the historical circumstances within which Erekle's decision can be sensibly envisioned:

> Beginning in the 15th century, Georgian kings were looking for an ally in their struggle against Muslim invaders. With this aim they tried to form an alliance with Russia along with other Christian states in Europe. After the fall of Byzantine Empire (1453) Russia remained as [Georgia's] closest Orthodox [Christian] country and the desire for its support and partnership occurred naturally to Georgian politicians … Russia had its own interests and … when the time came, Russia did not pay attention to the destiny of a country fighting for its survival. It singlehandedly, piece-by-piece annexed [Georgia] and erased from the map a country of great historical past and culture.

This narrative places the decision to ally with Russia within the larger context of struggle against pressure from the non-Christian powers. At the time Georgia was at risk of remaining under pressure from two Muslim empires, the Ottoman and the Persian. But more importantly the framing that derives its authoritative force by projecting current aspirations for Eurointegration into the remote past links this particular historical reality with Georgia's long-lasting mission to find its rightful place in the greater European community and the Christian oecumene. It is within such a discursive framing that one can come across the justificatory logic that underlines the importance of Russian-Georgian religious kinship. And it is here, then, that the Orthodoxy becomes much more than a mere interjection of faith and nationhood.

In a column titled 'Erekle II – The Tragedy Of An Enlightened King' that was published in 2013 in a popular online magazine *Georgia Today*, the authors pose 'Erekle's Dilemma' in the following manner:

> The country was too weak to remain independent, and Erekle was forced to sup with the devil. Faced with the choice of making a pact with greedy Russians in the North, who were Orthodox Christians, or with the less

imperialistic but more aggressive Persians in the South, who were Muslims, he opted for the Russians. How would you have decided?

At the same time, many Georgians evaluate Erekle's move as a political failure, a misjudgement of Russia's political agenda based on naiveté and the weakness of Erekle's character. For instance in the same article the authors write:

> Erekle arguably underestimated what it meant to invite the Russian Bear to his kingdom, and probably he did not expect his decision to have consequences that would reach into the 21st century. Nonetheless, he well understood that Russia was a dangerous ally, and he tried hard to instead get the French on board.

Once, when discussing Georgia's 'western orientation' and ongoing memory battles on Russian-Georgian relations, Dimitri, a historian in his 60s, who was at the time working on the history textbook '200 years of Russian-Georgian relations', pointed out:

> At the time [18th century Georgia], although I am utterly against Russian politics, I think that Russia of the time, despite its barbaric nature, compared to Qizilbash and Ottoman countries was kind of a European state. A brilliant Russian aristocracy was raised on French and European literature and this was the Napoleonic period … French was in fashion … and our aristocracy imitated Russian aristocracy. At least Russia was a window to Europe. That is why I do not criticise this big decision of Erekle's … but I completely dissociate myself from these Russophiles … these Russophiles use Erekle's personality as their flag.

In Dimitri's view, Erekle's main aim was not to preserve the statehood but to 'move Georgian people and the country away from any sort of Asian developmental path … Georgia's Europeanisation was his major strategy … even if it cost him the loss of the statehood' (personal communication). In his effort to reason with the king's geopolitical logic, Dimitri (like many others I have spoken with) employed two binarisms both of which construe a frame of argumentation that are culturally meaningful and were at the time aligned with the political rhetoric and geopolitical agenda of the state. One is the juxtaposition between Georgians' Europeanisation vis-á-vis the environment of 'Ottoman-Kizilbash' influence, as he himself coined it. This dichotomy inherently embodies religious dimension, since in Georgian historic consciousness the term 'Ottoman-Kizilbash' is synonymous with 'faithless' and more importantly with the 'threat to Christian tradition'. Thus, on Erekle's part 'moving away' from the 'Ottoman-Kizilbash' environment amounted to saving Georgian Christianity. Another binarism that Dimitri resorts to embodies the concept of a nation as a two-dimensional entity, an understanding that devises analogy between the human and the nation. 'States are much like humans' Dimitri explained,

> A nation is a living organism and is like individuals ... So, here I am asking you as an individual and we can discuss this together: Is a human's sole purpose his/her physical existence? Well there are people for whom it is the only purpose, but aren't there people who along with physical existence deem spiritual, intellectual ... development to be important?! Is that not so?! So I think, Erekle viewed his state from this perspective.

Of course Dimitri's reasoning is not unique and these excerpts from the interview here serve the demonstrative purpose to showcase what is a culturally given, transmitted and circulated form of conceptualisation that is deeply embedded in historical consciousness. This is so, particularly, because of the manner in which historical truth is posited by the memory narrative. Cultural imperative reinforced through such a symbolic medium is what makes it possible for a Soviet generation historian and an 18-year-old student to rely on the identical notions of the nationhood, in order to claim either political legitimacy or cultural continuity:

> To me, generally, a nation does not mean a group of people who have territories and sovereign state. A nation may not be independent, but it still exists as long as it preserves its culture and traditions.

Tengo, an 18-year-old high school graduate wrote this in his essay on tradition and modernity, to claim that preserving culture is of utmost importance for the Georgian nation. Such an interpretation of nationhood stems from the conception of Georgia's past as a repeated cycle of invasions and occupations. From this perspective, Georgians preserved their nationhood under the rule of various invaders because of cultural and spiritual steadiness. This memory maxim underpins both Dimitri's and Tengo's reasoning mode, as well as of that of the historian Putkaradze, quoted earlier in this paper.

Orthodox brotherhood versus Western orientation

What one can infer from these contemplations on Erekle is the significance of two discursive elements – Orthodox faith and Western 'orientation' – that frame competing representations of the Russian-Georgian past, but also transpose cultural and political imperatives of modern Georgian nationhood. It is along the lines of these politico-religious paradigms that the altercation – at times veiled and disguised through indirect addresses and rhetoric – between pro-Western government and Orthodox Church unfolded.

Although traces of Georgia's European aspirations can be discovered throughout different historical periods, it was Saakashvili's reformist administration that mobilised a wide range of ideological and political resources toward a cohesive and tenacious action-plan for Georgia's integration into Western alliances. The main motivation behind this newly revamped geopolitical agenda, more than anything else, had to do with the desire to divorce Georgian statehood from Russia's political orbit. Georgia was no longer to belong to the Russian or Soviet imperial margins, but instead was reconceived as an outskirt of the European geopolitical landscape. Orthodoxy came to stand in the way of this ambitious yet auspicious objective in somewhat subtle ways.

It was in the context of the power vacuum and the crisis of legitimacy of state institutions following the collapse of the USSR that the Georgian Orthodox Church gained momentum. Since then it empowered the notion that a successful Georgian state cannot be realised beyond the boundaries of a particularly Georgian Christianity. While not always tangible, the Church harvested the anti-Western sentiments through a subtly subliminal rhetoric. To be sure, rather than loudly declaring these ideas and cursing the West openly, Church leaders have gradually and subtly insinuated these sentiments between the discourse on pure Georgian culture vis-à-vis dangerous foreign ideas. The following excerpt from Patriarch's Christmas Epistle is one of the more sharp declarations of such discontent toward the 'West': 'The West is the world where everything is permitted and violence dominates. It is materially rich but spiritually poor, so it is strange and difficult for Georgians to accept.'[5]

Instead of going against EU openly, the Church has stressed the importance of 'unadulterated culture' and harnessed scepticism toward the feasibility of Georgia's European aspiration. So for instance, while Saakashvili often spoke of a multi-ethnic Georgia, one of religious diversity, and the 'historically tolerant nature of Georgian people', the Church leaders have often reiterated the importance of Orthodox Christianity in sustaining the Georgian State, culture and national identity and veiled anti-Western sentiments in their insistent rhetoric about pure Georgian traditions and culture.

Such a tactic played well into the nationalist vulnerabilities and aligned public perceptions of the present with the pre-existing conceptions of the past, while reinforcing certain discursive frames within which to conceive Georgia's future. This was possible, especially because of the complex cultural construct for imagining nationhood in which nationalism and orthodoxy interweave as mutually constitutive forces, as interdependent sources of moral authority and cultural legitimacy. The centre of power both for the State and for the Church, then, is not self-sustained, self-oriented (i.e. nation and religion respectively), certainly not divorced in the dichotomy of secular versus sacred, but rather gravitating toward one another. In other words, the State lends its legitimacy from the Church. It has to, because the Church is declared as the single most authoritative and trustworthy institution among some 80 per cent of the Georgian population (according to several surveys). Yet, this very power of the religious institution rests on its capacity to insinuate itself between the sacred and the secular of the nationalist ideology. Thus the Church's authority is not singular, it is not self-derived, but it has to annex the secular symbols of nationhood in its own domain to harvest the full right of enforcing ideological obedience in its subjects.

This, of course, has antecedents from different historical pasts that act upon current context in ample ways. Nationalism, as Bruce Kapferer has put it 'makes the political religious and places the nation above politics' (1988: 1). In Georgia this came to be realised in a most literal sense, as the Georgian Orthodox Church institutionalised the ethno-nationalist doctrine into its orthodox practice, thus making religion political. In Viktor Shnirelman's (1998) words, since late 1980s Georgian nationalism emphasised the role of Georgia as a 'stronghold of Christianity' in a hostile Muslim environment (p. 58). So, after the collapse of the Soviet Union, not only did nationalism become a hegemonic ideology, but in subsequent years religious essentialisation of such elements of collective identity as ethnicity and faith fed into social and political frictions, struggles for power, and eventually resulted in a civil war and multiple ethnic conflicts (see Pelkmans 2006; Grant and Yalçın-Heckmann 2007).

Because of the pervasive power of the nationalist sentiment, beginning from early 1990s, the Orthodox Church started to consolidate its power through appropriation and incorporation of secular spaces into its sacred domain. The most common practice of this became canonisation of secular figures that had significance for the national narrative or nationalist ideology, among them the nation's founding fathers, kings symbolizing Georgia's Golden Age or public figures who have played an important role in the process of Georgian nation-making, but had no connection to the Church or religious activism in any meaningful way. Canonisation, as a religious and cultural practice, is an act of monumentalisation and sacralisation that is aimed at producing a crystal-lised image of a symbolically meaningful figure. As canonical symbols, historical figures become both intractable and intact, their name can only enter public debate from a single, univocal perspective. Such images cease to be reflected upon, critically discussed, inflected or contested, instead they can only be upheld as the icons that signify the power of a religious institution and are venerated as authorities of the divine nature.

By usurping and consecrating secular spaces and discourses, the Church asserted its ownership over 'Georgianness' as a category of its authority and inscribed it into Georgian Orthodoxy. As Patriarch Ilia II stated in one of his sermons made in early 1990s in an effort against rising popularity of the Jehovah's witness: 'Every person who betrays the Orthodoxy and our Church [...] will be betrayer of his/her nation, thus, every men who contributes to spreading sectarian teachings and different religions will be declared as the enemy of Georgian nation.'[6]

It is from this powerful symbolic position nested in-between secular nationalism and Orthodox patriotism that the Georgian Church has been advancing its political and geopolitical doctrine. This has had ample and vividly demonstrable impact on Georgian public space and popular opinions, especially to the extent of Georgia's 'pro-European' vis-à-vis 'pro-Russian' orientation. Georgia's Patriarch has promoted ideas on the 'purity of Georgian culture' with a veiled anti-Western sentiment, from as early as the 1990s. The following excerpts from his speeches are illustrative:

> High culture and developed technology are not sufficient for people's happiness. There are values which are formed in a nation's life over the centuries, and losing them is a crime. For us such is Orthodox Christianity: bestowed by disciples, music that astonishes everyone [he has Georgian folk music in mind], our language and script filled with mystery and majesty, spectacular art, iconography, architecture, our beautiful customs. Which traditions of East and West can be compared to this? Unfortunately, we have not yet fully comprehended the treasure we own.
> (Patriarch Ilia II, Christmas Message, 1994–1995)

> Today the times have changes and with that the methods of evil, too. Today nobody uses force to disgrace national pride and impinge upon religious beliefs. Degrading our traditions and ways of life is accomplished through different methods ... So today every one of us is facing a choice: abandon the normal path of the homeland or internalise imposed false culture? Resist informational pressure (he implies the internet) or preserve the heritage of our ancestors and enduring values?
> (Patriarch Ilia II, 2008)

As Kapferer points out,

> [when] made into a religious object, culture becomes the focus of devotion. It can have the character of a religious fetish, an idol, a thing which has self-contained magical properties capable of recreating and transforming the realities of experience in its image.
> (1988: 2)

In the practice of religious nationalism, culture becomes an accessory to power when a 'threat to culture' is invented and some 'other' is construed in terms of the threat. In the Patriarch's words trading the 'national treasure', which includes Orthodoxy as its defining element but is not its singular denominator, for the West with its 'high culture and technological development' is 'a crime'. This statement sets up a conflict in which the Georgian language, folk music, traditional culture and art are endangered by the 'other's culture' which cannot even 'be compared' to the Georgian one. His dictum is clear: Georgians need no model to which to aspire, what it needs is to preserve the 'treasure' it owns, the cornerstone of which is Orthodox Christianity. As the Patriarch related on a different occasion 'In our ancestors' consciousness, love for religious belief and love for the homeland were as undivided as was the divine and human nature of Christ'.[7] Such statements inscribe both

Georgian identity and patriotic duty in the domain of Orthodox Christianity; Georgianness becomes indissolubly attached to Orthodoxy while the Church acquires unquestionable authority in both secular and sacred dimensions of nationhood.

With such sacralisation of the secular and secularisation of religious, the Church has attained two-fold power and has become a major rival (if not superior and hegemonic) vis-à-vis the State. Such fusion of religion, nation and Georgian statehood in a single indissoluble whole has been often expressed in statements like: 'Orthodox faith is the spine of our national body' by Patriarch Ilia II (*Easter Message,* 1992).[8] The shrine set up in the school hallway in one of Tbilisi's private schools provides an ample example of the social ramifications of this discursive synthesis of sacred and secular.

Hence, regardless of Saakashvili's attempt to inscribe 'Europeanisation' into the nation's memory and define Europe as Georgia's natural historical landscape, predetermined by the nation's ancestral 'compass', for many Georgians the 'West' was an unfamiliar cultural terrain. The idea of cultural relatedness to some 'other' went against a nationalist cosmology that emphasised Georgia's cultural unbelonging, its immutably sharp boundedness. Many Georgians had been in the habit of acknowledging a singular form of relationship to the rest of the world, and it was not one of 'belonging' to somebody else's civilisation, not of being similar, a borrower. Instead, it is one of dissent and difference, maintaining cultural singularity through resistance and dissension.

'The fake music of Orthodox brotherhood'

The discourse on Orthodoxy is significant not only as part of cultural identity and nationalist rhetoric, but in terms of its capacity to have geopolitical implications. Namely, the issue with the Orthodox imperative is that it insinuates on favouring the Orthodox 'familiar-neighbour' Russia over the non-Orthodox 'stranger' West. This is where the tension between 'friend' versus 'occupant' has most political implications. It is this colonial linkage of Orthodoxy and Russia and the post-colonial power of this frame to shape national and political subjectivities that problematise State–Church relations. Orthodoxy becomes a geopolitical cost, but only in the narrative frame of 'friendship' and 'spiritual preservation'. This is why much political and ideological capital has been spent by Saakashvili's administration to dismantle the myth on Russia's 'orthodox benevolence'. The Museum of Soviet Occupation in the centre of Tbilisi is one limpid instantiation of this counter-ideological impetus and is providing an unquestionable proof that Russia had invested considerably in annihilating Georgia's religious elite and that Soviet regime acted on its deliberate intention to destroy the nation's religious heritage, by destroying churches throughout the entire country. This latter, for instance, is represented in the form of an archival exhibition of several hundred documents that provide clear evidence of the damages inflicted upon churches and religious clergy over several decades.

Such a breach between the State rhetoric and the country's most author-itative institution's ideology did not always float to the surface, exactly because of the mutual interdependence of the State's and Church's authority. For most of it, such altercation materialised in indirect addresses that ampli-fied the subterranean tension and enforced a sense among many that Russia, after all, may not be 'that much of an enemy'.

Conversely, Saakashvili's allies but also liberal intellectuals and progressive elite increasingly and more intensely alienated themself from the Church, and became more vocal in overt criticism. Some labelled the Georgian Church Russia's 'Trojan horse' – an institution that has served its imperialist agenda since the Tsarist regime. For instance, the right-wing liberal magazine 'Tabula' featured a column *The Law of Russian-Georgian Eternity* (*qartul rusuli maradisobis kanoni*) outlining the long history of relations between Russian and Georgian Churches in a section 'Trojan Horse'. The following quote highlights the general pathos of the author's opinion: 'in reality, this naive hope in a common faith (*ertmortsmuneoba* in Georgian literally is commonfaith-ness) played the role of a real Trojan horse in the preparation for [Georgia's] occupation and annexation' (22 February 2013).

On 25 September 2013, President Saakashvili delivered one of his final speeches at the United Nations. In it, he spoke of Russia's aggressive politics and the threat to freedom in the face of the Eurasian Union. Half of his speech was possibly meaningless to his immediate audience, but made lot of sense in the context of the Georgian discursive battlefield:

> When we hear the fake music of the Orthodox brotherhood sung by Russian imperialists, can't we hear the true voice of the Patriarch Kirion, who was assassinated, or the eternal voice of the Patriarch Ambrosi Khelaia, who was tortured during days and weeks only because he appealed to the Geneva Conference against the invasion of his country? And he told his Russian interrogators: 'You can have my body, my flesh, but you will never have my soul.' Are we so deaf as not to hear the voices of the killed bishops and priests, tortured by Russian imperialists and Russian communists? Are we so uneducated that we do not recall who has repainted our churches and erased our sacred frescos?
>
> Are we so blind today not to see the destruction of our churches by the same people, who erased our churches in [inaudible] now in the occupied territories?
>
> (Civil.ge. 2013)

For the Western audience, neither Patriarch Kirion nor Ambrosi Khelaia awake any meaningful associations, let alone have any weight for the kind of moral argument Saakashvili was making. But for Georgians these are both religious and national heroes who have been sacrificed at the altar of the nationhood by the hands of the Russian 'occupants'. In making his point he deviated from what the imminent, immediate issue was, to speak of what was temporally distant and conceptually remote from his immediate audience, yet what he spoke of was at the heart of his nation's 'webs of meanings' (Geertz 1973). His concluding remarks speared through the discursive, ideological and political intricacies fleshed out in this chapter and while his moral argument employed whole another set of terms and frameworks to persuade Western audience of the 'evil' of Russia, for his own national public he relied on the culturally embedded symbols to dismantle the myth of Russian-Georgian brotherhood.

While religion and politics are inescapably tied to one another almost anywhere, it is especially in the domain of Eastern Christianity that we find the most intricate cultural and historical ties between faith and nationalism. Within that, the Georgian paradigm of 'Orthodoxy' represents a distinctly complex construct that creates the knot between religious and political through multi-vocal and multivalent symbolics. Meanings that are weaved into the 'Orthodox faith' have connotations for the Georgian national identity, memory myths pertaining to the very images of national character and spirituality. At the same time this same construct emanates the power of the Church as a religious and as a national institution, but most significantly it embodies the notion of 'Orthodox brotherhood' between Russia and Georgia, perhaps one of the most complex and contested relations between a former Empire and a post-colony that infringes upon current geopolitical battles in the region.

Notes

1 Translation by D. M. Lang, from *Lives and Legends of the Georgian Saints*, London: George Allen & Unwin 1956, pp. 13–39.
2 This chapter is based on the extensive field research conducted between 2010–2013 in Georgia, and the analysis of extensive textual data, which involved school curriculum, history textbooks, media sources and over 300 essays written by young Georgian students.
3 Title of the head of the Georgian Orthodox Church, used since early 11th century.
4 In the mythic ideation of Georgian history, national narrative creates a paradigm of the nation's destiny one that suggests that when united and mobilised Georgians can defeat any enemy, but internal friction and treason is what tips the fate in favour of their invaders (see Wertsch 2005; Wertsch and Batiashvili 2012; Batiashvili 2012). Thus, according to this patterned representation, Georgianness as both a hypothetical and normative model simultaneously embodies two polarities of the character: self-sacrificing heroism and self-defeating betrayal.
5 Christmas Epistle of 1994–1995, Epistles, Speeches, Teachings, Vol. I. Tbilisi, 1997.
6 Ilia II *epistoleni, sityvani, qadagebani,* [Epistles, Speeches, Sermons] Volume II, Tbilisi 1997, see www. orthodoxy.ge.
7 www.orthodoxy.ge.
8 Patriarch Ilia II, 'Epistles, Speeches, Preachings', Volume 1, Tbilisi 1997.

References

Aleksidze, N. 2016. 'A Nation among Other Nations: The Political Theology of the Conversion of Georgia.' In *Quisest Quiligno Pugnat? Missionaries and*

Evangelization in Late Antique and Medieval Europe (4th–13th Centuries). Edited by E. Piazza, pp. 227–245. Verona: Alteritas.

Batiashvili, N. 2012. 'The "Myth" of the Self: The Georgian National Narrative and Quest for "Georgianness".' In *Memory and Political Change*. Edited by A. Assmann and L. Shortt, pp. 186–200. New York: Palgrave Macmillan.

Civil.ge. 2013. 'Saakashvili's Speech at the UN General Assembly – 2013.' *Civil.Ge Daily News Online*. Last access: 30 March 2014.

Geertz, C. 1973. *The Interpretation of Cultures: Selected Essays*. New York: Basic.

Grant, B. and L. Yalçın-Heckmann. 2007. *Caucasus Paradigms: Anthropologies, Histories and the Making of a World Area*. Münster: Lit.

Gurchiani, K. 2017. 'How Soviet Is the Religious Revival in Georgia: Tactics in Everyday Religiosity', *Europe-Asia Studies* 69(3): 508–531.

Karpov, V., E. Lisovskaya, and D. Barry. 2012. 'Ethnodoxy: How Popular Ideologies Fuse Religious and Ethnic Identities', *Journal for the Scientific Study of Religion* 51(4): 638–655.

Kapferer, B. 1988. *Legends of People, Myths of State: Violence, Intolerance, and Political Culture in Sri Lanka and Australia*. Washington: Smithsonian Institution.

Pelkmans, M. 2006. 'Assymetries on the 'Religious Market' in Kyrgyzstan'. In *The Postsocialist Religious Question: Faith and Power in Central Asia and East-Central Europe*. Edited by Ch. Hann and the 'Civil Religion' Group, pp. 29–46. Münster: LIT Verlag.

Putkaradze, T. n.d. *History of Georgia: A Short Version* (*sakartvelos istoria: mokle varianti*), unpublished manuscript, available online: www.scribd.com (last accessed 15 September 2018).

Rayfield, D. 2012. *Edge of Empires: A History of Georgia*. London: Reaktion.

Shnirelman, V. 1998. 'National Identity and Myths of Ethnogenesis in Transcaucasia'. In *Nation-Building in the Post-Soviet Borderlands: The Politics of National Identities*. Edited by G. Smith, V. Law, A. Wilson, A. Bohr and E. Allworth, pp. 48–67. Cambridge: Cambridge University Press.

Tabula 2013. 'The Law of Russian-Georgian Eternity', *Tabula Online Magazine. Tabula*, 22 February (last accessed 5 April 2014).

Vinitzky-Seroussi, V. 2002. 'Commemorating a Difficult Past: Yitzhak Rabin's Memorials', *American Sociological Review* 67(1): 30.

Waal, Th. De. 2011. *Georgia's Choice: Charting a Future in Uncertain Times*. Washington DC: Carnegie Endowment.

Wertsch, J. 2005. 'Georgia as a Laboratory for Democracy', *Demokratizatsiya: The Journal of Post-Soviet Democratization* 13(4): 519–535.

Wertsch, J. V. and N. Batiashvili. 2012. 'Mnemonic Communities and Conflict'. In *Trust and Conflict: Representation, Culture and Dialogue*. Edited by I. Marková and A. Gillespie. Hove, East Sussex: Routledge.

White, H. 1981. 'The Value of Narrativity in the Presentation of Reality'. In *On Narrative*. Edited by J. T. W. Mitchell, pp. 1–23. Chicago, IL: University of Chicago Press.

10 The end of the pro-Orthodox consensus

Religion as a new cleavage in Russian society[1]

Dmitry Uzlaner

In their famous study of cleavages, Lipset and Rokkan (1967) list 'religious vs secular' as one of the key lines that historically divide modern national societies. Opposition between secular and religious groups is an important dimension of political confrontation. Although the logic of this argument is solid, post-Soviet Russia has heretofore been a curious exception in this respect. Religion did not become socially insignificant and irrelevant as a result of the process of Soviet secularisation. On the contrary, after the fall of the USSR, religion attracted much attention, but with little confrontation or tension. There are, of course, disagreements among different religious organisations or even within them (Kostiuk 2002). There are 'cult controversies', including a significant debate concerning so-called sects and new religious movements (Shterin 2012). And the long and difficult struggle against militant Islamism continues. But religion in general – at least in its traditional form – has largely been a matter of consensus, not cleavage, for Russian society.

This peculiar post-Soviet, or 'post-atheist', situation is called the 'pro-Orthodox', or sometimes the 'pro-religious', consensus in academic literature. In this chapter, I will analyse this peculiar consensus, which I argue is now falling apart. We are witnessing a slow but dramatic break-up of this pro-Orthodox consensus.

What is the pro-Orthodox (pro-religious) consensus?

Before discussing the pro-Orthodox consensus in detail, I will make certain theoretical clarifications. Following Karel Dobbelaere (2002; 2004: 230), I consider secularisation and desecularisation to be multi-dimensional concepts. These processes can happen on three distinct levels: the macro-level (Dobbelaere 2002: 29–35; the level of social structure or *societal* secularisation/desecularisation), the meso-level (Dobbelaere 2002: 35–38; the level where society and the individual meet, such as a community or an organisation) and the micro-level (Dobbelaere 2002: 38–43; the *individual* level or the level of personal beliefs and practices). I refer to the meso-level not only in the sense of organisational secularisation/ desecularisation, as Dobbelaere implied, nor merely in the sense of 'change occurring in the posture of religious organizations … in matters of belief, morals and rituals' (Dobbelaere 2002: 25), but rather in a broader sense that includes popular attitudes to these organisations, public approval or disapproval of their activities, public trust or distrust towards their representatives, or a willingness or lack of willingness to follow their advice. In this sense, the concept of a 'pro-Orthodox consensus' refers to the meso- and partially to the macro-level, where the latter is seen as the logical continuation of the former.

The term 'pro-Orthodox consensus' was coined by Furman and Kaariainen (2007a). These scholars consider the pro-Orthodox consensus to be one of the most vivid manifestations of a so-called religious renaissance in post-Soviet Russia. With this concept, they basically wanted to communicate a very simple idea: 'The "good" and "very good" attitude to Orthodoxy becomes the firm and 'definitive' attitude of the overwhelming majority, virtually universal' (Furman and Kaariainen 2007a: 20–22). This consensus is 'nationwide, inasmuch as the proportion of people whose attitude to Orthodoxy is "good" and "very good" is significantly larger than the proportion of believers' (Furman and Kaariainen (2007a: 22). Paradoxically, 'the "good attitude" to Orthodoxy is typical not only for believers, but also for the overwhelming majority of those who identify themselves as "undecided", "unbelievers" and even "atheists"' (Furman and Kaariainen (2007a: 22; see also Ładykowska in this volume). According to Furman and Kaariainen (2007b: 81), therefore, 'atheists and unbelievers are in a sense also part of this "pro-Orthodox consensus"'. So the pro-Orthodox consensus basically signifies the general acceptance of Russian Orthodoxy, and of the Moscow Patriarchate as the institutional embodiment of Orthodoxy, which is shared by everyone regardless of class, gender, income, occupation and even regardless of one's belief or unbelief.

Sergey Lebedev (2015: 14), the author of the only article that tries to elaborate this concept further, identifies three meanings of the pro-Orthodox consensus:

> A trust within society toward the Church as represented by the Russian Orthodox Church; the prevalence of a positive image of Orthodoxy and the Church; the predominance of positive social expectations from the Church and religion, and from their interaction with society.[2]

This is the pro-Orthodox consensus at the meso-level.

But how do Furman and Kaariainen conceptualise the macro-level of the pro-Orthodox consensus? They consider it to be a logical continuation of the meso-level. As if projecting the pro-Orthodox consensus into the future, they write,

> in the religious sphere, these peculiarities of Russian society and its post-Communist development are manifested in the proclivity for a state Church, for the conferral to Orthodoxy of the status of an official ideology and for the limitation of the activities of other religions that are mostly new to Russian society … The old tsarist formula of 'Orthodoxy,

Autocracy, and Nationality' and the Soviet formula of 'moral-political unity' are seemingly being re-created in a watered-down version, along with other ideological symbols ... The Church and state power are together once again, and as they did before the Revolution of 1917, they are strengthening one another. A sort of 'interchange' of popularity and authority is taking place between the Church and the President of Russia, which enhances the further strengthening of the 'pro-Orthodox consensus' and the role of religion as a symbol of national unity.

(Furman and Kaariainen 2007b: 94)

Basically, Furman and Kaariainen connect the pro-Orthodox consensus with the traditional practice of close State–Church relations analysing the meso- and macro-levels as mutually enhancing one another. Lebedev (2015: 15) also considers these two levels to be seamlessly connected: 'The institutional element of the pro-Orthodox consensus is based upon the aligned interests of the two basic social institutions: the state and the Church (as represented by [the Moscow Patriarchate of the Russian Orthodox Church])'.

I will demonstrate below that this connection is highly problematic, and includes tensions and conflict too (see Köllner 2016; 2018). At the very point of transition from the meso- to the macro-level, the pro-Orthodox consensus is gradually beginning to disintegrate. The disintegration of this consensus on the meso-level is both the reason for and the consequence of the continuing movement of the pro-Orthodox consensus to the macro-level.

But what about the pro-religious consensus? Furman and Kaariainen state quite clearly that this consensus is 'actually "pro-Orthodox", and not "pro-religious" per se'. They make this claim, because they believe that in Russia, 'the Russian Orthodox Church is thrown into sharp relief among all religions, towards most of which the [popular] attitude is considerably worse – and towards some of which it is simply negative' (Furman and Kaariainen 2007a: 22). Yet, I still insist that this consensus is 'pro-religious'. By 'pro-religious', I mean the general positive attitude towards religion in the sense of a broad approval of the transcendent dimension of human existence, as opposed to what Taylor (2007) called the 'immanent frame' and 'closed world structures'.

Although the concept of a pro-Orthodox consensus as such is not particularly important for scholars who study religion in Russia, since it was not developed any further since Furman and Kariainen first coined it, it is still very significant as a 'background concept'. Religious processes in Russia are still analysed against the backdrop of a pro-Orthodox consensus and a religious renaissance. These assumptions are taken for granted, too obvious to be discussed in detail within concrete studies of religious education, of 'the turn to traditional values', or of new legal initiatives in the religious sphere, among others. The pro-Orthodox consensus is mentioned as a matter of fact, and then the discussion moves on (see Willems 2012: 30).

If we problematise this assumption, showing that the 'religious renaissance' is over and that the pro-Orthodox consensus is foundering, we would be able to analyse many events and ideas from a more robust perspective. We would be able to see, for example, the current religious processes that are going on in Russia in a multidimensional perspective. It is this intuition that guides my analysis.

Methodological reflections: what is happening to the pro-Orthodox consensus?

The main and sometimes the only instrument of the sociological analysis of religion in Russia is the opinion poll. Opinion polls show only slight variations in the pro-Orthodox consensus. In this sense, the position of the Russian Orthodox Church seems secure (Levada Centre 2017). For this reason, many scholars continue to mention the pro-Orthodox consensus as a given. Yet, what is it that makes me think that something else is going on here?

I strongly maintain that opinion polls, though revealing some important information, conceal important currents. A growing new reality, which is not yet fully visible, is beginning to undermine the status quo of the pro-Orthodox consensus and the religious renaissance. In order to notice this new reality, however, one needs to shift one's perspective.

Vyacheslav Karpov, in his conceptual analysis of desecularisation, makes an important distinction between the 'European' and the 'American' understandings of culture. In this context, he writes:

> The former tends to view culture as comprising supra-individual symbolic systems and steers clear of methodological individualism in its analysis. The latter more typically approaches cultures as aggregates of beliefs, values, attitudes, and norms shared by society's members and attributable to the individuals' locations in society.
>
> (Karpov 2010: 241)

This second 'American' approach to culture and cultural change still prevails. Karpov (2010: 241) continues: 'While survey-based assessments of religious trends have proliferated in recent decades, large-scale content-analytical studies of the arts, literature, philosophy, and other cultural subsystems have been marginal if not altogether forsaken by social scientists'. He then concludes, 'in the absence of long-term content-analytical studies of culture (including its contemporary audio-visual and digital manifestations), research on current secularizing and counter-secularizing trends produces an incomplete and potentially distorted portrayal of religion's status in modern society' (Karpov 2010: 242).

Karpov gives illustrative examples of how this overemphasis on opinion polls can distort our understanding of religious processes. For example,

> the actual and potential influence of radical Islamism may appear very small if we solely use survey data on Muslims' opinions to measure it.

Yet, a different assessment of radical Islamism's influence could result from a study of religio-political ideas prevalent in school textbooks, state-controlled TV broadcasts, and numerous radical Internet sites.

(Karpov 2010: 242f.)

Karpov then provides an even more telling example:

A 1945 survey found that no Germans at all (0 percent) said Hitler was right in his treatment of the Jews, 19 percent thought he went too far, and 77 percent opined that Hitler's actions were in no way justified ... Based on this post-factum conducted survey, the Holocaust becomes a fully incomprehensible event.

(Karpov 2010: 243f. citing Gordon 1984: 198)

In my analysis of the pro-Orthodox consensus, I will follow Karpov's intuition and move beyond the standard analysis of opinion polls. In their stead, I plan to examine a broader cultural landscape in order to assess which new trends and developments have become visible since 2012.

The end of the Pro-Orthodox consensus

Other scholars have already begun to note problems with the pro-Orthodox consensus (see also Batiashvili, Iordache and Živković in this volume on other Orthodox countries). Alexander Agadjanian (2015: 254) writes, 'in spite of the common "pro-Orthodox consensus" and the reports of high approval ratings for the Church in surveys, some new groups and actors emerged who consciously resisted the rise of religion's public presence'. Likewise, Aleksandr Verkhovskii (2014: 69) has noted that 'the term "pro-Orthodox consensus," used until now by Russian political observers, is ceasing to be applicable, because for the opposition, criticism of the ROC [Russian Orthodox Church] is becoming not only permissible but also unavoidable'. Although such observations are prescient, no one has yet provided a systematic analysis of these new challenges and their influence on the pro-Orthodox/pro-religious consensus.

The Pussy Riot case as a turning point

Jürgen Habermas (2009: 55) once said that an intellectual's most important ability is 'an avantgardistic instinct for relevances'. In the Russian context, the task of intellectuals is performed by artists who possess this necessary 'modicum of the courage required for polarizing, provoking, and pamphleteering' (Habermas 2009: 55). Correspondingly, it is exhibitions and works of art that have become the first sites of cultural change. As Agadjanian (2015: 254) writes,

the most visible and widely mediated anticlerical activities happened to emerge in the sphere of the contemporary arts. A few exhibitions and performances directly targeted 'clericalisation', such as the 'Beware: Religion!' exhibition in 2003, that became a *cause célèbre* in courts, [and] a few exhibits at galleries owned or directed by Marat Guelman.

These performances turned out to be merely the prolegomena to a much more significant event.

Any analysis of contemporary religious life in Russia should begin with the Pussy Riot case as a key turning point, as the very episode that revealed what was hidden below the surface of the Russian religio-political iceberg. It revealed the 'social guts' that had until then remained cloaked beneath a smooth social fabric. While one would be hard-pressed to argue for the artistic dignity of Pussy Riot's 'punk prayer' performance in February 2012, the debates that followed set the stage for many further trends and developments (see Uzlaner 2014). Literally all of the cultural phenomena that I consider here are rooted in the 'punk prayer' in the broadest sense (i.e. not just in the performance itself, but also in the debate that ensued, in the legal consequences, etc.). The whole story could be seen as a 'social drama' that, in the words of Victor Turner (1975: 35), brought:

> fundamental aspects of society, normally overlaid by the customs and habits of daily intercourse, into frightening prominence. People have to take sides in terms of 'deeply entrenched moral imperatives', and they must then weigh their 'loyalty and obligation' to specific social affiliations.

The Pussy Riot incident revealed what Turner calls the 'root paradigms' of Russian society concerning Church–State relations, the presence of religion in the public sphere and much more (see Schroeder and Karpov 2013).

The 'punk prayer' took place at a peculiar moment – a period of mass political protests against alleged electoral falsifications during the Parliamentary elections of 4 December 2011, which marked 'a watershed in the political history of post-Soviet Russia' (Yablokov 2014: 622) and the beginning of a new electoral cycle that would end with Vladimir Putin being elected to become President of the Russian Federation for the third time on 4 March 2012. Patriarch Kirill, the head of the Russian Orthodox Church since 2009, had made certain statements that were widely interpreted as supportive of Putin's return to the presidential post and as disapproving of anti-government civil protests.[3] The 'punk prayer', which would itself become a watershed in the religious history of post-Soviet Russia, was a reaction to this sequence of events, reflected in its text:

> Patriarch Gundiaev[4] believes in Putin
> Would be better, the bastard, if he believed in God!
> The Virgin's belt won't replace political gatherings
> The eternal Virgin Mary is with us in our protests.[5]

The full lyrics express a list of tensions connected to the Russian Orthodox Church – the dark Soviet past of the Church hierarchy, the limitations of basic liberal freedoms in the name of religious traditions, the persecution of homosexuals, discrimination against women, the luxurious lifestyle of some priests, the financial machinations of the Church, the penetration of religion into secular schools and, of course, the support of the ruling political regime. This constitutes a nearly exhaustive list of ongoing conflicts surrounding Orthodoxy.

The Pussy Riot case turned out to be a catalyst of the two processes. On the one hand, Church–State relations intensified with a strong turn to 'traditional values' and a public resurgence of Russia's civilisational identity as the last bastion of traditional Christian values (Sharafutdinova 2014; Stepanova 2015; Tsygankov 2016; Agadjanian 2017; Østbø 2017; Robinson 2017), in addition to a new legal reality of laws supporting Russian Orthodox positions and giving the Church real legal instruments to fight its critics and rivals.[6] This is probably what Furman and Kaariainen (2007b: 94) had in mind when they wrote that 'the Church and state power are together once again', as a logical extension of the pro-Orthodox consensus to the macro-level. On the other hand, the tension between parts of civil society and the Russian Orthodox Church was also beginning to grow. The 'punk prayer' was just the beginning of a cascade of media scandals that significantly aggravated the Church's reputation – the apartment with dust,[7] the Patriarch's vanishing watch (Schwirtz 2012; Jarzyñska 2014), pedophilia and homosexuality scandals,[8] and a series of car accidents involving drunken priests.[9] This negative wave of media attention was so strong that Church officials began to claim that there was a targeted campaign and even an 'information war' against the Church.[10] A segment of Russian society was none too pleased about this new stage of State–Church relations.

Contrary to expectations, the extension of the pro-Orthodox consensus to the macro-level turned out to be its death knell. Instead of remaining a matter of consensus, religion was quickly becoming a matter of constant tension and confrontation. Patriarch Kirill acknowledged this fact when he explained the reason for this 'information war' against the Church through a self-justifying interpretation:

> The Church has become 'uncomfortable' for a certain part of society, because it has raised its pastoral voice louder and louder to testify to the world about the Truth, [to distinguish between] what is God's truth and what is a lie.[11]

To a certain extent, the Patriarch is quite correct in his reflections. Scholars who study religious developments in Russia, including Agadjanian (2006: 174), have directed attention to:

> a striking gap between both the dynamics and the values of … two sets of data: ideational religiousness has rapidly risen and come close to

European and world averages, but practical religiousness has not changed much and remains one of the world's lowest.

Agadjanian (2006: 174) indicates that by this, he means that religion matters as 'a working symbolic resource which is still "good to think with" concerning the basic foundations of society'. But this vague 'semiotic religiosity', as Agadjanian (2006: 174) calls it, has very little relevance for actual social practices, for the way people live and make important decisions. What Patriarch Kirill has attempted to do is to transform this symbolic resource – including the pro-Orthodox consensus – into something more tangible, by way of real influence on state decisions, real legal privileges, real influence on the way people live, love, have sex and raise children (see Filatov and Malashenko 2011). In that sense, he has disrupted the post-Soviet religious *status quo* described by Agadjanian as the high symbolic significance of religion that is compensated by its almost total absence in everyday existence. It is, therefore, no surprise that such a disruption has quickly created high levels of tension around religious issues. The pro-Orthodox consensus has begun to break up, and religion has quickly turned into one of the most fraught cleavages in Russian society.

All these tendencies were revealed during the Pussy Riot case, which has henceforward marked the formation of a new religious landscape in Russia. Below, I will describe the most interesting cultural phenomena that illustrate my thesis that we are on the verge of a collapse of the pro-Orthodox consensus.

Leaving the Russian Orthodox Church – the phenomenon of ex-believers

One of the most significant signs of dramatic change in the religious landscape is the phenomenon of ex-believers. People often leave churches, but only in the second decade of the twenty-first century have these former believers revealed themselves to be such a visible cultural 'event'. By 'ex-believers' I mean those who previously had a lengthy, intense experience within the Russian Orthodox Church – as monks, priests or pious laymen – but who, for one reason or another, decided to quit the Church. These people, moreover, decided not only to quit, but also to make their negative experiences available for public consumption.

This phenomenon has come about for several reasons. First, the generation that was attracted to the Church during the religious renaissance and the pro-Orthodox consensus is beginning to reflect on what went wrong with what Patriarch Kirill calls 'the miracle … of the rebirth of the faith'.[12] In addition, thanks to social media we now have new sources of information beyond the vertical sources under state or Church control. Finally, something has changed in the cultural climate that has persuaded people to remain silent no longer, but to speak openly in public. They feel that their experience has relevance not only for their personal lives, but also for a wider audience.

There are numerous examples of ex-believers who are publicly active, but I will limit this discussion to the three most significant. Maria Kikot' (2017) published a bestselling autobiography, *Confession of a Former Lay Sister*. This book began as a series of blog posts (Kikot' 2016), which attracted much attention (with thousands of comments under each new post) and was eventually published by a leading Russian publishing house. *Confession* tells the story of a young woman who sincerely and deeply converted to Orthodox Christianity and became a novitiate in one of the most famous convents of Russia. Instead of experiencing a deep spiritual transformation, however, she experienced a humiliating life in a quarrelsome community of women headed by a tyrannical Mother Superior who was literally creating a cult around herself. In the end, the heroine decided to leave the convent, having become deeply disillusioned with her former ideals and spiritual advisers. The popularity of this book could be explained by the intimate way the author describes the underbelly of the Russian religious revival and the supposed triumph of the Christian faith. *Confession* was not the only book of its kind published in recent years. A former priest, Dmitry Savvin (2017), has published a similar book which describes the everyday life of a typical Orthodox diocese.

Grigorii Baranov, a former monk (Monk Mikhail) who spent dozens of years at a distant monastery before deciding to leave, is another telling example of an ex-believer. After quitting Orthodoxy, Baranov launched a vigorous social media campaign on *YouTube*, reflecting on his personal experience and inviting other people with similar experiences to share their stories with the general public. He conducts interviews with leading Russian atheists (Nevzorov and Baranov 2013) and creates video content with telling names like 'Orthodoxy as a way to degeneration', 'Orthodoxy in law' and 'The Orthodox Taliban'.[13] In 2014, with a goal to offer 'assistance in the deliverance from Orthodox dependency', Baranov started the project 'Rastserkovlenie' ('De-Churching', meaning gradual deliverance from Church life, a deliberate wordplay on 'votserkovlenie', the Church's recent conscious effort to 'in-church' nominal Orthodox believers).[14] This project offers psychological support for those who have decided to quit Orthodoxy but have encountered problems as they have moved in that direction.

The online mass media project called 'Ahilla' serves as our final example. Created in 2017 by a former priest, Alexei Pluzhnikov,[15] Ahilla's main goal is to offer 'reflections on the life of the Russian Orthodox Church [and] an independent look from the inside, as well as from the outside'.[16] In Ahilla's manifesto, one encounters a typical story of an ex-believer who has experienced disappointment on his spiritual path and has decided not to remain silent, but to make his disappointment public.[17]

Ahilla publishes online materials that tell the stories not only of former priests or monks, but also of anonymous people from within the Church. The latter are the voices of those who want to talk about the problems they are experiencing, but who are not yet ready to join the group of 'exes'.[18]

The members of this group of 'exes' are far from univocal. Some of these former Orthodox Christians, like Baranov, have turned to atheism and anti-religious ideas. Others have remained loyal to Christianity, but have begun a serious public reflection on what has gone wrong with the Church and what should be done next in order not to allow Russian society to spurn Christianity completely. In this regard, the statement of The Society of Christian Enlightenment, a community of believers who, after a negative experience with the Russian Orthodox Church, decided to start an independent reflection on the fate of Christ's teachings, is illustrative:

> The Pussy Riot incident and the unprecedented reaction to it by Church and state authorities testifies that today in Russia a dangerous situation for our society has taken shape, leading to the discrediting of Christianity and of the Russian Orthodox tradition in people's eyes. The anti-clericalism of part of [Russian] society is acquiring radical atheistic forms and is leading to the total negation of our national religious tradition.[19]

The phenomenon of the 'exes' is the clearest manifestation that the pro-Orthodox consensus, together with the religious renaissance, is over. Even if not all former believers turn to atheism or any other form of antireligious ideas, the naïve 'trust' and 'positive expectations' that existed when the pro-Orthodox consensus was forming within Russian society no longer exists.

Orthodoxy as a new site of conflict

Another new reality is that religion has become an issue around which constant conflicts, broadly debated in mass media, are erupting. This is a new and quite recent phenomenon. Sergey Filatov (2014: 17) argued that:

> since the end of the 1980s, an informal consensus has existed in Russian society concerning the inadmissibility of criticizing the activities of priests and especially of the leaders of the Russian Orthodox Church. The very few mass media outlets that have violated this consensus were not that popular. This informal ban on criticism was connected to the compassionate attitude to the Church and to believers, who suffered greatly under the Soviet regime.

Thus, the Church was until recently virtually exempt from criticism and free to do whatever it pleased. The situation is changing, however, with the 'punk-prayer' as the critical turning point, and this change has been quite painful, as more recent conflicts have shown. These constantly erupting conflicts are numerous, covering a wide range of spheres – including the political, legal and economic spheres. I have narrowed my analysis here to the cultural sphere specifically. I will assess two types of cultural opposition: one concerning the struggle for property and the other concerning the freedom of artistic expression and the various attempts to limit this freedom for the sake of traditional moral norms.

The Church vs museums

The process of the restitution of Church property has led to intense public debates in Russia concerning the reasonableness of such a practice (Köllner 2018).[20] This has become especially heated when the property in question has been occupied by a museum or another cultural site such as a school or a university.

The biggest debate of this kind is the case of Saint Isaac's Cathedral in St Petersburg, the largest cathedral in the city. It is currently occupied by a museum – the Saint Isaac's Cathedral State Museum-Memorial. In 2015, the Russian Orthodox Church launched a campaign to return this cathedral to its control. In January 2017, the governor of St Petersburg declared that the cathedral would soon be returned to the Church. St Petersburg's Union of Museum Workers considered this statement to be the start of the process of liquidating the museum. Mass demonstrations for and against the return of the cathedral, involving thousands of people, ensued.[21] The fate of the cathedral has yet to be decided. The case of Saint Isaac's Cathedral is probably the most famous recent example, but similar conflicts are taking place around a museum on the Solovetsky Islands (Soldatov 2016) and the Museum of Chersonesus in the Crimea.[22]

This is not simply a conflict over property. Rather, it is a much more serious question over who will control museums and which version of history will be promoted. For this reason, such conflicts have become a matter of great public concern and have engaged many people who are not directly connected to one or another particular museum.

The freedom of expression vs religious feelings

As mentioned above, one of the first conflicts around religion centred on art. 'Ostorozhno, Religiia!' ('Beware, Religion!') (2003) and 'Zapretnoye Isskustvo' ('Forbidden Art') (2006) were just a prelude to a whole chain of similar conflicts. As argued above, the Pussy Riot case was a turning point. After this affair, which resulted not only in the imprisonment of Pussy Riot members but also in the enactment of a special law aimed at punishing those who offend the feelings of religious believers, conflicts of this type have become an ordinary reality of Russian society.

To a certain extent, this is a sign that the religious situation in Russia is beginning to resemble Western patterns more closely. Agadjanian (2006: 177f.) notes:

> Russia faces a common, if not a global, quandary: a conflict between the freedom of speech and cultural (ethnic, religious) feelings ... [as] the

conflict between individual freedom and collective cultural 'feelings' became a subject of ongoing litigation in national and international courts.

What makes the Russian situation less common, at least as compared with Western countries, is the number of such conflicts in a relatively short time span, as well as the intensity of these confrontations. Below, I assess the most noteworthy cases.

On 26 January 2015, Tikhon, the Archbishop of Novosibirsk and Berdsk, sent an official letter to the prosecutor of the Novosibirsk region of the Russian Federation. In the letter, the archbishop expressed his indignation at a performance in the Novosibirsk Opera and Ballet Theatre, where the theatre director Timofey Kuliabin staged a provocative interpretation of Wagner's Tannhäuser, featuring Christ indulging in carnal pleasures in Venera's grotto. According to the archbishop, such a performance offended believers and hurt their feelings.[23] As a result, the head of the theatre was soon replaced with a new Orthodox director, who immediately cancelled the performance.[24]

On 14 August 2015, a group of Orthodox radicals smashed some works by Soviet sculptor Vadim Sidur at an exhibition in Moscow called 'Sculptures that we don't see'.[25] Sidur's works were severely damaged. The perpetrators explained this act of violence by stating that these works offended believers.

Alexei Uchitel' directed the movie 'Matilda' (released in October 2017), which is devoted to the love affair of the future Tsar Nicholas II and Polish ballet dancer Matylda Krzesińska. Since the Russian Orthodox Church has canonised Tsar Nicholas II, a group of Orthodox activists, supported by some deputies in the Russian Duma, launched a campaign to prevent this film from being shown in Russian cinemas. Natalia Poklonskaia, a Duma deputy, has even threatened that those who watch this film would be banned from taking holy communion.[26] In August 2017, an obscure extremist group called 'Christian State – Holy Rus' sent letters to film distributors threatening to burn cinemas that would show 'Matilda'.[27] On 4 September 2017, a man then attempted to set a large cinema in Ekaterinburg on fire by ramming its entrance with a car full of gas balloons and exploding his vehicle. The media calls this man simply 'a Matilda opponent'.[28]

The famous Russian film director Kirill Serebrennikov, whose previous works have explored the question of religious fanaticism,[29] was planning to stage the ballet *Nureyev* (2017) at the Bolshoi Theatre. This ballet is about the well-known Soviet dancer Rudolf Nureyev. In his adaptation of the ballet, Serebrennikov concentrated on the homosexual aspect of Nureyev's life, which led to the delay of its premier.[30] On 22 August 2017, Russian authorities arrested Serebrennikov under suspicion of embezzling government funds through a theatre production company he led called Studio Seven. The underlying reason for this persecution is not clear, but in public opinion, this case is often presented as the punishment of a freethinking artist for his assault on 'traditional values'.[31]

It would not be fair to interpret all of these conflicts as the Russian Orthodox Church standing against artists or against the freedom of expression. In most cases, official representatives of the Russian Orthodox Church have either abstained from taking a position or have tried to be very moderate in their public statements. But in all cases, groups representing at least part of the Orthodox community have initiated the conflicts and have tried to bring them to the desired outcome of limiting artists' activity. Similarly, there is always an opposing group – with fewer and fewer resources – which tries to prevent censorship and to defend the freedom of artistic expression.

The broader cultural sphere

Thus far, I have only discussed those aspects of cultural life that are directly related to religion. But in order to get a fuller picture, it is necessary to take a broader look at what is taking place within Russian culture in general. A content analysis of the most popular groups on Vkontakte (the largest social media site in Russia with 97 million users),[32] including MDK or Lepra, as well as the most popular vloggers on YouTube would reveal much in terms of cultural changes around the pro-Orthodox consensus.[33] Additional cultural phenomena that would require further research include the musical group 'Leningrad', youth culture with rap battles (tens of millions watch these battles on YouTube, which basically means that every young man in Russia is involved), and public opinion leaders. In the absence of such an analysis, however, I will draw the reader's attention to just one case that can tell a lot about what is taking place in Russia.

Ruslan Sokolovsky, a popular YouTube vlogger, was given a suspended sentence of 3.5 years in May 2017 for insulting the feelings of believers, on the basis of the new legal norms that were enacted in the wake of the Pussy Riot case.[34] According to the judge, Sokolovsky made several videos earlier in 2017 that insulted believers. In public opinion, however, this is a case of a vlogger who was arrested merely for catching a Pokemon while playing 'Pokemon Go' in a church. Rather than analyse this case at length, since it is only one of numerous recent cases involving conflict around religion, I will focus on one peculiar detail of this case: motives of the blogger.

When Judge Ekaterina Shoponiak asked Sokolovsky during the trial why he decided to make videos with a clear anticlerical and antireligious message, he was very forthright:

QUESTION: Why did you decide to touch on the issue of religion?
SOKOLOVSKY: Because everybody today brings it up. Because there are many believers online, and there is ongoing social conflict. This is a hotly debated issue.
QUESTION: But for what purpose did you choose such a hotly debated topic?
SOKOLOVSKY: Because it is interesting to me and to [other] people.
QUESTION: Because you get views with this?

SOKOLOVSKY: Yes.

QUESTION: Views in order to get fame and money?

SOKOLOVSKY: Yes to both.

QUESTION: Did you have other motives?

SOKOLOVSKY: No, I didn't have other motives.

QUESTION: What other hot social topics are [debated on the internet]?

SOKOLOVSKY: Too many to mention. The political situation in the country and the way Mentos reacts with Coca-Cola — this gets millions of views.[35]

In these excerpts Sokolovsky utters with striking frankness the essential intuition that seems to drive bloggers and public opinion leaders to talk about religion. They do so not only to express their views (atheistic or not), but also to receive attention, fame, money and millions of views – and all this by way of an issue that is at the centre of social conflict, is as heated as the political situation and attracts as many viewers as videos that show the chemical reaction that occurs when Mentos sweets are thrown into a bottle of Coca-Cola. This strongly confirms my thesis that profound cultural changes are taking place with respect to religion. Religion is becoming a site of constant struggle, tension, and spectacle.

The reaction of the Russian Orthodox Church

My argument concerning the end of the pro-Orthodox consensus can also be illustrated from another angle – the way the Russian Orthodox Church continues to react to these new cultural trends and developments. Again, the turning point was the Pussy Riot case, which has become the model for further (re)action. Soon after the 'punk-prayer', Patriarch Kirill began to talk about an 'information war' against the Church.[36] As Ilia Yablokov (2014: 628) writes:

> From April 2012 onwards, the narrative of a war against the Orthodox Church has dominated the speeches of pro-Kremlin intellectuals and Church representatives, who interpreted public criticism of the Russian Orthodox Church as part of the conspiracy of the West against the Russian nation.

But this was not just the Church's narrative, it was also the political regime's new ideological manoeuvre: 'The confrontational division of Russian society into "the people" and "the conspiring Other" closely connected with the West promoted an image of a loyal majority of Russian citizens who opposed a tiny minority backed by the powerful West' (Yablokov 2014: 633). This was the beginning of a new quality of Church–State relations, which I interpret as an attempt to extend the pro-Orthodox consensus to the macro-level.

This info-wars interpretation, which came on the heels of Pussy Riot's 'punk prayer', has become a model for the reaction to all further cultural developments described above. The logic is as follows:

> Something is happening, but this is not a problem between the Church and 'the people', rather it is a problem of a small minority of enemies who are inspired by the West and who are attacking not just the Church but the core of Russian national identity and culture.

This logic has inspired several restrictive legal initiatives including those against the offence of believers' feelings, against 'homosexual propaganda', and against foreign (and domestic) missionaries, to name a few. Such ideological man-oeuvres could be seen as a desperate attempt to increase the cohesion of the 'Orthodox majority' in order to explain away the growing internal antagonism and to conceal evident cracks in the once-solid pro-Orthodox consensus.

Numerous other cases could add even more detail to our picture. Such cases might include the imposition of religious education at schools and universities (Köllner 2016)[37] and the situation in Ukraine in which Orthodox unity is breaking up as part of the Orthodox flock in Ukraine has become alienated from the Russian Orthodox Church as a result of the ongoing conflict over Eastern Ukraine. Each case considered separately would not allow us to make such far-reaching conclusions, but when we put all of these cases together, we begin to see a new cultural backdrop that seems to be incompatible with the vision of the pro-Orthodox consensus as described by scholars in the first decade of 2000s. In that sense, Karpov (2013: 276) was right when he predicted the growth of critical reactions to Russia's 'desecularisation from above', especially when he foresaw 'an increasingly critical stance towards the ROC-MP [Moscow Patriarchate of the Russian Orthodox Church] and other official religious groups among younger, urban, well-to-do and educated Russians' who, he suggested, would be 'increasingly repulsed by the nationalistic, undemocratic and repressive ethos of official religion'.

Concluding remarks

The concept of a pro-Orthodox consensus was developed on the basis of opinion polls. It would be safest to proclaim the final end of this consensus only once opinion polls were to show significant changes in people's attitudes. This has yet to happen; according to opinion polls, the pro-Orthodox consensus still exists, at least partially. For example, the Levada Centre (2017), one of Russia's leading pollsters, recently reported:

> Orthodoxy remains the dominant confession in Russia. The absolute majority of Russians – 92 to 93 percent of respondents – regard Orthodox believers with respect and benevolence, which means that not only they

themselves [Orthodox believers] but also people of other faiths or atheists share a positive attitude towards them.

The only aspect in which this pro-Orthodox consensus is changing is in the attitude towards the idea that the Church should influence state decisions. The number of people who disapprove of this idea is increasing – from 27 per cent in 2005 to 36 per cent in 2017, whereas the number of those who approve is decreasing – from 16 per cent in 2005 to just 6 per cent in 2017. The same trend is evident in the way these individuals evaluate the influence the Church has on state politics in Russia. The number of those who think that this influence is excessive is increasing, whereas the number of people holding the opposite view is decreasing (Levada Centre 2017). In light of these figures, I can therefore conclude that my argument about the end of the pro-Orthodox consensus is only partly supported by opinion polls results.

I have chosen not to discuss the reliability of these figures for the reason that they are the only data that we have. From the methodological discussion above, however, I argue that the discrepancy between opinion polls and the underlying reality is not a particularly Russian phenomenon, but is rather something that occurs quite frequently elsewhere.

Thus, despite the fact that opinion polls only partially support my argument, a closer look at the level of cultural trends and developments reveals quite significant changes. The Russian Orthodox Church has become the source of nearly endless conflict. The negativity associated with Orthodoxy, and with religion in general (in the sense of the spiritual dimension of life), is rising to the extent that almost every rumour, every accusation – even those that are unfair – is 'hyped' in order to attract extensive public attention. This is true at least within the media that are not controlled by either the Church or the state. In official propaganda, however, this negativity is interpreted as an 'information war' and even a global conspiracy against the Church.

Throughout this chapter, I have avoided any discussion of sociological numbers or the demographic substrate behind this end of the pro-Orthodox consensus. I am not claiming that antireligious sentiment is the new mainstream. I do not know definitively which social groups are no longer part of the pro-Orthodox consensus. Nor am I certain that the trends I have described will not eventually be violently eradicated and suppressed by the state (perhaps at the request of the Church) as elements of foreign aggression against the Russian nation. Rather, my thesis is much more modest – that Russian Orthodoxy and religion in general are no longer factors of national consensus. From now on, it will be a factor of national conflict, just another cleavage that runs along Russia's national community. This is a paradox not anticipated by the scholars who began to talk about the pro-Orthodox consensus. As the Russian Orthodox Church has become more and more integrated into the state, it has become a key ideological element of Russia's 'conservative turn' and has received legal and material benefits. Yet, this macro-level success has coincided with the Church's failure to maintain a popular consensus at the meso-level, the very level at which its positions have thus far been perceived as strong and seemingly unshakable.

This chapter began with a reference to the classical research by Lipset and Rokkan. From their point of view, we can interpret the end of the pro-Orthodox consensus as the normalisation of the religious situation in Russia to a situation of political cleavage between the religious and the secular. Thus, the pro-Orthodox consensus was a peculiar post-atheist phenomenon that could not last long. The conflict over the Church and religion is a sign that Russia is returning to the standard situation of the Western nations, which are deeply divided over religion. Yet Furman and Kaarianen (2007a: 7–11), who introduced the concept of the pro-Orthodox consensus, offer an alternative interpretation: they talk about pendulum swings in Russia's societal reaction to religion from total acceptance to total denial and back again. From this perspective, we may be witnessing a new swing of the pendulum from hegemonic religiosity back to its no-less-hegemonic denial. So, is this a normalisation or a new swing of the Russian pendulum? Let us leave this as an open question that requires ongoing analysis.

Notes

1 This chapter was prepared with the support of Postsecular Conflicts project at the University of Innsbruck (funded by the Austrian Science Fund Project Number Y919-G22; 2015 676804; Principal Investigator: Dr Kristina Stoeckl).
2 This translation differs slightly from the one provided in the article's English abstract.
3 In a conversation with Putin, Patriarch Kirill called Putin's rule 'God's Miracle', see http://www.patriarchia.ru/db/text/2005767.html. The patriarch also said 'Orthodox people do not know how to participate in demonstrations […] We do not hear their voices; they pray in the silence of monasteries, in cells, at home. But they worry with all their heart about what is happening today to our people. They make clear historical parallels between the dissoluteness (*besputstvo*) and forgetfulness (*bespamiatstvo*) of the pre-revolutionary years and the mess, swaying and destruction of the country in the 1990s', see http://www.bbc.com/russian/russia/2012/02/110802_russia_patriarch_rallies.
4 The real second name of the Patriarch Kirill.
5 See http://pussy-riot.livejournal.com/12442.html and https://www.theatlantic.com/international/archive/2012/11/what-pussy-riots-punk-prayer-really-said/264562/.
6 These tendencies were visible earlier, but from 2012 on, there has been a qualitative shift in issues such as Church restitution, religious education, and bans of certain religious minorities (e.g. the Jehovah's Witnesses). Geraldine Fagan (2011) provides a detailed analysis of how, preceding this qualitative shift, Russia had already begun moving from total religious freedom to the gradual limitation of freedoms and a privileged status for the Russian Orthodox Church (and some other traditional religions).
7 This refers to a story of a woman living in an apartment belonging to Patriarch Kirill (likely his distant relative), who had a conflict with her neighbour who was making a repair. The dust from this repair reached Kirill's apartment. The woman in Kirill's apartment claimed that the dust caused nearly one million dollars damage and tried to take possession of the neighbour's apartment as compensation, see http://www.rosbalt.ru/moscow/2012/03/22/960327.html.

8 The most famous of such stories involve Father Gleb Grozovsky, as well as Deacon Andrei Kuraev's exposé on the Kazan seminary in 2013, see diak-kuraev. livejournal.com.
9 See http://politsovet.ru/49100-top-10-skandalov-s-uchastiem-rpc.html.
10 See http://www.pravoslavie.ru/58456.html.
11 See http://www.pravoslavie.ru/58456.html.
12 See https://russian.rt.com/article/148812.
13 See his YouTube vlog: https://www.youtube.com/channel/UCE0LAd6n6Ew9-Pm IZ6VzMAA.
14 See http://rascerkovlenie.ru/.
15 See http://www.colta.ru/articles/media/13974.
16 See http://ahilla.ru/76-2/.
17 See http://ahilla.ru/manifest-ahilly/.
18 See http://ahilla.ru/ya-nadeyus-na-revolyutsiyu-v-rpts/.
19 See http://pravoslav-ru.livejournal.com/4996912.html.
20 See   http://www.aljazeera.com/indepth/features/2017/08/evictions-trials-russian-church-claims-property-170822103042061.html.
21 See https://www.gazeta.ru/comments/2017/02/13_e_10523465.shtml#page2.
22 See https://lenta.ru/articles/2017/01/25/hersones/.
23 https://lenta.ru/articles/2015/02/26/tangezerdoc/.
24 https://iz.ru/news/584779.
25 http://www.rbc.ru/politics/14/08/2015/55ce15bb9a79474f19c056c8http://www.rbc.ru /politics/14/08/2015/55ce15bb9a79474f19c056c8.
26 See http://www.rbc.ru/society/21/06/2017/594a43609a794777237c25d7.
27 See   https://www.znak.com/2017-08-26/pravoslavnye_aktivisty_vnov_ugrozhayut_p odzhech_kinoteatry_iz_za_prokata_matildy.
28 Ekaterinburg is the location where Tsar Nicholas II and his family were killed by Bolsheviks in 1918. See also http://ria56.ru/posts/5424584582458245.htm.
29 He directed the movie 'The Pupil' (2016), which portrayed the danger of religious fanaticism through the story of a schoolboy who becomes a religious fanatic and begins to terrorise his entire school.
30 See https://meduza.io/feature/2017/07/10/mozhet-vyzvat-nepriyatie-pochemu-bolshoy-tea tr-sorval-premieru-nureeva-baleta-o-velikom-russkom-tantsovschike-i-otkrytom-gee. The premier happened in December 2017.
31 See https://www.youtube.com/watch?v=ZSsSfOuhvDY.
32 Statistics about VKontakte [https://vk.com/page-47200925_44240810].
33 MDK's site (https://vk.com/mudakoff) has 8.3 million users, and the Lepra ('Leprosy') site (https://vk.com/public30022666) is also quite popular.
34 Sokolovsky's sentence was reduced to 2.25 years of probation in July 2017, at which time he was also absurdly put on Russia's federal 'terrorist and extremist' list, see https://www.kommersant.ru/doc/3294094.
35 See https://zona.media/article/2017/27/04/pokemon_sokolovsky.
36 See http://www.pravoslavie.ru/58456.html and also http://izvestia.ru/news/520710.
37 This would also include the case of state-supported theology programmes in universities.

References

Agadjanian, A. 2006. 'The Search for Privacy and the Return of a Grand Narrative: Religion in a Post-Communist Society', *Social Compass* 53(2):169–184.
Agadjanian, A. 2015. 'Vulnerable Post-Soviet Secularities: Patterns and Dynamics in Russia and Beyond'. In *Multiple Secularities beyond the West: Religion and*

Modernity in the Global Age. Edited by M. Burchardt, M. Wohlrab-Sahr and M. Middell, pp. 241–260. Berlin: de Gruyter.

Agadjanian, A. 2017. 'Tradition, Morality and Community: Elaborating Orthodox Identity in Putin's Russia', *Religion, State and Society* 45(1): 39–60.

Dobbelaere, K. 2002. *Secularization: An Analysis at Three Levels*. Brussels: Peter Lang.

Dobbelaere, K. 2004. 'Assessing Secularization Theory'. In *New Approaches to the Study of Religion, Volume 2: Textual, Comparative, Sociological, and Cognitive Approaches*. Edited by P. Antes, A. W. Geertz and R. R. Warne, pp. 229–253. Berlin, New York: de Gruyter.

Fagan, G. 2011. *Believing in Russia: Religious Policy after Communism*. London: Routledge.

Filatov, S. 2014. 'Russkoe pravoslavie, obshchestvo i vlast' vo vremena politicheskoi turbulentnosti: RPTs posle oseni 2011 g.' [Russian Orthodoxy, society and authorities in times of political turbulence: The Russian Orthodox Church after the autumn of 2011]. In *Montazh i demontazh sekuliarnogo mira* [Assembly and disassembly of the secular world]. Edited by A. Malashenko and S. Filatov, pp. 9–41. Moscow: ROSSPEN.

Filatov, S. and M. Malashenko (eds.). 2011. *Pravoslavnaia tserkov' pri novom patriarkhe* [The Orthodox Church under the new Patriarch]. Moscow: Moskovskii Tsentr Karnegi.

Furman, D. and K. Kaariainen. 2007a. Religioznost' v Rossii v 90-e gody XX – nachale XXI veka [Religiosity in Russia in the 1990s and the beginning of the twenty-first century]. In *Novye tserkvi, starye veruiushchie; starye tserkvi, novye veruiushchie: Religiia v postsovetskoi Rossii* [New Churches, Old Believers; Old Churches, New Believers: Religion in Post-Soviet Russia]. Edited by K. Kaariainen and D. Furman, pp. 6–87. St Petersburg: Letnii sad.

Furman, D. and Kaariainen, K. 2007b. 'Religioznost' v Rossii na rubezhe XX–XXI stoletii' [Religiosity in Russia at the turn of the twenty-first century], *Obshchestvennye nauki i sovremennost'* 2: 78–95.

Gordon, S. 1984. *Hitler, Germans, and the 'Jewish Question'*. Princeton, NJ: Princeton University Press.

Habermas, J. 2009. *Europe: The Faltering Project*. Cambridge: Polity Press.

Jarzyńska, K. 2014. 'The Russian Orthodox Church as Part of the State and Society', *Russian Politics and Law* 52(3): 87–97.

Karpov, V. 2010. 'Desecularization: A Conceptual Framework', *Journal of Church and State* 52(2): 232–270.

Karpov, V. 2013. 'The Social Dynamics of Russia's Desecularisation: A Comparative and Theoretical Perspective', *Religion, State and Society* 41(3): 254–283.

Kikot', M. 2016. *Ispoved' byvshei poslushnitsy* [Confessions of a former lay sister]. LiveJournal of Maria Kikot'. Available online: https://visionfor.livejournal.com/.

Kikot', M. 2017. *Ispoved' byvshei poslushnitsy* [Confessions of a former lay sister]. Moscow: EKSMO.

Köllner, T. 2016. 'Patriotism, Orthodox Religion and Education: Empirical Findings from Contemporary Russia', *Religion, State & Society* 44(4): 366–386.

Köllner, T. 2018. 'On the Restitution of Property and the Making of 'Authentic' Landscapes in Contemporary Russia', *Europe-Asia Studies* 70(7) 1083–1102. doi:10.1080/09668136.2018.1484077.

Kostiuk, K. 2002. 'Tri portreta: Sotsial'no-eticheskie vozzreniia v Russkoi pravoslavnoi tserkvi kontsa XX veka' [Three Portraits: Social-ethical Views in the Russian Orthodox Church at the End of the Twentieth Century], *Kontinent* 113: 252–287.

Lebedev, S. 2015. 'Propravoslavnyi konsensus v Rossii nachala XXI veka kak fenomen religioznoi situatsii' [The Pro-Orthodox Consensus in Russia at the Beginning of the Twenty-first Century]. *Nauchnyi rezul'tat: Seriia 'Sotsiologii i upravlenie'* 1: 14–21.

Levada Centre. 2017. 'Religioznost' [Religiosity], *Levada-Tsentr*, 18 July. Available online: https://www.levada.ru/2017/07/18/religioznost/.

Lipset, S. M. and S. Rokkan. 1967. 'Cleavage Structures, Party Systems, and Voter Alignments: An Introduction'. In *Party Systems and Voter Alignments: Cross-National Perspectives*. Edited by S. M. Lipset and S. Rokkan, pp. 1–64. New York: Free Press.

Nevzorov, A. and G. Baranov. 2013. 'Aleksandr Nevzorov i monakh Grigorii Baranov'. YouTube Channel of 'Mikhail Monakh Grigorii', 26 February. Available online: https://www.youtube.com/watch?v=lXvZc43aObY.

Østbø, J. 2017. 'Securitizing "Spiritual-Moral Values" in Russia', *Post-Soviet Affairs* 33(3): 200–216.

Robinson, N. 2017. 'Russian Neo-patrimonialism and Putin's "Cultural Turn"', *Europe-Asia Studies* 69(2): 348–366.

Savvin, D. 2017. *Prevyshe vsego: Roman o tserkovnoi, netserkovnoi i antitserkovnoi zhizni* [Above It All: A Novel on Church, Non-Church and Anti-Church Life]. Moscow: EKSMO.

Schroeder, R. L. and V. Karpov. 2013. 'The Crimes and Punishments of the "Enemies of the Church" and the Nature of Russia's Desecularising Regime', *Religion, State and Society* 41(3): 284–311.

Schwirtz, M. 2012. '$30,000 Watch Vanishes Up Church Leader's Sleeve', *The New York Times*, 5 April. Available online: http://www.nytimes.com/2012/04/06/world/europe/in-russia-a-watch-vanishes-up-orthodox-leaders-sleeve.html?_r=.

Sharafutdinova, G. 2014. 'The Pussy Riot Affair and Putin's Démarche from Sovereign Democracy to Sovereign Morality', *Nationalities Papers* 42(4): 615–621.

Shterin, M. 2012. 'New Religious Movements in Changing Russia: Opportunities and Challenges', In *Cambridge Companion to New Religious Movements*. Edited by O. Hammer and M. Rotstein, pp. 286–303. Cambridge: Cambridge University Press.

Soldatov, A. 2016. 'Glamurnyi GULAG' [Glamorous GULAG], *Novaia gazeta*, 15 July. Available online: https://www.novayagazeta.ru/articles/2016/07/15/69269-glamurnyy-gulag.

Stepanova, E. 2015. '"The Spiritual and Moral Foundation of Civilization in Every Nation for Thousands of Years": The Traditional Values Discourse in Russia', *Politics, Religion & Ideology* 16(2/3): 119–136.

Taylor, Ch. 2007. *A Secular Age*. Cambridge, MA: Harvard University Press.

Tsygankov, A. 2016. 'Crafting the State-Civilization: Vladimir Putin's Turn to Distinct Values', *Problems of Post-Communism* 63(3): 146–158.

Turner, V. 1975. *Dramas, Fields, and Metaphors: Symbolic Action in Human Society*. Ithaca, NY: Cornell University Press.

Uzlaner, D. 2014. 'The Pussy Riot Case and the Peculiarities of Russian Post-Secularism', *State, Religion and Church* 1(1): 23–58.

Verkhovskii, A. 2014. 'The Russian Orthodox Church as the Church of the Majority', *Russian Politics & Law* 52(5): 50–72.

Willems, J. 2012. '"Foundations of Orthodox Culture" in Russia: Confessional or Nonconfessional Religious Education?', *European Education* 44(2): 23–43.

Yablokov, I. 2014. 'Pussy Riot as Agent Provocateur: Conspiracy Theories and the Media Construction of Nation in Putin's Russia', *Nationalities Papers: The Journal of Nationalism and Ethnicity* 42(4): 622–636.

Part V
Orthodoxy in the international arena

11 Guided by a 'symphony of views'

The Russian Orthodox Church's role in building Russia's symbolic capital[1]

Alicja Curanović

Introduction

This chapter takes a closer look at one specific sphere of relations between the Russian Orthodox Church (ROC) and the Russian State, that being foreign policy. In this particular domain the State has the dominant position. It is the subject of international law and the sovereign actor. In order to follow its goals in the international arena, the State has at its disposal the whole machinery of administration, a legion of well-trained diplomats, the mass media etc. Considering the fact that Russia is a secular country governed by a people who not so long ago showed considerable adherence to the Communist party/ideal, one would not expect the religious factor to manifest itself in Russian foreign policy. And yet the role of the Church in Russia's activity in the international arena is noticeable. It is not merely a result of the attractiveness of the ROC's material assets such as the infrastructure outside Russian territory or the Church's own diplomatic network. What makes the ROC so valuable for Russian foreign policy is its capacity to act as a norm entrepreneur as well as a dispenser of meanings and symbols. It's another sphere where one can observe the complex dynamics of the 'entangled authorities' (on an ideological, institutional as well as personal level, as defined by Köllner (2018)) of the Russian State and Church.

I argue that the ROC is playing an important role in the Kremlin's strategy aimed at restoring Russia's major power status. The Church is one of the few (if not the only one) institutions able to legitimate the historic continuity of the Russian statehood and thus can supplement the Kremlin's political projects with an aura of 'natural (eternal) legitimacy'. In other words, the ROC can create the 'effect of symbolic capital' so crucial for Russia's ability to build up its own authority and undermine the dominant normative order and the international hierarchy. This chapter provides a short analysis of Russia's striving for status in the context of symbolic and political capital – concepts coined by Pierre Bourdieu. An examination of Russia's conduct within this conceptual framework highlights the importance of the ROC in Russia's symbolic struggle. What is more, analysing the Church–State relations in regard to foreign policy and symbolic power enables a verification of the utility of the concept of symphony. I argue that the complexity of interactions between the ROC and the Kremlin exceed the ideal of harmonious relations. The visible 'symphony of views' of the two parties is as much a consequence of the Soviet past as of the Byzantium legacy. This 'symphony of views' can result in different sets of situations between the State and the Church: one of harmony as well as of tensions.

The chapter starts with a conceptualisation of the link between status, symbolic and political capitals. Next, the actions of the ROC and the Russian State within the symbolic struggle are analysed and illustrated by examples of the ideological project of *Russkii Mir* (Russian World) and Russia's policy in the region of the Arctic and the Middle East.

Status and symbolic capital

To the classic triad of a state's national interests (security, autonomy, prosperity) Alexander Wendt (2003: 236f.) added a fourth – self-esteem. Status plays an important part in nurturing a positive self-image. No formal principle of equal sovereignty can change the fact that there is a hierarchy of prestige attributed to states (nations) (Dore 1975). To T.V. Paul et al. (2014: 7), status is a set of 'collective beliefs about a given state's ranking on valued attributes (wealth, coercive capabilities, culture, demographic position, socio-political organisation and diplomatic clout)'. Status is both membership in a particular club of actors and the relative standing within this club (Paul et al. 2014). It is characterised by three properties. It is collective, since it cannot be achieved exclusively by the actions of the status seeker. It is subjective because it is founded not only on objective material criteria but also (if not mostly) on the perception of others. Finally, it is a positional good, each time defined in relation to other actors (Paul et al. 2014: 9). Status adds to a state's self-esteem if the position attributed to it by other countries corresponds with this state's sense of its own rightful place in the international hierarchy. In other words, a state's self-esteem is high, when its self-attribution is correlated with the recognition it receives. Status is attributed according to both material as well as ideational (moral) resources (Neumann 2008: 131). It may happen that a particular state is given a higher rank than its material potential would suggest. This is the case of an overachiever. Consequently, an underachiever is a state which is ranked below its capacity (Volgy and Mayhall 1995). States compete for status not only because it increases their self-esteem but also because it is an important source of authority (Clunan 2014: 274).[2] And authority lends legitimacy to a state's actions. As Stephen Brooks and William Wohlforth (2008: 173) put it, 'legitimacy is a set of beliefs about the propriety, acceptability, or naturalness of an action, an actor/role, or a political order'. And they conclude: 'Legitimacy is thus the great resource-multiplier' (p. 174).

Pierre Bourdieu (1968) also sees legitimacy as crucial. To him, legitimacy is what makes power relations and dependencies constituting society invisible.

Constant power struggle is the essence of social dynamics and forms the main division line between dominant and subordinated groups. Without a sense of legitimacy this system of subordination would not last.

Although Pierre Bourdieu himself dealt mostly with social relations within a state, David Swartz (1997, 2013) rightly notices that the French scholar rejected the artificial differentiation between domestic and foreign policy. And as Rebecca Adler-Nissen (2013) convincingly claims, Bourdieu's perspective can help to shed new light on how states behave in the field of international relations. When thinking about status and authority, Bourdieu's concepts of symbolic power, capital and violence seem to be a useful tool which could add to our understanding of interstate dynamics.

Individuals and groups compete for power using different resources which Bourdieu called *capitals*. Different types of capitals are correlated with different spheres of rivalry (called *fields*) (Bourdieu 1968). Bourdieu understood symbolic power as the capacity to produce symbolic meanings and forms; the capacity to shape perceptions of social reality by imposing the cognitive categories through which one understands the social world; the capacity to conserve or transform social reality by shaping its representations (Bourdieu 1968: 22f.; see also Swartz 2013: 83). Symbolic power is a cultural expression of domination and the power to form social identities. Symbolic power undergoes a process of naturalisation and is experienced by subordinated groups as an inevitable state of affairs. According to Bourdieu, the deep internalisation and acceptance of one's own subordination is an effect of symbolic violence.[3] Symbolic violence results in subordinates practically adapting themselves to existing hierarchies.

Symbolic capital makes the efficient exercise of symbolic power possible. It should be understood as a credit, an accumulated authority which enables a state to act in a way which other actors perceive as legitimate (Bourdieu 1991: 163–170; Williams 2007: 40). In describing symbolic capital Bourdieu et al. (1994) referred to authority, prestige and recognition. This brings us back to status. The status of a state depends on its accumulated authority. Symbolic capital is, to a certain extent, as David Swartz (2013: 103) put it, a property of the position a state holds in the hierarchy. It is the symbolic capital of the major powers (i.e. the states ranked the highest in the hierarchy) which enables them to preserve the very hierarchy, dominant norms, classifications and criteria of authority. And, consequently, symbolic capital is needed to challenge the established order.

It is important to emphasise the difference between symbolic capital and soft power or ideology. In Bourdieu's understanding, symbolic capital refers to deeply internalised, subconscious schemes (predispositions), which he called *habitus*. Individuals act upon them instinctively but cannot instrumentalise them. Ideology, in turn, is a political vision which can be instrumentalised. However, there is a connection between symbolic capital and ideology. Ideology can resonate with people because of their *habitus*, in other words, because of symbolic capital's 'invisible' functioning. Similarly to ideology, soft power (appeal) (see Nye 2005) often comes as a result of conscious effort by the state (e.g. public diplomacy). Therefore, in Bourdieu's classification, both ideology and soft power belong to the field of politics. 'The political field is that arena of the struggle for political power where other forms of capital are transformed into the capital of social support' (Swartz 2013: 68; Bourdieu 1991: 170f.). The struggle for power in the political field is explicit. The main goal is to impose one's vision of the world. To achieve this, it is necessary to mobilise people and garner their support, i.e. political capital is required (Bourdieu 1991: 194–202). Although they are not synonymous, both types of capital – symbolic and political – are interrelated, because political capital is a form of symbolic capital. The political field is one of symbolic domination and an arena of the struggle over belief (Bourdieu 1991: 170ff.; Swartz 2013: 79). When viewed as a whole, both symbolic and political powers are about legitimacy. However, in case of the latter the claim for legitimacy is, we could say, more 'visible'. It is expressed not in practises and practical adaptation (*habitus*) but in discourse. This nevertheless depends on symbolic capital. According to Bourdieu, symbolic capital is *meta-capital*, the 'glue' which maintains social order and underpins its hierarchies.

Russia and its status strategy

For reasons which have been exhaustively analysed (Tsygankov 2013; Prizel 1998; Blum 2008; Clunan 2009; Laruelle 2012; Morozov 2015) a coherent national identity has been one of fundamental concerns of Russian elites since the fall of the USSR. Major power status is a permanent component of Russia's self-image and much of Russia's behaviour is motivated by seeking recognition in the international arena. Russia sought recognition mostly from its Significant Other, i.e. the West – Europe and, since the 20th century, also the US. According to Iver Neumann and Vincent Pouliot (2011), much of Russian policy towards the West could be explained by Russia's striving for recognition rather than material gains. Tensions in relations with the West were fuelled by what Russia felt was insufficient recognition.

The collapse of the USSR had a great impact on new Russia's international status. Although the material parameters of Russia's standing noticeably decreased in comparison to those of the Soviet Union (see Ringmar 2002), the West did not question some formal attributes, such as its permanent seat at the UN Security Council, and offered Russia membership in the G8. From the perspective of the West, the Russian Federation was an overachiever (see Freire 2011). But Russia perceived itself as an underachiever which was not shown the respect it deserved. Events like the war in the former Yugoslavia, the bombardment of Kosovo or the invasion of Iraq only reaffirmed Moscow's conviction that it was not being treated as an equal by NATO members.[4]

The so-called 'colour' revolutions[5] in the post-Soviet area represent – in Russia's reasoning – the culmination of the degradation that started with the fall of the USSR. They were perceived by the Kremlin as an attempt to deprive Russia of its crucial attribute of power – its own sphere of influence.[6] The 'Rose Revolution' in Georgia (2003) and especially the 'Orange Revolution' in Ukraine (2004/2005) undermined Russia's authority in the so-called 'Near Abroad'.[7] From the point of view of the Russian elites, all the efforts and good will shown to the West in the 1990s brought nothing but humiliation. Not only was Russia not given its rightful recognition—its will to cooperate was also understood as a weakness and encouraged the West to advance into the post-Soviet territory.

'Colour' revolutions mark a shift in Russia's approach to the West and its understanding of today's world politics in general. One noticeable change, discernible in state doctrines on foreign policy,[8] is the tendency to frame global dynamics in terms of a civilisational rivalry. In consequence of this, the sphere of norms and values has assumed an important place in Russian strategic thinking and it is not surprising that Russia has made investments in soft power one of its priorities (see Sherr 2013).

Since the 'colour' revolutions, the Russian State has moved to the position of a challenger of the existing hierarchy not just in terms of geopolitics (a multipolar world vs *Pax Americana*) but also in terms of the normative order (see Uzlaner in this volume; Stoeckl 2014). Since Russia could not achieve what it felt was its rightful recognition by playing by the rules set by the West, it decided to formulate its own classifications, or at least its own interpretation of these rules. Russia's difficulty in adjusting to the order set by the West has a long record. I. Neumann and V. Pouliot look for an explanation in the late and never successfully finalised process of socialisation (see Neumann and Pouliot 2011; Neumann 2011). In their research they refer to Bourdieu's notion of *hysteresis*.[9] Within Bourdieu's conceptual framework, Russia's *habitus* is not synchronised well enough with its position in the *field*. This chronic lack of synchronisation fosters Russia's inclination to question the existing hierarchy. Russia's ambition to provide an alternative to the Western dominance in the sphere of symbols demonstrates its increasing concern with its own symbolic capital. The so-called conservative (moral) turn in Russian politics is the best manifestation of this tendency.

The conservative turn

After over a decade of a declared strong commitment to de-ideologised pragmatism (Tsygankov 2005), the Russian government again started to talk about values. One of the best examples are the statements of Sergei Lavrov, a Soviet-trained diplomat and, since 2004, the Minister of Foreign Affairs. Lavrov declared that Russian foreign policy should be guided by moral values,[10] and was convinced that the basic values shared by the world religions should become the foundation of the international order.[11] In 2014, in the face of the escalations of the Ukrainian conflict, Lavrov insisted that the reason for the deterioration of Russia's relations with the West was Russia's return to its traditional values.[12] Finally, referring to the sources of Russian soft power, Lavrov paraphrased the words of Alexander Nevsky – 'God is not about power but about the Truth'.[13]

According to the new narrative which since 2012 has gradually begun to dominate the public debate, Russia is one of the last strongholds of traditional values and morality in a secularised Europe (Laruelle 2014). What is more, according to this narrative, Russia – if it is to stay true to its values and principles – should not only protect its own civilisational sovereignty but also help other countries which suffer from the pressure of the cultural hegemony of the West. Equipped with a (new) identity (distinctive autonomous Russian/Orthodox/Eurasian civilisation) and mission (saving Europe from immorality and forming a better, more just world order), Russia is trying to position itself as a provider of a global normative alternative.[14] The conservative turn is a political project aimed at helping Russia in its symbolic struggle with the international hierarchy.

With the conservative turn, Russia is seeking to weaken the West's moral authority. The idea of questioning the moral leadership of the US or the EU by emphasising a commitment to traditional (interpreted as religious) values might seem risky coming from a country governed mostly by a post-Communist elite.[15] But it can be observed that the newly adopted conservative stance has provided Russia with an effective ideological platform capable of encompassing different allies. The narrative regarding traditional values appeals to Islamic countries (Laruelle 2014), American and European conservative groups,[16] and even pragmatic Communist China.[17] The role of the guardian of values, to which Russia should – according to the Kremlin and the ROC – aspire, adds to Russia's authority. It positions Russia as a noble power, able to stand up to the West not only militarily but also in the normative sphere. This particular conservative framework elevates the significance of the ROC for accumulating Russia's symbolic power.

The significance of the ROC

Marked by the conservative turn, the change of Russia's status strategy elevated the significance of the Church due to its role as a producer and dispenser of meanings and symbols.

Considering the fact that traditional values are interpreted in the Russian public discourse as religious ones (Curanović 2015), it becomes clear why the ROC's role is crucial in legitimising Russia's symbolic struggle. So far, only the Moscow Patriarchate together with the World Russian People's Council[18] have made an effort to define Russian traditional values. In other situations these are used in the public discourse as a vague notion. In 2011 a document entitled 'The Basic Values: The Fundaments of National Unity' was published with a catalogue of 17 values. It strengthened the ROC as the only legitimate dispenser of traditional values. Hence only the Church has the necessary credentials to support the Kremlin's claim to the moral leadership of the conservative part of the international community.

Furthermore, the ROC's rhetoric enhances the anti-Western edge of the conservative turn. The Church is making good use of negative stereotypes rooted in the Russian tradition to invigorate reluctance felt towards the West. For example, hierarchs compare the EU and the US to the decadence of the Roman Empire and recall the prosecutions of the first Christians when they refer to today's victims of aggressive European secularism.[19] Within this narrative the immoral West is juxtaposed with a Russia presented as having been a moral (noble) power since its early days and throughout its history. According to the representatives of the ROC, Russia was the first country to have introduced the principle of the equality of all the nations, which only after World War II was internalised by international society.[20] In the ROC's narrative, the Soviet Union followed this noble path – it saved the world from fascism and dismantled the colonial system. And now the Russian Federation, faithful to its historic destiny, must save the world from the aggressive secularism promoted by the West.[21]

This vision shows a characteristic feature of the Church's rhetoric, that being the emphasis on Russia's role as a global norm entrepreneur combined with the continuity of Russian statehood. As a result, an idealised vision of Russia is revealed which in each of its historic embodiments made an invaluable contribution to the normative order. In other words, the world would be a far worse place, if had it not been for the Russian State. Patriarch Kirill summed it up by saying that each Russian state has always striven for social justice.[22] This long historic record is one of the foundations of contemporary Russia's claim to moral leadership and a means to build up its symbolic capital. Symbolic capital is crucial if the challenger of the existing order wants to subvert the international hierarchy without physical violence in a way that would seem legitimate to other actors. The Kremlin is aware of the weakness of Russia's symbolic power. The problem is the deficit of authority in the international arena. Without the required legitimacy, imposing one's own vision of the world is impossible. It will be dismissed as propaganda or an ideological bluff. Therefore, Russia makes an effort to, putting it metaphorically, 'stylise' its political capital as a symbolic one, to accumulate political capital which would have 'the same effect as the symbolic one'. The references to the past serve to create an impression of Russia's well-established, historically accumulated authority.

To achieve such an ambitious goal, the Russian State needs an institution which represents historic continuity and can thus legitimate claims to this accumulated authority. The ROC is the best partner the Kremlin can find for this task. It would be false to suggest that the ROC is merely an instrument of the Kremlin. The fact that both actors increasingly often interpret international dynamics in terms of symbolic rivalry fosters the bilateral rapprochement.

It is hard to avoid noticing the similarity of views of the Church and the Kremlin.[23] The notion of sovereignty provides a good example. As Vladimir Putin stated at the Valdai Summit in 2013, 'striving for independence, for spiritual, ideological (...) sovereignty is an indispensable part of (the

Russian – A.C.) national character'.[24] The majority of Orthodox hierarchs are also committed to the idea of Russia's civilisational (also referred to as humanitarian, cultural or spiritual) sovereignty. The World Russian People's Council defined it as:

> a set of cultural, religious, socio-psychological factors which enable a nation and a state to reproduce own identity and to avoid a socio-psychological and cultural dependency upon external centres of influence. (...) It is the capacity to defend independence from the impact of soft power, which in the XXI century became the main instrument of expansion of powers aspiring to global hegemony.[25]

It is striking to what extent this definition is marked by thinking in terms of geopolitics rather than religion. Civilisational sovereignty is perceived by the representatives of the Moscow Patriarchate as a *sine qua non* of Russia's major power status. The intensity of preoccupation with status is well illustrated by Patriarch Kirill, who noticed that Russia cannot play any other role but that of a power in the international arena.[26] Even spheres which might seem free of major power rivalry, such as the dialogue of civilisations, are perceived by the ROC as a geopolitical battlefield. For example, to Vsevolod Chaplin, the former chairman of the Synodal Department for the Cooperation of Church and Society, this dialogue was one of the key spheres of the civilisational race and so he believed that it is crucial for Russia to establish its own institutions dealing with this issue, which would be independent from external influence.[27]

This geopolitical 'sensitivity' (awareness) of Russian hierarchs corresponds with the mindset of the Russian elites and has its roots in the common Soviet experience. The Moscow Patriarchate does not only pay attention to the spiritual sphere but also to earthly matters such as state prestige and status. The ROC's involvement in building Russia's symbolic capital is thus often voluntary and so not merely the result of the state's pressure.

A 'symphony of views' instead of a symphony

This noticeable convergence of views between the ROC and the Kremlin invites the question regarding the adequacy of *symphonia* for understanding the relation between these two parties. The concept of symphony refers to the ideal vision formed in the Byzantine Empire of how relations between Church and State should look. As Lucian Leuştean (2011) notices, symphony promotes equality and an intimate relationship between these institutions – each of them has its own domain, priorities and methods of operating. Symphony assumes neither interdependency nor a complete separation. In the days of Byzantium, as Tamara Prosić (2014: 181) explains, symphony, with harmony as a guiding principle 'meant being in accord with two basic Christian ideas: the idea of Christ's divine-human nature and the trinity'. Symphony was thus about 'diversity, equality and unity through diversity'. Lucian Leuştean, Tamara Prosić and Zoe Knox (2003: 576) suggest that symphony should be approached today as a political ideal which, embedded in tradition and coded in symbols, continue to influence contemporary Orthodox Christian socie-ties.[28] However, this does not mean that establishing symphony is a part of the actual agenda of any of the Orthodox Churches, including the ROC (see Knox 2003). Moreover, as Cyril Hovorun (2016) points out, many among Orthodox clergy either don't know about the historic reality of *symphonia* or they intentionally 'tailor the Byzantine past to their current political expedience'.[29] In fact in many scholarly analyses the notion of symphony is used in a metaphorical sense, with the emphasis on the lack of genuine equality between the ecclesiastical (*sacerdotium*) and temporal (*imperium*) authorities. For instance, in reference to Russia, James Warhola (2004: 97) writes about 'an imbalanced *symphonia*' and John Anderson (2007) writes of 'asymmetric *symphonia*'. The notion of symphony does not thus add to our understanding of the complexity of relations between the Church and the State. Therefore, while approaching the State-Orthodox Church nexus, one should go beyond the concept of symphony.

Regarding the foundations of today's relations between the ROC and the Kremlin, I agree with John Anderson who points to the significance of the shared Soviet past which brings together the 'altar' and the 'throne'. Anderson (2007: 188) argues that 'both sides are very much products of the Soviet era, with the Church still largely dominated by individual hierarchs whose biographies are very familiar to the successors of the KGB and who were appointed under Communist party guidance'. One area in which this shared Soviet experience manifests itself is the similarity of the views of the hierarchs and the State offi-cials on foreign policy issues such as: Russian identity, major power status, sovereignty, the post-Soviet area as Russia's sphere of influence, the threat posed by the West, and globalisation. In fact it is the realm of ideas where the harmony between the Church and the State can be observed to the largest extent. Therefore, I use the notion of a 'symphony of views' instead of 'symphony'.

The 'symphony of views', however, is just the departure point and does not guarantee a harmonious cooperation between the ROC and the Kremlin in the international arena. In reality this convergence of views may turn out to be superficial and fragile when tested by geopolitical reality. The three examples discussed below show the complex Church–State dynamics – the interaction between these two 'entangled' authorities. Tobias Köllner emphasises the inter-dependency and the dynamic nature of the Church–State's authority building strategies.[30] In the given cases, the State refers to the authority of the Church to legitimate its own claims (e.g. the idea of *Russkii Mir* after the annexation of Crimea). In building-up Russia's symbolic capital, the State relies on the authority of the Church. At the same time the ROC also takes advantage of the capacity of the Russian State (e.g. the issue of protecting Christian mino-rities in the Middle East). Let us thus note again that, contrary to common knowledge, the Church is not merely an instrument of the State.

All the examples discussed below refer to Russia's current political actions which are relevant for the symbolic struggle. They aim at changing the international hierarchy and at legitimating Russia's status as a world power. All the cases are status markers – *Russkii Mir* designates the Russian sphere of influence, the Arctic policy is a token of prestige, while the engagement in the Middle East is intended to confirm Russia's capacity to solve major crises.

The Arctic: sweet harmony

The Arctic plays an important role in global symbolic rivalry. An efficient and often conspicuous manifestation of a state's presence in this region has become a status marker at the beginning of the 21st century. The Russian government shows great determination to strengthen its presence in the High North (see Klimenko 2016; Laruelle 2013; Hønneland 2016; Sergunin & Konyshev 2017). Placing a Russian flag on the sea bed of the Arctic Ocean in 2007 was one of the most spectacular acts of symbolic meaning and it was praised by Patriarch Alexy II.[31] Significantly enough, the Arctic policy is a tool of status signalling not only for the Kremlin but also for the ROC. Since 2010 the Moscow Patriarchate has been developing its own project, *Russkia Arktika* (the Russian Arctic).[32] Under the aegis of this project, the ROC focuses mostly on symbolic actions, such as baptising the North Pole (2012), the Northern Sea Route (2013), or marking the Northern frontiers of *Russkii Mir* with new Orthodox chapels.[33] Furthermore, it has become a new custom for Orthodox priests to give a blessing to polar expeditions. This is a case of harmonious State–Church bilateral cooperation supplemented by parallel actions fuelled by a similar understanding of the strategic importance of the Arctic.

The main goal of *Russkaia Arktika* is to strengthen Russian civilisational sovereignty in the region.[34] The ROC pays much attention to the 'spiritual revival' of the Arctic and believes in its importance for Russia's power status. It is indicative in this regard that the main executor of the project, Bishop Yakov of Naryan-Mar and Mezensky, always emphasises the project's strategic meaning for the state and for its status. For instance, he talked about his parishioners as if they were a stake in a geopolitical rivalry – he stated for example that the Nenets people must remain a part of the Russian cultural sphere since they were the key to controlling the Arctic, which was of strategic significance due to present and prospective transport routes and natural resources.[35]

The fact that the ROC's activity in the Arctic is so closely correlated with state policy presents an example of a political project aimed at strengthening symbolic capital. It is important to note that also in this case the Church fosters the narrative of an uninterrupted accumulation of Russia's authority. Bishop Yakov, for instance, grasped the *longue durée* perspective by saying that Russians had discovered the Arctic for the world just as Columbus had discovered America and that since that historic moment the region had been civilised by a common effort of polar explorers from the Russian and the Soviet empires.[36] This narrative emphasises on the one hand Russia's uninterrupted historic presence (the accumulated authority) in the region. Equally importantly, though, it also emphasises its exceptional role as one of the greatest discoverers (comparable to Columbus) which has an unquestioned mandate to govern this territory (to fulfil this historic mission).

Russkii Mir: a symphony hijacked by the State

Russkii Mir is one of the best-known examples of the common cause of the Kremlin and the ROC. According to different versions – coined either by the presidential administration or the Moscow Patriarchate – it was laid out by the Kremlin in 2007 when it established the Russkii Mir Foundation (Laruelle 2015; Suslov 2014: 68). It was conceived as an ideological project aimed at strengthening the sphere of Russian cultural influence – a crucial attribute of a major power status. It was intended to replace the increasingly archaic 'post-Soviet' framework and to create a new sense of community, and a sense of a shared past and fate for the former Soviet societies.

Russkii Mir is a political project which is 'stylised' to have the 'effect of symbolic capital'. Russia's mandate to promote *Russkii Mir* and act as its main guardian and advocate is based in part on the assumption about the 'natural' continuity between Kievan Rus, the Russian Empire and the USSR. The Russian Federation is thus the rightful successor of the princedom ruled by Prince Vladimir – the founder of Kievan Rus. And the ROC is the only institution which can make Moscow's claim credible and Kiev's claims illegitimate (see Stahlberg in this volume).

The Russian State's and Church's interpretations of *Russkii Mir* were not identical from the very outset (Laruelle 2015; Suslov 2014: 68; Petro 2015) (both parties have enthusiastically made use of it).[37] Nevertheless this concept had seemed to foster symphonic cooperation between the ROC and the Kremlin in the post-Soviet area. This harmony was seriously damaged by the annexation of Crimea and the ongoing conflict in Eastern Ukraine. Under these circumstances the political function of *Russkii Mir* is beyond any doubt (Laruelle 2015; Jilge 2014). According to the dominant narrative in the Russian mainstream mass media, Ukraine has fallen victim to civilisational rivalry and Russia is the only ally which can help Ukraine to save its true (i.e. Orthodox, Eastern Slavic) identity, tradition and values. In other words, Russia is Ukraine's only hope to preserve its civilisational sovereignty. The ROC shares this narrative (it always refers to the situation in Ukraine as a civil war) but it does not openly support the policy of the Russian government (Suslov 2016). In order to avoid antagonising Ukrainian citizens (the members of the Ukrainian Orthodox Church of the Moscow Patriarchate), the ROC is much more cautious in using the notion of *Russkii Mir* since this is perceived as a propaganda tool of the Kremlin. Hence, what was once a common flagship project of the Church and the State has been hijacked by the latter for its own purposes. The ROC has found itself in a difficult position, trying not to offend the feelings of Ukrainian parishioners and at the same time not to undermine Russian policy.[38] However, even in such a demanding situation the Moscow Patriarchate is capable of creating the 'effect of symbolic capital'. In the public speeches made by the patriarch in the last years, the tendency to omit the notion 'Kievan Rus' (legitimating sovereign Ukraine) can be observed; this has been replaced by 'Rus', 'ancient (*drevnaia*) Rus' or 'Holy Rus'.[39] This case shows that the Kremlin has the upper hand and that its actions have forced the ROC to adapt its own narrative.

The Middle East: a symphony encouraged by the ROC

The talks held in Astana in 2017 on settling the conflict in Syria with representatives of Iran, Turkey and Russia with the complete absence of the West (the US or the EU) should be acknowledged as a spectacular diplomatic success for Moscow. It is the first time in decades (if not centuries) that the West does not have a say on a conflict which puts Europe's security in danger. Russia's engagement in Syria is commented on as being proof of Russia regaining the status of a major power (see Herbst 2016; Stent 2016; Trenin 2016). Also in this case the ROC has played a noticeable role in the Kremlin's foreign policy. The Moscow Patriarchate has provided the Russian government with a 'noble cause' which allowed it to move beyond the logic of geopolitics. Contrary to the West,[40] Russia's current involvement in the Middle East is not motivated by oil. According to the ROC, Russia in sending its troops to Syria has once again proved its readiness for self-sacrifice.[41] Patriarch Kirill referred to Russian military actions in Syria as a 'peace-keeping mission' and praised Russia for fighting ISIS.[42] He compared Islamic State to fascism and thus presented Russia's policy as once again standing up to Evil for the sake of humankind.[43]

Presenting Russia's engagement in the Middle East as fulfilling moral obligations adds to Russia's symbolic capital. It is worth noting that a long historic perspective is also employed in framing Russia's activity in this region. The ROC is crucial in the attempt to revive the authority of the Russian Empire. While talking to the representative of the Assyrian Church of the East, Patriarch Kirill said that 'just as the Russian Empire saved Assyrians from genocide while the Ottoman Empire was crumbling, today's Russia follows this tradition and protects the Christians of Syria'.[44]

The protection of the Christian minorities is presented as one of the main motives of Russia's engagement in the Middle East.[45] It is also one of the arguments voiced by the Church in Russia to support the regime of President Bashar al-Assad since he is the only guarantor that Christians' rights will be respected. The Russian government's prioritising the protection of the persecuted Christians shows the impact of the ROC's activity on the State's agenda. It was the Moscow Patriarchate which had consistently appealed to the Kremlin to offer its support to Christians. The Church started its campaign long before the Syrian crisis by establishing contacts with Syriac Christians from Iraq in 2006–2007 (Curanović 2012: 210). The Moscow Patriarchate has become the main advocate of these minorities[46] which is confirmed by the fact that the Patriarchates located in the Middle East recognise this role and actively seek Russian support (from both the State and the Church).[47] The ROC's capacity to help beyond the usual framework of humanitarian aid stems from the fact that the Church can rely on the diplomatic resources of the Russian State. The mission to protect Christians encouraged by the ROC has resulted in concrete actions from Russia. For instance, in 2011 the ROC initiated Resolution 1957 of the Parliamentary Assembly of the Council of Europe on 'Violence against Christians in the Middle East'. In 2013 the Interfaction Group in Defense of Christian Values of the Russian Duma issued an appeal to other members of the parliament of European countries to support the Christian minorities in the Middle East.[48] On 14 November 2014 the Russian State Duma issued the Declaration 'On the grievance and mass violation of the rights of religious and ethnic minorities in connection with the deterioration of the situation in Syria and Iraq'.[49] The Imperial Orthodox Palestine Society (IOPS)[50] prepared the declaration 'On protecting the Christians of the Middle East and Northern Africa' which resulted in a common resolution brought by Russia, the Vatican and Lebanon to the debate in the UN Human Rights Council in 2015, signed by 65 states so far.[51]

The initiatives listed here reveal the close cooperation between the Russian Church and State in the international arena. It is worth keeping in mind, though, that this 'symphony' was at first encouraged and then carefully nurtured by the ROC.

Conclusion

All the examples given above are related to Russia's identity. Whether it is about *Russkii Mir*, the Arctic or the conservative turn, it all comes down to the question of Russia's self-image and its role in post-Cold War order. After what the Kremlin feels were its failed attempts to gain recognition from the West by playing by the West's rules, Moscow decided to challenge Western dominance. And, importantly, it decided to challenge it in the sphere of symbols. The 'colour' revolutions in the former Soviet republics made the Kremlin aware of its weakness in this regard and mobilised it to invest in its soft power and to launch ideological projects, such as *Russkii Mir*.

In Pierre Bourdieu's classification, all those initiatives are connected to the political field. However, they ultimately aim at rebuilding symbolic capital. It is therefore not surprising that they are all promoted by referring to Russia's long accumulated authority. In this way a narrative is being created of Russia as a distinct civilisation with its own set of values, its own tradition and a distinctive spirituality, characterised by a moral superiority (especially in comparison to the West). This image of Russia is legitimated by the Russian Orthodox Church – a crucial ally of the Kremlin in its efforts to build up Russia's symbolic capital. The area of symbolic rivalry illustrates the dynamics between the secular and ecclesiastical authorities well. Although it is rooted in the 'symphony of views', this rivalry goes beyond the ideal of *symphonia*. The State benefits from the ROC's ability to provide legitimacy but the Church can also make a good use of Russia's diplomatic capacity.

Status in international relations is not ascribed merely on the basis of military and economic prowess. And a state cannot be regarded as a major power if it does not have an authority to implicitly impose normative values. I agree with Deborah Welch Larson and Alexei Shevchenko (2003: 78) that Russia is taking on the role of a noble leader to help it achieve the desired equal footing with the major powers. Aware of its objective material shortcomings vis-à-vis the West, Russia is trying to offset them by demonstrating its own moral superiority. Moral leadership thus functions as a 'shortcut to greatness' (Larson and Shevchenko 2003: 78) – a pass to the exclusive club of the top powers. Russia has chosen to assume the role of 'the guardian of values'. With this narrative Russia draws a sharp dividing line between the West and the others. Moreover, it tries to position itself as the leader of the non-West. This polarisation has a strong geopolitical dimension but it resonates well with so many different countries since it uses a clear normative criterion, i.e. traditional (religious) values. Although the Kremlin's policy of retraditionalisation is strongly fuelled by the ongoing Ukrainian crisis, it is important to keep in mind that this policy predates the conflict. Therefore, even a successful peace process will not necessarily result in a reversal of this policy. As I have tried to show, Russia's focus on symbolic struggle has deeper roots than purely practical consideration and could therefore have long-term consequences not only for its relations with the West but first and foremost for Russia's process of self-identification.

Notes

1 This research has been conducted as part of the project SONATA no. 2015/19/D/HS5/03149, financed by the National Science Centre, Poland.
2 On this issue I tend to agree with Anne Clunan rather than with David Lake, who suggests making a distinction between status and authority. The Soviet past plays a part in how contemporary Russia understands authority in the international area.
3 'Symbolic power creates a form of violence that finds expression in everyday classifications, labels, meanings, and categorisations that subtly implement a social as well as symbolic logic of inclusion and exclusion. Symbolic violence also finds expression though body language, comportment, self-representation, bodily care, and adornment. It has a corporal as well as cognitive dimension' (Swartz 2013: 39).
4 Hanna Smith (2014) suggests creating a special definition for Russia's case: 'a country that believes itself to be a great power, but does not have all capabilities of a great power according to certain definitions, and which only enjoys limited recognition as a great power internationally'.

5 'Colour' revolutions refer to the series of mass protests in former Soviet republics which resulted in a change of the government and sometimes led to regime change, *inter alia* in Georgia, Ukraine, Kyrgyzstan, Moldova.

6 According to Tudor A. Onea (2014) it can be argued that the 'colour' revolutions led to Russia experiencing status anxiety, i.e. fear of losing its rank.

7 The Near Abroad refers to the former Soviet republics with the exception of the three Baltic states, which make up the Russian sphere of geopolitical influence and exclusive interest.

8 In 'The Concept of the Foreign Policy of the Russian Federation' issued in 2008 it is said: 'It is for the first time in contemporary history that global competition is acquiring a civilisational dimension which suggests competition between different value systems (...) A religious factor in shaping the system of contemporary international relations is growing, inter alia, as regards its moral foundation. This problem cannot be resolved without a common denominator that has always existed in major world religions.'

9 A state of hysteresis is caused by the discrepancy between one's *habitus* and one's position in the field.

10 See http://ria.ru/society/20121216/915004621.html (16.12.2012).

11 See http://www.interfax-religion.ru/?act=news&div=49296 (17.12.2014).

12 See http://www.interfax-religion.ru/?act=news&div=55525 (5.06.2014).

13 See http://www.patriarchia.ru/db/text/2623344.html (30.11.2012)

14 See Putin's 2013 Valdai Discussion Club Speech.

15 Even Vladimir Putin in his interview for 'The Time' admitted that true moral values cannot be anything but religious. See http://www.patriarchia.ru/db/text/340853.html (19.12.2007).

16 On 22 March 2015 the first International Russian Conservative Forum was held in Saint Petersburg and was attended by some 150 representatives of far-right parties across Europe. See http://www.nytimes.com/2015/03/23/world/europe/right-wing-groups-find-a-haven-for-a-day-in-russia.html?_r=0 (22.03.2015).

17 During his visit to China in 2013 Patriarch Kirill on many occasions emphasised that Russian and Chinese civilisations share moral foundations. This argument was voiced also during his meetings with President Xi Jinping in 2013 and 2015.

18 The World Russian People's Council, established in 1993, is an international organisation under the ROC's auspices. Council sessions are attended by governmental representatives, leaders of public associations, the clergy, science and culture figures, and delegates of Russian communities from the near and far abroad.

19 See http://www.patriarchia.ru/db/text/173859.html (22.12.2006); http://www.patriarchia.ru/db/text/3800077.html (18.10.2014) and http://www.patriarchia.ru/db/text/1062197.html (3.02.2010).

20 See http://www.patriarchia.ru/db/text/103233.html (6.04.2006) and http://www.patriarchia.ru/db/text/4013160.html (14.03.2015).

21 As Vsevolod Chaplin noticed, every time that Russia's role decreased in global affairs, mass atrocities always started, see http://www.patriarchia.ru/db/text/4071923.html (8.05.2015).

22 See http://www.patriarchia.ru/db/text/3334783.html (31.10.2013).

23 For more on the similarity of views of the ROC and the Kremlin in the area of foreign policy, see Curanović (2012).

24 See Putin's 2013 Valdai Discussion Club Speech.

25 See http://www.patriarchia.ru/db/text/2505633.html (3.10.2012).

26 See http://www.patriarchia.ru/db/text/3748114.html (17.09.2014).

27 See http://www.interfax-religion.ru/orthodoxy/?act=news&div=50857 (17.04.2013). The ROC's commitment to civilisational dialogue is correlated with 'The State Doctrine of Foreign Policy'. The authors of this document consider this dialogue Russia's priority and claim that Russia should become its main initiator and

moderator. They justify this claim by reference to Russia's civilisational 'know-how' (Russia provides an example of a country where for several centuries Christians and Muslims lived peacefully and where there have been no religious wars) and its accumulated authority. See also http://www.interfax-religion.ru/orthodoxy/?act=news&div=50815 (15.04.2013).

28 Tamara Prosić (2014: 186) argues that 'symphony persisted in Russian consciousness through non-legal constructs, most notably through the concept of *sobornost*.' The symphonic (*sobornost*) ideal reflected in the structure of the first soviets was one of the reasons why Russian people embraced the early system introduced by Bolsheviks.

29 See also Jianu in this volume.

30 The issue of religious education in Russian schools makes a good case. See Köllner (2016).

31 See http://www.interfax-religion.ru/?act=news&div=57668 (22.01.2015).

32 See http://www.interfax-religion.ru/?act=news&div=54618 (28.02.2014).

33 New chapels were built in Novaya Zemlia, Franz Josef Land, Tiksi (Taymyr Peninsula).

34 Bishop Yakov stated that the Nenets people (indigenous people of Arctic) became an object of foreign aggression committed by protestant sects from Canada, Norway and the US. See http://www.interfax-religion.ru/?act=interview&div=392 (31.03.2014).

35 See http://eparchia.patriarchia.ru/db/text/3815182.html (28.10.2014).

36 Ibid.

37 In case of the ROC, it could be seen for instance in how the composition of *Russkii Mir* has evolved. At the beginning Kirill, while still a metropolitan, considered it foremost a cultural, civilisational space of Eastern Slavs. Later on, the Russia-Ukraine-Belarus triad was expanded to include Moldova. And in recent statements even Kazakhstan is mentioned as a part of *Russkii Mir*.

38 A well-known example of this 'balancing act' was the absence of the patriarch at the ceremony of the annexation of Crimea held in the Kremlin on 18 March 2014.

39 See http://www.patriarchia.ru/db/text/3334783.html (31.10.2013).

40 As Hilarion – the head of the Department for External Contacts of the Moscow Patriarchate – said in one of his interviews, there were only two things which interested the West in the Middle East: Israel and oil. The fate of the persecuted Christians was not one of them. Therefore, as he explained, the Christians of the region have stacked all their hopes on Russia and Vladimir Putin. See http://www.patriarchia.ru/db/text/3503307.html (26.05.2011).

41 See http://www.patriarchia.ru/db/text/4407803.html (19.03.2016).

42 See http://www.patriarchia.ru/db/text/4697676.html (23.11.2016).

43 Ibid.

44 See http://www.patriarchia.ru/db/text/3662948.html (29.05.2014).

45 See http://www.patriarchia.ru/db/text/2939370.html (17.07.2013) and http://www.interfax-religion.ru/?act=news&div=58385 (3.03.2015). However, one should keep in mind the significant geopolitical context of Russia's engagement, starting with the Kremlin's close relations with Bashar al-Asad's regime before the war, the Russian naval facility in the Syrian port of Tartus, the Russian Khmeimim Air Base near Latakia and last but not least the role of the Middle East conflict in the major powers' game. See also Stepanova (2016) and Shumilin (2016).

46 The ROC's engagement in the Middle East is also driven by the on-going competition between the Moscow Patriarchate and the Ecumenical Patriarchate for the informal leadership within the World Eastern Orthodoxy. Being able to rely on the diplomatic resources of the Russian State the ROC is more efficient in voicing the problems of the persecuted Christians than the Ecumenical Patriarchate which is forced to tread carefully with the Turkish government.

47 See http://www.patriarchia.ru/db/text/3693190.html (18.07.2014).
48 See http://www.patriarchia.ru/db/text/2926271.html (23.04.2013).
49 See http://www.patriarchia.ru/db/text/3960558.html (22.1.2015)
50 Among Russia's instruments for rebuilding its symbolic capital among Arabs, the Imperial Orthodox Palestine Society (connected also to the ROC) holds a special place. The reactivation of this institution, established originally in 1882, is particularly telling. It provides a symbolic arch between the Russian Empire and the Russian Federation. The Society, supported by the Russian Ministry of Foreign Affairs, organises centres for promoting the Russian language and culture. The project is labelled as reviewing *Russkaia Palestina* and its ambition is to restore the heritage of the Russian Empire in the Holy Land. See http://www.patriarchia.ru/db/text/2619703.html (28.11.2012).
51 It is worth emphasising that Russia raises claims to the role of protector of Christians also in other parts of the world. For example, in 2015 Sergei Lavrov voiced concerns about the situation of Christians in Kenya. See http://www.interfax-religion.ru/?act=news&div=58385 (3.03.2015).

References

Adler-Nissen, R. 2013. *Bourdieu in International Relations: Rethinking Key Concepts in IR*. New York and London: Routledge.

Anderson, J. 2007. 'Putin and the Russian Orthodox Church: Asymmetric Symphonia?', *Journal of International Affairs* 61(1): 185–201.

Blum, D. W. 2008. *Russia and Globalization: Identity, Security, and Society in an Era of Change*. Washington: Johns Hopkins University Press.

Bourdieu, P. 1968. *Social Space and Symbolic Power*. Lecture delivered at the University of California, San Diego, March 1968.

Bourdieu, P. 1991. *Language and Symbolic Power*. Cambridge: Polity Press.

Bourdieu, P., L. J. D. Wacquant and S. Farage. 1994. 'Rethinking the State: Genesis and Structure of the Bureaucratic Field', *Sociological Theory* 12(1): 1–18.

Brooks, S. G. and W. C. Wohlforth. 2008. *World out of Balance: International Relations and the Challenge of American Primacy*. Princeton,NJ: Princeton University Press.

Clunan, A. 2009. *The Social Construction of Russia's Resurgence: Aspirations, Identity, and Security Interests*. Washington, DC: Johns Hopkins University Press.

Clunan, A. 2014. '*Why Status Matters in World Politics*'. In *Status in World Politics*. Edited by T. V. Paul, D. W. Larson, W. C. Wohlforth, pp. 273–296. Cambridge: Cambridge University Press.

Curanović, A. 2012. *The Religious Factor in Russia's Foreign Policy*. New York and London: Routledge.

Curanović, A. 2015. 'The Guardians of Traditional Values: Russia and the Russian Orthodox Church in the Quest for Status', *Transatlantic Academy Paper Series* 1: 8–10.

Dore, R. P. 1975. 'The Prestige Factor in International Affairs', *International Affairs* 51(2): 190–207.

Freire, M. R. 2011. 'USSR/ Russian Federation's Major Power Status Inconsistencies'. In *Major Powers and the Quest for Status in International Politics: Global and Regional Perspectives*. Edited by T. J. Volgy, R. Corbetta, K. A. Grant and R. G. Baird, pp. 55–76. Basingstoke: Palgrave MacMillan.

Herbst, J. 2016. *How Syria Catapulted Russia from Mideast Pawn to Power Broker*. Available online: http://www.realclearworld.com/articles/2016/10/31/how_syria_ catapulted_russia_from_mideast_pawn_to_power_broker.html (accessed 31. 10. 2016).

Hønneland, G. 2016. *Russia and the Arctic: Environment, Identity and Foreign Policy.* London and New York: I. B. Tauris.

Hovorun, C. 2016. 'Is the Byzantine 'Symphony' Possible in Our Days?', *Journal of Church and State* 59: 1–17.

Jilge, W. 2014. *Analyse: Die Ukraine aus Sicht der 'Russkij Mir'.* Available online: http://www.bpb.de/internationales/europa/russland/186517/analyse-die-ukraine-aus-s icht-der-russkij-mir (accessed 17. 06. 2014).

Klimenko, E. 2016. 'Russia's Arctic Security Policy: Still Quiet in the High North?', *SIPRI Policy Paper* 45.

Knox, Z. 2003. 'The Symphonic Ideal: The Moscow Patriarchate's Post-Soviet Leadership', *Europe-Asia Studies* 55(4): 575–596.

Köllner, T. 2016. 'Patriotism, Orthodox Religion, and Education: Empirical Findings from Contemporary Russia', *Journal of Religion, State and Society* 44(4): 366–386.

Köllner, T. 2018. 'On the Restitution of Property and the Making of "Authentic" Landscapes in Contemporary Russia', *Europe-Asia Studies* 70(7): 1083–1102. doi:10.1080/09668136.2018.1484077.

Larson, D. W. and A. Shevchenko. 2003. 'Shortcut to Greatness: The New Thinking and the Revolution in Soviet Foreign Policy', *International Organization* 57(1): 77–109.

Laruelle, M. 2012. *Russian Nationalism, Foreign Policy and Identity Debates in Putin's Russia: New Ideological Patterns after the Orange Revolution.* Stuttgart: Verlag.

Laruelle, M. 2013. *Russia's Arctic Strategies and the Future of the Far North.* London and New York: Routledge.

Laruelle, M. 2014. 'Beyond Anti-Westernism: The Kremlin's Narrative about Russia's European Identity', *PONARS Eurasia Policy Memo* 326.

Laruelle, M. 2015. *The 'Russian World': Russia's Soft Power and Geopolitical Imagination.* Washington, DC: Center on Global Interests.

Leuştean, L. N. 2011. 'The Concept of Symphonia in Contemporary European Orthodoxy', *International Journal for the Study of the Christian Church* 11(2–3): 188–202.

Morozov, V. 2015. *Russia's Postcolonial Identity: A Subaltern Empire in a Eurocentric World.* Basingstoke: Palgrave Macmillan.

Neumann, I. 2008. 'Russia as a Great Power, 1815–1917', *Journal of International Relations and Development* 11(2): 128–151.

Neumann, I. 2011. 'Entry into International Society Reconceptualised: The Case of Russia', *Review of International Studies* 37: 463–484.

Neumann, I. and V. Pouliot. 2011 'Untimely Russia: Hysteresis in Russian-Western Relations over the Past Millennium', *Security Studies* 20(1): 105–137.

Nye, J. S. 2005. *Soft Power: The Means to Success in World Politics.* New York: Public Affairs.

Onea, T. A. 2014. 'Between Dominance and Decline: Status Anxiety and Great Power Rivalry', *Review of International Studies* 40(1): 125–152.

Paul, T. V., D. W. Larson and W. C. Wohlforth (eds.). 2014. *Status in World Politics.* Cambridge: Cambridge University Press.

Petro, N. N. 2015. *Russia's Orthodox Soft Power.* Available online: http://www.carne giecouncil.org/publications/articles_papers_reports/727 (accessed 23. 03. 2015).

Prizel, I. 1998. *National Identity and Foreign Policy: Nationalism and Leadership in Poland, Russia and Ukraine.* Cambridge: Cambridge University Press.

Prosić, T. 2014. 'Between Support for the State and Its Betrayal: The Contradictions of the Eastern Orthodox Christian Concept of Symphonia', *Political Theology* 15 (2): 175–187.

Ringmar, E. 2002. 'The Recognition Game: Soviet Russia against the West', *Cooperation and Conflict: Journal of the Nordic International Studies Association* 37(2): 115–136.

Sergunin, A. and V. Konyshev. 2017. *Russia in the Arctic: Hard or Soft Power?* Stuttgart: Verlag.

Sherr, J. 2013. *Hard Diplomacy and Soft Coercion: Russia's Influence Abroad*. London: Chatham House.

Shumilin, A. 2016. 'Russia's Diplomacy in the Middle East: Back to Geopolitics', *Russie. Nei.Vision* 93 (May).

Smith, H. 2014. 'Russia as a Great Power: Status Inconsistency and the Two Chechen Wars' *Communist and Post-Communist Studies* 47(3–4): 355–363.

Stent, A. 2016. 'Putin's Power Play in Syria', *Foreign Affairs*, January/February.

Stepanova, E. 2016. 'Russia's Policy on Syria after the Start of Military Engagement', *PONARS Eurasia Policy Memo* No. 421.

Stoeckl, K. 2014. *The Russian Orthodox Church and Human Rights*. New York and London: Routledge.

Suslov, M. 2014. '"Holy Rus": The Geopolitical Imagination in the Contemporary Russian Orthodox Church', *Russian Politics and Law* 52(3): 67–86.

Suslov, M. 2016. 'The Russian Orthodox Church and the Crisis in Ukraine'. In *Churches in the Ukrainian Crisis*. Edited by A. Krawchuk and T. Bremer, pp. 133–162. Basingstoke: Palgrave Macmillan.

Swartz, D. L. 1997. *Culture and Power: The Sociology of Pierre Bourdieu*. Chicago, IL: Chicago University Press.

Swartz, D. L. 2013. *Symbolic Power Politics and Intellectuals: The Political Sociology of Pierre Bourdieu*. Chicago, IL: University of Chicago Press.

Trenin, D. 2016. *Russia in the Middle East: Moscow's Objectives, Priorities, and Policy Drivers*. Available online: http://carnegie.ru/2016/04/05/russia-in-middle-east-m oscow-s-objectives-priorities-and-policy-drivers-pub-63244 (accessed 5. 4. 2016).

Tsygankov, A. P. 2005. 'Vladimir Putin's Vision of Russia as a Normal Great Power', *Post-Soviet Affairs* 21(2): 132–158.

Tsygankov, A. P. 2013. *Russia's Foreign Policy: Change and Continuity in National Identity*. Lanham, MD: Rowman & Littlefield.

Volgy, T. J. and S. Mayhall. 1995. 'Status Inconsistency and International War: Exploring the Effects of Systemic Change', *International Studies Quarterly* 39(1): 67–84.

Warhola, J. 2004. 'Religiosity, Politics, and the Formation of Civil Society in Multinational Russia'. In *Burden or Blessing? Russian Orthodoxy and the Construction of Civil Society and Democracy*. Edited by Ch. Marsh and N. Gvosdev. Boston, MA: Boston University Press.

Wendt, A. 2003. *Social Theory of International Relations*. Cambridge: Cambridge University Press.

Williams, M. C. 2007. *Culture and Security: Symbolic Power and Politics of International Security*. London and New York: Routledge.

12 Surrendering to public pressure

The 'Macedonian Orthodox Church' and the rejection of the Niš Agreement in 2002

Nenad Živković

Introduction

Unlike their Western counterparts, it would appear that the Orthodox Churches never truly came to terms with the civil power. In other words, they did not go through a separation process, which would have allowed them to exist and act independently from the civil power (cf. Kalaitzidis 2014; Makrides 2012; McGuckin 2003). Instead, even under secular or at times aggressively atheist regimes, such as Soviet communism was, they maintained a distinctive and somewhat servile relation to the state. The background of such relations may be brought into connection with the notion of 'ethnodoxy', i.e. a specific link between the ethnic identity and the prevalent religion of a group, as well as the implications that arise from such a link (Karpov, Lisovskaya and Barry 2012). There is, of course, a certain amount of generalisation in the previous remark. This is because the Orthodox ecclesiastical structure is quite decentralised on a global level, meaning that practically every independent Orthodox Church had and has to deal with this issue on its own. Historically, the dynamics of those relations has its beginnings in the Eastern Roman Empire. The model that was devised there, and which is usually described as *symphony* i.e. harmonic cooperation of imperial and ecclesiastical factor, remained essentially an ideal rather than reality (cf. McGuckin 2003; see also Jianu's chapter in this volume). Nevertheless, the interplay between *imperium* and *sacerdotium* in the Byzantine Empire, as well as their adapted implementations by the peoples under direct political influence of Byzantium and religious influence of its imperial Church, left an imprint on the overall dynamics of the relations between the state and the Church in the Orthodox tradition until today (Dvornik 1966: 839–840, and the whole chapter *Imperium and Sacerdotium* in general; see also Curanović's, Cîrlan's and Stahlberg's chapters in this volume).

However, this model went through some changes in the course of history, especially after the fall of Byzantium in 1453. For instance, it was in the Ottoman Empire, within its legal framework, that the Orthodox Church for the first time in its history received *civil* authority and acted in the name of the Ottoman state bureaucracy. The Ecumenical Patriarch was made civil head of all of the Orthodox subjects of the Empire, while the Church was invested with administration and arbitration in the legal affairs among the Orthodox population (Papadakis 1988: 45–47). Out of such circumstances arose, presumably, an even more symphonic or servile relationship with the state, than it was the case in the pre-Ottoman times. The Church effectively became a part of the Ottoman imperial administration and carried out its civil duties under the Biblical maxim that one must 'give back to Caesar what is Caesar's, and to God what is God's' (Luke 20, 25). This arrangement came handy for the Church administration as well, since it considerably increased its power in the Ottoman state.

This symphonic model, however, experienced further changes. Arguably the most significant transformation occurred with the emergence of nations during the nineteenth century. Since neither the earlier, Byzantine constellation *empire-church-emperor* nor the latter, Ottoman one, was further sustainable, it would appear, as Vasilios N. Makrides indicated, that it has been superseded by the *state-church-nation* constellation (Makrides 2013: 332). The implications of such a model included perception as well as self-perception of a nation's Church as its perennial guardian, which, eventually led to incorporating the Church 'into the national mythology of the respective states' (Makrides 2013: 332). It is precisely at this point, I believe, that a particular interplay between Orthodox Churches and their respective states can be observed in our time, even though this interplay does neither necessarily nor actually involve some kind of symphony or *symphonic harmony* between the state and the Church. It is rather a *nation*, often understood as sacrosanct, as inviolable, that a particular – *national* – Church nurtures exclusive relationship with. This relationship often comes as a result of a turbulent history, in the course of which the ecclesiastical factors assumed, during the Ottoman rule by necessity, the role of national leaders or national guardians. In such circumstances, as perverse as it may be, by being the highest national authority, a particular Church may find itself trapped by the very responsibility it has in the course of time gained in the terms of a distinctive patronage over a nation. I would argue that this kind of relationship can prevent it from taking actions which would even remotely contradict or unsettle such perception, let alone endanger national interests. In other words, I would like to draw on my own observations and point to another, less observed aspect of the generally assumed symphonic relationship between the Church and the state in the Orthodox tradition where the 'harmonious' relationship is being challenged (see also Batiashvili's and Iordache's chapters in this volume). Do we, thus, witness the end of the concept of symphony?

As a case in point I will focus on the Macedonian[1] ecclesiastical schism and the final rejection of the Niš Agreement in May/June 2002. In order to do so, I will try to present the means through which the public actors, such as government bodies and the media, created a specific milieu with the aim of fomenting resentment among the common people and the public in general toward the leadership of the Macedonian Church. For this purpose, I used various newspaper reports, interviews and articles published by the two daily newspapers from Skopje, *Dnevnik* (The Daily) and *Utrinski vesnik* (Morning News), in the last days of May and beginning of June 2002.

The primarily applied research method is critical discourse analysis, accompanied by content analysis (Van Dijk 1988; Van Dijk 2008; Krippendorf 2012). Analysing language used by public actors in reference to the proposed agreement, on the one side, as well as the meaning of the message which was thereby being sent, on the other, is, I contend, quite suitable here. It offers insight into the level of meaning, as well as into the specific choice of words and expressions, and hence reveals the positions of the actors involved.

The chapter is structured in the following way. In the first section, I offer a short outline of the historical context of the schism in the Republic of Macedonia. In the second section, the focus is set on the textual solutions of the Draft Agreement and their implications that initiated the debate on the pro and against. The final section turns to the analysis of the public reaction to the agreement and deals with political actors, government officials and the media. In the conclusion I summarise the findings and highlight a few relevant aspects.

Contextualising the ecclesiastical schism in Macedonia – a historical perspective

Although the ecclesiastical schism in the Republic of Macedonia officially dates back to 1967 when dioceses of the Serbian Orthodox Church (the SOC) in the then Socialist Republic of Macedonia unilaterally declared autocephaly, the foundations of the schism were laid down immediately after the Second World War. Simply put, the process of separation from the SOC and the declaration of autocephaly occurred in three major steps, the three so-called *clergy-laity councils* convened in Macedonia between 1945 and 1967.

The first declaration of autocephaly

After the liberation from the Bulgarian occupation forces, the new Yugoslav authorities were reluctant to allow the two bishops of the SOC in charge of the dioceses in Macedonia, who were forced to leave upon the occupation, to return to their seats. Instead, the *Initiative Committee for the organisation of church life in Macedonia* was formed in October 1944 only to be renamed a few months later, towards the beginning of 1945, to the *Initiative Committee for the foundation of the independent church in Macedonia and the renewal of the Archbishopric of Ohrid* (Zečević Božić 1994: 27–28; Radić 2002: 284). The *Initiative Committee*, formed by several local priests and de facto administrating the Church there, prepared and, as early as March 1945, convened, what would be known as the *First clergy-laity council*. This assembly of the local clergy and lay people, albeit in the absence of bishops, was held in Skopje, the capital city of the Republic of Macedonia, with the support and in the presence of several high-ranking local and federal officials, as well as of representatives of the Catholic Church and Islamic community (Sl. Dimevski 1989: 1029). The council proclaimed restoration of the ancient Archbishopric of Ohrid as the independent Macedonian Church, but asserted that, once the Yugoslav Patriarchate, a Church envisaged by the Yugoslav communist authorities to replace the national Serbian Church, was formed, the Macedonian Church would join it. However, this proclamation was shortly lived, since already in May 1946 a *Conference of priests of PR Macedonia* was convened, where the requests of the supporters of autocephaly were confronted by the growing number of those supporting autonomy inside the Serbian – and possibly – the 'Yugoslav' Church, producing a resolution which had much more moderate demands than that of 1945 (Zečević Božić 1994: 38–40; Ilievski 1973: 78–79). The Patriarchate in Belgrade did not recognise the canonicity of the council held in Skopje and pointed out that not only did not a single bishop of the SOC participate at this gathering, but its decisions contradicted the Tomos of the Ecumenical Patriarchate from 1922 which granted jurisdiction over the dioceses in question to the Serbian Orthodox Church (Radić 2002: 287, for details on the process of unification and the establishment of the SOC see Veselinović 1971). Although there were further contacts between the *Initiative Committee* and the Patriarchate, the *Initiative Committee* basically continued to administer the dioceses in the Republic of Macedonia without consent or any kind of oversight from the Patriarchate, let alone from the two bishops of the local dioceses, metropolitan of Skopje, Josif Cvijović and bishop of Zletovo-Strumica, Vikentije Prodanov, who were not able to return to their seats (Radić 2002: 289–290).

The restoration of the Archbishopric of Ohrid

After the latter assumed the patriarchal throne in 1950, relations gradually improved leading eventually to considerably moderate demands on the behalf of the *Initiative Committee*, such as simply retaining 'the local bishops and the national characteristics in the church through the use of the Macedonian literary language in church administration and everyday Macedonian in sermons' (Ilievski 1973: 89). However, the failure of the Episcopal Assembly of the SOC to actually fulfil these demands as well as the sudden death of Patriarch Vikentije in July 1958 led the *Initiative Committee* to convoke the *Second clergy-laity council* in October 1958 (Sl. Dimevski 1989: 1056), this time in Ohrid, where the seat of the ancient Archbishopric of Ohrid was. It was declared anew that the Archbishopric of Ohrid would be restored as the Macedonian Orthodox Church (the MOC). The vicar bishop of the patriarch, Dositej Stojković (or Stojkovski, which would be the Macedonian pronunciation; 1906–1981), despite the open and harsh objection of Patriarch German Đorić, answered positively to the invitation of the *Initiative Committee* to come to Ohrid. He did not actually take part in the session at which the restoration of the Archbishopric of Ohrid was declared, but was, nevertheless, elected its first metropolitan with the title 'the Archbishop of Ohrid and Skopje and Metropolitan of Macedonia' (Zečević Božić 1994: 94–95, fn. 45 and 46). This council passed the Statute of the MOC and established the jurisdiction of the MOC as corresponding to the borders of the PR Macedonia (Zečević Božić 1994: 62–79; 91–96; Puzović 1997: 51–54; Ilievski 1973: 93–97). Finally, it was made clear that the MOC aimed to maintain ecclesiastical unity with the Orthodox Church through the recognition of the highest orthodox ecclesiastical authority in Yugoslavia, that being the Patriarch of the SOC (Ilievski 1973: 94). A year later the SOC accepted its decisions and after new bishops were elected and ordained for the dioceses in Macedonia, the SOC tended to consider this issue resolved (cf. Puzović 1997: 61; Zečević Božić 1994: 100–109).

The Macedonian Orthodox Church declares autocephaly

It soon became apparent that the two parties differently interpreted the actual status and ecclesiastical competence of the Church in Macedonia. For instance, soon after it was granted autonomy, the MOC engaged in establishing separate parishes and dioceses in North America and Australia for the Macedonian communities abroad (Sl. Dimevski 1989: 1123–1126). Such possibility was envisaged in the Statute of the MOC from 1958, but only after the consent of the Patriarch had been obtained, which did not seem to have been the case. Since the existing situation proved that there was in fact a parallel ecclesiastical structure, the hierarchy of the SOC saw itself forced to re-evaluate the position of the MOC. Basically, the SOC was confronted with a direct request from the MOC, as well as with political pressure, to grant autocephaly to the MOC (Zečević Božić 1994: 145–146; on political pressure and involvement in this issue see Nikolić & Dimitrijević 2013: 196–197; Risteski 2009: 163–165). When the Episcopal Assembly of the SOC in May 1967 chose not to recognise the MOC as autocephalous, the hierarchy of the Macedonian Church decided to convene the *Third clergy-laity council*.

As was mentioned at the beginning of this section, the final declaration of autocephaly took place at the *Third clergy-laity council*, convened in Ohrid in July 1967, which coincided with the 2nd centenary of the abolishment of the ancient Archbishopric of Ohrid (abolished in 1767 by the Ecumenical Patriarchate, see Roudometof 1998: 19–20). The SOC refused to recognise the autocephalous status of the MOC, which was, and to this day remained, the position of all Orthodox Churches as well. Every further attempt to overcome the schism simply failed, since none of the two Churches was willing to step down from their positions.

The final attempt to restore unity

Towards the end of the twentieth century, the SOC and the MOC engaged in a new round of an official dialogue concerning the status of the Macedonian

Church. Archbishop Jovan of the Orthodox Archbishopric of Ohrid (OAO, autonomous under the SOC) wrote that it was in fact his initiative to resume the negotiations, which he launched upon his election to a bishop's degree in 1998 (when he was still a cleric of the MOC). Furthermore, he claimed that it was through him that then Archbishop of Athens Christodoulos agreed to appear as a mediator between the SOC and the MOC (Vraniškoski 2008: 86–87). After approximately four years and several adjustments to the proposed text of the agreement on restoring Church unity between the SOC and the MOC, these negotiations culminated in the signing of a draft of the agreement on 17 May 2002 in Niš, Southern Serbia. As the final step towards ecclesiastical unity, it was left to be ratified by the two respective synods at the earliest opportunity.

The document envisaged the MOC as the autonomous Archbishopric of Ohrid within the SOC – as was basically the solution from 1958/59 (cf. *Draft Agreement on Establishing Church Unity* 106–107). Due to unusually large freedom of self-administration, which the proposal entailed, the envisaged model of autonomy was interpreted by many on the Serbian side as *de facto* autocephaly and was therefore expected to be ratified in Macedonia. For instance, in addition to the provisions which foresaw that the Patriarchate would not interfere with any internal decision-making process, such as forming new eparchies, electing and appointing new bishops as well as the archbishop, the final version of the agreement also envisaged that the MOC could partake in inter-orthodox conferences and consultations without previously acquiring the otherwise customary special approval from the patriarch (cf. *Draft Agreement on Establishing Church Unity*, 106–113).

However, it soon became clear that not everyone found the proposed solution acceptable. Upon returning to their country, and after the text of the agreement was made public, the Macedonian ecclesiastical delegation and the higher hierarchy of the MOC as well faced severe criticism and even accusations of committing treason against the Macedonian nation and state (cf. Sa. Dimevski 2002). Eventually, the Holy Synod of the MOC rejected the proposed agreement together with the overall results of the negotiations that led to it in the first place. This, and the fact that bishop Jovan Vraniškovski of the MOC decided to enter into unity with the SOC, triggered a whole chain of events and actions which ever since have rendered the relationship between the SOC and the MOC highly volatile. As a result, the MOC remains unrecognised by the community of the Orthodox Churches while since 2004 a parallel ecclesiastical structure exists in the Republic of Macedonia: the unrecognised Macedonian Orthodox Church and the autonomous Archbishopric of Ohrid, formed under the auspices of the SOC and thus in communion with other Orthodox Churches.

The problematic implications of the Draft Agreement on Establishing Church Unity

The Macedonian question as a whole is quite multifaceted, to put it mildly. Its ecclesiastical aspect i.e. the 'Macedonian schism' is thus in no way separable from the wider notion of the 'Macedonian question'. In other words, the ecclesiastical issue in Macedonia is not purely ecclesiastical. The general question is, however, if any ecclesiastical issue is and can ever remain solely ecclesiastical (cf. Roudometof 2014: 80–101, and specifically 88–91). On the other hand, the 'Macedonian question' is a topic of its own that has been drawing the attention of researchers as well as of the general public for decades, especially after Macedonia gained independence in 1991 (see Munck & Risteski 2013; Roudometof 2002; Roudometof 2000; Pettifer 1999). One of the most intoxicating and most complicated aspects of this issue is probably the problem of the country's and accordingly nation's and Church's name: *Macedonia, Macedonians* and *Macedonian* Orthodox Church. As such it is beyond the scope of this chapter to deal with the whole Macedonian issue extensively. However, for the purpose of this chapter it is important to shed light on the confusion and in a certain way the hysteria that surrounded the signing of the Niš Agreement. In order to do so and in order to deal with the reasons that triggered the whole campaign against the agreement, one should take a look at how the text of the agreement treated the designation *Macedonia(n)*.

The text of the agreement consists of: a) the preamble; b) seventeen articles, each of those defining the status, rights, place in respect to the SOC and other Orthodox Churches, and, as a sign of Eucharistic unity, duties of the Church in Macedonia; and c) a short agreement on pastoral cooperation between the two Churches. In the context of the present topic, it would be of use to take a closer look at the preamble, the fourteenth and the fifteenth article, as well as the final section of the agreement, concerning pastoral cooperation.

In the preamble one reads that a 'broad church independence, that is, broadest church autonomy [is being recognised] to the existing eparchies of the orthodox church in the Republic of Macedonia, that is, the Ohrid Archbishopric and its Diaspora...' (*Draft Agreement on Establishing Church Unity*, 106). As it occurs throughout the document, this sentence sends an ambivalent message to some degree, since in practice independence and autonomy are not the same thing. This, in a way mixed, terminology suggests that the authors tried to present the two as being synonymous in order to create an impression that although autocephaly had not officially (meaning: literally) been granted, the autonomy might temporarily be understood as such. However, in its final point the preamble left the final decision on the matter of granting autocephaly 'to the future pan-orthodox concord of the Fullness of the Church in the Holy Spirit' (cf. *Draft Agreement on Establishing Church Unity*, 106). In other words, it implied that not the SOC alone is entitled to make such decision, but that it is a matter of concord of all Orthodox Churches. Secondly, the name Macedonia is used in the context of the official Republic's name, according to the Macedonian constitution, and not as it is internationally recognised (as the Former Yugoslav Republic of Macedonia), while the respective Church is referred to as the Archbishopric of Ohrid (the official English translation uses the formulation Ohrid Archbishopric; cf. *Draft Agreement on Establishing Church Unity*, 106, 110). So, naming the

Church in Macedonia as Macedonian was avoided, while the name Serbian Orthodox Church was used twice, although once, at the very beginning, inter-changeably with the old name 'the Patriarchate of Peć.' This is interesting, since it reflects the ancient ecclesiology, where a certain ecclesiastical see is named after a place in which it resides. On the other hand, the interchangeability of the designations, which was used in the case of the SOC, was not applied to the MOC.

While the preamble merely anticipated it, the fourteenth and the fifteenth articles of the agreement explicitly defined and regulated the name of the autonomous Church in Macedonia as well as the title of its primate. They read as follows:

> 14. In accordance with the ancient Church Tradition and the historical practice, the name of the respective Church is the Ohrid Archbishopric. The Ohrid Archbishopric may, according to the long-established practice, use the name it has used so far in its internal official communication with the Patriarchate of Peć.
>
> 15. For the same reason, the Primate officially bears the title Archbishop of Ohrid and Metropolitan of Skopje, and the present title can be applied internally.
>
> (*Draft Agreement on Establishing Church Unity*, 110–111)

As it becomes clear, the distinction 'Macedonian' was completely omitted from the articles defining the name of the Church there. The discourse makes it very clear, although not explicitly stated, that the name *the Macedonian Orthodox Church* is not to be used in the external appearances of the MOC. Instead, the Church is being recognised as the Archbishopric of Ohrid, fol-lowing, as the fourteenth article states, 'the ancient Church Tradition and the historical practice' (*Draft Agreement on Establishing Church Unity*, 110). Putting aside the question of the justification of such reference it is worth mentioning that this formulation actually has the Archbishopric of Ohrid in sight, as it existed from 1018–1767. At the same time, both of the articles underline that the name that has been used so far as well as the title of the archbishop may further be used in official communication with the Patriarchate, which is again being referred to as the Patriarchate of Peć, although according to the statute of the SOC, the title of the patriarch is the 'Archbishop of Peć, Metropolitan of Belgrade-Karlovci and Serbian Patri-arch,' while his seat is in Belgrade (*Draft Agreement on Establishing Church Unity*, 110; cf. *Ustav Srpske pravoslavne crkve* [The Statute of the Serbian Orthodox Church] 1957, Articles 11, 13 and 14). It is notable how the authors of this agreement chose to use affirmative language while in fact imposing a prohibition of the name usage.

So, according to these provisions of the agreement the MOC was supposed to appear in the inter-orthodox world as the Archbishopric of Ohrid but clearly *not* as the *Macedonian* Orthodox Church, while in official internal communication with the patriarchate in Belgrade the old name would be used without limitations. This would imply that the composers of the text of the agreement aimed to avoid any inter-orthodox resistance to the reference of a strictly *Macedonian* Church. It is widely known that because of the Greek objection to the use of the name Macedonia, since 1993, when it became a full member of the United Nations, the country is internationally recognised as the Former Yugoslav Republic of Macedonia. Having this in mind, it appears proper to assume that such concession was undergone in order to avoid resistance from the Greek authorities (both ecclesiastical and secular) who may have objected the recognition of an autonomous Church bearing the name 'Macedonian'. In fact, this was precisely the stand taken by the three Macedonian bishops who signed the Draft Agreement in Niš, who also implied that the agreement signed in Niš is not final and that it is in need of improvement (cf. 'Avtonomna ohridska arhiepiskopija' 2002).

The final section of the agreement is entitled *Draft Agreement on the Pastoral Cooperation*. It aims to establish adequate

> pastoral care for the members of the Serbian people in the Republic of Macedonia as well as for the members of the Macedonian people in Serbia and other regions of Serbia, as well in Croatia, Slovenia and elsewhere in the canonical area of the Serbian Orthodox Church …
>
> (Draft Agreement on Establishing Church Unity, 110)

This care should be achieved by appointing priests of a respective nationality where it is necessary. While implying that the SOC still holds canonical right to Macedonia, the text clearly speaks of the Macedonian people, and addresses the country under its constitutional name.

In the integral text of the agreement there are three references to the distinction 'Macedonia'. Two of them are used in the context of the constitutional Republic's name, while the third refers to the Macedonian people. Nevertheless, regardless of different possibilities to name the Church in Macedonia, the fact is that 'the signifier of the national background of the Church […] is missing' (Risteski 2009: 177). In this way, it would appear, the name dispute infiltrated and influenced the process of the ecclesiastical reconciliation.

Overall, the text of the agreement proves, in certain points, somewhat ambivalent. But, since its aim is to reconcile the difficult demands posed by historical events and to finally make a successful compromise, acertain amount of ambivalence is to be expected. Its presence may have led some authors to conclude that the agreement in fact gave an independent status to the MOC, 'just short of *canonical* autocephaly' (Aleksov 2010: 182–183).

Reactions to the proposed agreement – an analysis

Soon after the contents of the agreement were made public in the Republic of Macedonia the signatories from the Macedonian delegation (the three metropolitans: Petar of Australia who served as the administrator of Prespa and Pelagonia, Timotej of Debar and Kičevo, and Naum of Strumica) faced a harsh media campaign directed against them personally, their alleged betrayal and the implications of the Niš Agreement. For instance, Metropolitan Petar was reportedly called 'a Serbian spy' and 'Judas' by a protesting group of the faithful. This may have had to do with the fact that he was presiding over the Macedonian delegation at the meeting in Niš. However, even within the higher hierarchy of the MOC itself there was a loud objection to the terms of the agreement, represented in the first place by Bishop Agatangel and Metropolitan Kiril. Bishop Agatangel openly threatened that, should the agreement be accepted, it would come to a schism within the MOC. Reportedly, on the eve of the first session of the Holy Synod he even omitted the archbishop's name from the church service (Gorǵevski 2002a; Gorǵevski 2002b). This was the atmosphere in which the members of the Macedonian delegation tried to defend the agreement and present the reasons why they found it acceptable. To that end they held a joint press conference on 28 May. This conference took place two days after the session of the Holy Synod of the MOC was held for the first time since the agreement was signed on 17 May (and as such was the first official occasion to discuss the agreement among the members of the Holy Synod). At their joint press conference the three bishops concurred that the Niš Agreement was the best proposal that had ever been made by the SOC and that it would most certainly lead toward an autocephalous status in the future. Metropolitan Petar emphasised that their agenda was that they did not want to remain in schism with the entire Orthodox world, while Metropolitan Timotej reminded that every Orthodox church which they contacted in the past assured them that they must seek a solution with the SOC, since none of the churches would recognise their autocephaly when declared in such 'a coup-like manner...' ('Avtonomna ohridska arhiepiskopija' 2002). Furthermore, Metropolitan Petar emphasised the fact that according to the all-orthodox agreement from Chambésy (Switzerland) autocephaly can be granted only through the consensus of all autocephalous Orthodox churches which also means that no individual church, in this case the SOC, has the authority to grant autocephaly to another church. In the same manner he pointed out that gaining autonomous status is the most secure and the most certain way towards autocephaly (Georgievska 2002a).

In addition to clarifying the ecclesiastical terms and conditions of the possible recognition of their church, they referred to the problematic solution of the name as well. They insisted that the concession that was made, as outlined in the previous section, was purely pragmatic. The reason was to avoid possible resistance from the bloc of Greek churches, they affirmed. At the same time, it was pointed out that with the exception of the Greek Orthodox Church all Orthodox churches refer to them as the *Macedonian* Orthodox Church (Georgievska 2002a; 'Avtonomna ohridska arhiepiskopija' 2002). The intention of this assertion was apparently to strengthen the argument that the limitation of the use of the designation Macedonian was actually not as grave as it may have seemed.

Despite the arguments and explanations brought out by the three bishops – or precisely because of them – the reactions intensified in the following days. They included more frequent coverage in the media (as it will be shown in the next section), as well as a special reaction of the *Government's Commission for relations with religious communities and religious groups.*

As a separate governmental body this commission essentially has been in existence since 1951, that is, since the early years of communist Yugoslavia. In the following five decades it changed its name four times. It has operated under the present name since 2000, when the director is appointed by the government. The basic function of this commission is the regulation of the legal status of religious communities, that is, the registration of religious communities before state, as well as the mediation between the state and the religious communities in legal and other affairs (see the internet presentation of the Commission: 'Komisija za odnosi so verskite zaednici i religiozni grupi,' n.d.). Some reference to the socialist-communist period of this commission will be mentioned in the next section.

Media coverage and political pressure

One important aspect of the reaction to these events is the way in which the media reported on this issue. I have limited myself to the coverage from two daily newspapers from Skopje, *Utrinski vesnik* (Morning newspaper) and *Dnevnik* (The Daily). These published a number of reports, interviews and articles in the days prior to the final decision on the agreement. Even a brief glance at the newspaper titles allows for a preliminary conclusion that these were biased. Translated into English some of them read as follows: 'The bishops put the MOC in the arms of the Patriarchate of Peć' (Ǵorǵevski 2002b), 'The proposal for the 'autonomous Ohrid Archbishopric' is hellish' (Ǵorǵevski 2002c), 'Autonomy means erasing the history of the Macedonian Church' (Cvetanoski & Poposki 2002), 'Shameful act of negating of sacred symbols' ('Sramen čin na negiranje na svetite simboli,' 2002), 'The bishops signatories should be ecclesiastically punished and should repent' (Sa. Dimevski 2002), 'Pressured by the faithful people, will the Synod reject the Niš Agreement?' (Ǵorǵevski 2002d), 'Independent countries have the right to independent churches' (Ǵorǵevski 2002e), 'Bishop Stefan promised that the Synod will vote for an autocephalous MOC' (Ǵorǵevski 2002f), 'Schism in the church if the Synod votes for autonomy?' (Georgievska 2002b), 'The people will not give the MOC to the SOC' (Georgievska 2002c), 'The Primate and the hierarchs would break their oaths by accepting autonomy' (Cvetanoski 2002) etc. Let us engage in the analysis of the content and the language they used.

The daily newspapers *Dnevnik* and *Utrinski vesnik* published an interview with Doné Ilievski on 28 May and 31 May respectively. Ilievski was secretary general and president of the *Commission for religious affairs* of the People's (after 1963 Socialist) Republic of Macedonia from 1953 to 1973 and an active participant of the events in 1958 and 1967. He published a work on the history of the struggle for autocephaly (Ilievski 1972; translated into English: Ilievski 1973) and was, to put it that way, the highest 'moral' authority on the matter. Implying that accepting the proposed agreement would mean losing nationhood, Illievski said: 'Someone wants the same thing to happen to our church, which is happening right now to the state so that we could completely lose our identity as a nation. [...] The people are not going to accept it' (Cvetanoski & Poposki 2002).[2] He also described the proposed agreement as 'hellish', saying that it denies everything that has been done in the history of the MOC. In addition, he insisted that the title of the archbishop must not be given up on, also pointing out that it deliberately contains the designations 'Ohrid and Macedonian', because in that way the past and the present are united (Ǵorǵevski 2002c).

The same text reported that the World Macedonian congress, a non-governmental pro-nationalist organisation from Skopje, strongly opposed the Niš Agreement and called upon the Synod of the MOC to reject it since it 'inflicts immeasurable damage to the ecclesiastical and national dignity of the Macedonian people and devastates the already realised autocephalous status of our church' (Ǵorǵevski 2002c). Some political parties also expressed their opinion on the matter. The ruling pro-nationalist party at that time VMRO-DPMNE (The Internal Macedonian Revolutionary Organisation – the Democratic Party for Macedonian National Unity) issued a statement saying that any change to the name of the MOC would be unacceptable, while the public relations officer of the Socialist Party of Macedonia, Zoran Vitanov, pointed out that the depersonalisation of the MOC at the same time implies the depersonalisation of the Macedonian State and nation (Ǵorǵevski 2002c).

The reactions especially intensified on the day before and on the very day of the session of the Holy Synod of the MOC, where the decision concerning the agreement would be made. For instance, the day before the session of the Holy Synod *Utrinski vesnik* once again consulted Doné Ilievski and, in another text, reported that on that very day the *Government's Commission for religious communities* will be discussing the proposed Niš Agreement in order to agree on the official position on the matter (Cvetanoski 2002). This author concluded: 'The opinion of this body is necessary because the bishops will be able to directly hear the voice of the people, that is, of the persons with competence regarding the proposal of the Serbian church' (Georgievska 2002c). In addition to reporting that the faithful people as well as many priests oppose the agreement and that the teaching council of the Theological faculty in Skopje finds it unacceptable (Ǵorǵevski 2002d), *Dnevnik* also published an interview with Jovan Belčovski, a Church history professor from the same faculty. Belčovski argued that according to the canon law of the Orthodox Church, as well as to the example of the SOC after the First World War, every independent state is entitled to an independent church. He concluded that it were historical circumstances which resulted in the fact that an autocephalous church became the main feature of an independent state (Ǵorǵevski 2002e). His overall message was that by that right, being an independent state, Macedonia is entitled to its own autocephalous national church which already exists and thus cannot be degraded to an autonomous status, let alone deprived of its name (Ǵorǵevski 2002e).

However, the pressure culminated with the aforementioned session of the *Government's Commission for relations with religious communities*. Its conclusions were published on the very day of the Synod's session under the headline 'The bishops signatories should be ecclesiastically punished and should repent' (Sa. Dimevski 2002). In short, this Commission strongly recommended to the Holy Synod of the MOC not to accept the agreement, describing it as detrimental for the Church, State and nation. In addition, it even asserted that the bishops who signed it had committed an act of treason. One of the members of the Commission, Eleonora Petrova, was of the opinion that by signing the agreement the three bishops were not simply expressing their personal positions, but that it had most likely been previously agreed to by the Holy Synod and that the whole event was intended to act as a trial balloon in order to test the Macedonian public. Another member of the Commission, Mihajlo Georgievski from VMRO-DPMNE, was assured that the struggle for the recognition of autocephaly would not be abandoned although the bishops made 'an impudent act of high treason' (Sa. Dimevski 2002). The Commission came to an unanimous conclusion that the Church should at no cost give up the name 'Macedonian'. In the end, the overall opinion prevailed that the issue was rather a political one and not an exclusively ecclesiastical one. The recognition of the MOC would only be possible when the Republic of Macedonia resolved its dispute with neighbouring Greece over the issue of the name of the country, concluded Petrova (Sa. Dimevski 2002).

This example of how the government apparatus had taken a stand against the agreement and how it openly suggested, in a manner that resembles more a command than a mere suggestion, that the agreement should be rejected, serves to support the general thesis of this chapter. The fact that the Commission was in session the day before the Holy Synod would meet, which also meant that its conclusions would be published on the day of the Synod's session, appears quite convenient. Furthermore, accusing the bishops of the MOC of *treason* as well as of an attempt to test the public opinion does not only directly undercut their authority as ecclesiastical officials. It also questions their loyalty to the Macedonian nation. As such, and especially so being sent from a government's body, this poses a strong message to the ecclesiastical hierarchy that ratifying the agreement would not be the right thing to do.

On the other hand, it is no less remarkable how the newspapers published such a meticulous report of the Commission's session under an openly admonitory title. Also, it is important to have in mind that this newspaper reported on the *day before* about this session and urged the bishops *in advance* to hear the voice of the people, which would be expressed in the opinion of the Commission. It is worth noting that there was a certain conviction that the Commission would rule in the way it in the end did.

The Commission's conclusions and suggestions to the Synod as well as the manner in which the media reported on the topic contributed to creating an atmosphere where the acceptance of the proposed agreement would be widely interpreted as treason and as an act against the nation's best interests. This becomes clearer if we take a closer look at the fact that the government's Commission suggested that the Church *punish* its bishops for the alleged act of treason. In doing so, this Commission not only implied that the representatives of the MOC did in fact do wrong, it also, by using the punishment terminology, sent a message, and a warning as well, that the bishops must amend. Putting all this aside, if a treasonous act had actually taken place then the power and the authority of the Church would have been fairly exceeded and it would in fact be the legal duty of the prosecutor's office to indict those under suspicion.

On the same day, that is on 6 June, *Utrinski vesnik* published two more related articles with the headlines, 'The Holy Synod facing an historic responsibility' and 'Bishops, hear the voice of the people!' (Georgievska 2002d; Duvnjak 2002). The first author reported that during the session of the Holy Synod there would be a peaceful protest by the *dissatisfied* faithful, who, as the author strongly asserts, 'object the eventual approval of, according to their opinion, a detrimental agreement for the future of the MOC' (Georgievska 2002d; Interestingly enough, the same author would later report that in spite of the announced protests of the faithful in front of the seat of the archbishop, only a few people appeared (cf. Georgievska 2002e). Once more it has been emphasised that the *Government's Commission for relations with religious communities* discarded the agreement as unacceptable and that, in addition to the dissatisfied citizens, the political parties also called for peaceful protests. Finally, it was emphasised that the Church communities of the Diaspora deemed it as 'negating the history of the Macedonian people and the church' (Georgievska 2002d). Similarly, the other author warned that '[i]f the few elected church officials, however, decide to go against the will of their own people it could easily happen that they find themselves being the only church in the world without its faithful' and openly called the Holy Synod to listen to the voice of its people, because they had already given the right answer (Duvnjak 2002).

The *Dnevnik* on the other hand published only one related article on that same day, however, one that was nonetheless important. Under the title, 'Bishop Stefan promised that the Synod will vote for an autocephalous MOC', this article also reported on the conclusions of the Commission, repeating that the bishops signatories had committed an act of treason (Ǵorǵevski 2002f). The negation of Macedonian nationhood and identity by the Niš Agreement was once again brought into question: '[…] it is tragic that at a time of contesting the Macedonian nation, our identity is being challenged from the inside, from an important institution such as the MOC' and 'Not only that the MOC is being placed under the control of the SOC, as a consequence the Macedonian nation is being denied' (Gorġevski 2002f). Even more importantly, this article reported that the president of the Commission, Gorgi Naumov, had met with Archbishop Stefan who *promised* him that the Synod would neither give up on the rightful and constitutional name of the Church nor on its autocephalous status. Furthermore, Naumov maintained that both of the highest two officials of the country, the president of the republic at the time, Boris Trajkovski, as well as the prime minister, Ljupčo Georgievski, were of the same opinion as the Commission on the matter (Gorġevski 2002f).

The abovementioned actions such as the rather instructive statements from the governmental structures and various political actors, or the manner and attitude of the media reporting on the matter indicate that an atmosphere was under construction, which would render the public pressure unbearable for the Church. The fact that President Trajkovski on another occasion made a strong correlation between the loss of the autocephalous status of the MOC and the loss of statehood of the Republic of Macedonia (see Cepreganov, Angelovska-Panova & Zajkovski 2014) only enhanced such an atmosphere.

In addition to almost permanently calling the statehood and nationhood into question quite illustrating is the discourse which was employed here. Abundant with admonitory tone it frequently used words and expressions such as *high treason, dissatisfaction* of the people, *historical responsibility* of the Holy Synod, *harmful* and *detrimental* agreement, *negation* and *denial* of national and Church history, *oath-breaking* bishops, *schism* in the Church, etc. Almost as a rule, negative formulations dominate. However, it is most striking how a straight and unambiguous correlation has been drawn between the status and the name of the Church in Macedonia, on the one hand, and the achieved or contested statehood and nationhood of the Macedonians, on the other. At the level of meaning, as well as at that of the discourse, the impli-cation was pretty clear – the acceptance of the proposed agreement would mean *depersonalizing, denying* and utterly *damaging* the nation, while those who would take this step would finally commit *treason*. They would betray *responsibility* which they willingly accepted when they received the episcopal rank. In all of this it is most indicating that the accent is primarily or even exclusively put on the national character of the Church. In other words, it seems that the Church is being seen primarily through the role of its *national responsibility* and mission. At the same time, maybe precisely in connection to this almost exclusively national understanding, the fact that the MOC would be recognised by the Orthodox Churches and would end its isolation was severely neglected in the reactions to the agreement.

Concluding remarks

My point of departure was to show that the generally assumed symphonic relationship between the Church and the state is not necessarily true (see also

Batiashvili and Iordache in this volume). A special relationship exists rather between a nation and its respective church, I asserted in the introductory section. In order to present a case in point I have concentrated on the controversy which arose upon signing of the *Draft agreement on restoring the church unity* between the SOC and the MOC, and on its final rejection. Although what has been presented here is but a sample, primarily regarding media coverage, the general direction is not difficult to identify, especially when it is seen through the lenses of various government officials, political and other public actors. To summarise, after the decision about the implementation or rejection of the Niš Agreement was being publicly interpreted as a decision *for* or *against* the Macedonian state and nation the Holy Synod of the MOC on its session from 6 June unanimously discarded and altogether rejected this agreement as unacceptable.

There is a point here, which deserves to be highlighted. It concerns the position of the Macedonian Church towards the state and nation, on the one side, and towards the global Orthodoxy on the other. In terms of doctrine i.e. Orthodox Christian belief and theological teachings the Macedonian Orthodox Church does not discern from other Orthodox Churches, but it is nevertheless being denied full canonical recognition within Orthodoxy. As the nation's perennial guardian, the Church was basically prevented to ratify the agreement allowing the political and public pressure to overcome the common ecclesiastical sense. So, its decision not to accept the proposed agreement was made at the costs of remaining in isolation towards the global Orthodoxy, but was, in the end, perceived by the public actors as the right decision for the wellbeing of the Macedonian nation and state.

This is a very dichotomous position and it indicates that there is a conflict between religious and secular authorities in post-socialist countries, where the secular bodies wish to control and steer religious actors in a very similar way as their socialist and communist predecessors had done earlier. There is, in other words, a lack of critical distance in regard to particular, national ideals and interests, which arises from the very nature of the relationship and the place of the national Church.

Finally, this example shows that there are Orthodox Churches that can only have a symphonic or cooperative relationship with the state when the interests of the nation do not conflict with the actions of the Church authorities. Certainly, I am not saying that this is only the case with the Church in Macedonia (see e.g. Curanović's 'symphony of views'). Although the spatial, as well as my own, limitations do not allow for a more comprehensive survey, this particular case should simply be understood as an example, an indicator of an issue that affects many if not most of the Orthodox Churches today. From this point of view one can thus conclude that the issue of symphony or symphonic harmony in the Orthodox tradition could often be described as a societal ideal and that it rather reflects certain periods of history of the Orthodox Church than the actual state of affairs. At the end, I would argue that under present circumstances such cooperative relationship between the Church and the state is only possible when the interests of the two align, in the ideal case as national interests.

Notes

1 I use the designation *Macedonia* as well as its derivations in reference to the terri-tory of the modern-day Republic of Macedonia and the respective Macedonian nation and church.
2 All translations from the newspaper articles are my own.

Bibliography

Sources

Draft Agreement on Establishing Church Unity (2005[2002]) in B. Vitanov (ed.), *Zaradi idnoto Carstvo, Tom I/For the Kingdom to Come, Vol. I*, pp. 106–111. Ohrid: Pravoslavna ohridska Arhiepiskopija.
Ustav Srpske pravoslavne crkve. 1957. Beograd: Sveti Arhejerejski Sinod.
Komisija za odnosi so verskite zaednici i religiozni grupi. (n.d.) Available online: http://www.kovz.gov.mk/?ItemID=1906BEA071923A40B2ECFB5752517506 (in Macedonian language).

References

Aleksov, B. 2010. 'The Serbian Orthodox Church: Haunting Past and Challenging Future', *International Journal for the Study of the Christian Church* 10(2–3): 176–191.
Cepreganov, T., Angelovska-Panova, M. and Zajkovski, D. 2014. 'The Macedonian Orthodox Church.' In *Eastern Christianity and Politics in the Twenty-First Century*. Edited by L. N. Leustean, pp. 426–438. London: Routledge.
Dimevski, Sl. 1989. *Istorija na makedonskata pravoslavna crkva*. Skopje: Makedonska kniga.
Dvornik, F. 1966. *Early Christian and Byzantine Political Philosophy: Origins and Background. Vol. Two*. Washington, DC: The Dumbarton Oaks Center for Byzantine Studies.
Ilievski, D. 1972. *Avtokefalnosta na makedonskata pravoslavna crkva*. Skopje: Nova Makedonija.
Ilievski, D. 1973. *The Macedonian Orthodox Church: the Road to Independence*. Skopje: Macedonian Review Editions.
Kalaitzidis, P. 2014. 'Church and State in the Orthodox World. From the Byzantine "Symphonia" and Nationalized Orthodoxy to the Need of Witnessing the Word of God in a Pluralistic Society.' In *Religioni, Libertà, Potere. Atti del Convegno inter-nazionale filosofico-teologico sulla libertà religiosa, Milano, Università Cattolica del Sacro Cuore e Università degli studi, 16–18 ottobre 2013*. Edited by E. Fogliadini, pp. 39–74. Milano: Vita e pensiero.
Karpov, V., Lisovskaia, E. and Barry, D. 2012. 'Ethnodoxy: How Popular Ideologies Fuse Religious and Ethnic Identities', *Journal for the Scientific Study of Religion* 51: 638–655.
Krippendorf, K. 2012. *Content Analysis: An Introduction to Its Methodology*. Thousand Oaks, CA: Sage.

Makrides, V. N. 2012. 'Orthodox Christianity, Modernity and Postmodernity: Overview, Analysis and Assessment', *Religion, State & Society* 40(3–4): 248–285.

Makrides, V. N. 2013. 'Why Are Orthodox Churches Particularly Prone to Nationalization and Even to Nationalism', *St Vladimir's Theological Quarterly* 57(3–4): 325–352.

McGuckin, J. A. 2003. 'The Legacy of the 13th Apostle: Origins of the East Christian Conceptions of Church and State Relations', *St Vladimir's Theological Quarterly* 47 (3–4): 251–288.

Munck, V. C. D. and Risteski, Lj. (eds.). 2013. *Macedonia – the Political, Social, Economic and Cultural Foundations of a Balkan State.* London: Taurus.

Nikolić, M. and Dimitrijević, D. 2013. '"Macedonian Orthodox Church" in former Yugoslav State', *Politikologija religije/Politics and Religion/Politologie des Religions* 7(1): 193–215.

Papadakis, A. 1988. 'The Historical Tradition of Church-State Relations under Orthodoxy.' In *Eastern Christianity and Politics in the Twentieth Century.* Edited by P. Ramet, pp. 37–58. Durham and London: Duke University Press.

Pettifer, J. (ed.). 1999. *The New Macedonian Question.* Basingstoke: Macmillan.

Puzović, P. 1997. *Raskol u Srpskoj pravoslavnoj crkvi – makedonsko crkveno pitanje.* Beograd: Sveti arhijerejski sinod Srpske pravoslavne crkve.

Radić, R. 2002. *Država i verske zajednice: 1945–1970. Deo 2, 1954–1970.* Beograd: INIS.

Risteski, Lj. S. 2009. 'Recognition of the independence of the Macedonian Orthodox Church (MOC) as an Issue Concerning Macedonian National Identity', *EthnoAnthropoZoom* 6, 145–185.

Roudometof, V. 1998. 'From Rum Millet to Greek Nation: Enlightenment, Secularization and National Identity in Ottoman Balkan Society, 1453–1821', *Journal of Modern Greek Studies* 16: 11–36.

Roudometof, V. (ed.). 2000. *The Macedonian Question: Culture, Historiography, Politics.* Boulder, CO: East European Monographs.

Roudometof, V. 2002. *Collective Memory, National Identity and Ethnic Conflict – Greece, Bulgaria and the Macedonian Question.* Westport, CT: Praeger.

Roudometof, V. 2014. *Globalization and Orthodox Christianity: The Transformations of a Religious Tradition.* New York: Routledge.

Van Dijk, T. A. 1988. *News Analysis: Case Studies of International and National News in the Press.* Hillsdale, MI: Erlbaum.

Van Dijk, T. A. 2008. *Discourse and Power: Contributions to Critical Discourse Studies.* Houndsmills: Palgrave MacMillan.

Veselinović, R. L. 1971. *Ujedinjenje pokrajinskih crkava i vaspostavljanje patrijaršije.* In Srpska Pravoslavna Crkva 1920–1970. Spomenica o 50-godišnjici vaspostavljanja srpske patrijaršije. Edited by Metropolitan Vladislav et. al., pp. 14–35. Beograd: Sveti arhijereski sinod Srpske pravoslavne crkve.

Vraniškoski, J. 2008. *Brief History of the Ohrid Archbishopric – Kratka istorija na ohridskata arhiepiskopija.* Ohrid: Arhiepiskopija ohridska i Mitropolija skopska.

Zečević Božić, J. 1994. *Die Autokephalieerklärung der Makedonischen Orthodoxen Kirche.* Würzburg: Augustinus Verlag.

Newspaper articles

'"Avtonomna ohridska arhiepiskopija" ja vodi crkvata do avtokefalnost' (2002, 29 May). *Dnevnik.* Retrieved from http://star.dnevnik.com.mk/?pBroj=1860&stID= 3136. Last accessed 16 March 2017.

Cvetanoski, V. (2002, 5 June). 'Poglavarot i arhijereite so avtonomijata Ќe gi pogazat dadenite zakletvi.' *Utrinski vesnik*. Retrieved from http://star.utrinski.com.mk/?pBroj=884&stID=11993&pR=2. Last accessed 15 March 2017.

Cvetanoski, V. and Poposki, K. (2002, 31 May). 'Avtonomijata znači brišenje na istorijata na Makedonskata crkva.' *Utrinski vesnik*. Retrieved from http://star.utrinski.com.mk/?pBroj=880&stID=11621&pR=3. Last accessed 23 March 2017.

Dimevski, Sa. (2002, 6 June). 'Vladicite-potpisnici crkovno da se kaznat i da se pokajat.' *Utrinski vesnik*. Retrieved from http://star.utrinski.com.mk/?pBroj=885&stID=12046&pR=2ed. Last accessed 15 March 2017.

Duvnjak, G. (2002, June 06). 'Vladici, slušnite go glas na narodot.' *Utrinski vesnik*. Retrieved from http://star.utrinski.com.mk/?pBroj=885&stID=12074&pR=8. Last accessed 5 April 2017.

Georgievska, V. (2002a, 29 May). 'Vladikata Petar go brani niškiot sporazum.' *Utrinski vesnik*. Retrieved from http://star.utrinski.com.mk/?pBroj=878&stID=11450&pR=2. Last accessed 22 March 2017.

Georgievska, V. (2002b, 4 June). 'Raskol vo Crkvata ako Sinodot izglasa avtonomija?' *Utrinski vesnik*. Retrieved from http://star.utrinski.com.mk/?pBroj=883&stID=11904&pR=2. Last accessed 13 March 2017.

Georgievska, V. (2002c, 5 June). 'Narodot ne je dava MPC na SPC.' *Utrinski vesnik*. Retrieved from http://star.utrinski.com.mk/?pBroj=884&stID=11992&pR=2. Last accessed 13 March 2017.

Georgievska, V. (2002d, 6 June). 'Svetiot sinod pred istoriska odgovornost.' *Utrinski vesnik*. Retrieved from http://star.utrinski.com.mk/?pBroj=885&stID=12045&pR=2. Last accessed 3 April 2017.

Georgievska, V. (2002e, 7 June). 'Sinodiot ednoglasno go otfrli niškiot nacrt-dogovor.' *Utrinski vesnik*. Retrieved from http://star.utrinski.com.mk/?pBroj=886&stID=12176&pR=2. Last accessed 4 April 2017.

Ѓорѓevski, B. (2002a, 25 May). 'Vladicite ja turkaat MPC vo pregratkite na Peќkata patrijaršija.' *Dnevnik*. Retrieved from http://star.dnevnik.com.mk/?pBroj=1857&stID=2968. Accessed 16 March 2017.

Ѓорѓevski, B. (2002b, 27 May). 'Vladicite Kiril i Agatangel gi vratija 'avtonomistite' na patot za samobitnost.' *Dnevnik*. Retrieved from http://star.dnevnik.com.mk/?pBroj=1858&stID=2977. Last accessed 20 March 2017.

Ѓорѓevski, B. (2002c, 28 May). 'Predlogot za 'avtonomna Ohridska arhiepiskopija' e pekolen.' *Dnevnik*. Retrieved from http://star.dnevnik.com.mk/?pBroj=1859&stID=3080. Last accessed 17 March 2017.

Ѓорѓevski, B. (2002d, 5 June). 'Pod pritisok na vernicite Sinodot ќe je otfrli spogodbata od Niš?' *Dnevnik*. Retrieved from http://star.dnevnik.com.mk/?pBroj=1866&stID=3412. Last accessed 9 March 2017.

Ѓорѓevski, B.. (2002e, 5 June). 'Samostojni državi imaat pravo na samostojni crkvi.' *Dnevnik*. Retrieved from http://star.dnevnik.com.mk/?pBroj=1866&stID=3413. Last accessed 9 March 2017.

Ѓорѓevski, B. (2002f, 6 June). 'Vladikata Stefan vetil deka Sinodot ќe glasa za avtokefalna MPC.' *Dnevnik*. Retrieved from http://star.dnevnik.com.mk/?pBroj=1867&stID=3418. Last accessed 13 March 2017.

'Sramen čin na negiranje na svetite simboli' (2002, 28 May). *Utrinski vesnik*. Retrieved from http://star.utrinski.com.mk/?pBroj=877&stID=11334&pR=2. Last accessed 10 April 2017.

Part VI
Afterword

13 Orthodox Christianity and State/Politics today

Factors to take into account

Vasilios N. Makrides

The relations between religion and politics, or more specifically between Church and State, in predominantly Orthodox contexts have, for a long time, constituted a specific area of scholarly interest. As it is hardly a new or under-researched topic, there are already copious amounts of related research from quite diverse perspectives, dealing with numerous epochs from the period of Byzantium and the Kievan Rus' to post-communist Eastern and South Eastern Europe. In actual fact, it was the latter transition that has triggered a renewed and enhanced interest in the whole theme, as ex-communist countries with a predominant Orthodox population and tradition began adopting Western standards of liberal democracy and concomitant models of regulating Church–State affairs. This process from communist totalitarianism to democratic polity was far from an easy and smooth one. On the contrary, it was in many cases quite conflictual and generated a lot of discussion and debate. Thus, there exists today plenty of information about this multi-faceted topic, which can serve as a basis for its comparative examination. We are talking about many locally or nationally defined Orthodox Churches and related Orthodox Christianities, whose relations to the respective states exhibit commonalities, yet are far from identical.

Is there a single or predominant Orthodox Christian model of Church–State relations? Such a perspective appears to be static and fails to do justice to the diverse Orthodox contexts and constellations. Aside from over-generalising, there is also another danger lurking behind, namely when modern terms and ideological constructions are uncritically projected onto the pre-modern past. A case in point relates to the notorious concepts of Caesaropapism in the Byzantine East and its opposite (the Papocaesarism) in the Latin West. Both terms are neologisms, first coined by the German Protestant theologian Justus Henning Böhmer (1674–1749), thereby criticising the Orthodox and Catholic traditions of regulating Church–State affairs (Hovorun 2016). The problem is, however, that especially the term 'Caesaropapism' became widespread in a negative sense, both in scholarly and general usage, as reflecting a problematic facet of Church–State relations in Byzantium and more broadly in the Orthodox world, given that the Church is subjected to the control of a powerful state. Such views were connected with the long-established negative views about the Byzantine Empire in Western scholarship and public opinion. Modern research has shown, however, that the situation in the East Roman Empire (Byzantium) was much more diverse, complex and multifaceted than the monistic term 'Caesaropapism' suggests. This is a reminder of the need for a more nuanced approach to the whole topic, considering the numerous Orthodox 'glocalisations' in history and at present (Roudometof 2013). But these caveats should not obscure the common elements among various Orthodox cultures, both historically and currently, which are not observed as such in Western Christianity. This concerns a particular Orthodox 'colouring' of the State and the public sphere, in official and unofficial forms alike, contesting the Western tradition of Church–State separation and the subsequent secularity or religious neutrality of the State. Another case relates to the usually strong connection between Orthodoxy and ethnic/national identity, as 'national churches' dominate the Orthodox world of today. A similar phenomenon can be *mutatis mutandis* observed in modern Western Christianity, yet with other facets and repercussions.

By way of conclusion, this chapter will attempt to sketch the ongoing dialectic between commonalities and diversity in the Orthodox world regarding Church–State relations drawing on selected historical and contemporary examples. There are some basic factors to be taken into account when talking about Church and State/politics in Orthodox contexts. The aim is not to give definitive answers, but rather to reflect on certain recurring, at times distinct and at times interconnected, phenomena, to look at several key issues, to raise various questions, and finally to try to adequately capture Orthodox Christian idiosyncrasies with regard to the State/politics.

The burden of the past: Church-State symphony and its diachronic mythology

A term that is widely known and utilised with reference to Church–State relations in Orthodox Christianity is 'symphony' (συμφωνία ἀγαθή, consonantia bona), which dates back to the time of Emperor Justinian I (527–565) and the famous 6th novella of his *Corpus Juris Civilis* (16 March 535). It is questionable, though, whether such a symphony between Church (*sacerdotium*) and State (*imperium*) ever existed in reality, not only in Justinian's time, but also later (cf. Hovorun 2016). The whole notion acquired a great symbolic significance in subsequent centuries, considering also that the Orthodox religious system massively relies on tradition, authority and veneration of the past. A problem arises, however, when this term is still uncritically and thoughtlessly used today by Orthodox and political leaders or functionaries for a variety of reasons, ideological or otherwise; for example, as a way of revitalising a pristine Orthodox tradition that was lost in the course of modern times in the wake of secularisation.

A case in point relates to the current post-Soviet Russian Orthodox Church, which emerged out of a long communist persecution and strove for a new close and productive relationship with the state, but without replicating the Tsarist period and its various drawbacks (e.g. when Orthodoxy represented a state Church). A symphony between Church and State does not figure prominently in the official post-Soviet Russian Orthodox discourse and does not possess a normative value. In the *Bases of the Social Concept of the Russian Orthodox Church* (III. 4), the term 'symphony' and its historical context are mentioned among many other models of Church–State relations in the Orthodox world. It is pointed out that the Orthodox Church does not show preference for one or another such model and that the modern situation, though not the ideal one, is quite different from the past and forces the Church to change and adapt itself. Nevertheless, we find the term used here and there on official occasions with a normative content. This was the case when current Patriarch Kirill was inaugurated to his office in the presence of then President Dmitrii A. Medvedev (2008–2012) on 1 February 2009 in Moscow. An eminent Russian Orthodox cleric, Vsevolod Chaplin, had also talked, after a meeting with Medvedev in 2011, about crafting a new symphony between Church and State. But Medvedev and ex-Serbian President Vojislav Koštunica (2000–2003) have also used the term to indicate the close Church–State relations in their predominantly Orthodox countries. Similar examples may be drawn on other Orthodox cultures, as well (Makrides 2012: 56; Leuştean 2014: 11f., 67, 107f.).

The question is what exactly is meant by such general utterances about a symphony between Church and State. If it is about a general cooperation between Church and State in various domains, then this is not exactly what the traditional model of symphony solely implied. Such a cooperation is nothing special and can be also observed in non-Orthodox contexts, thus it is questionable whether symphony is the right term to depict the present situation. The current use of this term aims at maintaining a necessary special connection between Church and State at all costs in an era when their separation is considered to belong to the cornerstones of modern statehood. Several scholars emphasise that the present situation between Church and State in Orthodox countries is not symphonic in the traditional sense, despite some apparent similarities. This is because in the modern context the State holds priority above all other institutions including the Church. Anderson (2007) has talked about an 'asymmetric symphonia' with regard to post-Soviet Orthodox Russia; Ghodsee (2009) has spoken of a 'symphonic secularism' in the case of post-communist Orthodox Bulgaria; Ramet (1988) has pointed to the various forms of co-optation when the Church is drawn into a cooperative relationship and an agreement of exchange with the State; finally, the present author (Makrides 2016) has referred to the phenomenon of 'asymmetric accommodationism', namely to the unavoidably partial and incomplete accommodation of the Church to modern exigencies.

It is thus false and illusory to talk today of a symphony and to recall past models of Church–State relations. There can be no such symphony in the traditional sense due to the structure of the modern nation-state and the present global order. Any closeness or alliance between Church and State, usually observable in predominantly Orthodox milieus, is not a symphony. Church and State in Byzantium were two *distinct* entities in theory, yet remained always connected to each other in practice. They were never heterogeneous and not *separated* in the modern sense with the clear demarcation between a secular and a religious realm. In the Byzantine perception, Church and State had a common divine origin and concomitant purpose within an eschatological frame. Further, the Byzantine concept of the worldly and temporal affairs, which were entrusted to the dealings of the State, was not identical with modern secularity and its multiple repercussions. Such a Byzantine model reflected the established Christology regarding the two distinct, yet not separated natures of Jesus Christ, divine and human, in one and the same person. Church and State were supposed to form two equally important parts of a single body, an idea often found in Byzantine thought, as in the collection of legal documents called *Epanagoge* of the 9th century. There was a 'division of labour' in this context, yet not in the modern sense when the State claims to be secular or at least religiously neutral.

Even the Byzantine tradition of symphony hardly reflected a harmonious relationship between Church and State. It was not a romantic cooperation and complementarity of two equal partners. Very often emperors intervened in Church affairs, not only in its administration, but also in internal matters related to the Church doctrine, and tried to implement their own view for political or other purposes. Justinian's policies vis-à-vis the non-Chalcedonian Christians and their aspired reintegration into mainstream Byzantine theology and by consequence into the Byzantine Empire are a case in point. The same holds true for the long iconoclast controversies (8th–9th c.), in which the law collection *Ecloga* during the Isaurian dynasty (717–802) appeared supporting the imperial control over the Church. This was also because the Byzantine emperor – in line with the previous Roman imperial tradition, but also with the Jewish tradition of the divinely sanctioned kinship – was thought to be endowed with a 'sacred authority', although he was not allowed to perform sacramental functions in the Church. Such a divine legitimation for the emperor can be located in various Byzantine traditions of all periods, starting from Eusebius, Bishop of Caesarea (4th c.), who especially praised the role of Emperor Constantine I in legalising Christianity in the Roman Empire. This dynamic slowly led to the higher position of the emperor vis-à-vis the Church and related claims for superiority in late Byzantium. Such claims were not automatically accepted by the Church. Patriarch Photios, to whom the *Epanagoge* collection is attributed, argued for a more balanced, reciprocal and equally adjusted Church–State relationship by strengthening the Church's own divine legitimation vis-à-vis the political power (Hovorun 2016).

Most of these discourses and debates were transferred later to Orthodox Russia, where they were adjusted to the Tsarist imperial ambitions and were occasionally drawn upon, as during the conflict between Patriarch Nikon

(1652–1658) and Tsar Alexei I Mikhailovich (1646–1682). In fact, the dependence of the Church on the State constitutes an old debate in Russian history; for example, in relation to the legitimacy of monastic property and the different trajectories taken by Nil Sorskii (1433–1508) and Joseph of Volokolamsk (1439/40–1515), the latter being in favour of Tsarist autocracy and a State-supported Church. Especially after the abolition of the Moscow Patriarchate in 1721 in the wake of the Petrine modernising reforms, the Church was largely subjected to the State and its control and became one of its administrative apparatuses.

Evidently, the above few examples do not support a diachronic application of the notion of symphony to Church–State relations. This notion was often bestowed with a quasi-ontological status as a trans-historical model of orientation within the Orthodox world. Characteristically, there is ample use of the term 'symphony' in Byzantine sources in numerous other contexts (e.g. agreement on doctrinal issues, consent among different nations), but not specifically with regard to Church and State. It was basically Justinian who applied this notion to Church–State relations framing it with an appropriate theological legitimation and legal tradition (Hovorun 2016). This speaks once more against the value uncritically attributed to this contingent and contextual category. The Byzantine symphonic tradition arose from a religiously dominated socio-political frame of reference, which is totally absent in modern statehood. This turns clearly against any attempt to revitalise elapsed Byzantine conditions, although there is still a widespread Orthodox penchant for bygone eras, filled with the aura of an ideal earlier situation. It is also a mistake to consider symphony in ecclesiological terms as referring to the nature of the Church itself.

Such a revitalisation of the symphonic tradition is definitely impossible today. Many Orthodox Churches and Christians live today with a minority status within another majority context, religious and otherwise (e.g. under Islam or in the West). Exactly this development renders any symphonic aspiration a priori to be impossible. Instead of articulating romantic regressions into the past and connecting the Church ideally with a specific political governance, it is more useful to examine the numerous and varied forms of Church–State relations that have been articulated across the long Orthodox history. It is also necessary to look for the recent and still ongoing transformations of the traditional closeness between Church and State, be it reciprocity, mutuality, partnership or cooperation (cf. Leuştean 2011). All this takes place in an environment mostly shaped by modernity, in which there might be a co-optation of the Church by the State and which exhibits particular features and unusual combinations, as the aforementioned 'symphonic secularism' clearly demonstrates.

The dialectic between imperial and national orientations

Another aspect of Church–State relations in the Orthodox world concerns the dialectic between the imperial and the national orientations. To begin with, the imperial feature is quite conspicuous across history, given that the

Orthodox Church lived and operated at the side of imperial political structures for centuries, and in some cases even up to today. A casual look at various aspects of the Orthodox tradition – its rich ritual, overall structure, architecture and iconography – reveals its predominant imperial splendour since Byzantine times. The Byzantine political ideology remained deeply imperial, even if the decline of the empire was evident. Indicative of this is the answer sent by the Patriarch of Constantinople Anthony IV (1389–1390, 1391–1397) in 1393 to the Grand Duke Basil I of Moscow (1389–1425) in favour of the necessary coexistence of empire and Church as a twofold indissoluble unit. This imperial ideology had also influenced the early Slavic would-be Empires of Tsar Symeon I of Bulgaria during the first Bulgarian Empire (893–927) and Stefan Uros IV Dusan of Serbia (1331–1355), who from 1345 bore the title 'Tsar of the Serbs and Greeks'. These were not national movements, but attempts to claim the principal imperial role of Byzantium for the Southern Slavs. The most important transfer of Byzantine imperial ideology (*translatio imperii*), however, related to Orthodox Russia, which after the fall of Byzantium in 1453 to the Ottomans claimed its imperial heritage as the protecting force of all Orthodox Christians. Ivan IV was named Tsar after 1547 until his death in 1584, and this coincided with the foundation of the Russian Tsardom (*Russkoe Tsarstvo*) between 1547 and 1721, leading later to the Russian Empire (*Rossiiskaya Imperiya*) between 1721 and 1917. The entire related discourse remained strongly imperial, and this is the role still claimed *mutatis mutandis* by the Moscow Patriarchate in post-Soviet times.

Orthodox Churches also existed alongside imperial structures that did not have a friendly disposition towards them. This happened during the long Ottoman Empire in South Eastern Europe and the Levant, as well as during the 'Soviet Empire'. It is thus obvious that most Orthodox Churches and Christians lived side by side with imperial political structures well into the 20th century. It is thus understandable why they often show related political preferences and why they have had 'problems' with modern secular statehood and liberal governance. This holds true for earlier periods, as well. The Phanariotes under Ottoman rule, a wealthy and politically active group of Orthodox families, were profoundly influenced by this imperial tradition and were hoping to reinstate the Byzantine Empire. Therefore, they were against the national aspirations of the Orthodox Balkan peoples for liberation and the foundation of independent nation-states.

The major challenge to this long-standing and powerful imperial tradition came from modern nationalism, which originated in Western Europe in the wake of the Enlightenment, the French Revolution and Romanticism and entered the Orthodox world through various channels. Already the official recognition of Moscow as a new Patriarchate (1589/1593) was undoubtedly a step towards the emergence of a distinct Russian Orthodoxy, yet this change should not be understood in a national sense. The Patriarchate of Constantinople had been also in 'Greek hands', but not a concomitant national character. The main currents of nationalism among the Orthodox became first evident in the late 18th century and dominant from the 19th century onwards with the foundation of many independent 'national' Orthodox Churches. This process was followed by conflicts and schisms from the Patriarchate of Constantinople, which has tried, albeit unsuccessfully, to maintain a supranational role in the age of nationalisms and preserve its ecumenical outlook and role due to its long imperial background. From the end of the 18th century, it had already become deeply aware of the dangers brought about by the budding nationalism of Western provenance and attempted to stop its intrusion into the Orthodox of the Ottoman Empire. This is why it also condemned various national insurrection plans and attempts against the Ottomans, including the Greek War of Independence in 1821. These fears were later materialised with the unilateral declaration of the autocephaly of the Greek Church in 1833 leading to a schism with Constantinople until 1850. Even so, this was not the end of related conflicts, as the Greek State and Church were still infatuated with nationalism and irredentism until the first decades of the 20th century.

This ecumenical, supra-national tradition of the Patriarchate of Constantinople is still present today, despite its close relations with the Greek State. This is particularly evident in the period of Patriarch Bartholomew (since 1991), whose strategy was to overcome provincialism and introversion and to bear witness to the universal and supranational orientation of the Patriarchate worldwide. His international ecological activities are a case in point. The ongoing globalisation process has led to a current re-adjustment of many Orthodox notions, which have acquired new dimensions and significance. In that sense, the Patriarchate of Constantinople is the sole major Orthodox actor today continuing the old imperial tradition in a modern frame without national aspirations. This became clear in the repeated problems between the Patriarchate of Constantinople and the Greek Orthodox Church, in spite of Constantinople's closeness with the Greek State (Roudometof 2014). Here it is about a clash between imperial and national orientations. The patriarchal throne of Constantinople generally enjoys a universal recognition today, evident in the convocation of the 'Holy and Great Synod of the Orthodox Church' (or the 'Panorthodox Council') in Crete in 2016, even if modern Turkey refuses to acknowledge its ecumenical role and tries to bestow a narrow 'Greek character' upon it.

The other historical centres of Orthodoxy in the East, namely the Patriarchates of Alexandria, Antioch and Jerusalem, although influenced by the Byzantine imperial tradition, did not raise such strong claims. Early enough, they were found under the rule of Islam, which in many cases holds true until today. Later on, a particular form of 'Orthodox nationalisation' took place there. Alexandria and Jerusalem are controlled today by Greek Orthodoxy and are supported by the Greek State, while Antioch became from the end of the 19th century through Russian intervention a bastion of Arab speaking Orthodoxy. Another Orthodox Church in which imperial and national orientations coexist and intermingle in a variety of ways is the Russian one. By virtue of the Stoglav Council (1551), the declaration of the autocephaly of the Moscow Patriarchate and the Petrine reforms, the Russian Church underwent a pre-modern ethnicisation (more in the sense of a Russification). This led later to its own nationalisation, but not at the cost of its imperial claims. It thus developed an overall profile supporting both orientations, as evidenced in the case of Pan-Slavism in the 19th century. The same is valid for the post-communist era. The Russian Church is nowadays the sole national Orthodox Church exhibiting global concerns, engaging itself on such a level quite ostentatiously and developing an analogous ideology, drawing on the Byzantine imperial tradition (cf. the film by now Bishop Tikhon Shevkunov *Gibel' Imperii: Vizantiiskii Urok* from 2008, and international activities of the foundation *Russkii Mir*). It thus presents a serious challenge to Constantinople's ecumenical role and appears to be its most direct rival in the global arena.

In principle, the imperial always runs contrary to the national. It is about a more holistic and integrative model against a specific and fragmented one. Eastern Orthodoxy has historically been much closer to the imperial tradition, and its intense nationalisation is basically a recent phenomenon, namely since the 19th century. Albeit at times very conflictual (Payne 2007), the latter exhibits a strong resilience and an impressive dynamic. In some cases, an independent autocephalous Orthodox Church had been even created before the independence of a respective state – so in modern Bulgaria, first the Church in 1870, and then the State in 1878. Many Orthodox Churches have no problem identifying themselves today with their national character, although they usually prefer to be called 'local churches' (*pomestnye tserkvi*), and not national ones. Various reasons and factors account for this national transformation of the entire Orthodox world in modern times and are closely related to Orthodox long-term traditions, structures and practices in pre-modern era. These include the modern transformation of the old Church–State relation into a Church-nation-relation; the dominant historical model of administrative pluralism in the East and the potential for Church independence (autocephaly); the widespread vernacularisation and indigenisation processes endemic in Eastern Orthodox missions; and the special strong nexus between people, motherland, as well as Christian and ethnic identity (Makrides 2013a).

Orthodoxy, autocracy and democracy: correlations and interactions

Is Orthodox Christianity closer to autocratic and even totalitarian regimes? Or is it perfectly compatible with a liberal democratic socio-political order? Such questions may appear at first glance superfluous, yet they have been vividly and controversially discussed on an international level in the wake of the collapse of communist regimes in Eastern and South Eastern Europe (1989–1991) where Orthodox Christianity had historically had a strong presence (cf. the notorious discussion of this topic by Samuel P. Huntington in the 1990s). This happened because ex-communist countries were supposed to make a rapid transition to democracy and develop according to (Western) liberal models (e.g. in politics, society, economy). But there were other forces within these countries including Orthodoxy, which were considered as obstructing this form of transition. This entire discussion was often highly ideological due to the widespread 'Orientalist' or 'Balkanist' discourses, revealing many lingering Western prejudices about the Orthodox world and culture.

The entire picture is rather a multifaceted and complex one. There are ex-communist countries like Romania and Bulgaria with an Orthodox majority population, which since 2007 have been full members of the European Union and do not appear to face problems adapting themselves to European norms and standards of governance. But there is also an Orthodox critique against liberality, democracy, secularity, individuality and various other developments connected with Western modernity, considered to be at odds with Orthodox orientations and ideal Church–State relations. The Russian Orthodox Church especially voices this criticism, most prominently in the *Bases of the Social Concept* of 2000 and in the document on human dignity and rights of 2008. There is an apparent incompatibility here in need of explanation. By going back to history and looking at Orthodox political preferences since Byzantine times, it becomes obvious that Orthodox cultures did not show a particular interest in democratic developments and preferred rather monarchic or auto-cratic regimes, which were theologically legitimated. The monarch (either an emperor or a king) was closely connected with the implementation of the will of God and Orthodoxy (= right faith) in society, even if by force and coer-cion. According to a negative Christian genealogy of political power and the state, their existence was regarded as a necessary and lesser evil. It has been allowed and imposed by God for the better regulation of human affairs and the reduction of sins in society. This explains why, ideally, every ruler had to be a pious, God-fearing person. A religiously homogeneous society was also preferred to a multi-religious one. Late Byzantine thinkers (e.g. Theodore Metochites, Nikephoros Gregoras) were critical of the early democratization processes in Italian city-states, which they considered inferior to their own political tradition, despite Byzantium's obvious decline (Syros 2010). This discrepancy became even more visible once West European modernity (including democratic governance) started to be articulated and implemented, and more radically so when it acquired a rather secular form. A constructive encounter of the Orthodox world with Western modernity has never taken place in a full sense. This explains the various Orthodox reactions against later democratisation processes; for example, in the wake of the French Revolution and the radical changes it was able to unleash.

The same is valid for the long tradition of Russian political autocracy from the time of Tsar Ivan IV and the *samoderzhavie* ideology in the 19th century up to Stalin's and Putin's autocratic characteristics, which enjoy admiration in various Orthodox circles. The canonisation of political figures in this context (e.g. of the last Tsarist family in 2000 by the Russian Orthodox Church) attests once more to this Orthodox preference for monarchy rather than for liberal democracy. A similar closeness between Orthodoxy and dictatorial, extreme right or totalitarian regimes can also be observed in the 20th century (cf. the fascist 'Iron Guard' movement in interwar Romania). Further, the Orthodox tradition of submissiveness to and collaborationism with non-democratic political regimes became quite evident during the 20th century under communism. This is why it was criticised both at that time (cf. Alexander Solzhenitsyn's 'Lenten letter' to Patriarch Pimen in 1972), but even more strongly in the aftermath. A case of submissiveness concerns the so-called Sergianism (*Sergianstvo*) in the Soviet Union, namely the declaration of loyalty to the Bolsheviks in 1927 by Sergii Stragorodksii, the *locum tenens* after Patriarch Tichon's deposition. Orthodox collaborationism with the communists, regardless if conditional or tactical, proved to be a source of huge problems and conflicts for several Orthodox Churches – consider the deep and long-standing intra-ecclesiastical schism in post-communist Bulgaria caused by such accusations. One may also locate forms of Orthodox light opposition to such autocratic regimes, yet these were not instrumental in enabling their fall. Basically, opposition came from the diaspora Orthodox Churches and other circles in the West and beyond the Iron Curtain, not so much from the inside.

In general, the Orthodox Church was historically hardly a revolutionary force in society, especially regarding socio-political upheavals and revolutions. Various Orthodox individual actors did exhibit occasionally an opposite attitude, but they usually did not represent the official Church hierarchy and the mainstream. The official Church attitude was mostly an accommodating one, looking for a rather good collaboration with whatsoever regime in power. Such a legitimation of power and lack of resistance were theologically legitimated by reference to the influential old Christian argument, namely that every political power in principle stems and is permitted from God (Rom. 13, 1–3; 1 Petr. 2, 13–16). Even in the case of an inimical political regime, the main Orthodox interest was not to undermine and overthrow it, but to secure a good status for the Church for the time being. There was a strong conviction that all historical developments had to be judged eschatologically, not from a limited temporal and contingent perspective. This explains the usual lack of official Orthodox resistance not only against totalitarian regimes, but also against any occupier or conqueror.

By contrast, if we look at the Protestant milieu of the former German Democratic Republic and the Catholic milieu of communist Poland, we observe a different situation. The respective churches there did play a role as forces of opposition against communism and were instrumental – along with other factors – in bringing its final demise. Their contribution has been widely recognised, both in the public discourse and the related literature. Historically, there exist long-standing lines of Church opposition to political power, social radicalism and a concomitant revolutionary potential in Western

Christianity, even in secularised forms. There are certainly various 'dark sides' in the Western Christian history; for example, the Church relations with National Socialism and Fascism and the phenomenon of the so-called 'Clerical Fascism'. But the tradition of Church resistance to inimical regimes is more strongly rooted in the Western than in the Eastern Christian tradition. Nobody has ever claimed that the Russian Orthodox Church has played a role in undermining Soviet communism and leading to its fall. In the case of the Ukraine, only the Uniate Church was considered as having played a role in the collapse of communism and the subsequent boosting of the democratisation process, not the pro-Moscow Orthodox Church. This Orthodox predilection relates to the long tradition of the necessary closeness to and dependence of the Church on the State. Interestingly, all this hardly means that the Orthodox are unable to perform changes in this domain. A case in point can be found in the Russian Orthodox *Bases of the Social Concept*. There the possibility of Church resistance is clearly an option when a political regime takes anti-Christian measures and follows related policies (III, 5; IV, 9). Such a change of perspectives is due to the previous communist period and experience when the Church was massively instrumentalised by the atheist regime for its own secular goals (Makrides 2015).

Does all this show an incompatibility between Orthodoxy and modern liberal democracy? Some scholars have attempted to find neglected 'democratic' and 'liberal' notions in specific Orthodox theological notions and perspectives (e.g. in the Orthodox personalist understanding of the Trinity in contrast to the Western essentialist one). There have been attempts to reconcile the Orthodox imperial autocratic tradition with modern democratic and secular politics or to revive past models of governance today, such as 'Political Hesychasm' (Stoeckl, Gabriel and Papanikolaou 2017). As with the previously discussed mythology about the Church–State symphony, such endeavours should be critically assessed, since they mostly represent romantic regressions into the past. But caution is warranted when talking indistinctly about an incompatibility between Orthodoxy and liberal democracy. The related problems are found on the level of principles, values and presuppositions, revealing a strong and pervasive longing for a pre-modern, romantic and ideal situation, which is supposed to solve or overcome all modern dilemmas. At the practical level, the Orthodox remain rather realistic, have no problems with liberal democratic regimes and adapt themselves to their secular exigencies. What the Orthodox still need is a deeper, serious and critical familiarisation with the logic of modern liberal democracy as such and, by extension, a constructive engagement with the overall project of modernity. This is again something that Western Christian Churches have accomplished more systematically, extensively and fruitfully throughout their modern history.

The significance of the Orthodox Church status: majority or minority?

Another issue to be taken into account in the current discussion of Church–State relations in Orthodox Christianity relates to the relevant status of an

Orthodox Church. Usually and predominantly, the Orthodox Churches representing the majority religion within a given state or territory are taken into consideration. It is actually in such contexts that Church–State relations were shaped in historical and modern times, both in Byzantium and in the various nation-states. There exist numerous Orthodox Churches and Christians with a minority status in quite diverse contexts (Western, Islamic). This entails significant consequences for their identity, policy and survival strategy including the area of Church–State relations. From the canonically recognised fourteen autocephalous Orthodox Churches today, half of them represent minority churches in their respective countries. Such Orthodox Churches do not enjoy any special privileges, official and unofficial alike, by the relevant states, at least as majority Orthodox Churches used to or still do. They have to coexist or even to constantly compete with other churches and religious groups for status, recognition and establishment in their milieus. This kind of competition, usually absent from Orthodox majority contexts, can render such churches more enduring, adaptable and stronger in the long run. The above observations pertain not only to Orthodox institutions, but also to various communities of Orthodox believers as religious minorities. These constitute facets of the broad Orthodox diasporic movement across the globe today, formed through various waves of emigration (Hämmerli and Mayer 2014).

What is characteristic of these Orthodox minority cases is their usually greater adjustment to the exigencies of their predominant cultural, religious and political milieu. This renders them different from the majority Orthodox Churches or mother-churches (in the case of diasporic communities). It also implies a greater openness towards modern secular developments including the Western regulation of Church–State affairs. In many cases, they are more innovative, experimenting with novelties and developing further, and fulfil numerous roles in society beyond the strict religious domain. Another consequence may be the greater independence from a mother-church and the articulation of a distinct Orthodox identity. A case in point is the Orthodox Church in America (OCA), whose autocephaly was initiated by the Moscow Patriarchate in 1970 without a Pan-Orthodox canonical recognition. However, this Orthodox Church hardly identifies itself with the Moscow Patriarchate, particularly with its post-communist course and outlook.

It goes without saying that a model of Church–State symphony is impossible under these circumstances. In a Western context, the Orthodox as a minority have usually no problem following the predominant separation between Church and State and the religious neutrality of the latter. They are normally registered with an official legal status and consequently must respect the legal system of their host country. Although cases of rigorist/fundamentalist attitudes are not altogether absent in such contexts (e.g. in the USA), the Orthodox mainstream shows an unproblematic compliance with the specific exigencies of such societies. This holds true even for the Orthodox in France, a country with a strong and strict tradition of laicism (Kazarian 2015). This proves that many historical, diachronic characteristics of the Orthodox

Church, including those pertaining to Church–State relations, are not onto-logical and essential, but were simply formed under specific socio-political circumstances. Hence, they have a relative value and can be modified or adapted in a novel situation without serious problems.

The same holds true for other developments in such minority contexts. Orthodox diasporic communities are affected by the de-territorialisation taking place within the broader globalisation process. New Orthodox identities may appear detached from particular historical territories and lands, leading to a de-coupling between Orthodoxy and a specific culture. Further, the process of transnationalism, namely when the jurisdiction of the mother-churches is extended to territories other than the traditionally national and canonical ones, may lead to the emergence of new 'transnational national communities' in host countries. These may be linked through faith beyond national and linguistic divisions, a fact attesting to the potential Orthodox adaptations to diverse and demanding new situations. Such a new model of transnational Orthodoxy may challenge the conventional diasporic one, which always keeps the strong bond between home and emigration country. This may lead, in turn, to reactions of mother-churches against transnationalism aimed at keeping the diasporic communities under control (Roudometof 2015).

In particular, the Orthodox in the West may develop in tune with the modern condition. Many novel ideas and promising suggestions did initially appear, both earlier and more recently, in such milieus. The close contacts with Western Christianity and the unavoidable mutual interactions possibly account for this. Not least, this relates to the central issue of Church–State relations. Several thinkers of the Russian Orthodox emigration in the West (e.g. Sergei N. Bulgakov, 1871–1944) supported the idea of a greater Church independence from the State and the need to overcome the old Constantinian and later Byzantine tradition of their close interdependence (Bulgakov 1999). The negative experience with the Tsarist protectionism of the Church, the rise of Marxism-Leninism and the subsequent persecution of the Church in the Soviet Union may explain this change. Such and similar critical ideas (e.g. against Orthodox ecclesiastical nationalism) are expressed especially in post-communist times by a new generation of Orthodox scholars and thinkers, mostly present and active in Western settings (Demacopoulos and Papanikolaou 2017). These attempted to initiate a fresh and open dialogue between Orthodox Chris-tianity and the modern world with a quite promising agenda. There is also a fruitful interaction with another young generation in the historical Orthodox heartlands seeking to overcome the hindrances of the past and to enable an Orthodox *aggiornamento*. The foundation of the 'International Orthodox Theo-logical Association' (IOTA) in February 2017 to coordinate all these endeavours is a case in point. All this speaks against a monolithic and arid Orthodoxy that allegedly remains fixed to its glorious and authoritative past.

However, the potential stemming from Orthodox diasporic communities and minority Orthodox Churches should not be overstated as the sole or most valuable basis for drawing conclusions about the current Orthodox world. These Orthodox are hardly representative of the entire Orthodox body, even more so from a historical perspective. Their relationship to the majority Orthodox Churches is asymmetric, given that the latter are far more powerful, influential and instrumental in defining normatively what the Orthodox mainstream is. The liberal positions of certain Orthodox raised in the West do not weight the same as the positions professed by a dominant majority Orthodox Church, especially when it comes down to a delineation and definition of Orthodox tradition and practice. If one wants to know more about the Orthodox evaluation of modern human rights, one cannot rely exclusively on the pro-liberal views formulated by progressive Orthodox thinkers in the USA (and elsewhere). Much more important on this topic is the related official and normative document of the Russian Orthodox Church of 2008, which is highly critical of modern human rights and evaluates them through Orthodox moral criteria. On the one side, there is an American Orthodoxy, which, although recognised and respected, is hardly a significant and decisive player within the overall American scene, religious and otherwise, as it represents a tiny minority (ca. 3 million) of the entire population. On the other side, there is a powerful Church institution like the Moscow Patriarchate with a global agenda influencing millions of people with its particular normative voice and discourse. No matter how promising and appealing many positions of the Orthodox in minority contexts are, they can hardly speak for the whole of the Orthodox world and represent normatively the Orthodox mainstream. The specific constellations of Church–State relations in an Orthodox minority context cannot be also transferred to the historical Orthodox heartlands, which usually have to address other challenges. Interestingly, many predominantly Orthodox countries, which have traditionally been places of emigration, have now turned into immigration countries, especially for Muslims coming from different geographical areas. Regardless if this leads to enhanced tensions or to greater religious plurality, it certainly asks for a re-evaluation of existing Church–State relations, which is already happening to some extent (cf. the case of Greece, which hosts thousands of legal and illegal Muslim migrants currently).

The latter issue brings forth another side of the Orthodox minority presence and history, both institutional and collective/individual, namely the Orthodox under Islam. We are talking here about a historically much longer period than the one with the Orthodox presence in the West. Amazingly quickly, from the early 7th century onwards, large parts of Byzantine Orthodox Christianity were captured by the Arabs and became minority churches. This process included, among other things, the three historical Patriarchates of the East: Jerusalem in 638, Antioch in 637 and Alexandria in 642. Later on, the Seldjuks and the Ottoman Turks progressively captured parts of the Byzantine Empire in Asia Minor, in the Balkans and other areas (1516 and 1517 Syria and Egypt respectively). The most important Orthodox See, namely that of the Ecumenical Patriarchate of Constantinople, is basically a minority church within a predominantly Muslim country, Turkey. All this had quite significant repercussions for local Orthodox identities and for Church–State relations in these contexts.

In such conquered areas, political power and control were taken over by Islam, yet the Orthodox Church managed in most cases to survive, to be recognised by the new rulers, and to undertake, more or less in an autonomous manner, various broader jurisdictions (e.g. social, political) beyond the strict religious domain. This was a kind of secularisation, as the Orthodox Church did not traditionally undertake such functions due to the old 'division of labour' established by the tradition of symphony. It does so solely in exceptional cases in order to fill the void left by an absent state and political power. This situation largely explains the lack of an organised Orthodox politicisation. Usually, there is not an explicit Orthodox political party supported by the Church, and Orthodox clerics are not allowed to be elected in the Parliament.

A characteristic case is found under Ottoman rule in the Balkans when such a broader role was undertaken by the Patriarch of Constantinople as the leader of the *Rum-Millet*. There also exist related cases, such as the priest-leaders (*vladika*) among the Montenegrin people from early 16th to mid-19th century – the most famous being the Prince-Bishop Petar II Petrović-Njegoš (1813–1851); or when the Orthodox Serbs emigrated in 1690 and in 1737–39 from the Ottoman to the Habsburg Empire and became recognised there as a 'Church-nation', with the Church playing a catalytic role in organising and holding them together. The interaction of Orthodox Serbs as a minority with the majority Catholic Habsburg culture was quite beneficial to them, as they were able to evolve in several domains (e.g. education). Another telling example of such a broader role of the Church is observable in the tradition of the ethnarch, namely the leader of the nation. This was embodied by Archbishop Makarios III of Cyprus, the first president of the Cypriote Republic after independence in 1959 until his death in 1977. However, his long presidency created quite some discontent within the ranks of the Cypriote Orthodox Church. This was mainly due to the permanent undertaking of such dual responsibilities, religious and political, by Makarios. This run contrary to the Orthodox Canon Law, which considers such an endeavour always provisional and temporary, especially in view of a critical moment in a nation's history.

The presence of numerous Orthodox Churches and Christians under a centuries-old Islamic rule did affect Church–State relations and had many repercussions. For the Orthodox, it was about a particular form of coexistence and occasional alliance out of various reasons and considerations. There was also an articulation of a specific Orthodox *modus vivendi* in such contexts in order to be able to survive and endure a foreign religious and political rule. This was perfectly complemented by the fundamental Orthodox lack of resistance to political power explained above, which went sometimes so far as to become a clear voluntary submission. This explains why the Patriarchate of Constantinople tried to legitimise Ottoman rule through theological arguments and to inhibit any insurrection plans among the Orthodox subjects around the end of the 18th century. Furthermore, at the political level, there are strong commonalities between Orthodox Christianity and Islam because of the common imperial tradition and outlook. Both had serious problems with the advent of the (Western) modern nation-state, which led to the fragmentation of the traditional pre-modern Orthodox (the Byzantine Commonwealth) and Islamic (the *ummah*) unity – a vision that the current Islamic State (IS) has also tried to re-activate in its own way. Finally, there was and there still exists a certain closeness between Orthodoxy and Islam in their common opposition and struggle against the West and Western Latin Churches, including their cultures, states and politics. Such attempts of cooperation have taken various forms, ranging from visions about an Orthodox-Islamic Commonwealth to an official religious dialogue between the two sides (e.g. the ongoing dialogue between the Russian Orthodox Church and Iranian Shia Muslims). The common critique directed against the West relates, among other things, to the construction and wider dissemination of the modern nation-state and its focal secular character and values, with which both Orthodox and Muslims still have great difficulties.

East and West: are they indeed so different?

In the previous sections, we often hinted at the differences between the Orthodox and the Western Christian regulation of Church–State relations. Such differences exist historically and are quite vital for understanding the respective developments in the East and West. They should not, however, be considered as ontological and intrinsic to the alleged 'nature' or 'essence' of the Churches under discussion. It all has to do with specific socio-historical developments, which came to be formed and crystallised in both areas of Europe. Seen in this way, it makes little sense to criticise the religious and political Papal authority and worldly power as a deviation from authentic Christianity, as F. M. Dostoevsky did in his famous legend about the Grand Inquisitor. It was an unavoidable process in the context of West European history and development.

Talking about the Latin West as a whole, the large variety of its forms and expressions in different regions should not be ignored. This issue also bears directly on Church–State relations. Further, the many 'grey areas' between East and West, especially evident in borderland regions, should not be overlooked; for instance, among the various Uniate cultures lying geographically between East and West. More important, though, are the elements that predominate, play historically a crucial role and have numerous significant consequences. This concerns the sensitive area of Church–State relations, as well. An East-West comparison should not be made on axiological terms with related value judgements. The aim should not be to prove the superiority of the one Christian tradition over the other and vice versa, as it has been done over and over again in the past. Diverging developments and trajectories were quite inevitable in the East and West. The Eastern model of symphony was totally impossible to apply in the West due to the lack of a central imperial authority there. By contrast, the Western model of a Church independent from political power could have never been implemented in the East because of the permanent existence of a central imperial authority there.

The same accounts for the lack of politicisation of Orthodoxy according to the Western pattern. On the one hand, following the Eastern model, the Church always needs a partner to co-exist and work with, for example, the empire, the state or otherwise. Ideally, it should never exist by itself alone. This leads to the privileged status (both official and unofficial) of many predominant Orthodox Churches nowadays in their respective states. On the other hand, following the Western model, the Church must always remain independent from the State and is even superior to it (cf. the doctrine of Pope Gelasius I, 492–496). The persisting tension between Church and State, pre-eminently evident in Augustine's work *De civitate Dei*, was thought to be resolved only eschatologically. Such a position reflects more or less the 'pessimistic' anthropology of the Latin West, which transposed ideas about the corrupted and fallen human nature and the need of divine grace for salvation to the prerogatives of a mundane political entity. This is contrasted with the more 'optimistic' anthropology of the Orthodox East, which was able to embrace and incorporate the imperial political entity in its salvific vision with fewer reservations. In addition, the Church in the West was able to acquire clear political power and its own territories. It thus started a long and fierce competition for superiority, power and control with the political rulers in the West (cf. the famous investiture controversy in the High Middle Ages). Later on, the Reformation emerged out of this long, pre-existing and influential Western tradition. Luther's idea about the 'two kingdoms' was aimed at supporting the Church's autonomy from State control. In the long run, all this was connected with the regulation of Church–State relations in modernity (cf. the notions of territorialism, separation, religious neutrality of the state, tolerance, secularity).

These developments are hardly found in the Orthodox East as such, which nonetheless was forced in the modern age *nolens volens* to accept them in the context of the nation-state. But the dominant Orthodox imaginary remained always critical of them, even if in practical terms accommodation and compromise were deemed necessary. Historically speaking, it is about diverging socio-political developments in East and West from the Late Antiquity onwards, when the two parts of the Roman Empire slowly drifted away from one another at many levels and in the end separated ecclesiastically in the long run. Here it is basically about the inexorable course of history, not about what is better or preferable.

Generally, one may locate both parallels and differences between East and West. We referred above to the general Orthodox lack of resistance towards political power, yet there has also been a strong Catholic tendency in favour of conservative, autocratic and even totalitarian regimes (cf. the collaborationist attitude towards the Vichy-Regime of Philippe Pétain in Nazi France).

The same holds true for a part of modern Protestantism if we look at the role of the *Deutsche Christen* in Nazi Germany. Especially the Roman Catholic Church had its own share of problems with democracy for many centuries, while things have only changed after the Second Vatican Council (1962–65). Further, the problems between Orthodox Christianity and modernity are no unique. The same appears to be the case with the predominant Catholic Church in Poland, which likewise criticises liberal and secular modern trends. In the latter case, this has mostly to do with the history of Polish Catholicism under communist rule, as it was never influenced by the innovative spirit of the Second Vatican Council. These cases reveal the wide intra-Catholic differentiation and variation.

The list of parallels and differences between Eastern Orthodox and Western Latin Christianity with regard to Church–State relations may be continued. In both cases, there exists an influential imperial tradition bequeathed by the Roman Empire, yet Orthodox universality is different from Roman catholicity in scope and outlook. In the East, this trend was historically part of the broader politico-religious ideology of the Byzantine Empire, whereas in the West it acquired a stronger religious aura, legitimation and inclination due to the all-encompassing claims of the Papal see as an autonomous religious institution independent of external political control. Both Rome and Constantinople exhibit today a related global and universal agenda, yet the differences between them are quite conspicuous. As already mentioned, the Moscow Patriarchate also intends to become a global player and does this successfully to a large degree by drawing on its own, centuries-old and powerful Russian imperial tradition. This underlines once more the particular problems of power constellation within the Orthodox Christian world because of its polycentric structure, a problem not faced by the Catholic Church.

Furthermore, we have talked about the nationalisation of the Orthodox world and its consequences, whereas the Catholic Church can be considered as the epitome of transnationalism. Although there are no Catholic national churches, the connection between Church and nation is still particularly strong on a local basis, for example, in Poland or in Ireland. We can also observe a strong connection between Church and nation in Protestant contexts, where Lutheranism, Calvinism or Anglicanism are often recognised as state religions. But the repercussions of this strong connection between Church and nation are quite different in the Orthodox East and the Latin West.

Bearing all this in mind, a comparative, non-axiological and balanced examination of Orthodox and Latin Christianity with regard to Church–State-politics relations may reveal highly interesting topics linked to their cultural specificities respectively. Why, for example, is the tradition of political saints (from the time of Emperor Constantine I onwards up to the canonisation of the last Tsarist family in Russia) much stronger in the Orthodox East than in the Latin West? Why is there a clear Orthodox predilection and preference for monarchy? Why does political theology remain underdeveloped in Orthodox contexts in contrast to the Latin West (Makrides 2017)? Why does the Orthodox Church generally lack a systematic social teaching in contrast to the highly reflected and developed Catholic social doctrine and Protestant social ethic? The only exception from the latter case is the Russian Orthodox Church, which in 2000 promulgated for the first time its official social concept (Makrides 2013b). Finally, why does the Orthodox Church generally show a limited potential for social revolution, reform and change in contrast to the Western Churches? These few indicative questions can show the merit of attempting such a comparative analysis of Eastern and Western Christianity, their parallel or different developmental courses, and the multiple, long-term consequences thereof. This pertains, among other things, to the central issue of the relations between Church, State and politics. Their systematic, case-oriented study will enable not only a contextual understanding of both commonalities and local specifics within the wider Orthodox Christian world (Kalkandjieva 2011), but also a better awareness of the crucial East-West dimension of the entire topic and its significance for the varied European and adjacent religious, cultural, social and political landscapes.

References

Anderson, J. 2007. 'Putin and the Russian Orthodox Church: Asymmetric Symphonia?', *Journal of International Affairs* 61(1): 185–201.

Bulgakov, S. 1999. *Towards a Russian Political Theology*. Edinburgh: T&T Clark.

Demacopoulos, G. E. and A. Papanikolaou (eds.) 2017. *Christianity, Democracy, and the Shadow of Constantine*. New York: Fordham University Press.

Ghodsee, K. 2009. 'Symphonic Secularism: Eastern Orthodoxy, Ethnic Identity and Religious Freedoms in Contemporary Bulgaria', *Anthropology of East Europe Review* 27(2): 227–252.

Hämmerli, M. and J.-F. Mayer (eds.) 2014. *Orthodox Identities in Western Europe: Migration, Settlement and Innovation*. Farnham: Ashgate.

Hovorun, C. 2016. 'Is the Byzantine "Symphony" Possible in Our Days?', *Journal of Church and State* 59(2): 280–296.

Kalkandjieva, D. 2011. 'A Comparative Analysis on Church-State Relations in Eastern Orthodoxy: Concepts, Models, and Principles', *Journal of Church and State* 53(4): 587–614.

Kazarian, N. 2015. 'The Orthodox Church in France Facing French Secularism ("laïcité")', *Religion, State and Society* 43(3): 244–261.

Leuştean, L. N. 2011. 'The Concept of Symphonia in Contemporary European Orthodoxy', *International Journal for the Study of the Christian Church* 11(2–3): 188–202.

Leuştean, L. N. (ed.). 2014. *Eastern Christianity and Politics in the Twenty-First Century*. London/New York: Routledge.

Makrides, V. N. 2012. 'Sind politische Voraussetzungen und Rahmenbedingungen für die Orthodoxen Kirchen absolut notwendig?', *Religion–Staat–Gesellschaft. Zeitschrift für Glaubensformen und Weltanschauungen* 13(1): 53–79.

Makrides, V. N. 2013a. 'Why are Orthodox Churches Particularly Prone to Nationalization and Even to Nationalism?', *St Vladimir's Theological Quarterly* 54(3/4): 325–352.

Makrides, V. N. 2013b. 'Why does the Orthodox Church Lack Systematic Social Teaching?', *Skepsis. A Journal for Philosophy and Interdisciplinary Research* 23: 281–312.

Makrides, V. N. 2015. 'Eastern Orthodox and Western Latin Churches under Communism: Differences and Parallels'. In *Romanica et Balcanica. Wolfgang Dahmen zum 65. Geburtstag.* Edited by T. Kahl, J. Kramer and E. Prifti, pp. 703–724. München: AVM – Akademische Verlagsgemeinschaft.

Makrides, V. N. 2016. 'Morality, Civil Law and Religion in Contemporary Greece. The Asymmetric Accommodationism of the Orthodox Church'. In *Evangile, moralité et lois civiles. Gospel, Morality, and Civil Law. Proceedings of the Colloquia at Bologna (2012) and Klingenthal (2014).* Edited by J. Famerée, P. Gisel and H. Legrand, pp. 267–285. Wien/Zürich: LIT.

Makrides, V. N. 2017. 'Political Theology in Orthodox Christian Contexts: Specificities and Particularities in Comparison with Western Latin Christianity'. In *Political Theologies in Orthodox Christianity: Common Challenges – Divergent Positions.* Edited by K. Stoeckl, I. Gabriel and A. Papanikolaou, pp. 25–54. London/New York: T&T Clark/Bloomsbury.

Payne, D. P. 2007. 'Nationalism and the Local Church: The Source of Ecclesiastical Conflict in the Orthodox Commonwealth', *Nationalities Papers* 35(5): 831–852.

Ramet, P. 1988. 'Autocephaly and National Identity in Church-State Relations in Eastern Christianity: An Introduction'. In *Eastern Christianity and Politics in the Twentieth Century.* Edited by P. Ramet, pp. 3–19. Durham/London: Duke University Press.

Roudometof, V. 2013. 'The Glocalisations of Eastern Orthodox Christianity', *European Journal of Social Theory* 16(2): 226–245.

Roudometof, V. 2014. *Globalization and Orthodox Christianity: The Transformations of a Religious Tradition.* New York/London: Routledge.

Roudometof, V. 2015. 'Orthodox Christianity as a Transnational Religion: Theoretical, Historical and Comparative Considerations', *Religion, State and Society* 43(3): 211–227.

Stoeckl, K., I. Gabriel and A. Papanikolaou (eds.). 2017. *Political Theologies in Orthodox Christianity: Common Challenges – Divergent Positions.* London/New York: T&T Clark/Bloomsbury.

Syros, V. 2010. 'Between Chimera and Charybdis: Byzantine and Post-Byzantine Views on the Political Organization of the Italian City-States', *Journal of Early Modern History* 14(5): 451–504.

Index